Doctor Who: A British Alien?

Danny Nicol

Doctor Who: A British Alien?

palgrave
macmillan

Danny Nicol
Westminster Law School
University of Westminster
London, UK

ISBN 978-3-319-88113-3 ISBN 978-3-319-65834-6 (eBook)
https://doi.org/10.1007/978-3-319-65834-6

Printed on acid-free paper

This Palgrave Macmillan imprint is published by Springer Nature
The registered company is Springer International Publishing AG
The registered company address is: Gewerbestrasse 11, 6330 Cham, Switzerland

To my mother

Preface

In the *Doctor Who* Christmas special "The Voyage of the Damned" (2007), Mr Copper, a pleasant ignoramus from another planet who fancies himself an expert on Earth, pronounces that Great Britain is part of "Europey" and that across the British Channel lie Great France and Great Germany. The Doctor corrects him: "no, no, it's just France and Germany: only Britain is Great".

The idea of *Doctor Who* as a love-letter to Britain has become a commonplace. In some ways, *Doctor Who* is simply *like* Britain: as a constitutional scholar, it is easy to see the parallels between *Doctor Who* and Britain's rules of governance. Unlike most American science fiction programmes, there was no grand design of the *Who*niverse—no sacred written constitution for the series—solemnly enshrined at the show's outset. Instead, like Britain's constitution, the production team have made it up as they went along. The British constitution is what happens: it lives on, changing from day to day. The same could be said of *Doctor Who*'s overarching narrative.

Since *Doctor Who* returned to our screens in 2005, I have been writing this book in my head. I had become an academic lawyer during the "hiatus" between classic-series *Doctor Who* (1963–1989) and new-series *Doctor Who* (2005–present), and when the show returned, I noticed that I was watching it without removing my academic hat. There was no book-length study of the way in which *Doctor Who* captures Britishness, politics and law, and so this book just *had* to be written.

I am grateful to the following for their advice, inspiration and encouragement: Steph Berns, Tony Bradney, Liz Duff, John Flood, Steve Greenfield, Matt Hills, Paresh Kathrani, Joan Mahoney, Chris McCorkindale, Frances Nicol, Sophie Nicol, Guy Osborn, Craig Owen Jones, Keith Say, Micky Silver, Alison L. Young and David Yuratich. Any errors remain my own. I am particularly grateful for the constant support I have received from my colleagues at Westminster Law School's Centre for Law, Society and Popular Culture in various *Doctor Who* projects: writing this book, guest-editing a special issue of the *Journal of Popular Television* on the law and politics of *Doctor Who*, and maintaining a blog on the same subject (politicsandlawofdoctorwho.blogspot.co.uk). I have benefitted greatly from the academic literature on *Doctor Who*, much of it strikingly recent.

I am not sure whether the word "fan" quite captures how I feel about *Doctor Who*. Certain scholars have argued that viewers tend to interpret *Doctor Who* to accord with their own political beliefs, yet some aspects of *Doctor Who*'s portrayal of Britishness delight me whilst others do not. Personally, I like contemporary *Doctor Who*'s suspicion of big business, cynicism over globalisation and casting of doubts on the merits of the Doctor's interventions. I am also rather partial to new *Who*'s edgy, more egalitarian version of unionism. I am less fond of the programme's slowness to escape its template of male domination, and hope that the long-awaited casting of a woman, Jodie Whittaker, to play the Doctor from 2018 onwards, will help remedy this. I also wish its admirable projection of a multi-racial Britain went hand-in-hand with less undervaluing of non-white characters and a more robust vision of racial equality. That said, I hope that this book will be equally useful for readers whose politics are entirely different from my own. More broadly, readers may not agree with all my interpretations of *Doctor Who*, but if my book makes people think about *Doctor Who* and the way it projects national identity, the effort will have been worthwhile.

London, UK Danny Nicol

Contents

1 *Who*nited Kingdom 1

2 "One Tiny, Damp Little Island": *Doctor Who*'s Construction of Britishness 29

3 "Lots of Planets Have a North!": Scottishness, Welshness and Northernness in *Doctor Who* 83

4 "The Enemy of the World": Globalised Law Versus British Self-Government 117

5 Is the Doctor a War Criminal? 159

6 From Davos to Davros: Corporate Power in Britain and in *Doctor Who* 209

7 Conclusion: *Doctor Who*'s Post-Democratic Britain 259

Index 281

List of Figures

Fig. 1.1	Brit by association. The Doctor is implicated by companion Rose Tyler's Union Jack t-shirt. *Doctor Who* (new series), "The Empty Child"/"The Doctor Dances", series 1, episodes 9 and 10, British Broadcasting Corporation, 2005	14
Fig. 2.1	The right to be oneself: the individualities of the Doctor and companion Polly form a contrast to a Cyberman. *Doctor Who* (classic series), "The Tenth Planet", season 4, serial 29, British Broadcasting Corporation, 1966	36
Fig. 2.2	Nothing out of the ordinary. The Doctor welcomes black lesbian companion Bill Potts into the *Who*niverse. *Doctor Who* (new series), "The Pilot", series 10, episode 1; British Broadcasting Corporation, 2017	74
Fig. 3.1	Eye candy of Cardiff. Gwen Cooper and Ianto Jones hold the fort at Torchwood. *Doctor Who* (new series), "The Stolen Earth"/"Journey's End", series 4, episodes 12 and 13; British Broadcasting Corporation, 2008	97
Fig. 3.2	Thoroughly British encounter. The Doctor and Scottish companion Amy Pond meet Winston Churchill. *Doctor Who* (new series), "Victory of the Daleks", series 5, episode 3; British Broadcasting Corporation, 2010	101
Fig. 4.1	Happy family. The Doctor with his UNIT colleagues of the early 1970s. *Doctor Who* (classic series), "Invasion of the Dinosaurs", season 11, serial 71; British Broadcasting Corporation, 1974	129

Fig. 5.1 Manhandling the unlike. Two Thals get physical with two Daleks. *Doctor Who* (classic series), "The Daleks", season 1, serial 2; British Broadcasting Corporation, 1963–1964 167
Fig. 6.1 Corporate army. The henchmen of International Electromatics arraign companion Zoe Heriot and friend before Tobias Vaughn. *Doctor Who* (classic series), "The Invasion", season 6, serial 46; British Broadcasting Corporation, 1968 247
Fig. 7.1 A mad man with a mask. The Master as British Prime Minister Harold Saxon. *Doctor Who* (new series), "The Sound of Drums"/"Last of the Time Lords", series 3, episodes 12 and 13; British Broadcasting Corporation, 2007 266
Fig. 7.2 His master-race's voice. British Commander Millington is too close to Nazism for comfort. *Doctor Who* (classic series), "The Curse of Fenric", season 26, serial 155; British Broadcasting Corporation, 1989 274

CHAPTER 1

*Who*nited Kingdom

Doctor Who, the British Broadcasting Corporation's (BBC's) longest-running television drama series, constantly projects imaginings of Britain and Britishness; the aim of this book is to explore them. Ostensibly, *Doctor Who* is a science fiction series (indeed, it is the world's longest-running science fiction programme), but it is as much a programme about what it means to be British. *Doctor Who*'s Britishness raises an array of questions: can a long-running and multi-authored programme like *Doctor Who* project a coherent vision of Britishness over time? Is the show's Britishness descriptive or normative, smug or critical, reactionary or progressive? How does *Doctor Who*'s Britishness confront pressing social issues such as class, gender, race and sexuality, as well as the tensions between the country's four nations? How does the presentation of Britishness respond to globalisation and to the rise of the transnational corporation? What impact have Britain's controversial military interventions made on *Doctor Who*'s depiction of national identity? These are the questions that this book seeks to answer.

This opening chapter has several objectives: first, it locates this study within the literature on national identity, politics and popular culture. It draws on John Street's and Liesbet van Zoonen's insights regarding the inseparability of political communication from popular culture.[1]

[1]John Street, *Politics and Popular Culture* (London: Polity, 1997), 57; Liesbet van Zoonen, *Entertaining the Citizen: When Politics and Popular Culture Converge* (Lanham, MD: Rowman and Littlefield Publishers Inc, 2004).

D. Nicol, *Doctor Who: A British Alien?*,
https://doi.org/10.1007/978-3-319-65834-6_1

The chapter also draws support from Michael Billig's and Tim Edensor's work on the relationship between national identity and popular culture.[2] The close interconnections highlighted by these writings show that programmes such as *Doctor Who* are in the business of national identity and politics and, as such, their contribution merits scholarly analysis just as much as the narratives advanced by politicians.

Secondly, the chapter shows why *Doctor Who* is a particularly fruitful source of commentary on national identity. The programme's template and tropes provide a multiplicity of avenues for its political output, and a wealth of opportunities for satire, allegory and metaphor.

Thirdly, this chapter aims to demonstrate how the exploration of national identity is pivotal to *Doctor Who*. Britishness is no peripheral matter. Rather, regardless of whether the Doctor's escapades are set in contemporary Britain, foreign climes, faraway planets or dystopian futures, *Doctor Who*'s characters are frequently coded as British and a judgement is handed down as to the merits or demerits of their British qualities.

Finally, the chapter considers the book's interpretative methodology, engaging with Alan McKee's well-known article "Is *Doctor Who* political?" and drawing upon the nature of legal interpretation.

National Identity: Politics, Law and Popular Culture

Doctor Who merits study because it makes a substantial contribution to debate surrounding British national identity and to the political controversies connected to it. The objection might be made that *Doctor Who* is a family-orientated and not particularly highbrow science fiction television programme, hardly deserving scholarly analysis. Yet in fact, there are sound reasons why works of popular culture such as *Doctor Who* warrant attention on matters of national identity, just as much as the pronouncements made about Britishness by the country's politicians. First, the importance of popular culture in a general sense has now been recognised by the academy. As Jim McGuigan observes, there is an increasing intellectual assumption that the symbolic experiences and practices of ordinary people are more important analytically and politically than

[2] Tim Edensor, *National Identity, Popular Culture and Everyday Life* (Oxford: Berg, 2002); Michael Billig, *Banal Nationalism* (London: Sage, 1995).

Culture with a capital "C". Writing in 1992, McGuigan identified as a great academic advance the fact that scholars were taking an appreciative, non-judgemental attitude to ordinary tastes and pleasures.[3] We should welcome academia treating popular culture more seriously because it impacts so deeply on the lives of millions of people.

Against this backdrop, there is a strong case to claim that the worlds of politics, national identity and popular culture, far from being discrete, are in fact intimately connected. A number of scholars have drawn attention to this close relationship. John Street, for instance, argues that both the popular media and politicians are engaged in creating works of popular fiction which portray credible worlds that resonate with people's experience.[4] To this extent, he maintains, political performance should be understood in similar terms to those which apply to popular culture. He further contends that popular culture plays a part in politics not so much through its explanatory power but rather by its ability to articulate the feelings and passions that drive politics.[5] In other words, for Street, the division between the pleasures and passions of politics and those of popular culture is almost entirely artificial. Furthermore, Street sees popular culture as being able to produce and articulate feelings which can become the basis of an *identity*. Popular culture, he argues, can become involved in politics through the way it offers forms of identity. Street contends that both within and between politics and popular culture, there is a constant struggle to articulate identities; that is, a battle is fought over the claim to represent competing identities, not least national identity.[6]

Liesbet van Zoonen goes further by arguing that works of popular culture actually *are* politics. This, she holds, is because politics is more than just what politicians do; politics is also a "field" existing independently from its own practitioners, one which accommodates the continuous struggle about power relations in society.[7] Politics, she contends, *has* to be connected to the everyday culture of the citizen, lest it become an alien sphere, dominated by strangers about whom no-one cares or

[3] Jim McGuigan, *Cultural Populism* (London and New York: Routledge, 1992), 4.

[4] Street, *Politics and Popular Culture*, 60.

[5] Street, *Politics and Popular Culture*, 191.

[6] Street, *Politics and Popular Culture*, 21–22.

[7] Van Zoonen, *Entertaining the Citizen*, 5.

bothers.[8] She suggests that the style of popular culture may offer a way into politics for people otherwise excluded or bored. She proposes that popular culture be acknowledged as a relevant resource for political citizenship, one which can make politics more engaging and more inclusive. On these readings, popular culture is politics pursued by other means. As such, it is as worthy of academic attention as the constant efforts of politicians to fashion national identities which resonate with voters.[9]

The relevance of popular culture to constructing a sense of Britishness is reinforced by Tim Edensor's work on national identity. Edensor argues that, until recently, "the masses" uncritically accepted "high" or "official" culture as the dominant signifier of national identity. He observes that of late, however, various accounts have suggested that popular culture has become important.[10] These accounts suggest that we now use a huge and proliferating resource of popular culture which operates to form a sense of national identity that is both dialogic and dynamic.[11] Television programmes have, therefore, become a most potent way of representing the nation. Furthermore, the globalisation of television has, he observes, unleashed a torrent of national representations, including some dissenting and dissonant ones.[12] Edensor also posits that national identities are fragmented. There are, he contends, multiple, chaotic ideas of Britishness, and this renders anachronistic any grand attempts to herd people around a single coherent vision.[13] In a similar vein, Michael Billig, in his book *Banal Nationalism*, argues that the ideological habits that reproduce and reinforce national identity are not removed from everyday life but are "flagged up" daily in the lives of citizens as part of the reassuring normality of life.[14] Billig highlights the constant nationality-flagging of British newspapers, which contributes daily to banal nationalism.[15] Moreover, he points out that we citizens participate in the priming of ourselves by reading, watching and interpreting the mass

---

[8] Van Zoonen, *Entertaining the Citizen*, 3.

[9] Van Zoonen, *Entertaining the Citizen*, 150–151.

[10] Edensor, *National Identity*, 10–11.

[11] Edensor, *National Identity*, 17.

[12] Edensor, *National Identity*, 141–142.

[13] Edensor, *National Identity*, 171–172.

[14] Billig, *Banal Nationalism*, 6.

[15] Billig, *Banal Nationalism*, 95.

media's assertions regarding national identity.[16] Billig's observations about Britain's newspapers apply just as much to a television drama such as *Doctor Who*.

Law, a secondary topic of this book, is also intimately connected to popular culture and to national identity. There are compelling arguments that law is inseparable from politics, indeed that law is *part* of politics.[17] If this be accepted, then the same arguments for envisaging a close link between politics, popular culture and national identity would apply as well to law, popular culture and national identity. In this regard, Steve Greenfield and Guy Osborn have argued that the relationship between law and popular culture is a valuable one, worthy of charting. They propose that understanding that relationship might enable more rigorous thinking about the relationship between law, politics and social change.[18] Law as an academic discipline tends to focus on the judgements of the courts and on legislation. Yet increasingly, legal scholars have come to accept that the social context of law is important. As Anthony Bradney has observed, what people think about law and about the content of legal rules helps to determine their behaviour.[19] To this end, he has analysed *Buffy the Vampire Slayer* (1997–2003) and its spin-off *Angel* (1999–2004) to explore, through a study of their two leading characters, the radically different attitudes to law that those subject to it may hold.[20] Through research like this, popular culture can give us important insights into legal philosophy. In this book, we engage with law's relationship with national identity in assessing *Doctor Who*'s treatment of the globalisation of law (Chap. 4), and the question of whether the Doctor is a war criminal (Chap. 5).

---

[16] Billig, *Banal Nationalism*, 127.

[17] See e.g. J.A.G. Griffith, *The Politics of the Judiciary* (London: Fontana Press, 1997); Danny Nicol, "Law and Politics after the Human Rights Act", *Public Law* (2006): 722–751.

[18] Steve Greenfield and Guy Osborn, "Law, Legal Education and Popular Culture", in *Readings in Law and Popular Culture*, eds. Steve Greenfield and Guy Osborn (Abingdon: Routledge, 2006), 8.

[19] Anthony Bradney, "The Case of *Buffy the Vampire Slayer* and the Politics of Legal Education", in *Readings in Law and Popular Culture*, eds. Steve Greenfield and Guy Osborn (Abingdon: Routledge, 2006), 17–21.

[20] Anthony Bradney, "For and Against the Law: 'Buffy the Vampire Slayer', 'Angel' and the Academy", *Entertainment and Sports Law Journal*, 9 (2011): 1.

Popular culture's potential to express and define Britishness was clearly demonstrated by the London 2012 Olympics opening ceremony, *Isles of Wonder*, directed by Danny Boyle. Indeed, the ceremony's resemblance to *Doctor Who* in terms of being a medium for projecting the nation was underlined by the fleeting appearance of the TARDIS (*Doctor Who*'s time-and-space machine) in the proceedings. *Isles of Wonder* sends up Britain's pre-industrial past by imagining a rural idyll being brutally uprooted by the country's energetic capitalists as the Industrial Revolution made Britain the workshop of the world. The ceremony is teasingly ambiguous as to whether this thrusting capitalism is a good or bad thing. In any event, the ceremony balances this narrative with a fulsome tribute to Britain's National Health Service (NHS) created in 1948 to provide, through general taxation, healthcare free at the point of need. In *Doctor Who* fashion, this segment combines the reassurance that the NHS offers its children patients with the frightening monsters of children's fiction (*Doctor Who* did something rather similar in "Smith and Jones" (2007) in which an NHS hospital is transported to the moon, where it suffers an alien incursion). The ceremony thereby places the NHS centre-stage as part of British national identity.

The opening ceremony certainly constituted popular culture, and to emphasise the point, it devoted a segment to celebrating British popular music and television. Furthermore, the event bore some striking parallels to *Doctor Who*.[21] For instance, the ceremony's memorable fantasy of the Queen jumping with James Bond from a helicopter matches *Doctor Who*'s light-hearted use of the Queen in "Silver Nemesis (1988) and "Voyage of the Damned" (2007). The Queen and Bond descend on Union Jack parachutes, an idea subsequently used by *Doctor Who* in "The Zygon Inversion" (2015). Similarly, the ceremony's heavy emphasis of Britain's multi-racial nature, expressed in the ceremony through a romance sequence between a black British boy and mixed-race British girl, mirrors contemporary *Doctor Who*'s persistent projection of Britishness as a multi-racial nationality, something we explore in Chap. 2. The response to the opening ceremony served as a reminder that portraying national identity is an unequivocally political act.

[21] It is noteworthy that Frank Cottrell Boyce, who worked on the ceremony, subsequently wrote two *Doctor Who* episodes: "In the Forest of the Night" (2014) and "Smile" (2017).

The ceremony's black-British romance and its putting the NHS at the heart of the nation attracted considerable hostility from some on the right of British politics, who found this version of the country's self-image too left-wing for their tastes.[22]

If, therefore, we are fully to chart the disagreements over Britishness, we cannot afford to limit ourselves to the generalisations advanced by the nation's political leaders: we should also examine important works of popular culture such as *Doctor Who*.

The Richness of *Doctor Who*

But why *Doctor Who* in particular? There are good reasons why *Doctor Who* is particularly fruitful in terms of projecting national identity. *Doctor Who* is a flagship BBC programme and the BBC is charged with developing a sense of British identity: over the years *Doctor Who* has come to play a special role in this regard, because its structure provides such ample scope for expressing the national story. In particular, *Doctor Who* is science fiction and it is widely accepted that science fiction tends to deal in metaphors.[23] For its part, *Doctor Who* has certainly demonstrated the genre's potential for allegory,[24] and has indeed used science fiction as a sustained means of satire.[25] Maura Grady and Cassie Hemstrom observe that regardless of whether *Doctor Who* covers historically themed, monster-driven or outer-space narratives, these are often thinly veiled allegories for British politics: the programme thereby holds a mirror to what is going on in British society.[26] In an assessment of classic-series *Doctor Who*, John Tulloch and Manuel Alvarado argue

[22] For instance, "Olympics opening ceremony was multi-cultural crap, Tory MP tweets", *The Guardian*, July 28, 2012; "Ministers 'pushed for changes' in opening ceremony", *The Sunday Telegraph*, July 29, 2012.

[23] Bernadette Casey et al., *Television Studies: The Key Concepts* (London: Routledge, 2002), 207–209.

[24] James Chapman, *Inside the TARDIS: The Worlds of Doctor Who*, 2nd ed. (London: I.B. Tauris, 2013), 5.

[25] Matt Hills, *Triumph of a Time Lord: Regenerating Doctor Who in the Twenty-First Century* (London: I.B. Tauris, 2010), 167.

[26] Maura Grady and Cassie Hemstrom, "Nostalgia for Empire, 1963–1974", in *Doctor Who in Time and Space: Essays on Themes, Characters, History and Fandom, 1963–2012*, ed. Gillian I. Leitch (Jefferson, NC and London: McFarland, 2013), 125–143.

that political external references have long been part of the show. This conclusion is no less valid with regard to post-2005 *Doctor Who*.[27] Additionally, the programme constantly asserts its Britishness and articulates a British identity.[28]

So what are the basic assumptions of the programme? *Doctor Who*'s hero is a character known as the Doctor, who—though humanoid—is not human. He comes from another world, another time. Six years into the show we discover that he is a Time Lord, a humanoid species with great powers over time travel. The Doctor lives in a time and space machine called the TARDIS, which is bigger on the inside than the outside and which looks like a 1960s police telephone box. For company, he acquires a series of mainly human companions with whom he has adventures. These adventures can take place at any point in time and space. Finally, the Doctor—when his body gets worn out or damaged—is able to regenerate, an ingenious device for refreshing the show with new lead actors. *Doctor Who* was broadcast from 1963 to 1989, and from 2005 to the present day. (In this book, I refer to the former as "the classic series" or "classic *Who*" and the latter "the new series" or "new *Who*".[29]) The sixteen-year period in which *Doctor Who* was largely absent from the screen (save for a one-off film *Doctor Who: The Movie* (1996)) provides additional academic interest, allowing scholars to identify changes in the projection of British identity over time. This gap is known as the "hiatus", yet as Miles Booy has shown, it actually proved to be a period in which fandom's creative energies thrived in the void created by the programme's absence.[30]

Doctor Who's template offers ample opportunity for metaphor, allegory and satire. Andrew O'Day, in a piece entitled "Towards a Definition of Satire in *Doctor Who*", draws attention to the variety of

---

[27] John Tulloch and Manuel Alvarado, *Doctor Who: The Unfolding Text* (New York: St Martin's Press, 1983).

[28] Hills, *Triumph of a Time Lord*, 30; Chapman, *Inside the TARDIS*, 8.

[29] I adopt these terms because they are widely used but do so reluctantly: the 1963–1989 series hardly seems old enough to be called classic, nor is it classic in terms of being of higher quality than the new series.

[30] Miles Booy, *Love and Monsters: The Doctor Who Experience, 1979 to the Present* (London: I.B. Tauris, 2012), 152.

outlets for satire in the show.[31] He argues, for instance, that the figure of the monster is key, functioning allegorically to demonstrate human traits. One might add that sometimes the idea of the monstrous is used to say something about British identity. This chimes with Tim Edensor's argument that a key element of fashioning national identity is to draw the boundaries between the self and the other. All forms of social identity involve an "Other", whether explicitly or implicitly[32]; and monsters of course represent "the Other" *par excellence*. Graham Sleight observes that in *Doctor Who*, the monstrous typically stands for something else: indeed, the portrayal of monsters is a kind of moral parable, an argument between competing systems of values.[33] For example, Sleight lists several *Doctor Who* monsters that are characterised by their warlike nature. Yet, in the wake of Britain's multiple interventions in Arab countries in the twenty-first century, it might be argued that the British political elite is itself warlike. Such self-doubt is reflected by *Doctor Who* sometimes portraying humans as being worse than monsters; for instance, in "The Curse of Fenric" (1989), a serial with a rich political content, a British military leader, Commander Millington, epitomises human monstrosity as he machinates to bring about the mass destruction of the Soviet people, at the British government's behest. Another example is "The Ambassadors of Death" (1970), where another British military figure, General Carrington, tries to start a war between humans and a non-belligerent species from Mars. Against this backdrop, Matt Hills is surely right to argue that the show's representation of monstrosity challenges assumptions about the monstrous, calling into question how we define and identify monstrosity.[34]

O'Day also contends that, from a satirical point of view, the recurring figures of rebels are significant. O'Day observes that, as a time traveller, the Doctor frequently arrives in a time and place where an initial equilibrium has already been disrupted and he must join with rebels to

[31] Andrew O'Day, "Towards a Definition of Satire in *Doctor Who*", in *Ruminations, Peregrinations and Regenerations: A Critical Approach to Doctor Who*, ed. Chris Hansen (Newcastle-upon-Tyne: Cambridge Scholars Publishing, 2010).

[32] David McCrone and Frank Bechofer, *Understanding National Identity* (Cambridge: Cambridge University Press, 2015), 2.

[33] Graham Sleight, *The Doctor's Monsters: Meanings of the Monstrous in Doctor Who* (London: I.B. Tauris, 2012), 2–3.

[34] Hills, *Triumph of a Time Lord*, 13.

bring about a new equilibrium. This scenario provides fertile ground for satire.[35] Whilst the Doctor's help may not be uncritical (for example, in "The Monster of Peladon" (1974), he favours moderate rebels against extremist ones, a metaphor for the internal conflicts within the National Union of Mineworkers during the miners' strikes of the 1970s), he normally sides with rebels against the source of their oppression, be that a government, corporation or supraplanetary organisation. These oppressive institutions in *Doctor Who* may represent a source of oppression in Britain.

There are other metaphors which O'Day does not mention. Most importantly, planets often act as metaphors for single states, allowing the show to satirise different forms of government, with an eye to the sort of country Britain risks becoming. Thus, the planet Terra Alpha in "The Happiness Patrol" (1988) is run as an authoritarian dictatorship, the Ood-Sphere in "Planet of the Ood" (2008) is a slave colony governed by a corporation, whereas in "Vengeance on Varos" (1985), the government of the planet Varos—whilst ostensibly independent and democratic—is under the thumb of a giant alien company. Occasionally, too, *Doctor Who* has played around with the idea of parallel universes. As Aidan Byrne and Mark Jones have observed, the mirror universe is an ideal vehicle for television shows to question the ethos, morality and politics of a given society, for the purpose either of self-congratulation or self-examination.[36] In *Doctor Who*, the idea of a parallel Britain has been used to advance cautionary tales about British politics. In "Inferno" (1970), for example, Britain has become a dictatorship, whereas in "Rise of the Cybermen"/"The Age of Steel" (2006), the corporate domination of Britain has reached new heights.

An allegory is an extended metaphor. Some *Doctor Who* stories are unequivocally allegorical in that they contain a multiplicity of metaphors linking the adventure to contemporary politics. For example, "The Curse of Peladon" (1972) is widely seen as an allegory for Britain joining the European Communities (EC; later the European Union). The serial was broadcast in the year that the British government signed the UK–EC accession treaty. The Doctor and companion Jo Grant

[35] O'Day, "Towards a Definition of Satire", 264–282.

[36] Aidan Byrne and Mark Jones, "Worlds Turned Back to Front: The Politics of the Mirror Universe in *Doctor Who* and *Star Trek*", *Journal of Popular Television*, 6(2) (2018).

visit the insular planet of Peladon, which is on the verge of joining the Galactic Federation, an organisation of planets which (like the EC) have relinquished war in favour of peaceful trade. Peladon (like Britain) is a monarchy whose political elite are split on the merits of pooling sovereignty. The Doctor is suspicious of one particular delegation: that of the Ice Warriors, who (like the Germans in the EC) have previously started wars but now vow to have rejected violence except in self-defence. The law of the Federation is (like EC law) supreme within its member planets but only within limited fields. Ultimately, the Doctor (like the British government of the day) thwarts those who want to sabotage accession to the organisation.

Another example of full-blown allegory in *Doctor Who* is "Warriors of the Deep" (1984). Set in Earth's near future in an underwater base (Britain's nuclear deterrent is submarine based), it imagines two human power blocs, fingers poised to annihilate each other. The sea base is run by one of the two power blocs but is invaded by Earth's earlier, reptilian inhabitants the Silurians and their aquatic cousins the Sea Devils. The reptiles' plan, which they perceive as merely a "defensive war", is to induce the two human blocs to use their nuclear arsenals to destroy each other. The tale contains an array of Cold War signifiers: brain control; secret agents; the oriental costumes of the Sea Devils (and mention of "triads"), which codes them as the Chinese cousins of the presumably Soviet Silurians; a weapon of mass destruction in the form of the Myrka, an electrocuting dinosaur; a missile which destroys organic tissue but leaves property intact; a successful bid by the Doctor at unilateral disarmament (he earns trust by surrendering his firearm); and at the end (unusually in a *Doctor Who* adventure) everyone dies, reptiles and humans alike, apart from the Doctor and his two companions. The Doctor's closing comment, "there should have been another way", serves as the show's verdict on "mutually assured destruction".

Other *Doctor Who* adventures may contain a single pivotal metaphor rather than a coherent collection of metaphors. For instance, "Aliens of London"/"World War Three" (2005) involves a takeover of the British government by the alien Slitheen, who are disguised as overweight humans. The idea of politicians being an alien race corresponds to perceptions which developed during the New Labour government 1997–2010 that they were indeed something of a species apart. Peter Oborne explores this idea in his book *The Triumph of the Political Class*, in which he argues that the British party system has collapsed in favour of a ruling elite estranged from civil society. Politicians, Oborne contends, have ceased to represent the voters and instead represent themselves. As a result, the real political divide is no longer between the main political parties but between the political class and the rest.[37] The likening of the Slitheen to the Blair government is consolidated when the Slitheen leader tries to start a nuclear strike on the grounds that there are "massive weapons of destruction capable of being deployed within 45 seconds", a satire on Tony Blair's justification for the invasion of Iraq (that Iraqi president Saddam Hussein could deploy weapons of mass destruction against British forces within 45 minutes of an order to use them). Terse witticisms such as this are an important part of *Doctor Who*'s satire, and we ought not to belittle their significance merely because of their brevity.

Despite *Doctor Who*'s constant satire, its treatment of British identity and politics has yet to be explored in depth. There has certainly been a welcome expansion of the academic literature on *Doctor Who*, particularly since 2010; yet few extended works have focused on the programme's engagement with national identity and its political and legal ramifications. To be sure, there have been some valuable chapters on *Doctor Who*'s Britishness in edited collections—by Barbara Selznick, Matt Jones and J.P.T. Brown[38]—but until the present monograph, there has been nothing of book length, which this multi-faceted subject surely merits. Among the books of collected essays, the only major work with a wholly political focus is the excellent *Doctor Who and Race*.[39] However, this book covers only one aspect of politics—race—and does not concentrate on Britain. There have also been a series of outstanding sole-authored monographs on *Doctor Who* in recent years, all of which have political content, but these books have tended not to have Britishness, politics and law as their primary focus. For example, John Tulloch and Manuel Alvarado's *Doctor Who: The Unfolding Text* explores the

---

[37] Peter Oborne, *The Triumph of the Political Class* (London: Simon and Schuster, 2007).

[38] Barbara Selznick, "Rebooting and Rebranding; the Changing Brands of *Doctor Who*'s Britishness"; Matthew Jones, "Aliens of London: (Re)Reading National Identity in *Doctor Who*", in *Ruminations, Peregrinations and Regenerations: A Critical Approach to Doctor Who*, ed. Chris Hansen (Newcastle-upon-Tyne: Cambridge Scholars Publishing, 2010); J.P.C. Brown, "*Doctor Who*: A Very British Alien", in *The Galaxy is Rated G: Essays on Children's Science Fiction Film and Television*, eds. R.C. Neighbors and Sandy Rankin (Jefferson, NC: McFarland, 2011).

[39] Lindy Orthia, ed., *Doctor Who and Race* (Bristol: Intellect, 2013).

programme from a variety of perspectives and engages with the political aspects pervasively but not extensively; Matt Hills' *Triumph of a Time Lord* concentrates on the success of new-series *Doctor Who*, again with recurring analysis of political discourses; James Chapman's *Inside the TARDIS* combines an account of *Doctor Who*'s evolution as a successful television series with a cultural history of the programme, Britishness being a pervasive theme rather than the overwhelming focus; Piers Britton's *TARDISbound* engages with the social rather than political aspects of *Doctor Who* and does not have a specifically British dimension; Lorna Jowett's *Dancing with the Doctor* critiques the show's treatment of one aspect of politics—gender—and, to a lesser extent, sexuality, in new *Who* and its spin-offs. Britishness is a theme of her book but the main theme is gender.[40] The present book attempts to fill the gap in the *Doctor Who* literature by offering an analysis of the programme that definitively gives pride of place to the show's presentation of Britishness and to the politics and law which underpin that identity.

This is a good time for such a study, because we live in an era in which the existence of Britain as a political entity and the nature of Britishness as a national identity have rarely been so contested. Pressure for—and resistance to—supranational governance on the one hand and for Scottish and Welsh independence on the other have cast doubt on Britain's viability as a united, self-governing state. In particular, the British electorate's historic decision in 2016 to leave the European Union both contributes to national identity whilst creating difficulties for that identity owing to the closeness and divisiveness of the referendum vote (52% leave, 48% remain). The EU vote also split the four nations of the United Kingdom, with England and Wales voting to leave and Scotland and Northern Ireland voting to remain. Differences over secession, European integration and globalisation make it problematic to define British national identity, as has the rise of alternative identities, including those associated with "Islamic" extremism. These questions of

[40]John Tulloch and Manuel Alvarado, *Doctor Who: The Unfolding Text* (New York: St Martin's Press, 1983); Hills, *Triumph of a Time Lord*; Chapman, *Inside the TARDIS*; Piers Britton, *TARDISbound: Navigating the Universes of Doctor Who* (London: I.B. Tauris, 2011); Lorna Jowett, *Dancing with the Doctor: Dimensions of Gender in the Doctor Who Universe* (London: I.B. Tauris, 2017).

Fig. 1.1 Brit by association. The Doctor is implicated by companion Rose Tyler's Union Jack t-shirt. *Doctor Who* (new series), "The Empty Child"/"The Doctor Dances", series 1, episodes 9 and 10, British Broadcasting Corporation, 2005

national viability are significant to the country at large, not just the academy. At such a time of crisis, the study of attempts to define the nation, including those attempts made by popular culture, become still more important.

CENTRALITY OF *DOCTOR WHO*'S BRITISHNESS

That Britishness is a central and pervasive theme of *Doctor Who* should be readily apparent to even the casual viewer. Russell T. Davies, showrunner of the revived post-2005 *Doctor Who*, explicitly intended it to be "very, very British".[41] The Doctor himself is a thoroughly British alien, invariably eccentric, often fond of tea and prone to "muddling through" his adventures, relying on brainpower more than firepower. When in *Doctor Who: The Movie* (1996), his one-off companion Dr Grace Holloway is seeking to reassure an American policeman that the Doctor is not reaching for a gun, she blurts out "he's, er, he's British", prompting the Time Lord's significant reply: "yes, I suppose I am". For good measure, the Time Lord's accents—most often southern English but sometimes northern English (ninth Doctor) and Scottish (seventh Doctor, twelfth Doctor)—mark him out as representing the United Kingdom.[42] Particularly striking is the Doctor's speech in "The Empty Child" (2005), set in London during World War Two, where he describes Britain as "one tiny, damp little island" single-handedly resisting Nazi domination, "a mouse in front of a lion". In the same episode, companion Rose Tyler sports a Union Jack t-shirt. Figure 1.1 shows how Rose's physical proximity to the Doctor is cleverly utilised to associate him too with the sense of Britishness signified by her t-shirt. Drawing the bodies of the Doctor and Rose together in this way serves to "Britishise" the Doctor, thereby setting the scene for his stirring patriotic speech. In a similar vein, in "The Idiots' Lantern" (2006), Rose lectures others on how to display the national flag. Companion Amy Pond's first couple of trips in the TARDIS involve meeting a future British queen and a past British prime minister, each adventure bedecked with Union Jacks.[43] Indeed, on occasion, the show seems to be satirising its own obsession with Britishness. For example, in "The Christmas Invasion" (2005), the Doctor completes one of his regenerations by dint of a flask of tea: it leaks into the inner workings of the TARDIS and he is revived by its vapours. In "The Zygon Inversion" (2015), the Doctor escapes a doomed plane in a Union Jack parachute. And in "Empress of Mars"

[41] Steve Clarke, "'Who' Dunnit Once…", *Variety* (March 21, 2005), 20.

[42] Jones, "Aliens of London", 98.

[43] "The Beast Below" (2010), "Victory of the Daleks" (2010).

(2017) the Doctor cannot resist a grin when, surrounded by Americans at NASA headquarters, he sees a picture relayed from Mars of the words "God Save the Queen" marked in boulders on the planet surface, indicating that the British had already visited the Red Planet. This somewhat relentless coding marks the Doctor, as well as *Doctor Who* as a programme, as representing Britishness.

Unsurprisingly, there is consensus among *Doctor Who* scholars that Britishness is indeed central to the show. Nicholas J. Cull observes that the supposedly alien Doctor's manners and adventures are deeply imbued with stories that the British people tell themselves about themselves.[44] Lorna Jowett characterises the Doctor as not a traditional hero but a very *British* one, tending to prevail through ingenuity and persuasion rather than firepower.[45] Maura Grady and Cassie Hemstrom judge *Doctor Who* to be "quintessentially British".[46] Matthew Jones sees the relationship between *Doctor Who* and Britain as "a defining element of the series", with "a British identity written into the very construction of the programme, beginning at its very roots": "a product of the UK, about the UK".[47] Barbara Selznick notes that whilst the programme can be analysed across an array of disciplines, including historically and philosophically, one common element with cuts across all these different studies is that *Doctor Who* is undeniably British, in its themes, style and character.[48] James Chapman observes that in an increasingly globalised television culture, *Doctor Who*'s insistence upon an almost parochial sense of Britishness is unusual.[49] Chapman also argues that the cultural politics and narrative ideologies of *Doctor Who* are unmistakably British in fostering toleration, non-conformity and difference.[50] Simone Knox notes that *Doctor Who* is marked by signifiers of Britishness in a whole

---

[44]Nicholas J. Cull, "TARDIS at the OK Corral: *Doctor Who* and the USA", in *British Science Fiction Television*, eds. John R. Cook and Peter Wright (London: I.B. Tauris, 2006), 55.

[45]Jowett, *Dancing with the Doctor*, 11.

[46]Grady and Hemstrom, "Nostalgia", 125, 139.

[47]Jones, "Aliens of London", 86, 89, 99.

[48]Selznick, "Rebooting and Rebranding", 68.

[49]Chapman, *Inside the TARDIS*, 8.

[50]Chapman, *Inside the TARDIS*, 7.

range of ways.[51] Matt Hills discusses the role of classic-series *Doctor Who* as an emblem of Britishness, articulating a British identity.[52] If anything, new-series *Doctor Who* appears to pursue Britishness with even greater gusto than the classic series, as evidenced by the critical mass of Union Jacks, Scots, the Welsh, cups of tea, prime ministers and queens. Indeed, new *Who* projects its image of Britishness in a more brazen fashion than classic *Who*.

Some commentators connect *Doctor Who*'s Britishness to the country's imperialism and neo-imperialism. In this regard, J.P.C. Brown argues that post-2005 *Doctor Who* is less preoccupied with Britishness as an animating *problem* than was the case in the programme's earlier years.[53] To be sure, the loss of the Empire has been receding into the country's past. However, there is ample evidence that the new series engages in sustained debate as to whether Britishness should embrace post-1979 neoliberalism at home and post-9/11 interventionism abroad. Dominic Sandbrook has attributed the show's success to the British loving stories of crusading heroes taking British values to the furthest reaches of the universe, characterising the Doctor as every inch the Victorian adventurer, an ideal hero for the post-imperial age.[54]

So pervasive is the Britishness metaphor in *Doctor Who* that it transcends time and space. Irrespective of whether a *Doctor Who* story is set in contemporary Britain, elsewhere in the world, or on some faraway world or space station, the culture is repeatedly earmarked as British.[55] Furthermore, there are a great many non-Earth humanoids in *Doctor Who*'s adventures.[56] These humanoids are frequently coded as British, regardless of whether their species is identified as human. An example is "Kinda" (1982). The Doctor and his companions land on the planet Deva Loka where they meet a small team of humanoid colonists. The dialogue and costumes of the two male colonists, Sanders and Hindle,

---

[51] Simone Knox, "The Transatlantic Dimensions of the Time Lord: *Doctor Who* and the Relationships between British and North American Television", in *Doctor Who: The Eleventh Hour*, ed. Andrew O'Day (London: I.B. Tauris, 2014), 112.

[52] Hills, *Triumph of a Time Lord*, 30.

[53] Brown, "*Doctor Who*", 179.

[54] *Dominic Sandbrook: Let Us Entertain You.* BBC Two, November 18, 2015.

[55] Tulloch and Alvarado, *Doctor Who*, 288.

[56] Indeed, only one *Doctor Who* story, "The Web Planet" (1965), has been bereft of humanoids (the Doctor and companions apart), an experiment that was not repeated.

match ideas of nineteenth-century British colonialism: they even wear the pith helmets of the British Empire. Subsequently, the time travellers encounter the Kinda, the native people of the planet. At first, the Doctor considers the Kinda to be primitive but, as John Tulloch and Manuel Alvarado observe, they actually form a highly advanced culture in terms of eliminating divisive aggression and individualistic assertion. Tulloch and Alvarado suggest that "Kinda" represents a debate about the superiority of individualist achievement and linear progress in contrast to communal harmony and a static history.[57] This in turn reflects arguments over the paternalistic assumptions of the British Empire. "Planet of the Ood" (2008) provides another example of a *Doctor Who* story set on a distant planet in a future epoch yet tackling aspects of contemporary Britishness. The Ood are the slave race of the Second Glorious and Bountiful Human Empire (an empire in which almost everyone has a British accent) and the story, set in the year 4126, can be interpreted as pitting "entrepreneurial, buccaneering Britain", in the form of the company Ood Operations which enslaves the Ood, against "fair-play Britain", in the shape of the Doctor, companion Donna and a political group Friends of the Ood which plots the Ood's liberation. Like the Kinda, the Ood seemingly resist the notion that everyone must emulate the West. Left to their own devices, they appear to eschew science, capitalism and individualism. *Doctor Who* has been accused of too often denigrating non-Western cultures and of assuming that societies should proceed in fixed stages towards the technologically and intellectually "superior" Western way of life, but this is not always the case.[58]

By the same token, *Doctor Who* stories set in foreign countries on Earth are often dominated by Britishness. "City of Death" (1979) takes place in Paris, yet any "Frenchness" in the story is at best marginal. By contrast, as Alan McKee rightly observes, Britishness is constantly expressed, in terms of amateurishness and playfulness.[59] Indeed, one

---

[57] Tulloch and Alvarado, *Doctor Who*, 269.

[58] Lindy A. Orthia, "Savages, Science, Stagism and the Naturalized Ascendancy of the Not-We in *Doctor Who*", in *Doctor Who and Race*, ed. Lindy Orthia (Bristol: Intellect, 2013), 269–288. Orthia herself instances "State of Decay" (1980) as a *Doctor Who* story that rejects a stagist or linear view of human development.

[59] Alan McKee, "Why is 'City of Death' the Best *Doctor Who* Story?", in *Time and Relative Dissertations in Space: Critical Perspectives on Doctor Who*, ed. David Butler (Manchester: Manchester University Press, 2007), 243.

seminal aspect of the Britishness of this adventure slips under McKee's radar: "City of Death" is to a significant extent the story of Duggan, a pleasant yet physically aggressive British police officer who accompanies the Doctor and companion Romana throughout the escapade, strikes the killer blow that thwarts the alien menace and receives the goodbye waves of the Doctor and Romana from the Eiffel Tower at the end of the story. The stocky Duggan can easily be read as a diminutive Britain punching above its weight in the international scene.[60] Another example of *Doctor Who* articulating Britishness in a foreign location is "The Impossible Astronaut"/"Day of the Moon" (2011), where an American setting is used to draw a pointed contrast between British reliance on brains and American reliance on guns.

The Doctor's succession of companions presents another way of telling the national story. In the classic series, all Earth companions bar two (Tegan Jovanka and Peri Brown) were British. Most companions acquired in outer space (Vicki, Steven Taylor, Zoe Heriot, Romana, Adric, Nyssa) were coded as British too. Romana, Nyssa and Turlough as non-human humanoids were afforded a mild degree of "Otherness" by being portrayed as upper-class British. All new-series companions have been British apart from Captain Jack Harkness. Indeed, in new *Who*, the use of companions as symbols of Britishness is even more pointed. For instance, Rose Tyler and Amy Pond are repeatedly filmed in proximity with the Union Jack; white companions often have black or mixed-race boyfriends to emphasise British pride in a multiracial society; and Martha Jones, Clara Oswald and Clara's boyfriend Danny Pink work for the country's great public services, the NHS and education, thereby highlighting the more egalitarian aspects of British identity. Even companions' choices of food and drink may serve to accentuate Britishness: it is Rose's mother who provides the tea which helps the Doctor regenerate in "The Christmas Invasion", whilst partly robotic companion Nardole also proffers tea and, in "Oxygen" (2017), urges the Doctor and companion Bill Potts to return to the "nice and cosy" TARDIS rather than risk a perilous adventure—a pointedly British invocation of the comforts and safety of home. Chips emerge as another signifier of national identity: much loved by Rose and family, savoured by Martha Jones and Captain Jack on their return to contemporary Britain, and

[60] "City of Death" was broadcast at a time of increasing supranationalism, with the first direct elections to the European Parliament taking place the same year.

served by Bill Potts in her job at a university canteen. (Their being called "fries" in the USA serves to make the term more exclusively British-and-Commonwealth.)

On occasion, *Doctor Who*'s writers even herd the Doctor's enemies into the British fold. "Victory of the Daleks" (2010) sees the Daleks recruited into the British army in the Second World War. They wear Union Jack insignia and ask their human colleagues whether they would care for some tea. Similarly, the Doctor's long-term Time Lord adversary, the Master, first appears in "Terror of the Autons" (1971) as a swarthy, bearded foreigner sporting a Nehru suit, only to regenerate into a British prime minister in "The Sound of Drums" (2007), a Britishness consolidated in "Death in Heaven" (2014) by a further transformation into the Scottish-accented Missy, who wears the attire of a Victorian governess.

Doctor Who's emphasis on Britishness is hardly surprising given that it is the flagship product of the British Broadcasting Corporation. According to Brian McNair, the Corporation was established partly to play the role, consciously articulated, of promoting a sense of Britishness and of national community.[61] For Linda Colley, the BBC is probably still the most reliable medium for creating some image of communion across the United Kingdom, having consistently and actively provided a cultural image of Britain.[62] Jean Seaton observes that the BBC has an obligation *to* the nation because it is *for* the nation. It therefore has to endlessly try and sort out what the nation is. Seaton argues that the BBC mainly metabolises the nation by worrying about it, thereby adding a reflexive anxiety and creative imagination to the problems it confronts. However, she contends, the BBC also trumpets Britain's good points.[63] As we shall see, *Doctor Who* does indeed project a combination of concern over British vices and pride in British virtue.

---

[61] Brian McNair, *News and Journalism in the UK*, 5th ed. (Abingdon: Routledge, 2009), 108.

[62] Linda Colley, "Does Britishness Still Matter in the 21st Century, and How Much/ How Well do the Politicians Care?", in *Britishness: Perspectives on the British Question*, eds. Andrew Gamble and Tony Wright (Chichester: Wiley-Blackwell, 2009), 25.

[63] Jean Seaton, "The BBC and Metabolising Britishness: Critical Patriotism", in *Britishness: Perspectives on the British Question*, eds. Andrew Gamble and Tony Wright (Chichester: Wiley-Blackwell, 2009), 78.

Interpreting *Doctor Who*'s Britishness

This book's focus is on the way in which *Doctor Who* presents Britishness *on television*; my analysis therefore omits the rich array of *Doctor Who* novels and audio adventures. An exclusive focus on television is a perfectly defensible choice[64]; *Doctor Who* as a television programme can be distinguished not least on the basis of the size of its audience compared to that for other outlets of *Doctor Who* fiction. As Neil Postman observes, "the single most important fact about television is that people watch it".[65] Where appropriate, I have included some analysis of *Doctor Who*'s major spin-offs, *Torchwood* (2006–2011), *The Sarah Jane Adventures* (2007–2011) and *Class* (2016). These apart, in the main I will make few comparisons between *Doctor Who* and other programmes or films, since the comparative task is already well performed by *Doctor Who* scholars from the fields of television and film studies.

A further methodological choice is between an "internal" analysis, where the researcher undertakes interviews and scours archives in search of the inside story of the writer's intention, and an "external" analysis, which interprets the end product with less emphasis on authorial intention. Again, both are valid approaches, and there are splendid examples of each in the existing body of *Doctor Who* scholarship, as well as hybrid methodologies. For the most part, this book adopts an external analysis, mindful of Graham Sleight's insight that authorial intention is one narrative among many.[66] After all, as Matthew Jones has argued, the concerns that underpin recent British history have emerged in *Doctor Who* regardless of whether the production team intended to invoke particular socio-political anxieties.[67] This approach avoids many of the difficulties to which the quest for authorial intention would give rise.

---

[64] Hills, *Triumph of A Time Lord*, 4. This choice is not intended to belittle *Doctor Who* tie-ins: as Matt Hills observes, they merit academic scrutiny. Piers Britton, in *TARDISbound*, has managed rather successfully to combine analysis of an array of *Doctor Who* fictional outputs.

[65] Neil Postman, *Amusing Ourselves to Death* (London: Methuen, 1996), 94.

[66] Sleight, *The Doctor's Monsters*, 3.

[67] Matthew Jones, "Army of Ghosts: Sight, Knowledge and the Invisible Terrorist in *Doctor Who*", in *Impossible Things, Impossible Worlds: Cultural Perspectives on Doctor Who, Torchwood and the Sarah Jane Adventures*, eds. Ross Garner, Melissa Beattie and Una McCormack (Newcastle-upon-Tyne: Cambridge Scholars Publishing, 2010), 45–61, 52.

These difficulties include the danger of retrospective falsification, the likelihood that authors of early *Doctor Who* serials would no longer be alive leading to a skewed analysis in favour of more recent *Doctor Who*; the problems of the show's multi-authored nature and the fluidity between the roles of writers, producers, executive producers and script editors, which makes "authorship" a nebulous concept in *Doctor Who*.[68]

So how then should we go about interpreting *Doctor Who*? In a well-known article, "Is *Doctor Who* political?", Alan McKee researched fans' views of *Doctor Who*'s classic series and concluded that most of them did not believe that *Doctor Who* was political, at least not in the sense of state-level politics. He contrasts that view with the interpretation put forward by John Fiske that *Doctor Who* advances a capitalist ideology (a stance with which I take issue later in this book). McKee contends that both interpretations of the programme are valid, having regard for the perspectives from which they arise, but that scholars should not claim an undue advantage for their interpretations by clothing them in the language of ideology.[69] McKee is surely right to argue that there are a range of reasonable interpretations of *Doctor Who*. As Rebecca Williams has observed, the idea of a singular, homogeneous and stable interpretation of *Doctor Who* which establishes an officially constituted reading formation can no longer be sustained.[70] But just as (*per* McKee) scholars'

---

[68] Dave Rolinson, "'*Who* Done it': Discourse of Authorship during the John Nathan-Turner era", in *Time and Relative Dissertations in Space: Critical Perspectives on Doctor Who*, ed. David Butler (Manchester: Manchester University Press, 2007), 176–189; Tom Steward, "Author Who?: Masterplanners, Scribermen and Script Doctors; the Producers, Writers and Script Editors of *Doctor Who*", in *Ruminations, Peregrinations and Regenerations: A Critical Approach to Doctor Who*, ed. Chris Hansen (Newcastle-upon-Tyne: Cambridge Scholars Publishing, 2010), 312–327. Rolinson observes that John Nathan-Turner's influence as *Doctor Who* producer in the 1980s was so profound that he was able to make recursion the common theme of the serials in his first season. Script editors Christopher H. Bidmead and Andrew Cartmel also both had great influence. Stewart argues that in the new, show Russell T. Davies' executive producer brief combined the roles of producer and script editor, allowing him to rewrite and redraft scripts.

[69] Alan McKee, "Is *Doctor Who* Political?", *European Journal of Cultural Studies*, vii/2 (2004): 201–217. I disagree with McKee that advancing an argument that *Doctor Who* projects an ideology somehow places a commentator such as Fiske in a privileged position. Quite the opposite: the claim makes Fiske more vulnerable to counter-argument.

[70] Rebecca Williams, "Desiring the Doctor: Identity, Gender and Genre in Online Fandom", in *British Science Fiction Television: Critical Essays*, eds. James Leggott and Tobias Hochscherf (Jefferson, NC: McFarland, 2011), 167–177, 177.

readings of *Doctor Who* are not beyond criticism, by the same token, neither should fans be cocooned from criticism. If academic interpretations of *Doctor Who* are fair game, then so too are those put forward by fans. There is a wealth of evidence that *Doctor Who* is a rich source of political references, so the fans in McKee's sample were not advancing a particularly strong argument.

Interpretation, then, is something we argue about. We all interpret from our own perspectives; but some readings are more plausible than others, so those interpretations vie with each other, all of them being contestable. This chapter has argued that one highly legitimate perspective takes account of the *national* context in which *Doctor Who* has evolved and in which it continues to be created. It should also be noted that McKee's article predated the publication of the main interdisciplinary works on *Doctor Who*—interpretations seen through the lenses of philosophy, religious studies and psychology.[71] Interdisciplinarity has enriched *Doctor Who* studies by adding another welcome array of perspectives by which meaning may be attributed to *Doctor Who*.

This malleability of interpretation is what John Tulloch and Manuel Alvarado notoriously dubbed the "semiotic thickness" of *Doctor Who*.[72] The idea of different readings of *Doctor Who* bustling for our attention resonates with the nature of legal reasoning. It is part of law's mystique that there exists a single "correct" interpretation of a legal provision. In reality, however, talk of "correctness", though it saturates the judicial psyche, masks the fact that there are usually a number of reasonable readings of the same text. Lawyers are really seeking the most compelling interpretation, supported by the most convincing evidence. In her book *Charter Conflicts*, Janet Hiebert questions the singularity of a "correct" judicial answer to disagreements over constitutional rights, arguing that such tensions are at heart philosophical and political, and that one should not deny the likelihood of reasonable disagreements over

[71] For example, Courtland Lewis and Paula Smithka, eds., *Doctor Who and Philosophy: Bigger on the Inside* (Chicago, IL: Open Court, 2011); Andrew Crome and James McGrath, eds., *Time and Relative Dimensions in Faith: Religion and Doctor Who* (London: Darton, Longman & Todd, 2013); Ian MacRury and Michael Rustin, *The Inner World of Doctor Who: Psychoanalytical Reflections in Time and Space* (London: Karnac, 2014).

[72] Tulloch and Alvarado, *Doctor Who*, 249. The phrase was satirised as pretentious in the *Doctor Who* serial "Dragonfire" (1987).

the limits of rights.[73] The same surely applies to readings of *Doctor Who*. On the other hand, this is not to say that anything goes. John Street rightly argues that works of popular culture ought not to be treated as blank screens onto which any idea can be written. Rather, there is a requirement for judgement and discrimination, a need to select between accuracy and distortion, between the genuine and the phoney. Street warns that one must immunise oneself against a populism which reads all popular culture as a form of political resistance.[74] Indeed, regardless of whether a reading of *Doctor Who* paints particular aspects of the programme as progressive or reactionary, one should not strain every sinew to extract contrived political meaning from the show. It is here that law's insistence on compelling evidence surely deserves to come to the fore. There may legitimately be a multiplicity of interpretations of *Doctor Who*, but we should only be interested in those interpretations that actually pass the test of being reasonably convincing.

Conclusion

In sum, a television programme seemingly about distant epochs, far-away planets and bizarre monsters is often really concerned with contemporary British identity, politics and law. When the TARDIS lands on a new planet, this frequently provides the opportunity to satirise some aspect of British life, so much so that *Doctor Who* can be considered a British institution and part of British identity. It is the *substance* of the programme's Britishness which this book aims to explore. In short, according to *Doctor Who*, what does it mean to be British?

Bibliography

Billig, Michael. *Banal Nationalism*. London: Sage, 1995.
Booy, Miles. *Love and Monsters: The Doctor Who Experience, 1979 to the Present*. London: I.B. Tauris, 2012.

[73] Janet Hiebert, *Charter Conflicts: What is Parliament's Role?* (Montreal and Kingston: McGill–Queen's University Press, 2001), 29–30. See also generally Jeremy Waldron, *Law and Disagreement* (Oxford: Oxford University Press, 1999).

[74] Street, *Politics and Popular Culture*, 19.

Bradney, Anthony. "For and Against the Law: 'Buffy the Vampire Slayer', 'Angel' and the Academy." *The Entertainment and Sports Law Journal* 9(1), 2011, 1.

Bradney, Anthony. "The Case of *Buffy the Vampire Slayer* and the Politics of Legal Education." In *Readings in Law and Popular Culture*, edited by Steve Greenfield and Guy Osborn, 15–30. Abingdon: Routledge, 2006.

Britton, Piers D. *TARDISbound: Navigating the Universes of Doctor Who.* London: I.B. Tauris, 2011.

Brown, J.P.C. "*Doctor Who*: A Very British Alien." In *The Galaxy is Rated G: Essays on Children's Science Fiction Film and Television*, edited by R.C. Neighbors and Sandy Rankin, 161–182. Jefferson, NC: McFarland, 2011.

Byrne, Aidan and Mark Jones. "Worlds Turned Back to Front: The Politics of the Mirror Universe in *Doctor Who* and *Star Trek*." *Journal of Popular Television* 6(2), 2018.

Casey, Bernadette, Neil Casey, Ben Calvert, Liam French and Justin Lewis. *Television Studies: The Key Concepts.* London: Routledge, 2002.

Chapman, James. *Inside the TARDIS: The Worlds of Doctor Who*, 2nd ed. London: I.B. Tauris, 2013.

Clarke, Steve. "'Who' Dunnit Once…", *Variety*, March 21, 2005.

Colley, Linda. "Does Britishness Still Matter in the 21st Century, and How Much/How Well do the Politicians Care?" In *Britishness: Perspectives on the British Question*, edited by Andrew Gamble and Tony Wright, 21–31. Chichester: Wiley-Blackwell, 2009.

Crome, Andrew and James McGrath, eds. *Time and Relative Dimensions in Faith: Religion and Doctor Who.* London: Darton, Longman & Todd, 2013.

Cull, Nicholas J. "TARDIS at the OK Corral: *Doctor Who* and the USA." In *British Science Fiction Television*, edited by John R. Cook and Peter Wright, 55. London: I.B. Tauris, 2006.

Edensor, Tim. *National Identity, Popular Culture and Everyday Life.* Oxford: Berg, 2002.

Grady, Maura and Cassie Hemstrom, "Nostalgia for Empire, 1963–74." In *Doctor Who in Time and Space: Essays on Themes, Characters, History and Fandom, 1963–2012*, edited by Gillian I. Leitch, 125–143. Jefferson, NC and London: McFarland, 2013.

Greenfield, Steve and Guy Osborn, "Law, Legal Education and Popular Culture." In *Readings in Law and Popular Culture*, edited by Steve Greenfield and Guy Osborn, 1–12. Abingdon: Routledge, 2006.

Griffith, J.A.G. *The Politics of the Judiciary.* London: Fontana Press, 1997.

Hiebert, Janet. *Charter Conflicts: What is Parliament's Role?* Montreal and Kingston: McGill–Queen's University Press, 2001.

Hills, Matt. *Triumph of a Time Lord: Regenerating Doctor Who in the Twenty-First Century.* London: I.B. Tauris, 2010.

Jones, Matthew. "Aliens of London: (Re)Reading National Identity in *Doctor Who*." In *Ruminations, Peregrinations and Regenerations: A Critical Approach to Doctor Who*, edited by Chris Hansen, 150–162. Newcastle-upon-Tyne: Cambridge Scholars Publishing, 2010.

Jones, Matthew. "Army of Ghosts: Sight, Knowledge and the Invisible Terrorist in *Doctor Who*." In *Impossible Things, Impossible Worlds: Cultural Perspectives on Doctor Who, Torchwood and the Sarah Jane Adventures*, edited by Ross Garner, Melissa Beattie and Una McCormack, 45–61. Newcastle-upon-Tyne: Cambridge Scholars Publishing, 2010.

Jowett, Lorna. *Dancing with the Doctor: Dimensions of Gender in the Doctor Who Universe*. London: I.B. Tauris, 2017.

Knox, Simone. "The Transatlantic Dimensions of the Time Lord: *Doctor Who* and the Relationships between British and North American Television." In *Doctor Who: The Eleventh Hour*, edited by Andrew O'Day, 106–120. London: I.B. Tauris, 2014.

Lewis, Courtland and Paula Smithka, eds. *Doctor Who and Philosophy: Bigger on the Inside*. Chicago, IL: Open Court, 2011.

McCrone, David and Frank Bechofer. *Understanding National Identity*. Cambridge: Cambridge University Press, 2015.

McGuigan, Jim. *Cultural Populism*. London and New York: Routledge, 1992.

McKee, Alan. "Is *Doctor Who* Political?" *European Journal of Cultural Studies* vii/2 (2004): 201–217.

McKee, Alan. "Why is 'City of Death' the Best *Doctor Who* story?" In *Time and Relative Dissertations in Space: Critical Perspectives on Doctor Who*, edited by David Butler, 233–245. Manchester: Manchester University Press, 2007.

McNair, Brian. *News and Journalism in the UK*, 5th ed. Abingdon: Routledge, 2009.

MacRury, Ian and Michael Rustin. *The Inner World of Doctor Who: Psychoanalytical Reflections in Time and Space*. London: Karnac, 2014.

Nicol, Danny. "Law and Politics after the Human Rights Act." *Public Law* (2006): 722–751.

O'Day, Andrew. "Towards a Definition of Satire in *Doctor Who*." In *Ruminations, Peregrinations and Regenerations: A Critical Approach to Doctor Who*, edited by Chris Hansen, 264–282. Newcastle-upon-Tyne: Cambridge Scholars Publishing, 2010.

Oborne, Peter. *The Triumph of the Political Class*. London: Simon and Schuster, 2007.

Orthia, Lindy, ed. *Doctor Who and Race*. Bristol: Intellect, 2013.

Orthia, Lindy. "Savages, Science, Stagism and the Naturalized Ascendancy of the Not-We in *Doctor Who*." In *Doctor Who and Race*, edited by Lindy Orthia, 45–60. Bristol: Intellect, 2013.

Rolinson, Dave. "'Who Done it': Discourse of Authorship during the John Nathan-Turner era." In *Time and Relative Dissertations in Space: Critical Perspectives on Doctor Who*, edited by David Butler, 176–189. Manchester: Manchester University Press, 2007.

Seaton, Jean. "The BBC and Metabolising Britishness: Critical Patriotism." In *Britishness: Perspectives on the British Question*, edited by Andrew Gamble and Tony Wright, 72–85. Chichester: Wiley-Blackwell, 2009.

Selznick Barbara. "The Changing Brand of *Doctor Who*'s Britishness." In *Ruminations, Peregrinations and Regenerations: A Critical Approach to Doctor Who*, edited by Chris Hansen, 68–84. Newcastle-upon-Tyne: Cambridge Scholars Publishing, 2010.

Sleight, Graham. *The Doctor's Monsters: Meanings of the Monstrous in Doctor Who*. London: I.B. Tauris, 2012.

Steward, Tom. "Author Who?: Masterplanners, Scribermen and Script Doctors; The Producers, Writers and Script Editors of *Doctor Who*." In *Ruminations, Peregrinations and Regenerations: A Critical Approach to Doctor Who*, edited by Chris Hansen, 312–327. Newcastle-upon-Tyne: Cambridge Scholars Publishing, 2010.

Street, John. *Politics and Popular Culture*. London: Polity, 1997.

Tulloch, John, and Manuel Alvarado. *Doctor Who: The Unfolding Text*. New York: St Martin's Press, 1983.

van Zoonen, Liesbet. *Entertaining the Citizen: When Politics and Popular Culture Converge*. Lanham, MD: Rowman and Littlefield Publishers Inc, 2004.

Waldron, Jeremy. *Law and Disagreement*. Oxford: Oxford University Press, 1999.

Williams, Rebecca. "Desiring the Doctor: Identity, Gender and Genre in Online Fandom." In *British Science Fiction Television: Critical Essays*, edited by James Leggott and Tobias Hochscherf, 167–177. Jefferson, NC: McFarland, 2011.

CHAPTER 2

"One Tiny, Damp Little Island": *Doctor Who*'s Construction of Britishness

Britishness is about the stories that the British tell each other about who they are. This chapter focuses on the stories that *Doctor Who* tells about being British. Britishness in *Doctor Who* also possesses a crucial internal dimension, in that the show has to mediate tensions between Britishness on the one hand, and, on the other, Englishness (southern and northern), Scottishness, Welshness and Northern Irishness. These issues will form the subject of Chap. 3. This chapter, however, investigates the external dimension: how *Doctor Who* delineates Britishness as a distinctive national identity vis-à-vis the rest of the world.

In interrogating *Doctor Who*'s Britishness, this chapter advances two main arguments. First, it proposes that *Doctor Who* not only offers a snapshot of the contemporary British, it also, having presented characters as British, frequently then goes on to indicate the moral worth of those characters in a way which points the viewer towards the show's preferred version of Britishness. It often does so by drawing a contrast between characters whose British qualities are deemed undesirable and characters who show the British nation at its best. *Doctor Who*'s assessment of Britishness is therefore partly empirical but primarily normative: to what sort of Britishness *should* the country aspire? As Lisa Kerrigan puts it, in *Doctor Who* "the knowledge of all that Britain *has been* is integrated with creative imaginings on what it *could yet be*".[1] In this regard, partly as a

[1] Lisa Kerrigan, "Not Sure if it's Marxism in Action or a West-End Musical: Class, Citizenship and Culture in New *Doctor Who*", in *Impossible Worlds, Impossible Things:*

D. Nicol, *Doctor Who: A British Alien?*,
https://doi.org/10.1007/978-3-319-65834-6_2

result of their political and normative nature, ideas about what it is to be British are both indeterminate and in constant flux. Britishness is thus constantly invented and reinvented over periods of time.[2] As a "site of endless transformations",[3] we may perceive *Doctor Who* as having tracked the changing imagining of Britishness.

Secondly, the chapter assesses the substance of *Doctor Who*'s Britishness in terms of its stance on entrepreneurialism, the public service ethos, race, class, gender and sexuality. In this regard, I contend that the show's conception of Britishness is something of a curate's egg: egalitarian in parts, conservative in others. All things considered, however, it will be argued that, despite smug and conformist elements, *Doctor Who* nonetheless offers a more progressive idea of Britishness than that put forward by the country's political establishment since the emergence of a neoliberal consensus in the 1980s.

Britishness: Politics or Brand Image?

It might be tempting to reduce Britishness to apolitical characteristics. To do so would, however, be misleading. National identity is above all a political construct. Britishness has always been porous, vague and fluid, a "mansion with many rooms".[4] In the absence of a clear, uncontested sense of British identity, there are (and always have been) *competing* versions of Britishness, general acceptance of which brings different political consequences.[5] Stories regarding national character may, if believed,

---

Cultural Perspectives on Doctor Who, Torchwood and the Sarah Jane Adventures, eds. Ross P. Garner, Melissa Beattie and Una McCormack (Newcastle-upon-Tyne: Cambridge Scholars Publishing, 2010).

[2] Mark Leonard, *Britain^{TM}: Renewing Our Identity* (London: Redwood Books, 1997), 71.

[3] John Tulloch and Manuel Alvarado, *Doctor Who: The Unfolding Text* (New York: St. Martin's Press, 1983), 5–6.

[4] Gary Younge, "No, Theresa May—immigration is not the real threat to national cohesion". *The Guardian*, October 6, 2015.

[5] Andrew Gamble and Tony Wright, "Introduction: The Britishness Question", in *Britishness: Perspectives on the British Question*, eds. Andrew Gamble and Tony Wright (Chichester: Wiley-Blackwell, 2009), 7; John K. Walton, "Introduction", in *Relocating Britishness*, eds. Steven Caunce, Ewa Mazierska, Susan Sydney-Smith and John K. Walton (Manchester and New York: Manchester University Press, 2004).

incline or disincline people towards different political futures for the country. In other words, contesting what it means to be British involves participating in the ongoing conversation as to the kind of country Britain *ought* to be. This is partly why British national identity is not a fixed entity but is constantly in the making.[6] Indeed, defining Britishness lies at the very heart of Britain's political battlefield. Thus, over the last forty years Britain's neoliberal political elite has promoted a conception of Britishness that fits its entrepreneurial ethos. In response, *Doctor Who* as a work of satirical science fiction fashions its own preferred version of Britishness. Studying these differences serves to bring to light the politically contested nature of national identity, as well as the contribution of popular television in creating Britishness.

To be sure, not every characteristic of Britishness which features in *Doctor Who* is heavily political. It would seem contrived, for instance, to attribute a political content to the emotional restraint, or "stiff upper lip", which marked the departures of companions in the programme's early years and which has been substantially abandoned in new *Who*, as British society became more tolerant of displays of emotion, not least in the wake of the death of Diana Princess of Wales in 1997. Nonetheless, numerous questions of national identity are substantially political. This is why attempts to define Britishness constantly work their way into the country's political discourse. Indeed, David Marquand contends that we have spent three hundred years arguing about Britishness.[7] To this day, Britain's political leaders persistently argue that their own favoured philosophy best accords to the British people's view of themselves. To see this in action, one need look no further than Britain's annual party conference season. Taking the 2015 conferences as an example, the Conservative Prime Minister, David Cameron, expressed his love for Britain as the "proudest multiracial democracy on Earth", a Britain based on equality of opportunity rather than outcome. He denounced the Labour Leader of the Opposition as "terrorist-sympathising [and] Britain-hating".[8] (A comedian rallied to the latter's defence arguing that

[6] Bhikhu Parekh, "Being British", in *Britishness: Perspectives on the British Question*, eds. Andrew Gamble and Tony Wright (Chichester: Wiley-Blackwell, 2009), 39.

[7] David Marquand, "Bursting with Skeletons: Britishness after Empire", in *Britishness: Perspectives on the British Question*, eds. Andrew Gamble and Tony Wright (Chichester: Wiley-Blackwell, 2009), 11.

[8] David Cameron, Conservative Party Conference, October 7, 2015.

"he's called Jeremy and dresses like a geography teacher—he couldn't be more British if he bled tea".[9]) For his part, the Labour leader, Jeremy Corbyn, argued that the "sense of fair play" was fundamental to the "shared majority values in Britain that are the fundamental reason why I love this country and its people".[10] As for the leader of the Liberal Democrats, Tim Farron argued that the government's refusal to help the refugees on the move across Europe was contrary to British values.[11]

Similarly, when in office, British politicians and officials cannot avoid using the state to indicate that those in Britain share certain things.[12] The election of the "New Labour" government in 1997 under Tony Blair's premiership saw the political character of Britishness being played down in favour of an emphasis on Britishness as a brand image. New Labour attempted to "rebrand" Britishness, with the aim of projecting Britain as a young country. Determined to replace "Rule Britannia" with "cool Britannia", Blair sought to associate his new government with Brit Pop celebrities, feting a succession of stars from music, film, television and fashion at Downing Street. The implications of treating Britishness as a brand image are drawn out by Mark Leonard in *Britain™: Renewing Our Identity.* Leonard argues that in order to redesign "UK plc", important lessons could be gleaned from businesses that successfully manage their identity. Leonard contends that forging a new British identity would create measurable economic benefits. He dismisses the objection that national identity is too complex and multivoiced to be "managed", arguing that, in reality, all modern nations fashion their identities in ways similar to the management of brands by companies.[13]

Commodification, however, is itself political: a decision to treat national identity as a brand image likens countries to companies, drawing the nation state into the business ethos. A practical example of this approximation of business and nation is put forward by Jim McGuigan, who argues that the Millennium Dome project constituted a bid by New Labour to abolish the past, by relinquishing the social democracy

[9]Frankie Boyle, *The Guardian*, September 21, 2015.

[10]Jeremy Corbyn, Labour Party Conference, September 29, 2015.

[11]Tim Farron, Liberal Democrats Party Conference, September 23, 2015.

[12]Varum Uberoi and Iain McLean, "Britishness: A Role for the State?", in *Britishness: Perspectives on the British Question*, eds. Andrew Gamble and Tony Wright (Chichester: Wiley-Blackwell, 2009).

[13]Mark Leonard, *Britain™: Renewing Our Identity* (London: Redwood Books, 1997).

previously associated with the Labour Party. He argues that the Dome exhibition projected Britain as a young, business-friendly country or even a nation of corporations. Altering the brand image of Britishness in this fashion can be read as part of New Labour's attempts to embrace rather than resist the neoliberalism bequeathed by the Conservatives.[14]

The brand-imaging of Britishness has been applied to *Doctor Who* by Barbara Selznick in a piece entitled "Rebooting and Re-branding: The Changing Brands of *Doctor Who*'s Britishness".[15] Selznick primarily addresses the selling of *Doctor Who* to an American television audience, and to her credit, she deploys branding in a way that does not conceal the political content of national identity. She identifies a "heritage brand" of Britishness, which emphasises clearly defined social rules, elitism and an orderly, all-white society. In this society, class struggle is, for the most part, charmingly sublimated into domestic foibles, as in television programmes such as *Upstairs Downstairs* (1971–1975, 2010–2012) and *Downton Abbey* (2010–2015). "Heritage Britain", in Selznick's view, glamourises the idea of the nation, glorifies Britain's past and is nostalgic for Empire. She contrasts "heritage Britain" with "cool Britain", a presentation of Britishness typified by "Brit Grit" films such as *The Full Monty* (1997), *Brassed Off* (1996), *Billy Elliot* (2000) and *Pride* (2014). Selznick explains that these films problematise the traditional image of proper British society. At the heart of "cool Britain" is the idea that the British nation has failed to take care of its people, obliging them to fall back on their own resources and rely on each other. "Cool Britain" thereby deals with significant themes of family, unemployment and corporatisation. Selznick's analysis is valuable, yet it has one shortcoming: in addition to giving an account of her "cool Britain" version of Britishness, she also fleetingly engages with the idea of "cool Britannia", which she describes as "the re-branding of Britain as a nation, a process which started with Tony Blair's New Labour government in the 1990s".[16]

---

[14]Jim McGuigan, "A Shell for Neo-Liberalism: New Labour Britain and the Millennium Dome", in *Relocating Britishness*, eds. Steven Caunce, Ewa Mazierska, Susan Sydney-Smith and John K. Walton (Manchester and New York: Manchester University Press, 2004).

[15]Barbara Selznick, "Rebooting and Re-branding: The Changing Brands of *Doctor Who*'s Britishness", in *Ruminations, Peregrinations and Regenerations: A Critical Approach to Doctor Who*, ed. Chris Hansen (Newcastle-upon-Tyne: Cambridge Scholars Publishing, 2010).

[16]Selznick, "Rebooting and Re-branding", 79.

"Cool Britain" and "cool Britannia" are similar-sounding phrases, and Selznick does not really draw out how very different these two ideals of Britishness are from each other. The difference is important, since post-2005 *Doctor Who*'s version of Britishness distances itself markedly from aspects of New Labour's "cool Britannia".

Doctor Who's Britishness: Entrepreneurs or Fair Play?

Doctor Who parts company from "cool Britannia" most strikingly when it comes to the merits of entrepreneurialism as a British characteristic. Imaginings of Britishness mediate a tension between a Britishness based on individual aspiration and one based on fair play (a term which tends to be interpreted as meaning substantive fairness). Mark Leonard in *Britain*^{TM} calls for a Britishness which would be seen as "open for business"—a country of entrepreneurs, open to the rest of the world, constantly innovating and inventing new ways of doing business. Yet, at the same time, he also wishes to project Britain as a nation of fair play: a country which sees itself as a team, marked by national solidarity, public service and support for the underdog rather than reliance on "trickle down" wealth.[17] The idea of "Britain open for business" pulls in favour of neoliberalism whereas the notion of "a Britain of fair play" militates towards social democracy. Leonard does not draw attention to this tension, nor does he specify what balance should be struck between entrepreneurism and national solidarity. New Labour, by contrast, had no such inhibitions, unequivocally privileging business over social welfare concerns, supercharging Thatcherism rather than abandoning it.[18] When Labour was finally replaced by a Conservative-Liberal Democrat coalition, there was no change in the governmental narrative regarding national identity: the new Prime Minister David Cameron (a self-styled "heir to Blair") persistently sought to characterise Britain as "this buccaneering, world-beating, can-do country", a nation of global businesspeople.[19]

---

[17] Leonard, *Britain*^{TM}, 57, 61.

[18] Mark Evans, "Neoliberalism and Policy Transfer in the British Competitive State: The Case of Welfare Reform", in *Internalizing Globalization: The Rise of Neoliberalism and the Decline of National Varieties of Capitalism*, eds. Susanne Soederberg, Georg Menz and Philip Cerny (Basingstoke: Palgrave Macmillan, 2005), 71.

[19] David Cameron introducing the Conservative Party manifesto, April 14, 2015.

Of course, a great many contemporary Britons are indeed business-orientated. Commerce has constantly manifested itself in characterisations of Britishness, from the traditional view of Britain as a nation of shopkeepers to the contemporary satire of thrusting Industrial Revolution capitalists in the 2012 London Olympics Opening Ceremony. However, the precise degree of business-orientation of the British people is not stable and has been substantially conditioned by politics: in particular, the shrinking of the state since the 1980s meant that former public employees and new entrants into employment were obliged to work for a private firm or be self-employed, leading to an erosion of the public service ethos in favour of the business culture. *Doctor Who* certainly perceives a commercial mentality as part of contemporary Britishness. When the TARDIS materialises above Starship UK in the distant future in "The Beast Below" (2010), the Doctor describes the vessel as "a whole country, living and laughing and…shopping!—and searching the stars for a new home." As Kate Flynn has pointed out, "shopping" seems an incongruous addition to the Doctor's list of the country's defining characteristics; he seems to be emphasising that consumerism looms large in the British psyche.[20]

It does not follow, however, that *Doctor Who*'s writers actually *approve* of materialistic and profit-seeking traits forming part of Britishness. National identity discourses are as much about normative debates as they are about empirical assessments, and so it is worthwhile considering *Doctor Who*'s stance on the British as entrepreneurs. This is particularly important because of John Fiske's theory about the Doctor himself. Fiske would have us believe that the Doctor's eccentricity symbolises an individualism which in turn connotes attachment to capitalism.[21] Undoubtedly, despite regenerations, the Doctor's whimsical, out-of-the-ordinary nature has, in one way or another, become an enduring element of *Doctor Who*. The programme has always emphasised the importance of being able to express one's individuality. Figure 2.1 shows the Doctor and companion Polly with a Cyberman, one of an alien race which has entirely eliminated individuality in favour of an improved ability to survive.

[20]Kate Flynn, "A Country Made from Metal? The 'Britishness' of Human-Machine Marriage in Series 31", in *Doctor Who in Time and Space*, ed. Gillian I. Leitch (Jefferson, NC: McFarland, 2013), 207.

[21]John Fiske, "Dr. Who: Ideology and the Reading of a Popular Narrative Text", *Australian Journal of Screen Theory*, 14 (1983): 69.

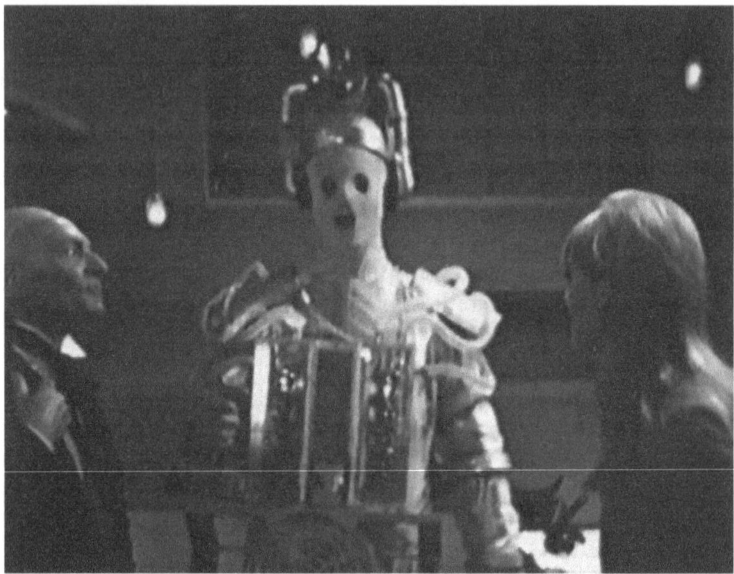

Fig. 2.1 The right to be oneself: the individualities of the Doctor and companion Polly form a contrast to a Cyberman. *Doctor Who* (classic series), "The Tenth Planet", season 4, serial 29, British Broadcasting Corporation, 1966

The image's positioning of the Doctor and Polly on either side of the featureless, expressionless Cyberman serves to highlight the differences between the two humanoids: the stiff, Victorian-looking Doctor and the softer, youthful, modern Polly. The stark difference between Doctor and companion is compounded by the contrast between them and the Cyberman, who has lost the very right to be different. The image therefore presents a potent message of the importance of being able to be oneself.

Too much emphasis on the individual can, however, be associated with a rather extreme form of capitalism. Jeffrey Richards argues that in Britain since the late 1970s "the self" took the direction of the aggressive pursuit of wealth, a hard-hitting individualism which has come to incorporate contempt for those who lack money.[22] However, the Doctor

[22] Jeffrey Richards, "Football and the Crisis of British Identity", in *Relocating Britishness*, eds. Steven Caunce et al. (Manchester and New York: Manchester University Press, 2004), 94.

himself does not fit snugly into the entrepreneurial mould. His gallivanting around the universe is not driven by pecuniary gain: rather, he is the benign aristocrat.[23] It is more convincing to argue that his eccentricity reflects his rebellious spirit.[24] Content with the seemingly inexhaustible comforts of the TARDIS, he appears disdainful of money, to the extent of refusing a salary from the United Nations Intelligence Taskforce (UNIT) when it recruits him in "Spearhead from Space" (1970). To emphasise the point, the Doctor is periodically contrasted with those who trawl time and space in search of profit.[25] Against this backdrop, the more compelling interpretation of the Doctor's eccentricity would be that it serves to symbolise Britain as a tolerant country, a quirky nation which cherishes difference and non-conformity.

The Doctor, therefore, is hardly a business figure; yet there are numerous minor characters in *Doctor Who* that are entrepreneurial and who could claim the mantle of Britishness. Let us consider four of them: Adam Mitchell in "The Long Game" (2005), Rickston Slade in "Voyage of the Damned" (2007), Purcell in "Night Terrors" (2011) and Pritchard in "Under the Lake" (2015). These four individuals are all new-*Who* characters and therefore reflect *Doctor Who* after Britain had experienced the full force of neoliberalism. All four are British or coded as British. Furthermore, they can lay claim to being "average Britons", none of them being the villains of their respective stories nor the leaders of corporations.[26]

1. *Adam Mitchell*

We meet Adam Mitchell, a young British man, in "Dalek" (2005) where he works as a buyer of extraterrestrial artefacts for a ruthless American capitalist. In "The Long Game" (2005), having travelled with the Doctor and companion Rose Tyler to a giant space station in Earth's future, Adam sneaks off on a money-making frolic of his own. He wants

---

[23] See generally Piers D. Britton, *TARDISbound* (London: I.B. Tauris, 2011), Chap. II.

[24] Gabriel McKee, "Pushing the Protest Button: *Doctor Who*'s Anti-Authoritarian Ethic", in *Time and Relative Dimensions in Faith: Religion and Doctor Who*, eds. Andrew Crome and James McGrath (London: Darton, Longman and Todd, 2013), 16–31.

[25] Examples include the Monk in "The Time Meddler" (1965) and Solomon the Trader in "Dinosaurs on a Spaceship" (2012).

[26] *Doctor Who*'s corporate magnates will be considered in Chap. 6.

to find out what replaced the computer microprocessor so that he can secure a commercial advantage when he returns to his own era. To this end, he even undergoes brain surgery to have a computer inserted inside his head. At the close of the episode the Doctor truncates Adam's adventures in time and space by taking him home, insisting that Adam just wanted to help himself, and that he (the Doctor) only takes the best—namely Rose. The Doctor's rejection of Adam as a companion can be interpreted as a rejection of profit-seeking as a motivation for time travel.

2. *Rickston Slade*

The Doctor encounters Rickston Slade in "Voyage of the Damned" (2007) when he becomes a stowaway on a large spacecraft called the Titanic, which offers cruises around the galaxy in which holidaymakers can experience primitive cultures, including that of Earth. The passengers, including Rickston, are humanoids from the planet Sto. However, much of the Titanic is earmarked as British: indeed, the first sight that confronts the Doctor as he emerges from the TARDIS is a Union Jack. Rickston too is coded as British, more specifically as a City of London type. When we first encounter him, he is wheeler-dealing on his mobile phone. The Titanic is sabotaged and left almost wrecked by the founder of the corporation that owns it, Max Capricorn. The Doctor leads a small band of survivors, including Rickston, to safety. Rickston's conduct throughout this rescue effort is marked by self-centred individualism and rudeness. In particular, he displays contempt for those who are not rich. He is unpleasant to the Doctor's one-off companion, the waitress Astrid Peth and he refers to the ship's steward as "a dead idiot". He brands a plump working-class couple, the Van Hoffs, "Mr. and Mrs. Fatso", and refuses to incur any risk to save them. Several people, including the Van Hoffs and Astrid, die in the course of the story, leaving Rickston one of the few survivors. At the end of the adventure, he hugs the Doctor, gleefully imparting the news that he sold all his shares in the Max Capricorn company and transferred them to its rivals, and that this has made him a rich man. He seems to expect the Doctor to share his joy at this financial good fortune. Our final sight of Rickston is once again on his mobile, as he orders that his shares be tripled-bonded and locked. Rickston provides a compelling example of the kind of capitalistic individualism of which John Fiske rather unconvincingly accuses the Doctor. Rickston's disdain for the have-nots reflects the mainstreaming of middle-class hostility towards working-class people that became commonplace from the 1980s onwards as the "legacy of a very British class war" waged by governments.[27] Rickston's apparent belief that selfishness is a virtue became widespread enough in Britain to spawn a literature on "selfish capitalism" in the early twenty-first century. Sue Gerhardt, in *The Selfish Society*, argues that selfishness is not merely an individual failing but the product of a society that sustains individualism, greed and materialism at the expense of collective interests and the needs of the social group as a whole. Using insights from developmental psychology, she argues for a more relational, collaborative society which sees selfishness as immature and anachronistic.[28] In *The Selfish Capitalist*, Oliver James warns that putting too much emphasis on possessions, money, appearances and fame has led to a substantial increase in emotional distress.[29] It is telling that *Doctor Who* too makes the link between neoliberalism and selfishness.

3. *Purcell*

We meet landlord Purcell in "Night Terrors" (2011), an adventure in which the Doctor and companions Amy and Rory receive a mayday call in the TARDIS which draws them to a council block, presumably in contemporary Britain. The trio knock on doors to try and locate the person in distress. Encountering Purcell, Rory is astonished to learn that he is landlord of the entire block. Purcell proves no model landlord. The block is run-down and he menaces his tenants for rent with the help of his large dog Bernard. Purcell's smug and solitary self-centredness is contrasted with the troubled but less selfish family life of the story's main characters—Alex, Claire and their little son George, who turns out to be the one who sent a message to the TARDIS. The fact that Purcell is very obviously working class conforms to the argument of the Thatcher governments in the 1980s that anyone, whatever their social class, could become a successful entrepreneur. In fact, by imagining Purcell, *Doctor Who* is being rather too charitable towards neoliberalism, the effect of

[27] Owen Jones, *Chavs: The Demonization of the Working Class* (London: Verso, 2011).

[28] Sue Gerhardt, *The Selfish Society: How We All Forgot to Love One Another and Made Money Instead* (London: Simon and Schuster, 2010).

[29] Oliver James, *The Selfish Capitalist* (London: Vermilion, 2008).

which has been to reduce rather than increase social mobility.[30] On the other hand, Purcell astutely represents the pattern of property ownership in contemporary Britain. For much of the twentieth century, council-owned houses and flats were a means of sheltering the less-well-off from the harshness of the housing market. In the 1980s, however, the Conservative government started to sell off these properties to tenants at subsidised prices. This policy was presented as liberating the individual: tenants could own their properties and bequeath them to their children. In reality, however, the policy led to some 40% of council properties being let out by private landlords, who charged rents of up to seven times the average social rent for the properties, resulting in a huge increase of evictions for rent arrears.[31] Purcell's ownership of the whole block neatly counters the narrative that sales of social housing benefit the individual tenant. More broadly, Purcell's story reflects the inequalities between landlords and tenants that came about during Britain's neoliberal era with the abolition of protected tenancies and rent controls. These reforms played a part in the housing crisis which developed in Britain in the new century, whereby housing (both to rent and for sale) became scarce and unaffordable for many young people. This situation was also reflected in the episode "Knock Knock" (2017) in which companion Bill Potts and her student friends are shown round risibly substandard houses by an estate agent before falling into the clutches of the sinister Landlord and his vast, alien-infested house.

4. *Pritchard*

The Doctor and companion Clara encounter Pritchard in "Under the Lake" (2015), a story set in the near future in an underwater mining facility in Scotland. Pritchard's main preoccupation is to advance the interests of the company for which he works, Vector Petroleum. The company has purchased the rights to all assets under the lake, so he wants to assert its property right to a spaceship that was found there. Pritchard also feels that he should assume leadership of the facility because of his company's financial stake. He is motivated throughout by

[30] Chrystia Freeland, *Plutocrats: The Rise of the New Global Super-Rich* (London: Penguin, 2012), Chap. 6.

[31] Pete Apps, "Right to Buy to Let: Scale of Re-lets Revealed: 40%", *Inside Housing*, August 14, 2015.

the desire not to lose a bonus. He comes to grief when he leaves the facility in search of power cells which he deems valuable, only to be killed on his return, seemingly by ghosts. Pritchard is delineated as a grasping yet rather one-dimensional individual: there is not much to him, other than his devotion to his company. He is contrasted with the other characters staffing the facility, who engage with each other far more, including romantically.

The examples of Adam, Rickston, Purcell and Pritchard therefore suggest that *Doctor Who* perceives entrepreneurism as a common British characteristic but not as a desirable one. It is enlightening to contrast the four British entrepreneurs with two American tycoons in new-series *Doctor Who*: Henry van Statten in "Dalek" (2005) and Luke Rattigan in "The Sontaran Stratagem"/"The Poison Sky" (2008). Both are more successful than their British counterparts, each possessing an extensive business empire. Furthermore, both come to a sticky end as the result of their entrepreneurial entanglements with hostile aliens. In the case of Luke Rattigan, American supremacy over the British is emphasised by the British students at his Rattigan Academy having to wear orange uniforms reminiscent of American prisons and Guantanamo Bay. As Nicholas J. Cull observes, *Doctor Who* has always had to assert national values at a time of American domination and British decline.[32] In this regard, it would be comforting to see Britain's adoption from the 1980s onwards of a more rugged and abrasive capitalism as, at least in part, an American import.

The show's unfavourable stance towards British entrepreneurialism is confirmed by comparing Adam, Rickston, Purcell and Pritchard with the Doctor's companions. Significantly, there has been no "entrepreneur companion". There has, by contrast, been no shortage of public servants. There have been teachers (Ian Chesterton, Barbara Wright, Clara Oswald), physicians (Harry Sullivan, Martha Jones and ultimately Nyssa) and a nurse (Rory Williams).[33] Furthermore, companions are frequently

[32] Nicholas J. Cull, "TARDIS at the OK Corral: *Doctor Who* and the USA", in *British Science Fiction Television*, eds. John Cook and Peter Wright (London: I.B. Tauris, 2006), 52–70.

[33] Even the minority of companions who work in the private sector—such as Sarah Jane Smith, Donna Noble and Amy Pond—hold posts which rely on skills other than business acumen. For instance, as an intrepid investigative reporter, Sarah Jane behaves more as if she were performing a public service, both in *Doctor Who* and in the spin-off *The Sarah*

deployed to draw contrasts with characters orientated towards financial gain. For instance, "The End of the World" (2005) makes a very explicit contrast between companion Rose Tyler and the "last human" Cassandra O'Brien, who intends to massacre her fellow business leaders having purchased shares in their rivals' companies. Similarly, "The Lazarus Experiment" (2007) counterposes companion Martha Jones, a medical student training at an NHS hospital, with Professor Lazarus and Lady Thaw, whose youth-restoring treatment would be the preserve of the rich.

Doctor Who therefore tends to express disapproval at the entrepreneurial vision of Britishness advanced by successive governments. Instead, it articulates Britishness in terms of social fairness. This idea of British identity is readily apparent in "The Doctor Dances" (2005), where the Doctor startlingly reminds 1940s Londoners not to forget to create the welfare state. It is also implicit in the sympathetic treatment of an NHS hospital in "Smith and Jones" (2007) contrasted to one run for private profit in "New Earth" (2006). No doubt, *Doctor Who*'s preference for the public service ethos over commercial endeavour reflects the difficulty in reconciling the elevation of the pursuit of self-interest with a philosophy that prioritises the coherence of Britain as a *community*.

Doctor Who's Britishness: In a Class of Its Own

Barbara Selznick's "heritage Britain" is the idea of Britishness based on respect for social hierarchy, as reflected in television dramas such as *Upstairs Downstairs* (1971–1975, 2010–2012) and *Downton Abbey* (2010–2015). In these shows, the rightness and virtue of the class system is generally unquestioned.[34] The vast majority of servants in these

Jane Adventures. Similarly, Donna works for private firms, yet her administrative prowess could just as easily be put to good use in the public services. Indeed, insofar as Sarah Jane and Donna deploy their professional skills in their adventures with the Doctor, they could actually be viewed as providing a public service. See, for example, "The Time Warrior" (1973–1974), "Robot" (1975–1976), "The Doctor's Daughter" (2008) and, in *The Sarah Jane Adventures* spin-off, "Invasion of the Bane" (2007).

[34] In contrast, the situation comedy *You Rang M'Lord* (1988–1993), a satire on *Upstairs Downstairs*-style dramas, featured as its lead character a butler who continuously asserted that his employers were not his betters, they merely had more money than he did.

two dramas never query the right of the Bellamy family in *Upstairs Downstairs* and the Crawley family in *Downton Abbey* to a lavish degree of domestic service: it is taken to be the natural order of things. Yet the rigid class hierarchy in these shows is made more acceptable by upper-class characters tending to treat the lower orders in a reasonably kindly fashion, even as their confidantes, an example of the "domestic foibles" which serve to soften the harshness of the class divide.[35] When it comes to new-series *Doctor Who*, Selznick discerns a shift from the "heritage" to the "cool" brand of Britishness.[36] However, I would argue that *Doctor Who* never really fitted Selznick's "heritage Britain" template. Of course, in the vast and sprawling *Doctor Who* canon there are bound to be some stories that apply "heritage Britain" ideas of class fairly forcefully; for example, "The Mark of the Rani" (1985) could be read in this way.[37] For the most part, however, *Doctor Who* tends to be critical of *overly oppressive* class systems. In this regard, Piers D. Britton puts forward the attractive thesis that the Doctor is persistently portrayed as aristocratic because in class terms this makes him an archaic fantasy figure, a socially neutral outsider who can thereby critique different kinds of class relations. This conceit, Britton observes, has remained remarkably durable in both classic and new *Who*.[38]

---

[35] Carl Freedman, "England as Ideology: From *Upstairs Downstairs* to *A Room with a View*", *Cultural Critique*, 17 (1990–1991): 79, 82.

[36] Selznick, "Rebooting and Rebranding", 84. By contrast, Simone Knox contests Selznick's binary view by arguing that Matt Smith's portrayal of the Doctor reflected not straightforward heritage but heritage-as-cool Britishness. However, Knox focuses more on the stylistic rather than the political significance of these distinctions. Simone Knox, "The Transatlantic Dimensions of the Time Lord: *Doctor Who* and the Relationships between British and North American Television", in *Doctor Who: The Eleventh Hour*, ed. Andrew O'Day (London: I.B. Tauris, 2014), 111–118.

[37] In "The Mark of the Rani", only working-class people are enslaved by the Rani, a renegade Time Lord; there is no tension between the employer (the local Lord) and his employees owing to his kindly ways, and Luddism is depicted as a form of Rani-induced madness. A potential working-class hero of the tale, Luke, comes to a sticky end so is not destined to be the star of the story. "The Mark of the Rani" is perhaps the closest that *Doctor Who* gets towards a *Downton Abbey* style acceptance of social rank as the natural order of things. Something of a corrective to "The Mark of the Rani" was "The Next Doctor" (2008) where Victorian orphans are forced to work in a factory to prepare for a Cyberman invasion.

[38] Britton, *TARDISbound*, Chap. II.

As Una McCormack observes, there is no shortage of *Doctor Who* adventures in which the Doctor has helped to overthrow iniquitous social systems on other worlds, from "The Space Museum" (1965) to "The Happiness Patrol" (1988).[39] He has prompted revolution in societies where the upper class of a planet has quite literally drained the life-force from the lower orders, as in "The Savages" (1966) and "State of Decay" (1980). More recently, in "Planet of the Ood" (2008), the Doctor and companion Donna Noble witness the liberation of a slave race, the Ood, from imperialist humans. Other worlds apart, there are also plenty of Earth-bound *Doctor Who* stories in which social class looms large. "The Green Death" (1973) counterposes Welsh working-class miners against the more prosperous English staff of the company Global Chemicals. Whilst the stereotypical portrayal of the miners leaves much to be desired, there is no question that the villains of the piece are the men of Global Chemicals.[40] In "Horror of Fang Rock" (1977), we meet working-class Edwardian lighthouse-keepers Vince, Ben and Reuben. They are joined by a thoroughly unappealing trio of upper-class people: Colonel Skinsale MP, Lord Palmerdale and his secretary Adelaide. The story persistently contrasts the keen sense of public duty of the lighthouse-keepers with the corruption and passion for private gain of Lord Palmerdale and Colonel Skinsale.

"The End of Time" (2009–2010) touches upon the way in which the upper class has morphed into something of a celebrity class. We are introduced to tycoon Joshua Naismith by former companion Donna buying his bestseller *Fight the Future* for her granddad for Christmas. This sets the scene for an adventure in which Naismith tries to secure immortality for his daughter Abigail. The quest for celebrity on the part of the economic elite established itself during the neoliberal era and stands in sharp contrast to earlier times. For instance, in 1911 the Liberal government sought a land tax which incurred particularly bitter opposition in the House of Lords because it would necessitate a survey of land ownership, revealing inequalities in wealth and property ownership

[39] Una McCormack, "He's Not the Messiah: Undermining Political and Religious Authority in New *Doctor Who*", in *The Unsilent Library: Essays on the Russell T. Davies Era of the New Doctor Who*, eds. Simon Bradshaw, Antony Keen and Graham Sleight (London: The Science Fiction Foundation, 2011), 47.

[40] This serial's treatment of Welsh people is considered in more depth in Chap. 3.

which peers wished to keep private.[41] In "The Empty Child"/"The Doctor Dances" (2005), set in Second World War London, a young woman called Nancy organises meals for working-class children who are homeless and living rough. They take food from the tables of the better-off during air raids. The Doctor entirely approves, quipping that he is not sure whether the scenario constitutes Marxism in action or a West End musical. "Human Nature"/"The Family of Blood" (2007) is set in a 1913 English public school and presents the rigid pre-war class divide as distinctly unappetising, not least when school nurse Joan Redfern tells companion Martha, posing as a maid, to remember her position and not to be over-familiar with the Doctor, who is working as a schoolteacher. Working-class people are treated as expendable in various stories: the catering staff are killed off *en masse* in "Mummy on the Orient Express" (2014) as a warning to the more valuable passengers, a group of scientists; less esteemed Britons are fed to a Star Whale in "The Beast Below" (2010); down-and-outs are first in line to be converted into Cybermen in "Rise of the Cybermen"/"The Age of Steel" (2006).

Doctor Who's satire of class is particularly trenchant in relation to the Doctor's own people, the Time Lords. Our first encounter with the Time Lords in "The War Games" (1969) lends them the air of a magisterial, supranational authority; but subsequent adventures develop them into an extended metaphor for the British class system.[42] In particular, it transpires that the Time Lords are not a species but an elite. On the planet Gallifrey, they sit at the pinnacle of a rank-obsessed, hierarchical society of chapters, cardinals, chancellory guards and the more plebeian classes.[43] Those who tire of their sclerotic system are banished to the desert wilderness of "outer Gallifrey".[44] Far from esteeming the Time Lords as a font of guiding wisdom, we eventually come to see treachery, corruption and a callous disregard for the right to life as their hallmarks.[45] As for the Doctor himself, his meddling often seems aristocratic in its arrogance. Sometimes the viewer is encouraged to condemn his

[41] Duncan Watts, *Whigs, Radicals and Liberals 1815–1914* (London: Hodder and Stoughton, 2002), 148.

[42] Britton, *TARDISbound*, 166.

[43] "The Deadly Assassin" (1976).

[44] "The Invasion of Time" (1978).

[45] See also "The Five Doctors" (1983), "Arc of Infinity" (1983), "The End of Time" (2009–2010), "Hell Bent" (2015).

patrician high-handedness, as in "The Waters of Mars" (2009), where he witnesses a catastrophe on the red planet but then, convinced that he has mastery over the laws of time, saves individuals who according to established history did not survive. On other occasions, however, the Doctor's lordly conceit is rather played down. For example, in "The Christmas Invasion" (2005), he deploys the dirty trick of spreading rumours of poor health to bring about the removal of Harriet Jones as British Prime Minister, but the episode does not signal much indignation at this interference in British democracy. Only in "The Sound of Drums" (2007), a year and a half later, do we discover that the political space left by Harriet Jones' departure enabled the Doctor's arch-enemy the Master to become prime minister, with calamitous results. Criticism of the Doctor is not only delayed but muted, with no character expressly mentioning that the Doctor might be to blame.

In the main, therefore, *Doctor Who* stories voice disapproval of class discrimination. On the other hand, the show does not want to rock the British ship of state too much. Most notably, the regular participation of British sovereigns in the Doctor's adventures has become part of *Doctor Who*'s Britishness, with monarchs being subjected to far gentler satire than that accorded to the Time Lords. In "Inferno" (1970), in a parallel-universe fascist Britain, the Doctor expresses sorrow at hearing that the Royal Family has been executed. It thereby associates the sovereign with the maintenance of British democracy, somewhat ironic for an unelected head of state. Queen Elizabeth II makes a cameo appearance in "Silver Nemesis" (1988), the show's twenty-fifth anniversary offering, and defies fears of alien intrusion by remaining in London over Christmas in "Voyage of the Damned" (2007). Queen Elizabeth I features in the fiftieth anniversary special, "The Day of the Doctor" (2013), as does Queen Victoria in "Tooth and Claw" (2006). Both these sovereigns ultimately fall out with the Doctor in dramatic fashion. In a disappointingly sexist depiction, Elizabeth I simpers over the Doctor, marries him in secret, and then—having been abandoned by him—orders his execution.[46] As for Victoria, having knighted the Doctor and made companion Rose a dame, she exiles the Time Lord and establishes the Torchwood Institute with the aim of defending Great Britain from the Doctor and other

[46]See "The Shakespeare Code" (2007) for Queen Elizabeth I's displeasure towards the Doctor.

"phantasmagoria". In the distant future, Britain's mixed-heritage sovereign Liz 10 (Queen Elizabeth X) catalogues the Doctor's capers with her regal predecessors. *Doctor Who*'s satire of successive British sovereigns does not smack of any great campaign for a classless society, but neither does it accord to traditional BBC fawning.[47]

Finally, it is enlightening to consider the Doctor's companions. They are rarely drawn from the ranks of the rich. Indeed, tellingly, his only truly upper-class companions have been non-human: Romana (a Time Lord) and Nyssa (a native of the planet Traken); an upper-class earthly companion comes forward in "Planet of the Dead" (2009) in the form of Lady Christina de Sousa, only to be rejected by the Doctor. Human companions are predominantly middle class, with the exceptions of working-class Ben Jackson, Rose Tyler and Bill Potts. The Doctor suggests to Lynda, an apparently working-class young woman from Earth's distant future, that she become a companion in "Bad Wolf"/"The Parting of the Ways" (2005), but she is killed by Daleks. He asks Perkins, a working-class, middle-aged engineer, to become a companion in "Mummy on the Orient Express" (2014) but Perkins declines. Furthermore, some companions such as Ace and certainly Donna Noble are pointedly presented as lower middle class.

Middle-class domination of the "companionariat" has enabled *Doctor Who* to reflect the more precarious lifestyles of the middle class under neoliberalism. This is reflected in the job/vocational changes of companions Donna Noble, Amy Pond and Clara Oswald, which contrast with the stable careers of companions in the show's earlier years. Piers D. Britton theorises that the show focuses on middle-class anxieties.[48] If so, then the job instability of recent companions provides good evidence of the expression of these anxieties. However, building on Britton's insight, it is worthwhile considering the *nature* of these middle-class anxieties. The show is far more focused on worries about domination by a corporate elite than on concerns about working-class militancy. The latter anxiety is expressed in "The Monster of Peladon" (1974), aired during a period of miners' strikes and power cuts, but it is difficult to discern

[47] *Doctor Who*'s gently ribbing support for the British monarchy is reinforced by the Doctor's seeming approval of the hereditary principle on other planets: see, for example, "The Krotons" (1969), "The Curse of Peladon" (1972), "The Monster of Peladon" (1974) and "The Horns of Nimon" (1979–1980).

[48] Britton, *TARDISbound*, 38–39.

any other *Doctor Who* serial or episode that expresses fear of the working class.

In conclusion, there are a good many *Doctor Who* stories that criticise rather than eulogise class systems, and on this basis, we can acquit *Doctor Who* of advancing the "heritage Britain" ideal. Whilst offering few visions of classless societies, *Doctor Who* tends to be especially critical of *harsh* class divides and *stultifying* ruling elites. This is particularly relevant in an era in British society in which contempt for working-class people has become alarmingly mainstream, and in which class discrimination has intensified as the distribution of wealth has polarised.[49]

Doctor Who's Britishness: Race, Empire, Empathy

The British Empire—the largest empire in world history—had a profound impact on Britishness. Indeed, *Doctor Who* may be read as an attempt to come to terms with Britain's loss of importance in the post-imperial era.[50] As John Vohlidka has observed, "Britain's view of itself was left without a rudder and the public needed a new form of self-identification defining their wants, values and composition. *Doctor Who* helped fill this need."[51] In a sense, the show provides an imaginary substitute for the country's imperial might: we can perceive the Doctor as exporting Britishness throughout the cosmos, without the need for conquest and colonisation.

To be sure, the British Empire's impact on Britishness has not been entirely reactionary: in particular, the end of Empire generated waves of immigration into Britain. Over time, these immigrations have engendered an attractive vision of Britain as proudly multiracial. As Mark Leonard observes, Britain is a hybrid nation: it does not mould ethnicities into a conforming whole. Instead it thrives on ethnic and cultural diversity as a way of renewing and re-energising itself.[52] This diversity is now a major signifier of Britishness. By the same token, however, Britain's failure to attain racial equality within its shores may also

[49] Jones, *Chavs*.

[50] Cull, "TARDIS at the OK Corral", 55.

[51] John Vohlidka, "*Doctor Who* and the Critique of Western Imperialism", in *Doctor Who and Race*, ed. Lindy Orthia (Bristol: Intellect, 2013), 125.

[52] Leonard, *Britain™*, 56.

be viewed as part of Empire's bequest, the subordinate status of the colonised being reflected in the inferior life-chances of the non-white British today. The present era's succession of British foreign policy adventures in the Middle East, frequently satirised in new-series *Doctor Who*, also conveys imperial overtones. It could indeed be argued that Britain has a foreign policy that does not reflect the country's diversity, setting the progressive and reactionary legacies of Empire at odds with each other. These tensions are readily apparent in *Doctor Who*. Indeed, it is much to *Doctor Who*'s credit that it frequently concerns itself with Empire and colonisation, subjects which have been written out from some celebrations of British heritage, notably the London Olympics Opening Ceremony in 2012.[53] *Doctor Who* regularly confronts the dark side of Empire; and without such engagement, we surely cannot converse healthily about Britishness.[54] Almost invariably, new-series *Doctor Who* celebrates Britain's diversity through the plentiful use of non-white characters in the Doctor's adventures. At the same time, *Doctor Who* is often justly accused of according inferior prominence to these characters. The show has also been charged with manifesting an imperialistic disdain for non-Western ways of life.

Before we consider *Doctor Who*'s use of non-white characters, it is worth observing how the centrality of Empire to *Doctor Who*'s Britishness is reinforced by the curious absence of Europeanism. Britain's vexed relationship with the European Union (previously, European Community) has loomed large in British politics since accession in 1973. Membership profoundly altered Britain's constitution by restricting the legislative ability of the British Parliament within the policy fields covered by the European treaties. Eventually, it also had a major social effect. In 2004, a number of Eastern European countries joined the European Union and their nationals took advantage of EU provisions on the free movement of persons far more extensively than the citizens of the older

---

[53] Irene Marra, *Britishness, Popular Music and National Identity* (New York and Abingdon: Routledge, 2014), 21. For an argument that *Doctor Who* has failed to show the postcolonial transition stages of societies, see Lindy Orthia "'Sociopathetic Abscess' or 'Yawning Chasm'? The Absent Postcolonial Transition in *Doctor Who*", *The Journal of Commonwealth Literature*, 45 (2010): 207–225.

[54] David Marquand, "'Bursting with Skeletons': Britishness after Empire", in *Britishness: Perspectives on the British Question*, eds. Andrew Gamble and Tony Wright (Chichester: Wiley-Blackwell, 2009), 10–21, 15.

EU Member States had ever done. This immigration had a significant effect on the composition of Britain's population. Public dissatisfaction with the influx of Eastern European workers was a major factor in the 2016 referendum vote to leave the EU.

Doctor Who's muted response to Eastern European immigration is all the more intriguing given that the show greeted Britain's entry into the European Community with something of a metaphorical fanfare. "The Curse of Peladon" (1972) and "The Monster of Peladon" (1974) are widely seen as allegories for British accession, with the Doctor by turns encouraging the isolated planet of Peladon to join a Galactic Federation, and later coping with popular discontent when some members of the Federation prove imperialistic. Subsequent adventures featured continental European characters only occasionally, sometimes helpful to the Doctor ("The Invisible Enemy" (1977)), more often hostile ("City of Death" (1979), "Nightmare of Eden" (1979) and "Silver Nemesis" (1988)). After the Peladon stories, however, there was no attempt in classic *Who* to resurrect allegories for European integration; this may well have been due in part to the relatively low profile of the European debate for much of the 1980s. British Euroscepticism only really advanced in the late 1980s, as it became evident that Britain had given up significant national sovereignty in order to bring the European single market into existence. It further intensified with the negotiation of the Maastricht Treaty in the early 1990s, which introduced the euro currency and created both the European Union and its common foreign and security policy.[55]

The onset of significant Eastern European migration virtually coincided with the start of *Doctor Who*'s 2005 reboot. Yet intriguingly, Eastern Europeans are almost entirely absent from the Doctor's new-series adventures. In "The Sontaran Stratagem" (2008), a Polish man claims to have been working twenty-four hours a day in a factory secretly controlled by the Sontarans, a warrior species. Whilst the story assumes that the entire workforce is under hypnosis, the choice of a Pole can also be seen as a sideswipe at fears of the Eastern European work ethic. There was widespread concern that Britons would be passed over for work in favour of industrious Eastern Europeans who would act as a source of

[55] Danny Nicol, *EC Membership and the Judicialisation of British Politics* (Oxford: Oxford University Press, 2001), Chaps. 6–7.

cheap labour. Months earlier, British Prime Minister Gordon Brown had promised to provide "British jobs for British workers", yet this pledge flew in the face of an EU legal prohibition on nationality discrimination and the idea was quietly dropped. Given the scale of immigration, the absence of Eastern European figures in new-series *Doctor Who* is a curious gap in the show's representation of contemporary Britain. It may reflect a lack of a heartfelt identification as European—many British people finding it difficult to enthuse about European integration, whatever their stance on EU membership. On this reading, modern *Doctor Who* is Eurosceptic by omission, insofar as European integration will not be allowed to sidetrack or dilute the show's dominant narrative of a multiracial Britain peopled by the descendants of Empire. The programme deals with the EU by ignoring it.

Tellingly, though, once Brexit (British exit from the European Union) was under way, the *Who*niverse felt able to introduce its first major Eastern European character in the form of Matteusz Andrzejewski, a Polish school student, in the spin-off *Class*, which was broadcast in the wake of the EU referendum. In the first episode, Charlie (an alien prince) invites Matteusz to be his partner for the school prom, prompting *Class*'s first gay kiss as well as Matteusz's comment "Oh yes my deeply religious parents are very happy I'm going to dance with a boy". It seemed as though, now that Brexit was happening, the *Who*niverse seemed more relaxed about making Eastern Europeans part of its national story. This was timely, as Poles had recently replaced Indians as Britain's most numerous ethnic minority. Also notable, however, is the "Britishisation" of Matteusz. In a fine act of stereotyping, his parents are represented as "the Other". First, they disapprove of Matteusz's relationship with Charlie; then they ground him; then they throw him out. It is not fanciful to see Charlie as a character who serves to make Matteusz more British. Despite being an alien, Charlie is someone who represents Britishness in *Class*, as the Doctor does in *Doctor Who*. By inviting Matteusz to the prom, Charlie initiates the gay relationship that detaches Matteusz from his Polish family and moves him into the multiracial British "family" of the *Class* team.[56] Ushering continentals into the

[56]With Brexit in the offing, Matteusz's Britishisation conformed to the trend towards Eastern Europeans living in Britain applying for British nationality. It is also worth noting here that *Class* is aimed at a different demographic audience compared to *Doctor Who* (a youth/BBC Three audience). The more accepting stance here perhaps anticipates or

British fold only in the wake of the Brexit decision is less disruptive of the story which *Doctor Who* really wants to tell: the story of Empire.

Let us, therefore, turn to the children of the Empire. *Doctor Who*'s long history has witnessed a dramatic shift in the treatment of black, Asian and oriental characters. In the programme's early years, there were few non-white characters, and those few were not depicted as being the equals of whites. The show's racism was indeed thunderous. For example, one of the earliest black characters was Toberman, in "The Tomb of the Cybermen" (1967). Toberman is the loyal servant of Kaftan, a continental European logician who, together with her colleague Kleig, intends to revive the dormant Cybermen. Toberman is characterised by his dumbness, loyalty, strength and self-sacrifice. Other silent characters included a muscular Turk in "The Evil of the Daleks" (1967) and a black circus strongman (played by the same actor who had portrayed Toberman) in "Terror of the Autons" (1971). Brawn is snidely presented as an alternative to brains; and through silence, marginalised people are projected as mindless, voiceless and subject to the whims of external authority.[57] This denial of autonomy is disturbing for a show which celebrates non-conformity. "The Talons of Weng-Chiang" (1977) marked a particular low point in *Doctor Who*'s portrayal of the non-white. In this serial, Chinese immigrants in Victorian Britain are typecast as members of secretive criminal cults, the Doctor blithely relating how he was attacked by "this little man and four other little men". George Ivanoff summarises the tale well: "the story...depicts Chinese people in a rather stereotypically unflattering light, using them only as villains: it's all opium dens, gangs and the abduction of young women".[58] To crown it all, the lead Chinese character was played by a white British man: only his underlings were genuinely Oriental. It took until the swansong years of the classic series for there to be a sea-change in the portrayal of Britain's ethnic minorities, with sympathetic non-white characters featuring in "Remembrance of the Daleks" (1988), "The Happiness Patrol" (1988),

---

projects the attitudes of a different generational audience towards the EU free movement of persons.

[57] Sandra Styles, "The Silent Monologue: The Voice Within the Space", *AlterNative: The International Journal of Indigenous Peoples*, 4(2) (2008): 89–101.

[58] George Ivanoff, "That was Then, This is Now: How My Perceptions Have Changed", in *Doctor Who and Race*, ed. Lindy Orthia (Bristol: Intellect, 2013).

"The Greatest Show in the Galaxy" (1988–1989), "Battlefield" (1989) and "Survival" (1989). Moreover, race emerges as a pervasive theme in "Remembrance of the Daleks" (1988), "Ghostlight" (1989) and "The Curse of Fenric" (1989).

Continuing this approach, and very different from most of classic *Who*, new *Who* has persistently tried to portray Britain's "tiny damp little island" as one which relishes its racial diversity. Lindy Orthia observes that classic *Who* emerged from Britain's post-Empire period when the formerly colonised people were migrating to Britain and were transforming conceptions of Britishness, whereas new *Who* embraces an assertive engagement with cosmopolitan Britain—diverse in terms of class, race, gender, sexuality, regionality and subculture.[59] Hence, in the new series, the Doctor gained his first black companions—Mickey Smith (fleetingly) in 2006 and Martha Jones in 2007. Furthermore, three of his white companions have had black or mixed-race boyfriends—Rose Tyler, Donna Noble and Clara Oswald (Donna had two). Use of one-off or recurring black and Asian characters also became extensive. To give a few examples: in "Fear Her" (2006), a black girl is taken over by an alien force against the backdrop of the London Olympics 2012; in "The Beast Below" (2010), a mixed-race Queen is sovereign of the United Kingdom in the distant future; in "The Bells of Saint John" (2013), companion Clara is carer for two mixed-race children Angie and Artie; in "The Caretaker" (2014), she has become a teacher at Coal Hill School with a large cohort of black pupils[60]; and in "Hell Bent" (2015), a white male Time Lord regenerates into a black woman. These examples merely give a flavour of the almost obsessive welter of non-white characters who feature in new-series *Doctor Who*. Occasionally the use of non-white characters has caused controversy. For instance, the black and Asian presence in crowd scenes in "The Shakespeare Code" (2007), set in the Elizabethan era, and "The Woman Who Lived" (2015), set in the eighteenth century, may be attacked as historically inaccurate, and (in the former case) of whitewashing Elizabethan racism and slavery.[61] The same charge may

[59] Lindy Orthia, "Introduction", in *Doctor Who and Race*, ed. Lindy Orthia (Bristol: Intellect, 2013), 3–4.

[60] This racial mix formed a sharp contrast to the all-white cohort which we see at the same school in the old show's opening episode "An Unearthly Child" (1963).

[61] Iona Yeager, "Too Brown for a Fair Praise: The Depiction of Racial Prejudice as Cultural Heritage in *Doctor Who*", in *Doctor Who and Race*, ed. Lindy Orthia (Bristol: Intellect, 2013), 23.

be levelled at "Empress of Mars" (2017), which optimistically featured a black British soldier in Victorian times.[62] But this criticism should be tempered by bearing in mind that the main purpose of *Doctor Who* is to represent contemporary Britain and contemporary British identity. Thus, in the show's historical stories we can see the black presence as an attempt at creative nostalgia, representing not the country in former times but the country today.[63]

Furthermore, hybridity has become a pervasive theme of *Doctor Who*, mirroring Britain's nature as a hybrid nation. Hybridity is repeatedly presented as a source of strength, with racial purity as a source of weakness. Moreover, hybridity is associated with being British. For example, "Remembrance of the Daleks" (1989) is a story set in London in 1963, which involves a conflict between two species of Daleks, each claiming racial superiority. The Dalek obsession with racial purity is brought into sharp relief by the Doctor's encounter with John, a Jamaican who lends a hand running a local café, and whose conversation with the Doctor touches on slavery and his African heritage. Whilst there is no explicit suggestion that John or his descendants may interbreed with white Britons—indeed, in the main, the story emphasises how British society was more racist in the 1960s than today—nonetheless, placing John in the heart of Britain, yet cheek by jowl with the Daleks' race war, serves to emphasise the potential for hybridity of the emerging cosmopolitan British nation. The merits of hybridity are emphasised in "The Stolen Earth"/"Journey's End" (2009), where companion Donna Noble fleetingly becomes the super-intelligent Doctor-Donna, a hybrid between herself and the Doctor, in which form she defeats the Daleks. Strength is once again linked to hybridity in "Hell Bent" (2015), where the Time Lords fear destruction by a being known as "the Hybrid". The episode concludes with the revelation that the Hybrid is half Time Lord and half human, and not one person but two: the dangerous combination of a passionate and powerful Time Lord (the Doctor) and a young woman companion (Clara Oswald) who is very similar to him. By contrast, the potential of hybridity to inspire peace is emphasised in "Daleks in

---

[62] "*Doctor Who* writer protested against problematic casting of black actor as Victorian soldier", *Telegraph*, June 11, 2017.

[63] *Doctor Who*'s approach is not entirely consistent. "Thin Ice" (2017) is set in Regency London and again features black characters, yet black companion Bill Potts suffers racism, which is swiftly avenged by the Doctor punching the perpetrator, Lord Sutcliffe.

Manhattan"/"Evolution of the Daleks" (2007), where the Dalek leader Sec, having hybridised with a human, proposes abandoning the Daleks' quest for supremacy, and asks the Doctor to find the new Dalek-human species a new planet in which to live rather than conquer Earth. The same theme recurs in "The Zygon Invasion"/"The Zygon Inversion" (2014), in which UNIT staff member Osgood has been appointed guardian of peace between the humans and Zygons, along with a Zygon which changes its appearance to resemble her. Osgood refuses to tell the Doctor whether she is human or Zygon, asserting that she and her "sister" were the living embodiment of the peace between the two species, so she is both human *and* Zygon. Osgood's claim raises the intriguing question of the extent to which hybridity is a state of mind rather than exclusively a physical state. In 2013, an insightful book of collected essays, *Doctor Who and Race*, was published which by and large criticised the show's stance on racial issues, including the treatment of non-white characters. Whilst many of the criticisms in *Doctor Who and Race* are valid, it is no less important to acknowledge *Doctor Who*'s improvement over time in terms of the way in which the show has fashioned a Britishness that celebrates the country's racial diversity and presents hybridity as a source of strength.

Thus *Doctor Who* now includes a plenitude of non-white characters and provides a positive imagining of hybridity. Yet this is not to say that new *Who*'s treatment of non-whites is entirely satisfactory. A "critical mass" of non-white characters is certainly present, but so too is the relegation of most of them to minor roles. Even the treatment of non-white characters with major roles has been criticised. For instance, it has been suggested that Martha Jones' period as companion was itself marked by the Doctor's racial discrimination against her. Linnea Dodson has complained that Martha is the "rebound companion" and that, by comparison to Rose Tyler, her predecessor as companion, the Doctor is constantly ungenerous towards her.[64] On the other hand, as Timothy

[64]Linnea Dodson, "Conscious Colour-Blindness, Unconscious Racism in *Doctor Who* Companions", in *Doctor Who and Race*, ed. Lindy Orthia (Bristol: Intellect, 2013). Similarly, Dodson complains of the show's racist treatment of Martha's family in the series finale "The Sound of Drums"/"Last of the Time Lords" (2007), where they are held captive and forced to act as servants. Yet it is actually the Doctor's arch-enemy, the Master, who forces the Jones family into this domestic service role reminiscent of the British colonies. On this reading, the show can be interpreted as disapproving of this racist treatment rather than tolerating it.

Mark Robinson has observed, one would be hard pressed to find a character as strong, capable and intelligent as Martha.[65] One should add that Martha remains one of the few companions in the new show to get the last laugh. It is she who chooses to leave the TARDIS, since the Doctor does not requite her love: she is speedily recruited to an important post in the Unified Intelligence Taskforce (UNIT), and has further adventures in both *Doctor Who* and the spin-off *Torchwood*. More importantly, she participates cheerfully in these post-TARDIS escapades. This connotes that Martha has moved on, that she has "got over" the Doctor. By contrast, we also meet Rose Tyler on various occasions after she has left the Doctor and, for the most part, she seems morose. Indeed, a number of white companions have come off worse than Martha when they leave the TARDIS—Rose, Donna Noble and Amy Pond. If we choose to give greater weight to what happens to companions after their stint with the Doctor, it becomes possible to take a more positive view of *Doctor Who*'s treatment of Martha and her strength of character.

A more substantial criticism of *Doctor Who*'s commitment to racial equality is that after Martha Jones' period as companion, the experiment of a non-white companion was not repeated until the arrival of Bill Potts in 2017. Several potential non-white companions never made it into the TARDIS. Thus, in "The God Complex" (2011) the TARDIS materialises in what seems to be a 1980s hotel on Earth. Here the Doctor and companions Amy Pond and Rory Williams meet a motley collection of characters who, it transpires, are the intended victims of an elusive creature which feeds off people's deepest fears. The most engaging of these intended victims is a young Asian woman, Rita. Like Martha, Rita works for Britain's National Health Service, a career which itself codes her as British. For good measure, she makes tea for the embattled group, explaining: "Of course! I'm British! It's how we cope with trauma. Well, that or tutting." Rita's characterisation is reminiscent of Yasmin Alibhai-Brown's observation that Black and Asian Britons ironically feel more deeply about their British identity than any of the indigenous groups, and that by embracing British identity they have redefined

[65] Timothy Mark Robinson, "Agency, Action, and Re-action: The Black Female Presence in *Doctor Who*", in *Ruminations, Peregrinations and Regenerations: A Critical Approach to Doctor Who*, ed. Chris Hansen (Newcastle-upon-Tyne: Cambridge Scholars Publishing, 2010), 159.

it.[66] When she hints at an attachment to Islam, the Doctor asks whether she is a Muslim and she responds that she is, adding: "Don't be frightened!" At the time in Britain, non-Muslims were indeed becoming frightened, as the perception of Islam became confused with terrorism perpetrated by those who claimed to be Muslims; British Muslims were becoming no less afraid at a rising tide of Islamophobia. Having Rita as a companion would have been a golden opportunity to interrogate these pressing issues, and indeed, the Doctor hints to her that she might join the TARDIS crew. However, Rita is killed off in "The God Complex". *Doctor Who* thereby deprived itself of a marvellous opportunity to explore the relationship between Britishness, Islam and allegedly Islamic extremism, at a time when such an exploration would have enriched the show. The failure to make Rita a companion was compounded by the ruling-out of two further possible non-white companions. In "Into the Dalek" (2014), the Doctor refuses a request from a mixed-race character, Journey Blue, to join his adventures, on the spurious grounds that she is a soldier. On the same grounds, it becomes evident in "The Caretaker" (2014) that companion Clara's mixed-race boyfriend Danny Pink, soldier-turned-maths-teacher, is not destined for the TARDIS either, since he does not hit it off with the Doctor. The question of the Doctor's militarism—whether he is a soldier or whether he is a "good man"—was the pervasive theme of the *Doctor Who* season in which Journey and Danny were passed over. Nonetheless, it is disappointing that the Doctor should reject two *non-white* "soldiers" when in fact non-whites are underrepresented in the British armed forces. These observations make it all too possible to read the fates of non-white characters as amounting to a narrative of rejection. Mickey Smith is rejected by Rose Tyler as a boyfriend; Martha is rejected by the Doctor as a girlfriend; the show rejects Rita as a companion by killing her off; and the Doctor rejects Journey and Danny as companions. This is a depressing litany, which may reflect a racist Britain *as it is* but fails as imaginative science fiction to project a non-racist Britain as a normative aspiration. The advent of Bill Potts as companion in 2017 was a step in the right direction, as was the Doctor punching a character in "Thin Ice"

[66]Yasmin Alibhai-Brown, "The Excluded Majority: What about the English?", in *Reclaiming Britishness: Living Together after 11 September and the Rise of the Right*, eds. Phoebe Griffith and Mark Leonard (London: The Foreign Policy Centre, 2002), 45.

(2017) for racially abusing her, but at the end of the series it was confirmed that Bill would be leaving *Doctor Who* and so would be merely a one-series companion (unlike white predecessors Amy Pond and Clara Oswald, both companions of several years' duration). The shortness of Bill's period as companion was softened by the somewhat ambiguous news that the Doctor in 2018 would be joined by "three new friends": Yasmin, an Asian woman; Ryan, a black man; and Graham, a middle-aged white man. More importantly still, in twelve regenerations, the Doctor has always been a white male: *Doctor Who* has yet to have a non-white Doctor. The *Doctor Who* canon does not dictate that the Doctor be white: in "The War Games" (1969), the Time Lords oblige the Doctor to regenerate and offer him a variety of possible faces, including that of a black man. Be that as it may, the Doctor's constant whiteness has acted as a conservative influence on the show's presentation of Britishness. Casting ethnic minority actors as the Doctor would make *Doctor Who*'s celebration of Britain's racial diversity more genuine. On this note, Mike Hernandez makes the strong point that continuing to cast exclusively white Doctors is actually contrary to the direction that *Doctor Who* has taken for some years, and that varying the Doctor's racial identity would help convey a more accurate conception of British culture and the more inclusive potential of British national identity.[67] Casting non-white Doctors would indeed be a powerful symbol of racial equality in Britain, since non-white actors would no longer be relegated to being the underlings of *Doctor Who* adventures but would have arrived at the show's pinnacle. Furthermore, some of the Doctor's adventures have always concerned Empire and colonisation, and on occasion, the show's—or the Doctor's—treatment of the colonised has left much to be desired. A non-white Doctor could well focus minds more acutely on the rights and wrongs of how the racial "Other" is treated. As Hernandez puts it, it would "allow the formerly imperial nation to fully see itself" and to imagine how the modern British *ought* to be, against the backdrop of how Britain *used* to be.[68]

---

[67] Mike Hernandez, "You Can't Just Change What I Look Like without Consulting Me!": The Shifting Racial Identity of the Doctor", in *Doctor Who and Race*, ed. Lindy Orthia (Bristol: Intellect, 2013).

[68] Lack of racial parity of esteem is also represented metaphorically in the treatment of aliens who wish to settle on Earth's surface. For instance, in "The Hungry Earth"/"Cold Blood" (2010) there are negotiations about dividing the Earth between Silurians (man's reptilian predecessors on the planet) and humans, but no talk of the possibility of living together. Similarly, in "The Zygon Invasion"/"The Zygon Inversion" (2015) the

So what of *Doctor Who*'s representations of the British Empire and the people Britain colonised? In a sense, the Doctor could himself be seen as a metaphor for the British Empire, colonising time itself, differentiating good beings from evil beings in black-and-white terms and often exterminating the latter. As Christine Gilroy has observed, *Doctor Who* "supports the Doctor's privileged position and his self-appointed responsibility by allowing him to override multilateral solutions as well as the self-determinations of racial others".[69] However, the Doctor's role will be considered in depth in Chap. 5, which examines whether he is a war criminal; the present focus will instead be on those *Doctor Who* stories which imagine extraterrestrial empires and the colonised. One crucial issue here, identified by Lindy Orthia, is the show's attachment to "stagism". This is the idea that society moves forward in linear fashion, going through fixed stages towards scientific achievement. This theory of history fosters an intolerance of non-Western ways of life, which in turn can be used to justify colonisation. The implication being that more "advanced" Europeans can thereby "raise up" those at the more "primitive" stages of development.[70]

Early *Doctor Who* plots involving colonisation betray a disturbing toleration of discrimination. For example, in "The Ark" (1966), the Doctor and companions Dodo and Steven land on a huge spaceship in the distant future. The ship is transporting the human race to a new planet, together with the Monoids, a species of one-eyed humanoids who perform acts of domestic drudgery for the humans. We are told that the Monoids' origin is obscure, that their own planet was dying and that they offered their invaluable services in order to embark upon this joint voyage with the humans, who are referred to as "the guardians". Shockingly, whilst the Doctor swiftly grasps that the Monoids are far cleverer than the humans realise, he expresses no disapproval at their

shape-shifting Zygons are permitted to settle on Earth only if they permanently conceal themselves as being human.

[69] Christine Gilroy, "The Doctor's Burden: Racial Superiority and Panoptic Privilege in New *Doctor Who*", in *Impossible Worlds, Impossible Things: Cultural Perspectives on Doctor Who, Torchwood and The Sarah Jane Adventures*, eds. Ross P. Garner, Melissa Beattie and Una McCormack (Newcastle-upon-Tyne: Cambridge Scholars Publishing, 2010).

[70] Lindy Orthia, "Savages, Science, Stagism and the Naturalized Ascendancy of the Not-We in *Doctor Who*", in *Doctor Who and Race*, ed. Lindy Orthia (Bristol: Intellect, 2013).

subordination. The TARDIS returns to the Ark many centuries later, to discover that the Monoids have staged a revolution and have enslaved the humans. With wondrous lack of even-handedness, the Doctor sides with the humans against the Monoids. Only at the conclusion of the adventure, where the two races are compelled to make peace with each other, does the Doctor criticise the ancestors of the humans for having treated the Monoids like slaves, pointing out that it was no wonder they were repaid in kind. This condemnation is welcome but comes several centuries too late.

Discrimination against the colonised and disdain for societies that depart from Western norms is also evident in "Colony in Space" (1971). This serial concerns the struggle for control of a planet between two rival white groups: a collective of environmentalist colonists anxious to escape an authoritarian Earth, and the staff of the Interplanetary Mining Corporation, a company intent on exploiting the planet's mineral reserves. However, the planet is also inhabited by an indigenous species known as the Primitives. Although it transpires that the Primitives are telepathic and intelligent, the story marginalises them. The main conflict is played out between corporation and colonists, the latter astonishingly asserting that the planet is their world since they were there first. By contrast, the Primitives are dismissed on the grounds that their science has deteriorated into a primitive religion, the assumption being that a technological society is the only valid social form. In fact, it transpires that the Primitives form part of a society that created an ultimate weapon of destruction, then turned away from science because of the chaos it wreaked. The story of the Primitives surely invites reflection on whether technological advance deserves to be the aim of every society. Disappointingly, there is no such discussion: instead, the Primitives' technological backwardness is merely taken as an appropriate self-punishment for the abuse of science. More troubling still, *Doctor Who*'s triumph of good over evil sees the environmentalist colonists, not the indigenous population, ending up with the planet.

Thankfully, as *Doctor Who* evolved, there were more stories that adopted a more robustly anti-colonialist stance. In a clear metaphor for the British Empire, "The Mutants" (1972) features a human empire in decline and poised to abandon and grant independence to one of its colonies, the planet Solos. However, the human forces are led by the Marshal, a character who has no wish to relinquish the planet. The show's normative political position is articulated by the likeable officer

Stubbs, who says: "Let's get off and home, plenty to sort out there". The regime perpetuated by the humans (known as the Overlords) has clear overtones of apartheid and the Marshal's strategy is transparently one of divide-and-rule. For his part, the Doctor aligns himself with the Solonians and their liberation struggle. The story's flaw is that it credits the colonised with too little intelligence. The story is called "The Mutants" because the Solonians undergo a regular mutation, usually over hundreds of years, changing from humanoids to insect-like creatures to super-beings. However, we are expected to believe that they are somehow ignorant of all of this, since their culture has been destroyed by the Overlords. Instead they have to rely on a human scholar, Professor Sondergaard, as well as on the Time Lords, to learn about their most basic lifecycle. This seems far-fetched. Nonetheless, the extremely unfavourable depiction of the Marshal and the story's powerful imperative towards Solonian independence confirms the conclusion of Maura Grady and Cassie Hemstrom that "The Mutants" counters pro-British Empire narratives and makes visible the concerns of colonial peoples.[71]

"The Power of Kroll" (1978–1979) pits a mining company against green humanoid Swampies who live a simple life in the marshes of Delta Magna. Graham Sleight puts forward a rather convincing argument that the story could have been a parable of colonial exploitation but that it sabotages itself by depicting the Swampies as primitive, superstitious, hidebound by tradition, and just as greedy for power in their own way as those running the rig.[72] However, although the Swampies are not morally uplifting, neither is most of the company staff. In this adventure, the Doctor is more agnostic about the Western social imperative of seeking technological advance: he opines that "progress" is a very flexible word, capable of meaning anything one wants. Indeed, at the end of the tale he suggests to the sole surviving company employee that he should try leading the natural life; he might actually enjoy it. Similarly, in "State of Decay" (1980), the Doctor repeatedly expresses the view that societies are entitled to opt for a semi-rural culture in preference to a scientific and technological one.

[71] Maura Grady and Cassie Hemstrom, "Nostalgia for Empire, 1963–1974", in *Doctor Who in Time and Space: Essays on Themes, Characters, History and Fandom, 1963–2012*, ed. Gillian I. Leitch (Jefferson, NC: McFarland, 2013), 132–133.

[72] Graham Sleight, *The Doctor's Monsters* (London: I.B. Tauris, 2012), 32.

A further step in the anti-imperialist direction was taken in "Kinda" (1982), which imagines the Kinda, a people on the planet Deva Loka, which is under assessment for colonisation. The Kinda are a sophisticated community but not in the Western sense. A matriarchal society, they are telepathic, peaceful and calm, and they regard the flow of time as a curse. This belief is significant, since it flies in the face of linear ideas of technological development. Lindy Orthia has suggested, however, that "Kinda" offers only limited respite from the show's propaganda in favour of the Western way of life. She bases her argument on a terse dialogue between the Doctor and the scientist Todd in which the Doctor mentions that the Kinda seem primitive and Todd disagrees because the Kinda's necklaces are shaped as DNA double helixes. Orthia argues that this means that the story is advancing the familiar ideology of stagism.[73] However, not only does this dialogue turn out to be fairly inconsequential (the scientific theme not being developed at all), but more importantly, the main thrust of the story is that the Kinda are radically different from Western society, and yet they peacefully triumph over the colonists, even recruiting a couple of them to their own way of life. It is therefore hard to conceive "Kinda" as a story which makes conformity to Western culture the measuring stick for judging the merits of a society. Finally, "Planet of the Ood" (2008) concerns a species enslaved by a human corporation, Ood Operations, and used for domestic labour by the citizens of the Second Great and Bountiful Human Empire. It seems that, left to their own devices, the Ood form a society which is again very different from Western culture: they are a peaceful species leading a life of song, empathy, telepathy and prophecy. The Doctor joins forces with the Ood and the human group Friends of the Ood, to free them from exploitation.

Allowing for the many inconsistencies of the voluminous *Doctor Who* canon, one can therefore discern a trend towards a more critical stance towards Empire and colonisation, and in some stories a greater open-mindedness towards non-Western ways of life. Matthew Jones has theorised that by the time Tom Baker assumed the title role in 1974, Britain was ready to shrug off its imperial heritage and the British, like Baker's Doctor, would be wandering carefree travellers.[74] A corresponding

[73] Lindy Orthia, "Savages".

[74] Matthew Jones, "Aliens of London: (Re)Reading National Identity in *Doctor Who*", in *Ruminations, Peregrinations and Regenerations: A Critical Approach to Doctor Who*, ed. Chris Hansen (Newcastle-upon-Tyne: Cambridge Scholars Publishing, 2010), 80–81.

evolution is evident in the way in which the show depicts British imperialists. A tendency to portray them as merely "good-natured bumblers" has been identified by Alec Charles.[75] The show, however, has eroded this depiction over time. The pith helmet may be sported by a good-natured bumbler in "Kinda" but becomes downright sinister in "The Greatest Show in the Galaxy" (1988–1989), where it is worn by a character, Captain Cook, who hides his homicidal intent under a thin façade of bumbling. By the time of "Planet of the Ood", the metaphor has moved on entirely, imperialists eschewing Victorian imperial attire in favour of the smart modern suits of contemporary neoliberalism.

For its part, new-series *Doctor Who* was confronted by Britain's shift towards neo-imperialist overseas adventures, with British forces being deployed successively in Afghanistan, Iraq, Libya and Syria. The show has satirised these somewhat endless interventions. For example, it poked fun at Tony Blair's notorious "45 minutes" claim in "Aliens of London"/"World War Three" (2005).[76] And in "The Zygon Invasion"/"The Zygon Inversion" (2015) the Doctor puts forward arguments against bombing the Zygons which matched those being used against British participation in the bombing of Syria. ("You start bombing them, you'll radicalise the lot. That's exactly what the splinter group wants.")

To sum up, over time, *Doctor Who* has come to project a Britishness of racial *diversity* but falls lamentably short of making racial *equality* its hallmark of Britishness. The non-white "Other" is still relegated to a subordinate position. There was a dismal slowness to repeat the experiment of a non-white companion and the role of the Doctor has up until now grimly remained a whites-only preserve. Yet, at the same time, credit must be given where credit is due: *Doctor Who*'s criticism of colonialisation has sharpened over time as nostalgia for Empire receded, and the sheer mass of non-white characters in new *Who* has made the country's multiracial nature an indispensable aspect of *Doctor Who*'s Britishness. As

[75] Alec Charles, "The Ideology of Anachronism", in *Time and Relative Dissertations in Space: Critical Perspectives on Doctor Who*, ed. David Butler (Manchester and New York: Manchester University Press, 2007), 119.

[76] Tony Blair had claimed in 2002 that the military planning of Saddam Hussein, the President of Iraq, allowed for some weapons of mass destruction to be ready within forty-five minutes of the command to deploy them. Tony Blair, Foreword, *Iraq's Weapons of Mass Destruction, Assessment of the British Government*, September 2002.

Jon Cook has observed, the very diversity and plurality that from one perspective threatens the core of British identity has now come to define that identity.[77] It is heartening that *Doctor Who* celebrates this diversity as a fundamental part of national identity. In short, to be multiracial is to be British.

Doctor Who's Britishness: A Gendered Nationality?

The identity of nations is often framed by the role that women play within them. In theory, it would be possible for *Doctor Who* to have constructed a normative Britishness made distinctive by women being the equals of men. In this regard, Lorna Jowett argues that science fiction, dwelling as it does on the novel and the strange, could indeed offer something new by way of gender representation.[78] Yet, so far, *Doctor Who* has failed to do so. For gender equality to constitute part of *Doctor Who*'s vision of Britishness the programme would need to show a wholehearted commitment to gender equality: in fact, there is plenty of evidence pointing in the opposite direction—towards male domination.

Any prospect of a commitment to gender equality has been compromised by the show's structural tradition: a dominant male character is accompanied by a succession of subordinate, mainly female companions. The show's treatment of the companions constitutes a good yardstick by which to determine whether gender equality is part of *Doctor Who*'s Britishness. After all, just as the Doctor is an emblem of Britishness, so too are the companions. Most of them are both human and British. In new *Who*, this Britishness tends to be emphasised, whether by Rose Tyler's affinity with the Union Jack, Martha Jones' association with the country's iconic National Health Service, or Clara Oswald's employment at a London secondary school, the multiracial character of which emphasises its Britishness.

In classic *Who*, the companion evolved as having a secondary role, with drama revolving around the Doctor: in new *Who* the companion became more central, yet is still subject to ultimate subordination by the

---

[77] Jon Cook, "Relocating Britishness and the Break-Up of Britain", in *Relocating Britishness*, eds. Steven Caunce et al. (Manchester and New York: Manchester University Press, 2004), 35.

[78] Lorna Jowett, "The Girls Who Waited: Female Companions and Gender in *Doctor Who*", *Critical Studies in Television*, 9 (2014): 77.

Doctor. Thus, despite the possibilities for experimentalism which science fiction offers, *Doctor Who*'s authors have allowed the show to remain constrained by its narrative tradition. Imaginatively handled, it might have been possible to have the companion being more the Doctor's equal without unduly undermining his status as the star of the show.

In the classic series, only very rarely was a companion allowed to play the decisive role in resolving an adventure by using her intelligence and resourcefulness. Companion Vicki inspires a rebellion in "The Space Museum" (1965), and companion Zoe Heriot deploys her mathematical skills in "The Invasion" (1968) to destroy a Cyberfleet: but such instances were few and far between. Indeed, it seems uncontroversial that some woman companions of the show's early years—dubbed "screamers" by Richard Wallace—conformed unequivocally to damsel-in-distress stereotypes.[79] Examples include Polly (1966–1967), Victoria Waterfield (1967–1968) and Jo Grant (1973–1974). Polly was a screamer *par excellence*, and whilst she showed initiative in some adventures, her initiatives often sprang from her traditional femininity. For example, she uses her womanly wiles with an English officer in "The Highlanders" (1966) and deploys nail varnish remover against Cybermen in "The Moonbase" (1967). Too often, she just needed to be rescued. When she leaves the TARDIS together with boyfriend Ben Jackson, the Doctor remarks that Ben can become an Admiral and Polly can look after Ben—and Polly agrees! We meet Victoria in "The Evil of the Daleks" (1967) where, as a prisoner of the Daleks, she is all crinolines, traditional femininity and passivity. She tries to investigate the Yeti in "The Abominable Snowmen" (1967) only to get hypnotised, and she makes little real impact in subsequent adventures. Victoria's status as a screamer was strikingly confirmed in "Fury from the Deep" (1968), where the Doctor deploys and amplifies her screams in order to destroy the monster he is fighting. At the end of this serial, Victoria expresses a wish to leave the TARDIS but it is the Doctor not Victoria who decides she should live with the Harrises, a married couple whom they have met in this adventure, so her departure is marked by a lack of agency. For her part, Jo Grant acts on her own initiative more than Polly and Victoria, but, without the Doctor in charge, these initiatives usually end in disarray. This is exemplified by her first

[79] Richard Wallace, "'But Doctor?'—A Feminist Perspective of *Doctor Who*", in *Ruminations, Peregrinations and Regenerations: A Critical Approach to Doctor Who*, ed. Chris Hansen (Newcastle-upon-Tyne: Cambridge Scholars Publishing, 2010).

adventure "Terror of the Autons" (1971), where a solo bid to investigate a plastics factory leads in short order to her capture by the Doctor's enemy, the Master. Jo is well summarised by James Chapman as "a well-meaning but rather accident-prone dolly bird".[80] Jo's successor as companion, Sarah Jane Smith (1973–1976), was originally intended to be a stronger, more feminist, character: in two of her earliest stories, "The Time Warrior" (1973–1974) and "The Monster of Peladon" (1974), she forcefully espouses pro-women's liberation views. Significantly, however, although Sarah Jane remained the Doctor's companion until the autumn of 1976, she never again voiced feminist opinions, reverting to a character rather more similar to Jo Grant's. Thus, the Doctor's frequent demands to his enemies of the whereabouts and safety of "Miss Smith" came to echo earlier entreaties he had made for "Miss Grant". The overriding impression is that the companion is a pretty young woman who gets into scrapes and needs to be saved by the Doctor. James Chapman observes that it seemed difficult to escape the limitations of the programme's format.[81] In any event, the *Doctor Who* production team seemed unwilling to transform that format.

Over time, *Doctor Who*'s authors tried on occasion to veer away from the damsel-in-distress model, yet these efforts did surprisingly little to remedy the show's male domination. Leela (1977–1978) was an Amazonian-type huntress from another planet. Something of an action woman, she frequently displays more courage than male characters (and fainting, panicking female characters) whom she encountered. Although the Doctor more than once lauds her for her bright ideas (for instance in "The Face of Evil" (1977) and "Horror of Fang Rock" (1977)), for the most part, her narrative emphasises her physicality, primitiveness and intuition. Her warrior nature serves to add a political dimension: she foments revolution in both "Underworld" (1978) and "The Sun Makers" (1977) and organises military action in "The Invasion of Time" (1978). Leela certainly provides relief from the dolly-bird tradition. Yet since the pervasive theme is that the Doctor is *educating* Leela, showing her the error of her primitive ways, this difference serves to reinforce the Doctor's male authority. She is also somewhat undermined by her departure, a rather unlikely falling-in-love with a military officer on the

[80] James Chapman, *Inside the TARDIS* (London: I.B. Tauris, 2013), 79.

[81] Chapman, *Inside the TARDIS*, 79.

Doctor's home planet. In any event, since we are focusing specifically on gender as a signifier of *Britishness*, it should be noted that it is difficult to conceive of Leela as British. She is "othered" by her unusual English, in that she does not use contractions such as "I'm", "don't" and so on. In terms of her timeline, she may be post-British and in metaphorical terms pre-British. Romana (1978–1981) was a Time Lord who was assigned to assist the Doctor in his search for the "Key to Time" in what was the show's first real story arc in 1978–1979. Yet although Romana could join in spouting the Doctor's technobabble, this was about all she could do. For instance, her very first episode, in "The Ribos Operation" (1978), culminated in her being (rather needlessly) trapped by a monster—a predicament from which the Doctor, of course, rescues her. Moreover, for all her vaunted intellect, Romana was not permitted to be the Doctor's equal in terms of solving the problems that she and the Doctor faced. In "The Power of Kroll" (1978), for example, the Doctor, Romana and another character are sentenced by the indigenous Swampies to die according to holy ritual. Whilst Romana expends a great deal of dialogue during this ritual complaining and wisecracking about their impending deaths, only the Doctor comes up with a way of actually avoiding this fate. The show's authors seemed unwilling ever to significantly reverse these roles; when, in "The Pirate Planet" (1978), Romana comes up with a tactical spark of genius, her display of intelligence is swiftly trumped by a more baffling idea of the Doctor's, which both she and the Doctor laud as "ingenious" and "fantastic". Romana's departure in "Warrior's Gate" (1981) shows her untapped potential in terms of initiative, independence and selflessness: she leaves the Doctor in order to help an alien species. Classic *Who*'s final companion, Ace (1987–1989) follows rather a similar pattern. Her narrative tries to buck the trend but again is never allowed wholly to succeed. Whilst Ace's character and fears are better developed than those of previous companions, and whilst she has elements of an action heroine, nonetheless the Doctor is particularly fatherly towards her, thereby preserving his domination.

It seemed that the post-2005 show might usher in companions who would be more the Doctor's equal partner. In this regard, Lee Barron argues that the new series transformed the politics of companions: no longer mere sounding-boards for the Doctor's brilliance nor damsels in distress, he contends that new-show companions play vital roles not merely in combating alien menaces but in teaching the Doctor how to be human.[82] To be sure, to *Doctor Who*'s credit, the companion's story tended to take centre stage in new *Who* far more than in the classic series. The companions' families also loomed larger than in the past, reflecting not only the show's adoption of a more soap opera-style intensity of drama but politically an acknowledgment of the growing role of family as the welfare state was pared back under British neoliberalism. Moreover, on a number of occasions the actions or insights of the companion save the day. Examples include Rose Tyler's derring-do in "Rose" (2005), Amy Pond's perspicacity in "The Beast Below" (2010) and "Victory of the Daleks" (2010) and Clara Oswald's leadership qualities in "Flatline" (2014).

It would be misleading, however, to assume that the new-series companions, for all their feistiness, embody gender equality. Several commentators have put forward the opposite view. For example, Dee Amy-Chinn argues that in new *Who*, acts of care, *when carried out by women*, limit agency and restrict the growth of the characters who embody them. She draws a contrast between companion Rose Tyler, whose care ethic is motivated by proximity to the recipient, and the Doctor, whose care ethic is based on broader moral principles. This difference means that Rose is destined to be a smaller moral actor than the Doctor, and this in turn perpetuates a conservative discourse of gender.[83] Whilst, in theory, Rose's caring and accepting responsibility for the welfare of others could have been put forward as an alternative framework for a positive representation of women, Amy-Chinn argues that *Doctor Who* too often paints her quality of caring as misguided and problematic, turning what might have been a source of female empowerment into a form of limitation. Amy-Chinn's thesis, however, disregards the self-seeking nature of Rose's caring: she is solicitous of her father in "Father's Day" (2005) and of Jackie Tyler's marriage in "Rise of the Cybermen" (2006) so that she, Rose, may have a complete family. Her "caring" for new acquaintances and for boyfriend Micky Smith amounts to very little. A different, more powerful argument is advanced by Lorna Jowett, who comments that the new show forcefully contrasts a solitary Doctor with female

[82]Lee Barron, "Intergalactic Girl Power: The Gender Politics of Companionship in 21st Century *Doctor Who*", in *Ruminations, Peregrinations and Regenerations: A Critical Approach to Doctor Who*, ed. Chris Hansen (Newcastle-upon-Tyne: Cambridge Scholars Publishing, 2010).

[83]Dee Amy-Chinn, "Rose Tyler: The Ethics of Care and the Limits of Agency", *Science Fiction Film and Television*, 1 (2008): 231.

companions *who are defined by relationships.* Jowett observes that sexual tension with the Doctor works to the detriment of female characters who often end up abandoned and waiting.[84] Thus, in new *Who*, travelling with the Doctor comes at a high price. For the (male) Doctor, the adventure goes on and on; for the (mainly female) companions, everything too often ends in tears.

The Doctor's women in new-series *Doctor Who* have indeed suffered a variety of miserable departures: Rose Tyler is banished to an alternative universe. Whilst she could thereafter upgrade her career from shop assistant to being a top officer of Torchwood, an organisation which combats alien invasions, this does not appear to make her happy owing to her sense of abandonment by the Doctor. Ultimately, she is palmed off with an unstable Doctor-substitute, a human clone of the Time Lord. As for Donna Noble, the experience of travelling with the Doctor appears to politicise her: she sides with the oppressed Ood in "Planet of the Ood" (2008) and criticises the militarism of UNIT in "The Sontaran Stratagem" (2008). At the end of her travels with the Doctor, she is transformed into a human-Time Lord hybrid, the Doctor-Donna. Had Donna remained in the TARDIS as the Doctor-Donna, even for a single episode, this might finally have presented the Doctor with a true equal. But such a challenge to the Doctor's supremacy was too radical for *Doctor Who*. Instead, it conveniently transpires that Donna's physiology cannot cope with the hybridity, and the Doctor is obliged to reverse her hybridisation and erase her memories of their adventures, returning her to her former life as a gossipy lightweight. Sydney Duncan and Andy Duncan point out that Donna's demotion is particularly disheartening because she is the only companion played by a woman who is over forty.[85] Amy Pond, along with husband Rory Williams, is zapped back in time to an unliberated 1930s America from whence she cannot return. Martha Jones is rare in controlling her own destiny, leaving the TARDIS having tired of the Doctor not reciprocating her romantic affections. She takes advantage of her experiences to build herself a career in UNIT. Even here, however, there is something to be said for

---

[84] Jowett, "The Girls Who Waited", 77.

[85] Sydney Duncan and Andy Duncan, "How Donna Noble Saved the Multiverse (and Had to Pay for it)", in *The Unsilent Library: Essays on the Russell T. Davies Era of the New Doctor Who*, eds. Simon Bradshaw, Antony Keen and Graham Sleight (London: The Science Fiction Foundation, 2011), 90.

Lorna Jowett's argument that since Martha leaves the TARDIS in order to heal her unrequited love for the Doctor, even this agency is undercut.[86] In any event, we can conclude that making *Doctor Who* "more emotional" has been exacted at the heavy cost of too often crushing the show's *women* through their departures, while the show's *man* perennially bounces back. As Noah McLaughlin has observed, whilst the new-series companions may be tough women, *Doctor Who* ultimately contains and even erases their challenges to the Doctor's masculine authority.[87]

Furthermore, on occasion, new *Who*'s strong women characters show a disturbing tendency to sacrifice themselves for the Doctor. Recurring character Professor River Song, for instance, is represented as being an assertive and independent woman, yet in her very first adventure with the Doctor, "Silence in the Library"/"Forest of the Dead" (2008), she chooses to sacrifice her life in order to save him. Tom Powers observes the paradox that, as a result, River is "strong and weak, independent and subservient, empowered and disempowered".[88] Like River, companion Clara Oswald is feisty. She metaphorically *becomes* the Doctor in "Flatline" (2014), where circumstances conspire to force the Doctor to remain in the TARDIS leaving Clara to rally the ranks in order to prevent an invasion of creatures from another dimension. She concludes: "I was you today. I was the Doctor, and apparently I was quite good at it!" In "Kill the Moon" (2014), she decides the fate of Earth's moon without the help of the Doctor, and in "Death in Heaven" (2014), she manages to convince Cybermen that she is the Doctor. This attempt to narrow the gap between the Doctor and his female companion is to be welcomed, not least because it paved the way for a woman—Jodie Whittaker—to be cast as the Doctor in 2017—something which could conceivably do much to remedy *Doctor Who*'s problem with representing women. Yet Clara's claim

[86] Jowett, "The Girls Who Waited", 84.

[87] Noah McLoughlin, "Gender Redux: *Bionic Woman*, *Doctor Who*, and *Battlestar Galactica*", in *Ruminations, Peregrinations and Regenerations: A Critical Approach to Doctor Who*, ed. Chris Hansen (Newcastle-upon-Tyne: Cambridge Scholars Publishing, 2010).

[88] Tom Powers, "A Muted Melody", in *Who Travels with the Doctor?* eds. Gillian I. Leitch and Sherry Ginn (Jefferson, NC: McFarland, 2016), 106.

to be a strong character is undermined by her over-arching narrative. The viewer's early encounters with Clara make her something of an enigma because the Doctor has already met two women practically identical to her at different points in time and space. The far-fetched solution to this mystery is uncovered in "The Name of the Doctor" (2013), which reveals that Clara was "born to save the Doctor". It transpires that Clara has spliced herself throughout time and space, being born, living and dying in numerous planets and epochs. The purpose of leading these multiple lives is to rescue the Doctor at various points in his own timeline from his alien enemy, the Great Intelligence. Whilst Clara's departure is more cheering than those of most of her new-*Who* predecessors—in "Hell Bent" (2015) she leaves, Doctor-like, to pursue her own adventures in her own TARDIS with a female companion of her own, Ashildr—nonetheless, the notion that the very purpose of her life/lives is to save/serve the Doctor undermines her claims to equality with him.

In sum, whilst the "screamers" of *Doctor Who*'s past certainly did not put forward a particularly positive representation of women, neither does the modern show unequivocally turn over a new leaf. Rather, it is egalitarian in some respects, reactionary in others.[89] In an article written by Alyssa Franke and myself, we argue that new *Who*'s combination of the feminist and the anti-feminist corresponds rather strikingly with the sensibility of post-feminism which has come to the fore in popular culture since the 1990s.[90] In any event, despite improvements in the show's representation of women since the early years, the female companion is still not the equal of the male Doctor. As a result, *Doctor Who* has not conveyed a gender politics sufficiently egalitarian to make gender equality a distinctive part of the show's Britishness.

[89] Dee Amy-Chinn describes this ambivalence in these terms: in recent years, the show has simultaneously promoted an agenda of liberalisation regarding choice and diversity and kinship matters, together with a conservative agenda in relation to gender, sexuality and family life. See Dee Amy-Chinn, "Amy's Boys, River's Man: Generation, Gender and Sexuality in the Moffat *Who*niverse", in *Doctor Who: The Eleventh Hour*, ed. Andrew O'Day (London: I.B. Tauris, 2014), 84.

[90] Alyssa Franke and Danny Nicol, "'Don't Make Me Go Back': Post-Feminist Retreatism in *Doctor Who*", *Journal of Popular Television*, 6(2) (2018). Alyssa Franke chronicles new *Who*'s treatment of gender on the Whovian Feminism blog, whovianfeminism.tumblr.com (last accessed June 18, 2017).

Britishness and Sexuality

Since the outset, *Doctor Who* has constantly emphasised non-conformity as a British characteristic, not least through the Doctor's own eccentricity. As James Chapman has observed, the cultural politics and narrative ideologies of *Doctor Who* serve to encourage difference. Chapman identifies the show as being imbued with an unmistakably liberal ethos but points out that one could easily substitute "liberal" with "British".[91] New-series *Doctor Who* often links Britishness with non-conformity, toleration and broad-mindedness on issues of sexuality. In this respect, new *Who* is very different from the classic series, which steered clear of anything other than heterosexuality and which in any event depicted the Doctor as asexual. Catherine Coker has observed that new-series *Doctor Who* addresses lesbian, gay, bisexual and transgender viewers as part of its regular viewership. She also notes that the focus tends to be on characters engaging in emotional intimacy and affection: the emphasis is not on sex but on feeling.[92] Conversely, Lorna Jowett notes new *Who*'s emphasis on heterosexual romance between the Doctor and his companions, which is aligned with the Doctor's presentation as a sexually attractive man.[93] It could be argued that the loss of the Doctor's asexuality makes new *Who* less welcoming for non-heterosexuals. Be this as it may, for our purposes, interest lies in the link which the show makes between non-straight sexuality and Britishness.

The new show's first serious brush with non-straight sexuality came in its very first year. In "The Empty Child"/"The Doctor Dances" (2005), we encounter Captain Jack Harkness, an omnisexual space agent attracted to men, women and an array of different species. Jack becomes a companion, albeit only for a short time. With his American accent and GI glamour, it may be awkward to envisage Jack as symbolising Britishness. However, the writers of *Doctor Who* and its spin-off *Torchwood* strengthened Jack's link with the country by putting him

[91] Chapman, *Inside the TARDIS*, 7.

[92] Catherine Coker, "Does the Doctor Dance? Heterosexuality, Omnisexuality and Spontaneous Generation in the *Who*niverse", in *The Unsilent Library: Essays on the Russell T. Davies Era of the New Doctor Who*, eds. Simon Bradshaw, Antony Keen and Graham Sleight (London: The Science Fiction Foundation, 2011).

[93] Lorna Jowett, *Dancing with the Doctor: Dimensions of Gender in the Doctor Who Universe* (London: I.B. Tauris, 2017), 18.

in charge of the Cardiff branch of that most British of organisations, Torchwood, where he has a relationship with Welsh Torchwood member Ianto Jones.

The association of Britishness with lesbian and gay equality was heavily underscored in "The Idiot's Lantern" (2006). This story is set in London in 1953 at the time of the coronation of Queen Elizabeth II. The Doctor and Rose, believing that there may be an alien presence in the house of the Connolly family, gain entry by posing as "patriotism inspectors", checking that the Connollys have decorated their house properly with Union Jacks. The time travellers are thereby delineated as the custodians of British values. Later, as friends and family gather round the Connollys' television set to watch the ceremony, the bullying head of the household, Eddie, describes his teenage son Tommy as a "proper little mummy's boy all round", prompting friend Betty to suggest that this is a sign of homosexuality which should be beaten out of him; Eddie agrees. Ultimately Tommy rounds on Eddie, declaring that the war was fought against fascism so that people could do what they wanted to do, and not be told with whom they should fall in love. *Doctor Who* thereby retells the story of the Second World War as a defence of British toleration of non-conformity, including homosexuality. Reality was very different: it remained a criminal offence to conduct male homosexual acts for a further decade and a half after the end of the war. "The Idiot's Lantern" is therefore another fine example of *Doctor Who*'s creative nostalgia: the revisioning of the past to address contemporary British issues.[94] At the end of the story, for all his patriotism, Eddie's intolerance is condemned as un-British, and he is rejected by his family and forced to leave the family home.

Over time, a succession of recurring characters helped to strengthen the link between acceptance of homosexuality and Britishness. These included Madame Vastra and Jenny, a lesbian mixed-species couple living in Victorian London. Vastra is a Silurian, one of a race of humanoid reptiles who ruled the Earth in the age of the dinosaur. She is nonetheless coded as British by her Scottish accent and by her Sherlock Holmes-style relationship with the Metropolitan Police (she solves murders then eats the perpetrators). Jenny Flint is her human, cockney wife, who poses as her maid for the sake of Victorian respectability. This couple help the

[94] See Grady and Hemstrom, "Nostalgia", 138.

Fig. 2.2 Nothing out of the ordinary. The Doctor welcomes black lesbian companion Bill Potts into the *Who*niverse. *Doctor Who* (new series), "The Pilot", series 10, episode 1; British Broadcasting Corporation, 2017

Doctor in a number of his adventures, alongside their droll Sontaran butler.[95] We belatedly learn that Clara Oswald is bisexual when she expresses an attraction towards Danish girl Ashildr in "The Girl Who Died" (2015). Ashildr is made immortal by the Doctor, and she eventually "becomes" British, being a highwayman in southern England in the seventeenth century and mayor of a hidden street of aliens in London in contemporary times. Clara ultimately leaves the Doctor for Ashildr in "Hell Bent" (2015). In the *Doctor Who* spin-off *Class* (2016),

[95]"A Good Man Goes to War" (2011), "The Crimson Horror" (2013), "The Name of the Doctor" (2013), "Deep Breath" (2014). "A Good Man Goes to War" involves a battle between the Doctor and his friends and the Church, which is imagined as a military organisation. The story also features a gay male married human couple, The Thin One and the Fat One, thereby associating gay marriage with the Church of England, the established church of the largest nation of the United Kingdom.

two school students, alien prince Charlie and Polish Matteusz, start a teenage gay relationship after Charlie invites Matteusz to the School Prom. As described earlier, we can see Matteusz as undergoing a process of "becoming British", prompted by his gay identity. The objection may be made that all the same-sex relationships in *Doctor Who* involve characters who are not human or not entirely so, and that this serves to exoticise same-sex relationships and set them apart from the show's "normal" ones. This complaint has some validity but is undermined by the way in which these relationships are "brought home" by being infused with a sense of Britishness.

The sense of Britishness was also evident when in 2017 there was a further leap forwards with the engaging Bill Potts, a British black lesbian, becoming the Doctor's companion. Bill reveals her lesbianism within seconds of her initial appearance, while her introductory episode, "The Pilot" (2017), revolves around her romance with another woman. The fact that Bill prefers women is treated as nothing out of the ordinary. This is emphasised in "The Eaters of Light" (2017), where she encounters a second-century Roman platoon from whom she expects anti-lesbian prejudice, but in fact she discovers that almost all the soldiers are bisexual and regard bisexuality as the norm, so that they find her homosexuality endearingly restrictive. In other episodes, Bill's lesbianism is hallmarked as "cool", for example by student suitor Paul, whose response when she tells him that she is only interested in women is "I was never in with a chance. Awesome!" ("Knock Knock" (2017)). Her love-life is also deployed as a source of good-natured humour. For instance, in "Extremis" (2017) and "The Pyramid at the End of the World" (2017), due to the Doctor's entanglements, one of Bill's romantic encounters at home with another woman is interrupted by the pope and another by the Secretary-General of the United Nations. Bill's Britishness is emphasised by her accent, humour and liking for chips, yet, intriguingly perhaps, her race and sexuality also actually serve to make her more British rather than less so. The presentation of Bill's lesbianism as by turns sweet, cool and banal brings us back to the *normative* dimension of *Doctor Who*'s Britishness. Figure 2.2 shows how the programme skilfully eases the introduction of Bill as the first lesbian companion. It places Bill's introductory scene in the midst of multiple signifiers of *Doctor Who*'s heritage. She sits at a desk in the Doctor's office amidst photographs of the Doctor's granddaughter Susan Foreman (1963–1964) and the Doctor's wife Professor River Song (2008–2015). Bill reaches for a jar containing not pens but a collection of the Doctor's trademark sonic screwdrivers. The TARDIS sits familiarly in the corner of the room bearing an out of order sign used in "The War Machines" in 1966. Bill is thereby immersed from the outset in the full richness of the *Doctor Who* canon. The viewer is invited to think: "She's a lesbian: so what? She goes with the grain of *Doctor Who*."

Conclusion

J.P.C. Brown has argued that *Doctor Who*'s assertion of Britishness is problematic since it involves asserting homogeneity in the face of diversity.[96] In fact, *Doctor Who* mitigates this difficulty by separating the empirical from the normative. It differentiates between what the British *are* and what they *ought to be*. So, for example, the show concedes that many Britons are highly entrepreneurial; it does so by having numerous minor characters who are driven by the profit motive. However, it certainly does not celebrate these business buccaneers as its role models for the British. Instead, it warns against a preoccupation with money-making and lauds the public service ethos.

This normative Britishness is progressive in some respects, reactionary in others. On class, to use Barbara Selznick's terminology, *Doctor Who* tends more towards a "cool Britain" than a "heritage Britain" model. Furthermore, the show has made a positive contribution towards embracing bisexuals, lesbians and gays within its construction of Britishness. On race, *Doctor Who* both cheers and disappoints. The modern show does not extol Empire and regularly celebrates Britain's racial diversity. The large number of black, Asian, oriental and mixed-heritage actors in new *Who* makes us feel good about Britain as a multiracial country. Yet the slowness to repeat the innovation of the non-white companion and the failure to cast a non-white Doctor compromises the show's capacity to present racial equality as an aspect of Britishness. *Doctor Who* is yet more dispiriting when it comes to gender. In classic *Who*, the Doctor's female companions were often damsels in distress; and however feisty new *Who*'s women, they nonetheless ultimately remain subordinate to the male Doctor. Moreover, despite pressure,

---

[96] J.P.C. Brown, "*Doctor Who*: A Very British Alien", in *The Galaxy is Rated G: Essays on Children's Science Fiction Film and Television*, eds. R.C. Neighbors and Sandy Rankin (Jefferson, NC: McFarland, 2011).

it took until 2017 to cast a woman to play the Doctor. Thus, *Doctor Who*'s treatment of women certainly does not set the British apart as having any distinguishing national commitment to gender equality. *Doctor Who*'s gender politics stands as an example of the show's vision of Britishness running behind the curve, justifying Lorna Jowett's criticism that the way in which the show represents the nation is not good enough.[97]

This combination of reactionary and progressive elements means that, like the London Olympics opening ceremony 2012, *Doctor Who* offers simultaneous celebrations of continuity and revolution, tradition and counterculture, custom and multiculturalism.[98] Alongside its perennial contrast between the British *as they are* and the British *as they ought to be*, these tensions serve to remind us that *Doctor Who* is a core product of the British Broadcasting Corporation, an organisation mandated to develop and disseminate a sense of Britishness. Let us return to Jean Seaton's observation that the BBC worries about the British but also emphasises the country's virtues.[99] On this reading, for all its shortcomings on race and gender, *Doctor Who* may be seen as projecting anxiety about British entrepreneurial selfishness, and trumpeting virtue by celebrating British diversity, public service and sense of fair play.

Bibliography

Alibhai-Brown, Yasmin. "The Excluded Majority: What about the English?" In *Reclaiming Britishness: Living Together after 11 September and the Rise of the Right*, edited by Phoebe Griffith and Mark Leonard, 44–50. London: The Foreign Policy Centre, 2002.

Amy-Chinn, Dee. "Amy's Boys, River's Man: Generation, Gender and Sexuality in the Moffat *Whoniverse*." In *Doctor Who: The Eleventh Hour*, edited by Andrew O'Day, 70–86. London: I.B. Tauris, 2014.

Amy-Chinn, Dee. "Rose Tyler: The Ethics of Care and the Limits of Agency." *Science Fiction Film and Television* 1(2) (2008): 251–267.

[97] Jowett, "The Girls", 89.

[98] Marra, *Britishness*, 188.

[99] Jean Seaton, "The BBC and Metabolising Britishness: Critical Patriotism", in *Britishness: Perspectives on the British Question*, eds. Andrew Gamble and Tony Wright (Chichester: Wiley-Blackwell, 2009), 78.

Apps, Pete. "Right to Buy to Let: Scale of Re-lets Revealed: 40%." *Inside Housing*, August 14, 2015, 1.

Barron, Lee. "Intergalactic Girl Power: The Gender Politics of Companionship in 21st Century *Doctor Who*." In *Ruminations, Peregrinations and Regenerations: A Critical Approach to Doctor Who*, edited by Chris Hansen, 130–149. Newcastle-upon-Tyne: Cambridge Scholars Publishing, 2010.

Britton, Piers D. *TARDISbound: Navigating the Universes of Doctor Who*. London: I.B. Tauris, 2011.

Brown, J.P.C. "*Doctor Who*: A Very British Alien." In *The Galaxy is Rated G: Essays on Children's Science Fiction Film and Television*, edited by R.C. Neighbors and Sandy Rankin, 161–182. Jefferson, NC: McFarland, 2011.

Chapman, James. *Inside the TARDIS: The Worlds of Doctor Who*, 2nd ed. London: I.B. Tauris, 2013.

Coker, Catherine. "Does the Doctor Dance? Heterosexuality, Omnisexuality and Spontaneous Generation in the *Who*niverse." In *The Unsilent Library: Essays on the Russell T. Davies Era of the New Doctor Who*, edited by Simon Bradshaw, Antony Keen and Graham Sleight, 93–106. London: The Science Fiction Foundation, 2011.

Cook, Jon. "Relocating Britishness and the Break-up of Britain." In *Relocating Britishness*, edited by Steven Caunce, Ewa Mazierska, Susan Sydney-Smith and John K. Walton, 17–37. Manchester and New York: Manchester University Press, 2004.

Cull, Nicholas. "TARDIS at the OK Corral: *Doctor Who* and the USA." In *British Science Fiction Television*, edited by John Cook and Peter Wright, 52–70. London: I.B. Tauris, 2006.

Dodson, Linnea. "Conscious Colour-Blindness, Unconscious Racism in *Doctor Who* Companions." In *Doctor Who and Race*, edited by Lindy Orthia, 29–34. Bristol: Intellect, 2013.

Duncan, Sydney and Andy Duncan, "How Donna Noble Saved the Multiverse (And Had To Pay for It)." In *The Unsilent Library: Essays on the Russell T. Davies Era of the New Doctor Who*, edited by in Simon Bradshaw, Antony Keen and Graham Sleight, 81–92. London: The Science Fiction Foundation, 2011.

Evans, Mark, "Neoliberalism and Policy Transfer in the British Competitive State: The Case of Welfare Reform." In *Internalizing Globalization: The Rise of Neoliberalism and the Decline of National Varieties of Capitalism*, edited by Susanne Soederberg, Georg Menz and Philip Cerny, 69–89. Basingstoke: Palgrave Macmillan 2005.

Fiske, John. "Dr. Who: Ideology and the Reading of a Popular Narrative Text." *Australian Journal of Screen Theory* 14 (1983): 69–100.

Flynn, Kate. "A Country Made from Metal? The 'Britishness' of Human-Machine Marriage in Series 31." In *Doctor Who in Time and Space*, edited by Gillian I. Leitch, 195–292. Jefferson, NC: McFarland, 2013.

Franke, Alyssa and Danny Nicol. "'Don't Make Me Go Back': Post-Feminist Retreatism in *Doctor Who*." *Journal of Popular Television* 6(2), 2018.

Franke, Alyssa. Whovian Feminism. whovianfeminism.tumblr.com. Last accessed June 18, 2017.

Freedman, Carl. "England as Ideology: from *Upstairs Downstairs* to *A Room with a View*." *Cultural Critique* 17 (1990–1): 79–106.

Freeland, Chrystia. *Plutocrats: The Rise of the New Global Super-Rich*. London: Penguin, 2012.

Gamble, Andrew, and Tony Wright, "Introduction: The Britishness Question." In *Britishness: Perspectives on the British Question*, edited by Andrew Gamble and Tony Wright, 1–9. Chichester: Wiley-Blackwell, 2009.

Gerhardt, Sue. *The Selfish Society: How We All Forgot to Love One Another and Made Money Instead*. London: Simon and Schuster, 2010.

Gilroy, Christine. "The Doctor's Burden: Racial Superiority and Panoptic Privilege in New *Doctor Who*." In *Impossible Worlds, Impossible Things: Cultural Perspectives on Doctor Who, Torchwood and The Sarah Jane Adventures*, edited by Ross P. Garner, Melissa Beattie and Una McCormack, 25–44. Newcastle-upon-Tyne, Cambridge Scholars Publishing, 2010.

Grady, Maura and Cassie Hemstrom, "Nostalgia for Empire, 1963–74." In *Doctor Who in Time and Space: Essays on Themes, Characters, History and Fandom, 1963–2012*, edited by Gillian I. Leitch, 125–143. Jefferson, NC and London: McFarland, 2013.

Hernandez, Mike. "'You Can't Just Change What I Look Like without Consulting Me!': The Shifting Racial Identity of the Doctor." In *Doctor Who and Race*, edited by Lindy Orthia, 45–60. Bristol: Intellect, 2013.

Ivanoff, George. "That was Then, This is Now: How my Perceptions Have Changed." In *Doctor Who and Race*, edited by Lindy Orthia, 77–82. Bristol: Intellect, 2013.

James, Oliver. *The Selfish Capitalist*. London: Vermilion, 2008.

Jenkins, Simon. *Thatcher and Sons*. London: Penguin Books, 2006.

Jones, Matthew. "Aliens of London: (Re)Reading National Identity in *Doctor Who*." In *Ruminations, Peregrinations and Regenerations: A Critical Approach to Doctor Who*, edited by Chris Hansen, 150–162. Newcastle-upon-Tyne: Cambridge Scholars Publishing, 2010.

Jones, Owen. *Chavs: The Demonization of the Working Class*. London: Verso, 2011.

Jowett, Lorna. "The Girls Who Waited: Female Companions and Gender in *Doctor Who*." *Critical Studies in Television* 9 (2014): 77–94.

Jowett, Lorna. *Dancing with the Doctor: Dimensions of Gender in the Doctor Who Universe*. London: I.B. Tauris, 2017.

Kerrigan, Lisa. "'Not sure if it's Marxism in Action or a West-End Musical': Class, Citizenship and Culture in new *Doctor Who*." In *Impossible Worlds, Impossible Things: Cultural Perspectives on Doctor Who, Torchwood and the Sarah Jane Adventures*, edited by Ross P. Garner, Melissa Beattie and Una McCormack, 145–160. Newcastle-upon-Tyne, Cambridge Scholars Publishing, 2010.

Knox, Simone. "The Transatlantic Dimensions of the Time Lord: *Doctor Who* and the Relationships between British and North American Television." In *Doctor Who: The Eleventh Hour*, edited by Andrew O'Day, 106–120. London: I.B. Tauris, 2014.

Leonard, Mark. *Britain™: Renewing Our Identity*. London: Redwood Books, 1997.

McCormack, Una. "He's Not the Messiah: Undermining Political and Religious Authority in New *Doctor Who*." In *The Unsilent Library: Essays on the Russell. T. Davies Era of the New Doctor Who*, edited by Simon Bradshaw, Anthony Keen and Graham Sleight, 45–62. London: The Science Fiction Foundation, 2011.

McGuigan, Jim. "A Shell for Neo-Liberalism: New Labour Britain and the Millennium Dome." In *Relocating Britishness*, edited by Steven Caunce, Ewa Mazierska, Susan Sydney-Smith and John K. Walton, 38–52. Manchester and New York: Manchester University Press, 2004.

McKee, Gabriel. "Pushing the Protest Button: *Doctor Who*'s Anti-Authoritarian Ethic." In *Time and Relative Dimensions in Faith: Religion and Doctor Who*, edited by Andrew Crome and James McGrath, 16–31. London: Darton, Longman and Todd, 2013.

McLoughlin, Noah. "Gender Redux: *Bionic Woman*, *Doctor Who*, and *Battlestar Galactica*." In *Ruminations, Peregrinations and Regenerations: A Critical Approach to Doctor Who*, edited by Chris Hansen, 117–129. Newcastle-upon-Tyne: Cambridge Scholars Publishing, 2010.

Marquand, David. "Bursting with Skeletons: Britishness after Empire." In *Britishness: Perspectives on the British Question*, edited by Andrew Gamble and Tony Wright, 10–21. Chichester: Wiley-Blackwell, 2009.

Marra, Irene. *Britishness, Popular Music and National Identity*. New York and Abingdon: Routledge, 2014.

Nicol, Danny. *EC Membership and the Judicialisation of British Politics*. Oxford: Oxford University Press, 2001.

Nicol, Danny. *The Constitutional Protection of Capitalism*. Oxford: Hart, 2010.

Orthia, Lindy. "'Sociopathetic Abscess' or 'Yawning Chasm'? The Absent Postcolonial Transition in *Doctor Who*." *The Journal of Commonwealth Literature* 45 (2010): 207–225.

Orthia, Lindy. "Introduction." In *Doctor Who and Race*, edited by Lindy Orthia, 3–11. Bristol: Intellect, 2013.

Orthia, Lindy. "Savages, Science, Stagism and the Naturalized Ascendancy of the Not-We in *Doctor Who*." In *Doctor Who and Race*, edited by Lindy Orthia, 45–60. Bristol: Intellect, 2013.

Parekh, Bhikhu. "Being British." In *Britishness: Perspectives on the British Question*, edited by Andrew Gamble and Tony Wright, 32–40. Chichester: Wiley-Blackwell, 2009.

Powers, Tom. "A Muted Melody." In *Who Travels with the Doctor?* edited by Gillian I. Leitch and Sherry Ginn, 106–122. Jefferson, NC: McFarland, 2016.

Richards, Jeffrey. "Football and the Crisis of British Identity." In *Relocating Britishness*, edited by Steven Caunce, Ewa Mazierska, Susan Sydney-Smith and John K. Walton, 88–109. Manchester and New York: Manchester University Press, 2004.

Robinson, Timothy Mark. "Agency, Action, and Re-action: The Black Female Presence in *Doctor Who*." In *Ruminations, Peregrinations and Regenerations: A Critical Approach to Doctor Who*, edited by Chris Hansen, 150–162. Newcastle-upon-Tyne: Cambridge Scholars Publishing, 2010.

Seaton, Jean. "The BBC and Metabolising Britishness: Critical Patriotism." In *Britishness: Perspectives on the British Question*, edited by Andrew Gamble and Tony Wright. Chichester: Wiley-Blackwell, 2009.

Selznick Barbara. "Rebooting and Rebranding: The Changing Brand of *Doctor Who*'s Britishness." In *Ruminations, Peregrinations and Regenerations: A Critical Approach to Doctor Who*, edited by Chris Hansen, 68–84. Newcastle-upon-Tyne: Cambridge Scholars Publishing, 2010.

Sleight, Graham. *The Doctor's Monsters: Meanings of the Monstrous in Doctor Who*. London: I.B. Tauris, 2012.

Styles, Sandra. "The Silent Monologue: The Voice Within the Space." *AlterNative: The International Journal of Indigenous Peoples* 4(2) (2008): 89–101.

Tulloch, John, and Manuel Alvarado. *Doctor Who: The Unfolding Text*. New York: St Martin's Press, 1983.

Uberoi, Varum and Iain McLean. "Britishness: A Role for the State?" In *Britishness: Perspectives on the British Question*, edited by Andrew Gamble and Tony Wright, 41–53. Chichester: Wiley-Blackwell, 2009.

Vohlidka, John. "*Doctor Who* and the Critique of Western Imperialism." In *Doctor Who and Race*, edited by Lindy Orthia, 125–139. Bristol: Intellect, 2013.

Wallace, Richard. "'The Sound of Empires Toppling': Politics, Public Service Broadcasting and *Doctor Who*." Conference paper, *Doctor Who: Walking in Eternity*, University of Hertfordshire, September 3–5, 2013.

Walton, John K. "Introduction." In *Relocating Britishness*, edited by Steven Caunce, Ewa Mazierska, Susan Sydney-Smith and John K. Walton, 1–16. Manchester and New York: Manchester University Press, 2004.

Watts, Duncan. *Whigs, Radicals and Liberals 1815–1914*, 2nd ed. London: Hodder and Stoughton, 2002.

Yeager, Iona. "Too Brown for a Fair Praise: The Depiction of Racial Prejudice as Cultural Heritage in *Doctor Who*." In *Doctor Who and Race*, edited by Lindy Orthia, 21–28. Bristol: Intellect, 2013.

CHAPTER 3

"Lots of Planets Have a North!": Scottishness, Welshness and Northernness in *Doctor Who*

The Doctor in "The Daleks' Master Plan" (1965–1966) is asked by a police officer first whether he is English, then whether he is Scottish, then whether he is Welsh. Denying all three identities in turn, the Doctor dismisses them as "too narrow, too small, too crippled", before famously declaring himself "a citizen of the universe, and a gentleman to boot!" Against this backdrop, this chapter examines *Doctor Who*'s treatment of Scottish and Welsh nationalities, as well as considering northern English identity. The United Kingdom is best characterised as a union state consisting of England, Scotland, Wales and Northern Ireland. With its four nations, it is a country in which people's identities have constantly been plural and shifting.[1] At times, people have felt more British, at other times they have felt more English, Scottish and Welsh and so forth.[2]

The United Kingdom is also characterised by English domination, insofar as England is by far the most populous of the four nations, accounting for some 55 million of the Kingdom's 65 million people.

[1] Linda Colley, "Does Britishness Still Matter in the 21st Century—And How Much/How Well do the Politicians Care?", in *Britishness: Perspectives on the British Question*, eds. Andrew Gamble and Tony Wright (Chichester: Wiley-Blackwell, 2009), 22.

[2] In Northern Ireland, the United Kingdom's smallest nation, British identity tends to be counterposed to Irish identity and is connected to the division between unionists, who tend to be Protestant, and nationalists, who tend to be Catholic. Northern Irish identity in *Doctor Who* will be briefly considered towards the end of the chapter.

D. Nicol, *Doctor Who: A British Alien?*,
https://doi.org/10.1007/978-3-319-65834-6_3

As a result, governments tend to be English dominated. This English preponderance contains the seeds of Scottish and Welsh discontents. At the same time, whether those who grow up and live in England choose to self-identify as English or British remains very much a question for the individual. Aside from certain sports, there is scant social necessity for an English person to identify as English rather than British. Though probably most choose to define themselves as English, some identify primarily as British while many others may express different identities in different contexts. There is also ambiguity over whether Englishness constitutes a nationality or an ethnicity, a haziness which impacts on whether non-whites in England favour a British identity over an English one. These sensitivities and nuances may create difficulties within *Doctor Who* studies, particularly for scholars not imbued with the lived experience of England. For example, in a chapter entitled "Rose *is* England", Tanja Nathanael argues that *Doctor Who* companion Rose Tyler represents England and that indeed "the body of Rose is conflated with England".[3] Yet Nathanael's account does not explain why Rose represents England *rather than* Britain and, on occasion, she uses the terms "England" and "Britain" interchangeably. There is, in fact, some evidence that Rose's narrative aligns her more closely with Britishness than with Englishness.[4]

Be this as it may, the state of flux over the United Kingdom's competing identities has become particularly evident during *Doctor Who*'s lifetime. Since the 1960s, tensions between British identity on the one hand and English, Scottish and Welsh identities on the other have intensified. This period has witnessed the growth of the nationalist parties, unsuccessful bids for devolution in the late 1970s, rising tensions under Tha tcherism/neoliberalism, the birth of devolution at the turn of the century and its evolution thereafter, and the Scottish independence referendum of 2014. Britain's withdrawal from the European Union has fuelled further calls for Scottish independence, with the likelihood of a second referendum on secession. Devolution has changed even the language by

[3]Tanja Nathanael, "Rose *is* England", in *Who Travels with the Doctor?* eds. Gillian I. Leitch and Sherry Ginn (Jefferson, NC: McFarland, 2016), 79–90.

[4]For example, Rose is the only companion to have adventures with the Doctor in England, Scotland and Wales, and she is closely connected to the Union Jack, the flag of the United Kingdom, in "The Empty Child"/"The Doctor Dances" (2005) and "The Idiot's Lantern" (2006). If she were representing England she would be aligned with England's own flag, the Saint George's Cross.

which the country is expressed: whilst it was usual in the 1970s to speak of Britain as constituting "the nation", it has become increasingly common to talk in terms of England, Scotland, Wales and Northern Ireland as being four nations, and as the United Kingdom as constituting their state. Against this backdrop, this chapter considers how *Doctor Who* engages with these internal strains on British identity.

Multiple stories in both classic-series and new-series *Doctor Who* have had Scottish and Welsh characters and settings. This chapter explores some of the key assumptions on which these stories are based. It considers how, in *Doctor Who*'s early days, Scottish and Welsh society tended to be portrayed as backward. Furthermore, Scottish and Welsh characters were frequently marked out by a lack of agency, displaying a remarkable passivity by comparison with characters with English accents. At the same time, whilst *Doctor Who* was fundamentally unionist, it did not seem to project a union based on much sense of equality between Britain's nations. This unionism has, however, changed in new-series *Doctor Who*, which often reflects more overtly the tensions between the nations of the United Kingdom, and mediates them to arrive at a unionism based on greater equality of esteem.

Britain: Newish State, Older Allegiances

The United Kingdom of Great Britain came into existence in 1707, a new state superimposed on older allegiances. The Kingdom of England (which had incorporated Wales in 1542) and the Kingdom of Scotland dissolved themselves into the new entity.[5] Since its formation, the fortunes of the competing national identities within the United Kingdom have ebbed and flowed. The new British identity has constantly vied with its English, Scottish and Welsh rivals. Sometimes (as at present), the competition has been overt; at other times, it has been low-key.

[5]The Treaty of Union came into force on May 1, 1707 and was incorporated into English and Scottish law by Acts of Union passed by the Parliament of England and the Parliament of Scotland. The two Parliaments thereby dissolved themselves to create the Parliament of the United Kingdom of Great Britain. Subsequently, the new state changed again, to become the United Kingdom of Great Britain and Ireland by virtue of the Treaty of Union 1800. In 1922, it became the United Kingdom of Great Britain and Northern Ireland when the Irish Free State acquired dominion status, becoming the Republic of Ireland in 1937.

Linda Colley has explained how in the eighteenth century—the British state's first century—the new collective identity was forged primarily by war. Whether they hailed from England, Scotland or Wales, Georgian-era Britons were brought into confrontation with a hostile Other in the form of France. As the world's foremost Catholic power, France united the English, Scots and Welsh by allowing them to define themselves as Protestants fighting for survival. It was, therefore, the Other beyond Britain's shores, and not cultural or political consensus at home, that encouraged the British to define themselves as a single people. Crucially, far from the English, Scots and Welsh dissolving into Britishness, they remained—and remain—distinct peoples in cultural terms.[6] Later on, British identity was again bolstered by the country's relationship with the rest of the world in the nineteenth century, where the victories and prosperity of the British Empire, together with the Otherness of the colonised peoples, buoyed up the public sense of Britishness. The First and Second World Wars once again made British national identity a stark matter of us-versus-them.[7] This high tide of British identity was sustained into the Second World War's aftermath, with the birth of the British welfare state and, in particular, the National Health Service. The new enterprise of social justice helped to reinforce British identity, in addition to the still strong enterprise of Empire. The weakening of these common enterprises, as Empire turned to Commonwealth and as the social democratic consensus became firmly entrenched, made the pull of Britishness less obvious.[8] By the middle of the twentieth century, the common bonds were starting to fade.

Thus, by the birth of *Doctor Who* in 1963, the collective British identity was beginning to weaken and English, Scottish and Welsh identities were coming more to the fore. The separatist parties Plaid Cymru—The

---

[6]Linda Colley, *Britons: Forging the Nation 1707–1837* (New Haven and London: Yale University Press, 1992), 5–6. Colley explains that for poor and less literate Britons, Scotland, Wales and England remained potent rallying calls and that even among the more politically educated it was common to think in terms of dual nationalities rather than a single British nationality. Colley, *Britons*, 373.

[7]This sense was reflected in *Doctor Who*'s celebration of British identity in "The Empty Child"/"The Doctor Dances" (2005) and "Victory of the Daleks" (2010).

[8]Andrew Gamble and Tony Wright, "Introduction: The Britishness Question", in *Britishness: Perspectives on the British Question*, eds. Andrew Gamble and Tony Wright (Chichester: Wiley-Blackwell, 2009), 2–4.

Party of Wales and the Scottish National Party were starting to make gains in local elections. In parliamentary by-elections, they garnered popularity on the back of disillusionment with the then-Labour government. Plaid Cymru's Gwynfor Evans won the Carmarthen by-election in 1966 and the SNP's Winnie Ewing won the Hamilton by-election in 1967. In 1973, Britain became a Member State of the European Communities, subsequently the European Union. With memories of the Second World War receding, European integration eroded the sense of a continental Other which made Britons feel that they had an identity in common. This contributed to the re-emergence of internal divisions and of English, Scottish and Welsh nationalism.[9] Jon Cook has emphasised the weakening of the political autonomy of the British state as a reason for the decline of British identity, noting that British decision-making now depends upon incorporation into orders defined elsewhere—globalisation, the USA and Europe.[10] British identity has weakened because the state underpinning it is no longer the confident structure it once was.[11] In the same vein, Marquand argues that the British state, traditionally seen as the chief agency for promoting social justice, is now broken-backed in that regard.[12]

In the 1980s and 1990s, the emergence of neoliberalism as a strong political consensus within all three UK-wide parties further galvanised support for devolution and for the pro-independence parties, since they could align Scottishness and Welshness with a distinctive, more social democratic politics. The Scottish Parliament and Welsh Assembly came into existence under the 1997 Labour government. Whilst the then British Prime Minister, Tony Blair, believed that devolution would eliminate the impetus to independence, the opposite transpired. The separatist Scottish National Party (SNP) outflanked Labour to the left and

[9] Colley, *Britons: Forging the Nation*, 6–7.

[10] Jon Cook, "Relocating Britishness and the Break-Up of Britain", in *Relocating Britishness*, eds. Steven Caunce, Ewa Mazierska, Susan Sydney-Smith and John K. Walton (Manchester and New York: Manchester University Press, 2004), 17–37.

[11] Andrew Gamble and Tony Wright, "Introduction: The Britishness Question", in *Britishness: Perspectives on the British Question*, eds. Andrew Gamble and Tony Wright (Chichester: Wiley-Blackwell, 2009), 1.

[12] David Marquand, "Bursting with Skeletons: Britishness after Empire", in *Britishness: Perspectives on the British Question*, eds. Andrew Gamble and Tony Wright (Chichester: Wiley-Blackwell, 2009), 14.

became first the main opposition party in the Scottish Parliament and subsequently the government. Originally returned as a minority government in 2007, the SNP became the country's first majority government in 2011: a remarkable achievement given the system of proportional representation used for elections to the Scottish Parliament. In 2014, the SNP government initiated a referendum on Scottish independence, in which Scottish voters decided by 55% to 45% to remain in the United Kingdom. In Wales, whilst the impetus towards self-government was less dramatic, nonetheless the Welsh electorate too showed an inclination towards differentiating themselves from the voters of the United Kingdom, electing a succession of Labour and Labour-coalition administrations even when the British electorate as a whole opted for Conservative or Conservative-coalition governments. In 2011, the voters of Wales resolved by referendum to grant the National Assembly full lawmaking powers in the policy areas devolved to it.

From the mid-1960s onwards, therefore, tensions between Scottish and Welsh identity on the one hand, and Britishness on the other, have gradually become more apparent. This roughly coincided with *Doctor Who*'s first foray into Scotland in "The Highlanders" (1966–1967). Subsequent *Doctor Who* adventures set in Wales and Scotland, such as "The Green Death" (1973), "Terror of the Zygons" (1975) and "Delta and the Bannermen" (1987), tracked the slow rise of Scottish and Welsh nationalism. The argument of this chapter is that these stories project a rather reactionary unionism. By comparison, post-2005 *Doctor Who*, which has been led by Welsh and Scottish showrunners and which has coincided with the early years of devolution, presents more of a unionism of equals. In this chapter, therefore, contrasts between classic and new *Who* are particularly significant. Let us start by considering the ways in which *Doctor Who*'s classic series portrayed Scottishness and Welshness.

The Classic Series: Postcolonial Scotland and Wales?

One controversial question is whether a postcolonial analysis is appropriate when considering the relationship between Scotland and Wales on the one hand and England/Britain on the other. Were Scotland and Wales colonies? If so, are they still colonies? Should one consider *Doctor Who*'s Scottish and Welsh characters and stories from that perspective?

Scotland's status as a colony has been considered by Liam Connell.[13] He deems the designation of Scotland as an English colony to be highly controversial, and argues that there is a danger of blurring colonisation with imperialism, which he defines as a global system of development in which capital is increasingly internationalised. Connell argues that the basis of postcolonial cultural explanations is fundamentally political. He is therefore critical of scholars of Scottish literature who seek to link their work to postcolonialism without undertaking political analysis. For instance, one of colonisation's most constant features is the transfer of indigenous control over social organisation to the colonial power, yet in the case of Scotland, according to Connell, almost the reverse is true, with Scots retaining high levels of autonomy and continuing to serve at the highest levels. Furthermore, Connell argues that in order to claim that Scotland was colonised, one must ignore the material indicators which suggest that Scotland generally benefited greatly from the modernisation processes which followed union with England—and indeed those were processes over which Scots exercised substantial control. So postcolonial ideas have to be used with sensitivity to their limitations in the Scottish context. Ellen-Raïssa Jackson confirms that postcolonial readings have, on the whole, been resisted and overlooked in Scotland in favour of core–periphery theories. Whilst Jackson seems to lament this neglect of postcolonialism, she furnishes no political evidence that Scotland is a colony.[14]

As for Wales, Chris Williams has argued that Wales is not a colony of England and has not been since 1536.[15] He contends that the ratio of English or British coercion to Welsh consent has always been low and that the Welsh have been the active agents in as well as passive subjects of Britain's imperial expansion. Indeed, far from being a colony, Wales was, from the nineteenth century, part of the most advanced imperial and commercial state in the world. All in all, Williams argues, the

[13]Liam Connell, "Modes of Marginality: Scottish Literature and the Uses of Postcolonial Theory", *Comparative Studies of South Asia, Africa and the Middle East*, 23 (2003): 26–39.

[14]Ellen-Raïssa Jackson, "Dislocating the Nation: Political Devolution and Cultural Identity on Stage and Screen", in *Scotland in Theory: Reflections on Culture and Literature*, eds. Eleanor Bell and Gavin Millar (Amsterdam and New York: Rodopi, 2004), 108.

[15]Chris Williams, "Problematizing Wales: An Exploration in Historiography and Postcoloniality", in *Postcolonial Wales*, eds. Jane Aaron and Chris Williams (Cardiff: University of Wales Press, 2005), 3–27.

Welsh experience does not translate into the standard language of Third World trajectories. There were and are, however, inequalities between the two societies, with Wales losing out in the distribution of wealth and resources. In particular, the Welsh economy has struggled to keep pace with the more prosperous parts of England since the 1920s, and it may be more appropriate to view Wales as a 'dependent periphery'. Williams argues, however, that the application of postcolonial concepts need not be confined to countries that were unambiguously colonies. Williams therefore applies postcolonial ideas of ambivalence, hybridity and post-nationality to Wales. Tellingly, both Williams and Connell advance the argument that those who argue that Scotland and Wales are colonies ignore the "colonisation of the English by the English state", in the form of the social exclusion of the English working class, culturally evidenced by the tendency to conflate English with standard English.

Thus, it is unconvincing to claim that Scotland and Wales are colonies of England. Nonetheless, it may be possible, following Williams, to deploy postcolonial concepts with due sensitivity to both countries. Some of these themes may be discerned in *Doctor Who*. One is the portrayal of backwardness—the notion that Scottish and Welsh society is more primitive than English society and needs to be raised to English levels. A second is the impression of a lack of agency: that Scots and the Welsh are reliant on English help in order to do what needs to be done. A third is the projection of a unionism which bases itself on the assumption that Scotland and Wales *need* England but not *vice versa*, and that the nations of Britain are better together primarily for this reason. Let us examine these themes in turn.

Backwardness

The depiction of Scottish and Welsh society as somewhat backward is readily apparent in classic-series *Doctor Who*.[16] This portrayal carries the suggestion that the English are a civilising force, brought to bear upon backward and incompetent natives.[17] "The Highlanders" is set in the

[16]This chapter's analysis of the classic series focuses on serials set in Scotland and Wales. Occasionally, however, Welsh characters in serials set in England have been depicted as backward, grasping and self-seeking—for example, Driver Evans in "The Web of Fear" (1968) and Mullins in "Spearhead from Space" (1970). By contrast see n. 20 below.

[17]Jackson, "Dislocating the Nation", 15.

Jacobite rebellion of 1745. It depicts the Scots as having been taken in by "romantic piffle", as the Doctor puts it, into going to war in support of Bonnie Prince Charlie. Whilst the English soldiers are portrayed as ruthless and racist, the Scots are no less so. For instance, when the Highlanders are locked in the hold of a ship together with the Doctor's cockney companion Ben, some of them suggest killing Ben because he is English. This would be "one more blow we can strike for Scotland, one more piece of vermin ... Tramp his English bones into the deck!" Thankfully this course of action is vetoed by other Highlanders, but the anti-English racism is hardly uplifting.

The projection of backwardness is also apparent in "The Green Death". Set in South Wales, the villain of "The Green Death" is the company Global Chemicals (and the computer which runs it). The company's dangerous processes are leading to the creation of deadly giant maggots. Global Chemicals, despite its international reach, is staffed by Englishmen. The Welsh miners are taken in by the company's promise of jobs, believing the manager Mr. Stevens' claim of "wealth in our time" (a satire on British Prime Minister Neville Chamberlain's 1939 promise of "peace for our time"). The miners display themselves indifferent to environmental dangers, even in the face of the claim that their children may be poisoned, arguing that they cannot afford to live the way they want. Their attitude to life does not seem to extend beyond their own livelihoods. "Terror of the Zygons" is set in rural Scotland and advances a kitsch, mists-and-myths, vision of Scottish society. UNIT soldiers stay in a pub run by Archie, a landlord who plays bagpipes and claims to have second sight. Colin McArthur argues that the association of Scots with the supernatural "is a discourse in which marginalised peoples throughout the world will recognise themselves".[18] Highland society is all delightfully feudal: the Duke of Forgill, an archaic, born-to-rule aristocrat, is the central Scottish character, and his ghillie wards off trespassers from his land using a shotgun, including anyone involved in the extraction of North Sea Oil. Metaphorically, the Industrial Revolution, taking the form of the Hibernian Oil Company, is made to feel unwelcome.[19] To add to the kitschness of this Highland yarn, the Brigadier

[18]Colin McArthur, *Brigadoon, Braveheart and the Scots: Distortions of Scotland in Hollywood Cinema* (London: I.B. Tauris, 2003), 18.

[19]This forms a contrast with the Doctor's foray into northern England in "The Mark of the Rani" (1984), which I consider later in this chapter.

dons a kilt and even the Doctor sports a tartan hat and scarf. In all three adventures, the marginalisation of Scottish and Welsh women also indicates backwardness.[20]

Lack of Agency

Welsh and Scottish characters tended to be sidelined in the classic series in the sense that they made scant contribution to bringing the adventure to its resolution. This lack of impact is rather obvious in "The Highlanders". In the latter episodes of this story, the Scots are for the most part imprisoned in the hulk of a ship, awaiting transportation as slaves to the Caribbean. They are not allowed to act for themselves; indeed, the only proactive prisoner is the Doctor's English companion Ben. Ultimately, the Scots are saved from slavery by the Doctor's cunning. There is a stark contrast as action flashes between impotent, incarcerated Highlanders not doing much, and the busy, machinating Doctor.

The lack of agency of the Welsh miners in "The Green Death" is no less striking. The miners feature in the opening episodes of this six-part story, yet by the climax they have all mysteriously disappeared. Even the young Welsh professor, Clifford Jones, is out of action for the final two episodes, having been bitten and infected by a giant maggot. Saving Wales (and the world) from the maggots and from a power-crazed computer responsible for their existence is left to the Doctor (a Time Lord with a received-pronunciation English accent) and UNIT's English troops. The same tendency is also evident in "Terror of the Zygons", which features several Scottish characters: a publican, a Duke, a ghillie and a stern nurse. The publican is killed by the Zygons even though he claims to have "second sight", the power to perceive things which are not detected by the senses. This does not say much for his abilities. The Duke, ghillie and nurse turn out to be not Scots but Zygons in disguise, since Zygons can change their physical appearance to replicate other beings. The "real" Scots are in suspended animation, stowed away on the Zygon spaceship. Once revived, their sole achievement is—at the Doctor's behest—to run out of the spaceship just before it blows up.

[20] It may be significant in this regard that by contrast in "Fury from the Deep" (1968), the chief executive of a public-sector sea gas company, Megan Jones, is a Welsh woman. The story is set in England in the present day or near future and Jones is the only Welsh character.

Unionism

Despite the unflattering depictions of Scots and the Welsh in classic-series *Doctor Who*, one can easily discern a unionist message. At first blush "The Highlanders" might appear not to be unionist. The English soldiers, we are told, gave no quarter to Highland men, women and children. They butcher the wounded and were preparing to hang the Highlanders, along with the Doctor and Ben. Yet the main narrative concerns a corrupt British official, Solicitor Grey, saving the Highlanders from being hanged in order to profit from selling them as slaves. Ultimately, the British state redeems itself by arresting Grey for slave-smuggling. Moreover, the Scots are rescued by the English-accented Doctor and Ben.

"The Green Death" can also be read as unionist. By the end of the adventure, only English soldiers are in action, which suggests that the Welsh can and should rely for their salvation on the English (Brigadier Lethbridge-Stewart, Captain Yates and Sergeant Benton, as well as the Doctor). Unionism also looms large in "Terror of the Zygons", in several respects. First, the national identity of the Brigadier is revealed. This popular and perennial figure may seem entirely English but his origins are Scottish, hence he wears his clan tartan in this adventure. Secondly, the story emphasises Britain as a small island: the Loch Ness monster speeds rapidly from Scotland to the Thames estuary, then up past the Houses of Parliament to the venue of the first international energy conference. Thirdly, the Duke turns out to be involved in the energy conference. The Zygon version of the Duke is projected as an anachronistic aristocrat, hostile to oil company staff crossing his land. By making the "real" Duke an important figure in the energy sector and by relocating him from his Highlands estate to a London conference, the script marks him out as part of the British state.

The unionism projected by these stories is alarmingly inegalitarian in terms of both ethnicity and social class. For instance, the Welsh miners in "The Green Death" play no part in saving Britain from the giant maggots, having bafflingly vanished in the final episodes. In "Terror of the Zygons", the Duke displays interests which go beyond the confines of the Scottish Highlands, but the ghillie, publican and nurse do not. The barring of working people of Wales and Scotland from *Doctor Who*'s normative unionism is disheartening. Their exclusion is particularly unfortunate in view of the way in which the show depicts its unionism as a rejection of profiteering. Britishness triumphs over business in both "The Highlanders", where Solicitor Grey ends up in prison, and "The Green Death", where the multinational company Global Chemicals is obliterated.

A modest turning-point in the programme's unionism came in "Delta and the Bannermen" (1987), a story in which the Doctor, in his first incarnation to use a Scottish accent, and English companion Melanie Bush, come to the aid of the staff and holidaymakers of a 1950s Welsh holiday camp. The camp comes under attack from the Bannermen, mercenaries from outer space who are on a seek-and-destroy mission to kill Delta, an alien queen who is the last of her kind. Unlike "The Green Death", Welsh characters engage throughout the escapade, including at its conclusion. However, the Welsh role is undermined by the rejection of a Welsh woman as the story's love-interest. The plot sees the romance between childhood sweethearts Billy and Ray (Rachel) fizzle out as Billy falls in love with Delta. Indeed, he self-administers a royal jelly cocktail in order to transform himself into a member of Delta's own green-hued species. Ray is Welsh, Billy's accent is English (though to be a childhood sweetheart he must surely have spent his childhood in Wales). Whilst the script throws Ray a few inconsequential lines in Welsh, perhaps in order to boost her exoticism, the overriding narrative is of the exoticism of Delta trumping the homeliness of Ray.

New-Series Doctor Who: Egalitarian Unionism?

The post-2005 revived *Doctor Who* had a Welsh showrunner, Russell T. Davies, from 2005 to 2010, followed by a Scottish showrunner, Steven Moffat, from 2010 to 2017. In view of the fact that Wales accounts for only 5% of the British population and Scotland for 8.5%, this must surely rank as one of the most remarkable coincidences in *Doctor Who*'s history. It was a coincidence which had a profound effect on the show's projection of the union, and on its portrayal of Welsh and Scottish characters. In addition, new *Who*'s unionism reflected the greater optimism and self-confidence of post-devolution Britain. The Scottish Parliament and the National Assembly of Wales were fresh institutions. As Murray Leith and Daniel Soule have observed, the first decade of legislative devolution witnessed an increase in everyday awareness of Scottish and Welsh national identity. There was a greater feeling that they were nations rather than merely "sub-national" components of the United Kingdom.[21] Thus, the third episode of new *Who*, "The Unquiet Dead" (2005), was set in Victorian Cardiff. This in itself forms quite a contrast with classic-series *Doctor Who*, which ran for over three years before broadcasting an adventure based in a non-English part of Britain in the shape of "The Highlanders". The first new-series story to be set in Scotland, "Tooth and Claw", was broadcast just a year later in 2006.

In "The Unquiet Dead", the Doctor and companion Rose Tyler encounter Welsh character Mr. Sneed, an undertaker, and his maid Gwyneth. With the help of Charles Dickens, the time travellers investigate corpses that seemingly come back to life. They discover that the corpses have been animated by the Gelth, an endangered race of disembodied aliens. It transpires that Gwyneth has "the sight" (for instance, she is aware that Rose's father is dead and she can visualise twenty-first century London). Gwyneth is convinced that she can use her powers to act as a bridge, transporting the Gelth to our own dimension. They can then inhabit the bodies of the deceased. Although Rose is disgusted by this plan, the Doctor supports it, likening it to recycling. Perceiving the Gelth as "angels", Gwyneth sacrifices herself to help them come to Earth, but as the Gelth materialise they reveal that their real intention is to create additional corpses for themselves by massacring humankind. At this point, Gwyneth manages to annihilate the Gelth by striking a match whilst they are still in gaseous form, causing a huge explosion. Afterwards, the Doctor claims that Gwyneth must have already been dead for five minutes before she destroyed them. By sheer will, it would appear, Gwyneth managed to act from beyond the grave, a magnificence reinforced by the visual panache with which she strikes the fatal match. The message that refugees conceal a wish to kill us is undoubtedly reactionary. Nonetheless, "The Unquiet Dead" serves to demarcate Gwyneth, a working-class Welsh woman, as a powerful actor. Whilst admittedly, the notion of possessing second sight conforms to *Celtic* stereotypes, Gwyneth's agency contrasts strikingly with the lack of agency of Archie, the Scottish publican in "Terror of the Zygons" thirty years

[21] Murray Leith and Daniel Soule, *Political Discourse and National Identity in Scotland* (Edinburgh: Edinburgh University Press, 2011), Chap. 8.

earlier, whose vaunted possession of "the sight" did not even empower him to differentiate humans from Zygons—with fatal consequences.[22]

Gwyneth's agency is reinforced by that of Gwen Cooper, a Welsh woman played by the same actress, in the *Doctor Who* spin-off *Torchwood* (2006–2011). Set in contemporary Cardiff, *Torchwood* imagines the Welsh division of Torchwood, the institute created by Queen Victoria in response to her encounter with the Doctor in "Tooth and Claw" (2006). Its aim is to protect Great Britain from alien invaders. *Torchwood* is simultaneously unionist and Welsh: Torchwood is a British institution, yet since its London headquarters had been destroyed in the *Doctor Who* adventure "Army of Ghosts"/"Doomsday" (2006), the Cardiff branch seems to enjoy complete autonomy to pursue the objective set by Britain's late sovereign. In that regard, it is outside the government, beyond the police. The organisation deals with the problems thrown up by a rift in time and space centred on Cardiff, which brings alien invaders into the city. *Torchwood* follows the career of Gwen Cooper as she is recruited to Torchwood from the bottom ranks of the local police force. The stories are often told predominantly from Gwen's point of view, and certain episodes, such as "Random Shoes" (2006), focus on Gwen's own investigations, with her colleagues relegated to a minor role. Lorna Jowett has observed how Gwen serves to represent emotion and human warmth and how her family keeps her grounded in the "real world", whereas by contrast, the group's leader Captain Jack Harkness frequently appears cold and calculating. These differences enable Gwen repeatedly to criticise Jack's leadership.[23] Furthermore, in episodes such as "Exit Wounds" (2008), she displays impressive leadership skills of her own. The show also sees the other Welsh member of the Torchwood team, backroom-boy administrator Ianto Jones, increasingly develop into a frontline figure. For good measure, Ianto has a gay relationship with Jack.

Figure 3.1 shows Gwen and Ianto in a scene from the *Doctor Who* episode "The Stolen Earth" (2008) in which they guest-starred. It exhibits the Celtic good looks of the two characters as they staff the Torchwood

---

[22]Too much should not be made of *Doctor Who* perpetrating *Celtic* stereotypes as regards second sight: in "The Daemons" (1971) the irreproachably English Miss Hawthorne has magical powers as a white witch.

[23]Lorna Jowett, *Dancing with the Doctor: Dimensions of Gender in the Doctor Who Universe* (London: I.B. Tauris, 2017), 25–27.

Fig. 3.1 Eye candy of Cardiff. Gwen Cooper and Ianto Jones hold the fort at Torchwood. *Doctor Who* (new series), "The Stolen Earth"/"Journey's End", series 4, episodes 12 and 13; British Broadcasting Corporation, 2008

Hub. Unlike Welsh characters in classic-era *Doctor Who*, the image unequivocally presents Gwen and Ianto as "eye candy", as befits stars of *Torchwood*. Here, they take responsibility for the Hub during the absence of Torchwood leader, Captain Jack Harkness. In this regard, Gwen's gesture to Ianto to keep quiet subtly indicates that she outranks him, a stark contrast to the "Green Death" ethos of visible Welsh men and practically invisible Welsh women. All in all, the pair present an attractive image of modern Welshness.

In the five-part adventure "Torchwood: Children of Earth" (2009), Gwen's husband, the homely Rhys Williams, gets co-opted onto the Torchwood team too. Gwen, Ianto and Rhys are therefore depicted as the rising characters in the organisation, and this can be read as a signal of Wales' post-devolution vitality. *Torchwood* also uses humour to assert its confidence in Welsh identity; for example, in "Torchwood: Children of Earth", Gwen and Rhys joke about needing injections as Gwen drives across the Severn Bridge from Wales into England. In "Torchwood: Miracle Day" (2011), Gwen and Jack are victims of a rendition from Wales to the USA. On board the plane, an American operative taunts Gwen by saying "If you're the best England's got to offer, God help you!" Gwen retorts "I'm WELSH!" and delivers a punch which knocks the American out. Quite apart from the agency of its Welsh characters, for the most part, *Torchwood* also seems to make a conscious effort to counter the image of Celtic backwardness.[24] The stars are youthful, the attitude towards sexuality progressive, and the Torchwood Hub is packed with technology.[25] Likewise, the Cardiff setting is represented primarily by the city's modern spaces, not by its Edwardian residential streets and ornate shopping arcades.[26] *Torchwood*'s emphasis on Wales-as-modern provides a definite contrast to the nostalgia of "Delta and the Bannermen" and the archaic portrayal of the Welsh miners in "The Green Death".

Cardiff's prominence was reinforced by "Boom Town" (2005), a *Doctor Who* adventure which imagines the city being run by an English mayor, Margaret Blaine. The story is in part a satire on New Labour deceptiveness (one of Tony Blair's policies was the promotion of directly elected mayoralties). As in "The Green Death", the English leader promises "jobs for all"—this time by dint of a new nuclear power station. In reality, her motives are self-seeking: she is an alien, a member of the Slitheen family, and she intends blowing up Cardiff so that she can generate the energy to escape Earth. In contrast to "The Green Death", the Welsh characters, scientist Mr. Cleaver and journalist Cathy Salt, have the intelligence to grasp the dangers of the project, although it is the Doctor and his companions who actually thwart Margaret's plans.

As for Scotland, the first Scottish adventure in new-series *Doctor Who* was "Tooth and Claw" (2006). Set in the nineteenth-century Highlands, it is a story in which Scottish aristocrat Sir Robert McLeish sacrifices his life to protect his sovereign, Queen Victoria, from a werewolf alien. It also transpires that McLeish's late father, together with Prince Albert, constructed as a precaution a means of destroying the werewolf—a means that the Doctor deploys. Whilst this tale accords agency only to the highest, male echelon of Scottish society, as represented by Sir Robert and his father, their agency nonetheless represented a modest

---

[24] A regrettable exception is "Countrycide" (2006), where the Torchwood team encounter a cannibalistic Welsh village, suggesting a difference between urban and rural Wales.

[25] For criticism that Torchwood's approach to homosexuality does not go far enough, see Sherry McGinn, "Sexual Relations and Sexual Identity Issues: Brave New Worlds or More of the Old One?", in *Illuminating Torchwood*, ed. Andrew Ireland (London: I.B. Tauris, 2010).

[26] Stephen Lacey, "'When You See Cardiff on Film, it Looks Like LA' (John Barrowman): Space, Genre and Realism in *Torchwood*", in *Torchwood Declassified*, ed. Rebecca Williams (London: I.B. Tauris, 2013), 137–153, 141.

improvement on the passivity of the Laird in "The Highlanders" and the Duke in "Terror of the Zygons".

More transformative was the impact of Steven Moffat's elevation to showrunner in 2010. This afforded the opportunity for a more striking change in *Doctor Who*'s treatment of Scottish characters, not least through the introduction of Scottish companion Amy Pond (2010–2012). When the Doctor shows Amy the TARDIS, she questions why he is so certain that she will run away with him. He replies: "you're a Scottish girl in an English village and I know how that feels". To be sure, Amy only ever self-identifies as Scottish, and yet she is repeatedly associated with Britain and Britishness. The complex identity of *Doctor Who*'s "Scottish girl in an English village" is reflected in Willy Maley and Sarah Neely's argument that traditional Scottish identification-with-place has been undermined by a rootless cosmopolitanism.[27] More generally, David McCrone has observed that under conditions of globalisation, we are confronted with a range of different identities appealing to different parts of ourselves.[28] Eleanor Bell identifies an apparent hesitancy in the case of Scottishness to address this individualisation of identity because it is "radically unaccountable and a menacing portent for the future". The national territory is no longer the place from which national attachments spring to life. Rather, a multiplicity of *terrae* emerges, sometimes restricted by no mere sense of place.[29] Amy Pond provides a prize example of this phenomenon.

Amy's first journey in the TARDIS in "The Beast Below" (2010) is to a distant future in which the human race has left for the stars to avoid the scorching sun. She and the Doctor arrive on Starship UK, the vessel on which the British people left Earth. Amy soon learns, however, that the Scots had insisted on a ship of their own. "Good for them", she quips, "Nothing changes." This revelation might be taken to indicate that "The Beast Below" has little to offer on Scots and Scottishness, yet

[27]Willy Maley and Sarah Neely, "Almost Afraid to Know Itself: Macbeth and Cinematic Scotland", in *Scotland in Theory: Reflections on Culture and Literature*, eds. Eleanor Bell and Gavin Millar (Amsterdam and New York: Rodopi, 2004), 101.

[28]David McCrone, *The Sociology of Nationalism* (London and New York: Routledge, 2008), 32–34.

[29]Eleanor Bell, "Postmodernism, Nationalism and the Question of Tradition", in *Scotland in Theory: Reflections on Culture and Literature*, eds. Eleanor Bell and Gavin Millar (Amsterdam and New York: Rodopi, 2004), 85.

this is not the case, owing to Amy's exceptional role. On Starship UK, the Doctor meets Liz 10, who turns out to be Queen Elizabeth X, the United Kingdom's sovereign. Liz is aware of a darkness at the heart of her nation, believing that her government is concealing the truth about Starship UK. Both she and the Doctor are particularly puzzled by the lack of vibrations on board the Starship, which would seem to indicate that the Starship has no engine. It transpires that the government is concealing the fact that Starship UK is powered by a huge alien creature, a Star Whale, which lives below the ship. The government constantly tortures the Star Whale with electrical charges, convinced that this is necessary to keep it moving. At the end of the story, Liz is confronted with a choice between pressing two buttons—one to "Forget" the secret of the Star Whale, the other to "Abdicate" and free the whale, prompting Starship UK to disintegrate. The Doctor swallows the government assumption that the Starship will indeed perish if the Star Whale is given its freedom. Whilst he agonises over whether to lobotomise the creature, Amy pieces together the evidence and has the insight to grasp that the Star Whale came to the rescue of the British people because it could not bear to see their children crying. Amy forces Liz's hand down onto the "Abdicate" button. After a jolt, there is surprise as the Starship increases speed. Amy retorts that it's got to help if you stop torturing the pilot. She explains that the Star Whale came because it volunteered: being old and kind, and the last of its species, it could not stand back and watch the children cry.

Iain MacRury and Michael Rustin argue that in freeing the Star Whale Amy makes an important contribution in breaking a malign cycle, and that this represents the idea that the young can find an alternative to present cycles of exploitation which are commonly dubbed "inevitable" and "realistic".[30] However, in addition to this, it is striking that a *Scot* rescues a country which the Scots have forsaken. This implies, paradoxically, something of an affinity between Scots and the United Kingdom. Such a reading is on all fours with Kate Flynn's observation that Amy is simultaneously dislocated from, and in keeping with, her environs. There are repeated references to her outsider status, and yet her contiguity with

[30] Iain MacRury and Michael Ruskin, *The Inner World of Doctor Who: Psychoanalytical Reflections in Time and Space* (London: Karnac Books, 2014), 171.

Fig. 3.2 Thoroughly British encounter. The Doctor and Scottish companion Amy Pond meet Winston Churchill. *Doctor Who* (new series), "Victory of the Daleks", series 5, episode 3; British Broadcasting Corporation, 2010

the Union Jack palette emphasises that she is "British".[31] Amy's ambiguous relationship to Britain reflects the contemporary ambivalence of the Scottish people towards the British state. Yet ultimately, it is Amy, a young Scottish woman, who saves the British state, and in so doing, she displays an exceptional degree of agency.[32] On this basis, one could argue that "The Beast Below" is far more unionist than the Scots' abandonment of Starship UK would suggest.

Amy's agency in "The Beast Below" was no flash in the pan. In the very next episode, "Victory of the Daleks" (2010), she once again

---

[31]Kate Flynn, "A Country Made from Metal? The 'Britishness' of Human-Machine Marriage in Series 31", in *Doctor Who in Time and Space*, ed. Gillian I. Leitch (Jefferson, NC and London: McFarland, 2013).

[32]As regards Amy's gender, Anne McManus Scriven argues that Scottish literature is phallocentric in that the word "Scottish" has usually signified maleness. Perhaps the same was true of *Doctor Who* until the introduction of Amy. See Anne McManus Scriven, "The Muted Scotswoman and Oliphant's Kirsteen", in *Scotland in Theory: Reflections on Culture and Literature*, eds. Eleanor Bell and Gavin Millar (Amsterdam and New York: Rodopi, 2004), 167–181.

plays a decisive role. "Victory of the Daleks" is set in London in the Second World War, an epoch in which the sense of Britishness was, by all accounts, particularly strong within the country's four nations. The Doctor and Amy meet the wartime Prime Minister Winston Churchill. Figure 3.2 shows this encounter. In the image, Amy is astutely placed equidistant between a Union Jack and Winston Churchill. To her left, we see the Doctor, his own eccentric attire adding to the image's sense of Britishness. It is difficult to see the smiling Amy as representing anything alien to the almost obsessive Britishness of the scene: she resonates with it, rather than being incongruous.

Churchill introduces them to his top scientist Professor Edwin Bracewell. Like Amy, Bracewell is Scottish. He believes he has invented a new type of robot, the Ironsides, who will help Britain win the war against the Nazis. In reality, the Ironsides are Daleks. They have inveigled their way into the British war effort with the sole aim of ensnaring the Doctor into providing "testimony" that they are indeed Daleks, since this testimony is required in order to trigger the creation of a new Dalek species. Having secured the Doctor's testimony, the Daleks quit the scene but not before revealing that Bracewell is an android that they will use as a bomb to destroy Earth.

Convinced that by activating Bracewell's human element the Doctor can stop him exploding, he tries to get Bracewell to remember experiences which hurt him, such as the deaths of his parents. But this does not succeed in getting Bracewell to cancel the detonation. Amy, by contrast, is able to establish a more intimate rapport with Bracewell by dint of their shared Scottishness. She calls him "Paisley boy" (Paisley being Bracewell's home town) since, as a Scot, she is able to place the subtleties of his accent. She dredges from his memory an early romance, and this serves to enable his human side to prevail, thereby preventing the detonation. At one and the same time, therefore, Amy projects both Scottish fellow-feeling and broad humanity. Whilst it was not unprecedented for a companion to play a decisive role in one of the Doctor's adventures, to do so twice and in two consecutive stories was remarkable. Amy showed agency again towards the end of her period as companion when, in "A Town Called Mercy" (2012), she upbraids the Doctor over his preparedness to sacrifice the life of another in order to save the people of an American frontier town. She shames him into changing his conduct.

Amy's impressive agency forms a contrast not only to the passivity of the Scottish characters in "The Highlanders" and "Terror of the

Zygons" but also with the Doctor's earlier Scottish companion Jamie McCrimmon (1966–1969). Like Amy, the kilted, eighteenth-century Highlander was a popular companion of long duration. However, unlike Amy, Jamie was not presented as intelligent. He had many admirable qualities; indeed, these were catalogued in "The Evil of the Daleks" (1967) and included courage, mercy, instinct, pity, chivalry, friendship and compassion. But in "The Krotons" (1968–1969), an advanced alien race assesses him as being of low intelligence whilst deeming the Doctor and (English-accented) companion Zoe Heriot to possess high intelligence. This aura of backwardness was accompanied on occasion by a lack of agency. A particularly striking instance of the young Scot's passivity is evident in "The Invasion" (1968), where he insists on falling asleep during the climax of an adventure, compelling Zoe to exclaim that there are Cybermen underneath London and all he can think about is his sleep.

Amy's ability to effect change is clearly more powerful than Jamie's. To draw a contrast, in "A Town Called Mercy", Amy's criticism of the Doctor alters his course of conduct whereas in "The Evil of the Daleks", Jamie castigates the Doctor, describing him as "callous"; however, it turns out that Jamie's criticism is based on a misunderstanding, so nothing changes as a result. Amy's agency reflects the growing self-confidence and assertion of the Scottish nation post-devolution. At the same time, however, it is difficult to read Amy's role in *Doctor Who* as a metaphorical plea for Scottish independence. Amy herself elects to remain in her English village as a young woman when she would have been perfectly at liberty to return to live in Scotland had she wished. Moreover, she chooses to marry English nurse Rory Williams. This edgy, uneasy unionism is confirmed by the multiple occasions on which she is filmed with the Union Jack.

A final sign of *Doctor Who*'s improving attitude towards Scotland relates to the two Doctors with Scottish accents: the seventh Doctor (1987–1989, played by Sylvester McCoy) and the twelfth Doctor (2013–2017, played by Peter Capaldi), as well as the shifting identity of the Doctor's arch-enemy the Master. Until the arrival of the seventh Doctor, all Doctors spoke in received-pronunciation southern English accents. Having the show's hero speaking with a Scottish accent was therefore a powerful symbol which placed Scotland at the helm and connoted a more egalitarian unionism. Certainly, putting a Scot in charge of the TARDIS countered the previous stereotypes of Celtic backwardness and lack of agency. By the time of the twelfth Doctor, the Scottish government and parliament have become established institutions of the British constitution. In this regard, it is significant that the twelfth Doctor makes more of his Scottishness than the seventh: "I'm Scottish!" he exclaims having regenerated in "Deep Breath" (2014), "I can complain!" In the same scene, he also jokes about his "angry" eyebrows having declared independence and ceded from his face, as well as about his likely propensity to blame the English for everything. In the same vein, in "Smile" (2017) companion Bill Potts light-heartedly asks the Doctor if there is Scotland in space, and he replies that there is, with the Scots demanding independence from every planet they land on. Humour is thereby deployed to carve out a distinctive Scottish identity in a way which would not have occurred in the McCoy years. This may be attributed primarily to Steven Moffat's writing style and his showrunner "voice" as *auteur*, but also reflects the way in which devolution has pushed Scottish national identity to the fore.[33] At the same time, the programme is repeatedly satirising the push for separatism.

As for the Master, in "Death in Heaven" (2014) it becomes apparent that the Doctor's long-term adversary has undergone not only a change in gender (becoming Missy) but also a change of national identity (becoming Scottish). This change serves to underline that "a darker Scotland has emerged blinking into the light",[34] replacing the kitsch signifiers and mists-and-myths of the classic series' Scottishness. It was accompanied by a general mainstreaming of Scottishness in the programme, whereby more and more one-off or recurring characters were given a Scottish identity, including (somehow) Vincent van Gogh in "Vincent and the Doctor" (2010), and the reptilian Madame Vastra in "A Good Man Goes to War" (2011) and several subsequent adventures. Finally, one of the last episodes of Peter Capaldi's tenure of the lead role, "The Eaters of Light" (2017), is set in second-century Scotland and features the diminutive female leader of a band of Picts, Kar, who ultimately disobeys the Doctor to defend Earth against creatures from a portal in time and space, aided by a small number of Roman soldiers. Kar's

[33] Leith and Soule, *Political Discourse*, Chaps. 7–8 attribute a growing everyday awareness of Scottish national identity to devolution. They observe that with devolution, all political parties in Scotland, not just the Scottish National Party, focused more on the sense of nation and nationhood, Scottishness and belonging.

[34] Maley and Neely, "Almost Afraid to Know Itself", 101–102.

courageous agency provides a particularly strong contrast to the enforced passivity of the Scots in "The Highlanders" fifty years earlier.

Northern England

Let us return to Connell's and Williams' observations about the colonisation of the English by the English state. Both scholars (apparently independent of each other) propose that those promoting the idea that Scotland and Wales were England's colonies have failed to take proper account of the social exclusion of the English working class, as exemplified by the domination of standard English over regional accents. Visions of Englishness, and indeed Britishness, have indeed often been based on the ideal of the *southern* English village. John Major, as prime minister in the 1990s, notoriously eulogised Britain as a country of long shadows on cricket grounds, warm beer and old maids bicycling to Holy Communion through the morning mist. This hardly captures Britain but rather typifies the more prosperous parts of southern England. *Doctor Who* engaged in this village idyll in "The Daemons" (1971) and "Amy's Choice" (2010); however, in both stories, the southern English village becomes sinister and alarming. In "The Daemons", the vicar summons up an alien who resembles the devil; in "Amy's Choice", the Doctor and companions Amy and Rory are pursued around a village by murderous zombies.

In any event, the village idyll scarcely represents the entire English nation. Indeed, representing Englishness is particularly problematic. Paul Mason has argued that, as for no other nation in the British Isles, what it means to be English is completely subordinate to class, region, ethnicity and local culture. Mason contends that when it comes to class there is no other nation in Britain where the cultural divides are so pronounced and persistent. Indeed, he predicts that if a greater sense of Englishness fails to emerge in response to the shock of the Scottish independence referendum, it will be because of the class and cultural divides within England.[35] To be sure, these divisions contribute towards rather stark differences between north and south. The south of England is largely more prosperous than the north. Politically, there is a preponderance

[35] Paul Mason, "I do not want to be English—and any attempt to create an English identity will fail", *The Guardian*, May 10, 2015.

of Conservative-held parliamentary constituencies in the south of the country, whereas Labour heartlands are disproportionately concentrated in the north. However, unlike in Scotland and Wales, northern English complaints of inequality and marginalisation do not generate momentum in favour of devolution and independence, there being no difference of national identity to sharpen complaints of discrimination.[36] Furthermore, there is only a fuzzy border dividing northern England, the English midlands and the South.

Nonetheless, as George Orwell put it, to go north is to enter a strange country.[37] This sentiment is echoed in "The Crimson Horror" (2013), when the Sontaran butler, Strax, reminds his mistress Madame Vastra with foreboding in his voice, "Remember, we are going to *the North*". Certainly, northern England was a place to which *Doctor Who* rarely ventured. Most *Doctor Who* stories are set in southern England, with southern English characters. In a cultural sense, therefore, *Doctor Who* contributed to discrimination against the north. Two rare instances of *Doctor Who* stories with a northern English setting are "The Mark of the Rani" (1985) and "The Crimson Horror". Dispiritingly, in both instances, the TARDIS arrives in northern England unintentionally, the Doctor having planned trips to London. The north's "Other-ness" was compounded by the industrial revolution, which replaced wildernesses of nature with wastelands of slagheaps. The importance of the industrial revolution is reflected in both "The Mark of the Rani" and "The Crimson Horror". Both are set in the nineteenth century, with industrialisation and mechanisation looming large.

"The Mark of the Rani" may, as argued in the previous chapter, be read as a rare example of *Doctor Who* eulogising the class system. Dodgy north-east accents aside, the tale features an excessively pleasant captain of industry, Lord Ravenworth, who boasts of an excellent relationship with his men, claiming to have always enjoyed their trust and respect. He nurtures protégés George Stephenson (father of the British railway system) along with a younger, purely fictional character, Luke Ward. This happy narrative of master and men working together is all rather

[36] A referendum in North East England in 2004 rejected the government's proposal of a regional assembly by 78% to 22%.

[37] Katie Wales, *Northern English: A Social and Cultural History* (Cambridge: Cambridge University Press, 2006), 27–28.

a whitewash: enlightened employers were in a small minority. In general, the landed gentry clung to their estates and privileges, making life for the poor very harsh. In real life, Stephenson was employed by a Northumbrian industrial group called the Grand Allies, who fought together to obtain rights of way so that they could lay tracks to the sea for their coal: Lord Ravensworth was a member of this group. A former Conservative MP, Ravensworth esteemed Stephenson because Stephenson's inventions saved him so much money. Commercial advantage, not philanthropy, was therefore his main motivation.[38] Yet in "The Mark of the Rani", the era's oppression and class conflict are muted. In this regard, new *Who* once again improves on the classic series. "The Crimson Horror" offers an altogether grittier representation of life in the north. Its villain, Mrs. Gillyflower, reverts to the *Doctor Who* norm of a malevolent employer in league with a monster, in this instance a prehistoric red leech attached to her body. She lures the poor to her factory by preaching that it will be a shining city on the hill, which will save them from damnation on the Day of Judgement. She thereby presents her exploitation as a source of universal good in the usual capitalist fashion. Once recruited, her workers are paralysed by the creature's poison and are either dumped in the canal as "rejects", or preserved to populate the world after an apocalypse which Mrs. Gillyflower and the leech are arranging. Contrary to Mrs. Gillyflower's spin, her huge factory does not produce goods. It does, however, conceal a rocket that will be used to distribute the leech's venom throughout the Earth's atmosphere and kill off the rest of humanity. By imagining a factory which purports to manufacture things but does not do so, the drama deftly combines the Victorian narrative of heavy industry with contemporary echoes of the post-industrial.

The industrial revolution is therefore prominent in the Doctor's engagements with northern England. Let us now turn to the north's post-industrial era. Britain's decline as a manufacturing country intensified in the 1980s, during the long premiership of Margaret Thatcher, which saw a switch away from domestic manufacturing as trade in goods became increasingly globalised and British business turned more towards the provision of financial services. This change had a profound

[38] Hunter Davies, *George Stephenson: The Remarkable Life of the Founder of the Railways* (London: The History Press, 2004).

effect on northern England. Dereliction of factories and widespread unemployment added to the north's image of Otherness. The north's decline was reflected in a succession of "Brit Grit" films, which emphasised how northerners had to rely on each other, having been abandoned by the state. It was against this backdrop that *Doctor Who* kickstarted its new show in 2005 with the innovation of a Doctor with a northern English accent: the ninth Doctor, played by Christopher Eccleston. Eccleston is himself on record as having wanted to perform in a northern accent in order to champion the representation of the north, arguing that he wished to challenge the stereotype that those with northern accents lacked intellect. Indeed, his choice of accent caused something of a rift with the production team, who would have favoured received-pronunciation, and this tension may have contributed to Eccleston only playing the Doctor for a single series.[39] The production team's stance was disappointingly unimaginative and lacking in egalitarianism. Be this as it may, the end result was that the programme nonetheless had its first northern Doctor, and when companion-to-be Rose Tyler queries how he could be an alien when it sounds as if he is from the north, he retorts "Lots of planets have a north!"

Having a northern Doctor changed *Doctor Who*'s conception of Britishness. Quite apart from not being southern, the ninth Doctor seemed less upper class and less eccentric (for instance, he sported an austere leather jacket in place of the customary Doctor attire drawn from the past).[40] In this regard, John Paul Green argues that the role of Doctor was recast to emphasise the ordinary rather than the alien.[41] The ninth Doctor's character was more hard-edged than some of his predecessors; and scholars have characterised him as an "angry young man"

---

[39] *Mirror*, April 14, 2015.

[40] It does not follow that the ninth Doctor was signalled as working class. In this regard, a distinction might usefully be drawn between upper class (with its overtones of heredity and tradition) and ruling class (which can and does co-opt a small working-class contingent). Piers Britton insightfully observes that whilst the Doctor's accent belied a ruling-class identity, his actions and attitudes serve to recuperate it. See Piers D. Britton, *TARDISbound* (London: I.B. Tauris, 2011), 37.

[41] John Paul Green, "The Regeneration Game: *Doctor Who* and the Changing Faces of Heroism", in *Impossible Things, Impossible Worlds: Cultural Perspectives on Doctor Who, Torchwood and the Sarah Jane Adventures*, eds. Ross Garner, Melissa Beattie and Una McCormack (Newcastle-upon-Tyne: Cambridge Scholars Publishing, 2010), 3–24.

type,[42] or as brash and impolite.[43] However, Piers Britton perhaps gets closer to the mark in suggesting that the hyper-masculinity denoted by his costume does not really stack up: "given his unpredictable bi-polar swings from tortured grief to Jack-o'-lantern grinning, the ninth Doctor seemed to be protesting his butchness rather too much through his dress, trying to 'pass' and not quite managing".[44] This tallies with Matt Hills' observation that Christopher Eccleston's performance embodied an emphasis on performance of the heroic *as a mask*.[45] James Chapman, too, notes a "portrayal of damaged masculinity".[46] It may not be entirely fanciful to suggest that the ninth Doctor's vulnerability reflected the economic vulnerability of northern England. Certainly, the show's 2005 series heavily associated the Doctor with trauma. His back-story is that he has been a leading figure in the Time War, a war between his people the Time Lords and the Daleks. Making the northern Doctor a traumatised individual reflected the way in which many communities in the north had been economically traumatised, a pervasive theme of the Brit Grit films. However, a second metaphor may also be at play. The new show was launched during the opening years of the wars in Afghanistan and Iraq. In the course of these conflicts, many soldiers returned home with post-traumatic stress disorder (PTSD). Whilst the Afghan and Iraqi conflicts obviously lacked the mutual annihilation of the Time War, they nonetheless resulted in trauma. The Doctor in his ninth incarnation appears to suffer from PTSD. Partly because of this "hard edge", the northern ninth Doctor was an asset for *Doctor Who*'s portrayal of Britishness, refreshing in its inclusivity after the classic series's overconcentration on southern England.

No less positive was the introduction of *Doctor Who*'s first northern English companion, Clara Oswald (2012–2015). Like Amy Pond before her, Clara enjoyed a high degree of agency compared to

42 Barbara Selznick, "The Changing Brand of *Doctor Who*'s Britishness", in *Ruminations, Peregrinations and Regenerations: A Critical Approach to Doctor Who*, ed. Chris Hansen (Newcastle-upon-Tyne: Cambridge Scholars Publishing, 2010), 81.

43 David Layton, *The Humanism of Doctor Who* (Jefferson, NC: McFarland, 2012), 24.

44 Piers D. Britton, *TARDISbound*, 99–100.

45 Matt Hills, *Triumph of a Time Lord: Regenerating Doctor Who in the Twenty-First Century* (London: I.B. Tauris, 2010), 154.

46 James Chapman, *Inside the TARDIS: The Worlds of Doctor Who*, 2nd ed. (London: I.B. Tauris, 2013), 191.

earlier companions. As related in Chap. 2, in "The Name of the Doctor" (2013), Clara is revealed to be "the girl who saves the Doctor"; she subsequently shows exceptional agency again in "Flatline" (2014), "Kill the Moon" (2014) and "Death in Heaven" (2014), episodes which tend to narrow the difference between Clara as companion and the Doctor. Yet conversely, Clara's status as a *northern* English companion is undermined by *Doctor Who* placing her in London, initially as carer for her friend's children, Anjie and Artie Maitland, and then as a teacher at Coal Hill School. Clara is thus effortlessly detached from her northern place of upbringing, Blackpool, which scarcely merits a mention, let alone a visit. The opportunity afforded by a northern companion of centring the Doctor's and Clara's adventures more in the north was therefore largely squandered.[47] When, in "The Zygon Inversion" (2015), the Doctor denounces London as "a dump", this contempt is belied by the show's tendency to set so many *Doctor Who* stories there.

In sum, *Doctor Who*'s strong preference for London and southern English settings and characters means that the programme still fails to represent England as a whole. Nonetheless, it is possible to discern some modest improvement over the years. "The Crimson Horror" offered a metaphor for the exploitation of the northern English working class which is more realistic than the kindly capitalism and cosy social consensus which imbues the earlier "Mark of the Rani". The ninth Doctor's northern English persona gave the north a prominence which further extended *Doctor Who*'s range of "ideal Britons" beyond its southern comfort zone, and Clara Oswald as the first northern English companion was feisty and proactive. These changes signal a welcome, if limited, improvement in *Doctor Who*'s treatment of the north.

Northern Ireland

Finally, a few words should be said about Northern Ireland, the least populous nation of the United Kingdom. Northern Ireland has been entirely neglected as a setting for the Doctor's adventures. At the time

[47] A more progressive stance would have easily been possible, and is apparent in the Big Finish *Doctor Who* audio dramas, in which a companion to the Eighth Doctor, Lucie Miller (played by Sheridan Smith) is also from Blackpool. The Doctor and Lucie have adventures both in Blackpool itself and in the Lake District, also in North-West England ("The Zygon Who Fell to Earth" (2008), "Death in Blackpool" (2009)).

of the classic series, there was good reason for the Province's exclusion. Northern Irish society was dominated by the so-called Troubles, the violent conflict between loyalists and republicans over whether Northern Ireland should remain part of the United Kingdom or become part of the Republic of Ireland. This constitutional conflict was driven by a religious divide, Protestants mainly favouring the United Kingdom, and most Catholics preferring the Irish Republic. The conflict came to an end, not completely but substantially, with the Good Friday Agreement of 1998, which brought about a power-sharing constitution. Yet the advent of relative peace still did not lead to the Doctor having a Northern Irish adventure. To be sure, there have been occasional Northern Irish characters: a businessman in "Terror of the Autons" (1971), a UNIT scientist in "The Day of the Doctor" (the show's fiftieth anniversary special, 2013) and the commander of a spaceship in "Into the Dalek" (2014); but there was clearly no appetite to locate any of the Doctor's escapades in Northern Ireland. By 2013, however, the BBC had broadcast a highly successful crime drama, *The Fall* (2013–2016), set and filmed in Northern Ireland, which scarcely touched on the sectarian conflict. Whilst it would still be sailing too close to the wind for a *Doctor Who* adventure to satirise unionist Orangemen or republican bombers it is regrettable that contemporary *Doctor Who* still has not sought to represent Northern Ireland as part of its portrayal of the United Kingdom.

Hybridity as a Pervasive Theme

Returning to Chris Williams' argument that it may be useful to apply postcolonial ideas to Wales even though we cannot convincingly regard Wales as a colony, one of the postcolonial concepts or approaches which Williams considers is hybridity. By this he means "the way in which migration, settlement and intermarriage have blurred Welsh frontiers of ethnic identification". Noting that only three-quarters of people living in Wales were actually born in Wales, Williams observes that "our preoccupation with cultural identity has gradually been relaxed from seeing identity in the singular (Welsh, English, Irish etc.) to being prepared to give identity as hybridized or hyphenated (Anglo-Welsh, English-speaking Welsh, Irish-Welsh, Black-Welsh etc.) and has moved on to embrace concepts of situational or multiple identities".[48]

[48]Williams, "Problematizing Wales", 3–27, 14–15.

As we have seen in Chap. 2, hybridity certainly looms large in *Doctor Who*, in the grand sense of humans hybridising with aliens (see, for example, the human-Daleks in "Daleks in Manhattan"/"Evolution of the Daleks" (2007), or the Daleks with the "human factor" in "The Evil of the Daleks" (1967)). Hybridity, however, has also become increasingly prominent in the show in terms of intermarriage of the nationalities that comprise the United Kingdom. Such intermarriage appeared in a rudimentary fashion in "The Green Death" (1973), where the Doctor's English companion Jo Grant agrees to wed the rather Doctorish Welsh scientist Professor Clifford Jones.[49] In new *Who*, such hybridity becomes more prominent, particularly during Steven Moffat's period as showrunner. Scottish companion Amy Pond marries English companion Rory Williams and bears a child who becomes an important recurring character (and the Doctor's wife), Professor River Song. River is not only a Scottish-English cross but, having been conceived in the TARDIS during time travel, she has some Time Lord characteristics including the ability to regenerate.[50] Hybridity also comes to the fore in "Hell Bent" (2015), when the twelfth, Scottish-accented Doctor plucks his English companion Clara Oswald out of time and space to rescue her from death. Doing so risks the very fabric of time itself. This raises the intriguing prospect that "the Hybrid" long feared by the Doctor's race, the Time Lords, is not one individual but two: the Scottish Doctor and the English Clara.[51] Together they are described as "a dangerous combination of a passionate and powerful Time Lord and a young woman so very similar to him, companions who are willing to push each other to extremes". As Chris Williams implies, hybridity softens and blurs Britain's national boundaries, rejecting essentialist characteristics of the four nationalities and advancing the idea of a multiple self.[52] This chimes with the inclusive spirit of new-series *Doctor Who*'s Britishness. But "Hell Bent" goes

[49] *The Sarah Jane Adventures* episode "Death of the Doctor" (2010) reveals that this is a union which proves fruitful in raising some highly internationalised descendants.

[50] See "Day of the Moon" (2011), "Let's Kill Hitler" (2011).

[51] "Hell Bent" pointedly draws attention to the Doctor's and Clara's difference in identities. Having forgotten Clara following a memory-wipe, the Doctor exclaims to her "You're English!" and Clara retorts "You're not!".

[52] Williams, "Problematizing Wales", 15.

further and also represents the British hybrid as powerful, perhaps dangerously so.

Conclusion

We can discern a marked improvement in the portrayal of the Scots, Welsh and northern English in new-series *Doctor Who* compared to the classic series. Scottish, Welsh and northern English characters have become more prominent, they display a greater degree of agency, and are less often depicted as backward. Thus, new *Who* projects a more egalitarian unionism, one which does not seek to defuse the edgy, conflictual rivalries between the competing identities but which celebrates these tensions as part of the endless drama of the union.[53] Britain, with its four nations, has been described as "a great and largely successful multicultural experiment", a framework into which Britain's past and present immigrant communities can easily fit.[54] In this regard, contemporary *Doctor Who*'s treatment of Scots, Welsh and northern English can be seen as a celebration of the capaciousness of "Britishness" as a mansion with many rooms, within which multiple identities and conflicting loyalties may flourish.

Bibliography

Bell, Eleanor. "Postmodernism, Nationalism and the Question of Tradition." In *Scotland in Theory: Reflections on Culture and Literature*, edited by Eleanor Bell and Gavin Millar, 83–96. Amsterdam and New York: Rodopi, 2004.

Britton, Piers D. *TARDISbound: Navigating the Universes of Doctor Who*. London: I.B. Tauris, 2011.

Chapman, James. *Inside the TARDIS: The Worlds of Doctor Who*, 2nd ed. London: I.B. Tauris, 2013.

Colley, Linda. "Does Britishness Still Matter in the 21st Century, and How Much/How Well do the Politicians Care?" In *Britishness: Perspectives on*

[53] One might even argue that there is actually something very British about Britain muddling through with British subjects in Scotland and Wales not considering themselves British.

[54] Bhikhu Parekh, "Being British", in *Britishness: Perspectives on the British Question*, eds. Andrew Gamble and Tony Wright (Chichester: Wiley-Blackwell, 2009), 37.

the British Question, edited by Andrew Gamble and Tony Wright, 21–31. Chichester: Wiley-Blackwell, 2009.

Colley, Linda. *Britons: Forging the Nation 1707–1837*. New Haven, CT and London: Yale University Press, 1992.

Connell, Liam. "Modes of Marginality: Scottish Literature and the Uses of Postcolonial Theory." *Comparative Studies of South Asia, Africa and the Middle East* 23 (2003): 26–39.

Cook, Jon. "Relocating Britishness and the Break-up of Britain." In *Relocating Britishness*, edited by Steven Caunce, Ewa Mazierska, Susan Sydney-Smith and John K. Walton, 17–37. Manchester and New York: Manchester University Press, 2004.

Davies, Hunter. *George Stephenson: The Remarkable Life of the Founder of the Railways*. London: The History Press, 2004.

Flynn, Kate. "A Country Made from Metal? The 'Britishness' of Human-Machine Marriage in Series 31." In *Doctor Who in Time and Space*, edited by Gillian I. Leitch, 195–292. Jefferson, NC: McFarland, 2013.

Gamble, Andrew and Tony Wright. "Introduction: The Britishness Question." In *Britishness: Perspectives on the British Question*, edited by Andrew Gamble and Tony Wright, 1–9. Chichester: Wiley-Blackwell, 2009.

Green, John Paul. "The Regeneration Game: *Doctor Who* and the Changing Faces of Heroism." In *Impossible Things, Impossible Worlds: Cultural Perspectives on Doctor Who, Torchwood and the Sarah Jane Adventures*, edited by Ross Garner, Melissa Beattie and Una McCormack, 3–24. Newcastle-upon-Tyne, Cambridge Scholars Publishing, 2010.

Hills, Matt. *Triumph of a Time Lord: Regenerating Doctor Who in the Twenty-First Century*. London: I.B. Tauris, 2010.

Jackson, Ellen-Raïssa. "Dislocating the Nation: Political Devolution and Cultural Identity on Stage and Screen." In *Scotland in Theory: Reflections on Culture and Literature*, edited by Eleanor Bell and Gavin Millar, 107–120. Amsterdam and New York: Rodopi, 2004.

Jowett, Lorna. *Dancing with the Doctor: Dimensions of Gender in the Doctor Who Universe*. London: I.B. Tauris, 2017.

Lacey, Stephen. "'When you see Cardiff on Film, it Looks Like LA' (John Barrowman): Space, Genre and Realism in *Torchwood*." In *Torchwood Declassified*, edited by Rebecca Williams, 137–153. London: I.B. Tauris, 2013.

Layton, David. *The Humanism of Doctor Who*. Jefferson, NC: McFarland, 2012.

Leith, Murray and Daniel Soule. *Political Discourse and National Identity in Scotland*. Edinburgh: Edinburgh University Press, 2011.

MacRury, Ian and Michael Rustin. *The Inner World of Doctor Who: Psychoanalytical Reflections in Time and Space*. London: Karnac, 2014.

Maley, Willy and Sarah Neely. "Almost Afraid to Know Itself: Macbeth and Cinematic Scotland." In *Scotland in Theory: Reflections on Culture and Literature*, edited by Eleanor Bell and Gavin Millar, 97–106. Amsterdam and New York: Rodopi, 2004.

Marquand, David. "Bursting with Skeletons: Britishness after Empire." In *Britishness: Perspectives on the British Question*, edited by Andrew Gamble and Tony Wright, 10–21. Chichester: Wiley-Blackwell, 2009.

McArthur, Colin. *Brigadoon, Braveheart and the Scots: Distortions of Scotland in Hollywood Cinema*. London: I.B. Tauris, 2003.

McCrone, David. *The Sociology of Nationalism*. London and New York: Routledge, 2008.

McGinn, Sherry. "Sexual Relations and Sexual Identity Issues: Brave New Worlds or More of the Old One?" In *Illuminating Torchwood*, edited by Andrew Ireland, 165–180. Jefferson, NC: McFarland, 2010.

Parekh, Bhikhu. "Being British." In *Britishness: Perspectives on the British Question*, edited by Andrew Gamble and Tony Wright, 32–40. Chichester: Wiley-Blackwell, 2009.

Scriven, Anne McManus. "The Muted Scotswoman and Oliphant's Kirsteen." In *Scotland in Theory: Reflections on Culture and Literature*, edited by Eleanor Bell and Gavin Millar, 167–181. Amsterdam and New York: Rodopi, 2004.

Selznick Barbara. "Rebooting and Rebranding: The Changing Brands of *Doctor Who*'s Britishness." In *Ruminations, Peregrinations and Regenerations: A Critical Approach to Doctor Who*, edited by Chris Hansen, 68–84. Newcastle-upon-Tyne: Cambridge Scholars Publishing, 2010.

Tanja, Nathanael. "Rose *is* England." In *Who Travels with the Doctor?* edited by Gillian I. Leitch and Sherry Ginn, 79–90. Jefferson, NC: McFarland, 2016.

Wales, Katie. *Northern English: A Social and Cultural History*. Cambridge: Cambridge University Press, 2006.

Williams, Chris. "Problematizing Wales: An Exploration in Historiography and Postcoloniality." In *Postcolonial Wales*, edited by Jane Aaron and Chris Williams, 3–27. Cardiff: University of Wales Press, 2005.

CHAPTER 4

"The Enemy of the World": Globalised Law Versus British Self-Government

Globalisation is a dominant characteristic of our age, significantly affecting British law and the way in which Britain is governed. At its heart lies the phenomenon whereby supranational institutions increasingly take on the roles of national authorities. More recently, there have been indications of greater intolerance among the British to remote rule, culminating in the vote to leave the European Union in the 2016 referendum. This chapter traces the evolution of *Doctor Who*'s stance on globalisation. It aims to show how *Doctor Who*, by deploying allegory, actively promoted an ideal of internationalised governance and law in the late 1960s and early 1970s, to an extent which now seems naïve. It contrasts this position to that of new-series *Doctor Who*, which places more confidence in Britain itself as proper locus of the country's governance and lawmaking.

This chapter aims to draw attention to the striking nature of this change, and to seek to explain it. The argument is that *Doctor Who*'s falling out of love with internationalisation largely explains the new show's "patriotic turn". Whilst there is some evidence of a new-found tenderness towards British institutions, the new show's zeal for British self-governance can be attributed primarily to the abandonment of faith in "international good, national bad", a stance which has not stood the test of time. In particular, in the period between *Doctor Who*'s classic series and new series, globalisation's neoliberal character came to the fore. This chapter will argue that during the late 1960s and early 1970s, *Doctor Who*'s authors misunderstood globalisation, assuming it to be entirely

D. Nicol, *Doctor Who: A British Alien?*,
https://doi.org/10.1007/978-3-319-65834-6_4

progressive. Viewing internationalisation through rose-tinted glasses, they seemed to think that it would eradicate nationalism's irrationalities and were oblivious to the risk of corporate domination. This misreading was understandable in an era in which economic globalisation had not yet fully developed. By the time of the new series, however, the power of the transnational corporations within the globalised construct was all too clear.

Intriguingly, this change in the politics of *Doctor Who* runs counter to the consistent position of the British political class. Among the country's ruling elite, there has been a strong, durable and long-standing consensus in favour of globalisation, coupled with the lack of a serious anti-globalisation force in British politics. Even after the banking crisis of 2008, the first glimmerings of a more critical approach to globalisation among the nation's politicians proved faint to the point of non-existent; and even after the EU referendum, Prime Minister Theresa May saw global free trade as the way forward for Britain.

New *Who*'s stance must be set against the backdrop of a protracted period in which politicians have rammed globalisation down the electorate's throat. It will be suggested that the gulf between *Doctor Who*'s writers and Britain's politicians in this regard exemplifies a more general phenomenon—the alien quality of the contemporary political class, something which itself has not escaped satire in *Doctor Who* (see for example "Aliens of London"/"World War Three" (2005)), and which will form the focus of Chap. 7.

The term "globalised law" is relatively new. During the period where *Doctor Who* showed its greatest zeal for globalised governance, the word "globalisation" was not in common use. People tended to talk of the *international* rather than of the *globalised*. "Globalisation" entered common usage in the 1980s and 1990s as neoliberal governments, transnational organisations and corporations intensified their efforts to remove barriers to economic interpenetration. Presently, the term "globalised law" may be used to embrace a spectrum of international legal systems. Traditionally, international law depended for its force on the goodwill of the countries which had made a treaty. Whilst most states obeyed most international agreements most of the time,[1] enforceability was

[1]Louis Henkin, *How Nations Behave: Law and Foreign Policy* (New York: Columbia University Press, 1979).

nonetheless always seen as a problem. International law was perceived as a weak form of law, substantially at the mercy of national sovereignty. Since the Second World War, however, and more particularly since the 1980s and 1990s, governments increasingly created or strengthened international institutions to ensure stronger enforcement of international rules.[2] The most impressive enforcement machinery is that of the European Union, since its legal system has a semi-federal nature, which deploys national courts to enforce EU rules as the supreme law of the EU Member States.[3] But there are other powerful systems besides, such as those of the World Trade Organization and European Convention on Human Rights. As a result, national sovereignty is no longer a magic wand which can be waved to ward off engagement in the international system.[4] Furthermore, international law no longer merely concerns keeping countries within their frontiers. Rather, a vast array of laws and policies, previously the cherished "internal" preserve of national governments, have been hived off to supranational regimes.

This has led to an intensification of globalised governance. The impact on British governance is that fewer important decisions are taken by the British Cabinet, British Parliament and devolved institutions, more by national leaders congregating in supranational forums. Globalisation has also ushered in the "rise of the unelected", whereby increasingly important policies are determined by expert bodies unaccountable to any electorate, such as courts and central banks.[5] More fundamentally still, globalised law has endowed private companies with constitutional rights of free trade, freedom to provide services, and freedom of unhindered foreign direct investment, which cannot be overturned by national

---

[2]David Kennedy, "The Move to Institutions", *Cardozo Law Review*, 8 (1986–1987): 841–988.

[3]All national courts and tribunals of the EU Member States are obliged to give effect to EU law, giving it priority over any conflicting national law. See the judgement of the European Court of Justice in Case 106/77 *Simmenthal* [1978] ECR 629, [1978] 3 CMLR. The supremacy of EU law was accepted by the UK's highest court, the House of Lords, in *Factortame* [1991] AC 603, 658. See generally Danny Nicol, *The Constitutional Protection of Capitalism* (Oxford: Hart, 2010), 90–94.

[4]John Jackson, *The World Trade Organization: Constitution and Jurisprudence* (London: Pinter, 1998), 77.

[5]Frank Vibert, *The Rise of the Unelected: Democracy and the New Separation of Powers* (Cambridge: Cambridge University Press, 2007).

parliaments, since supranational commitments tend to bind national political communities for the future. This, in turn, has served to foster the rise of the transnational corporation.

It should be emphasised that globalisation represents *a choice on the part of the political actors*. It has not occurred inevitably because of the growth of technology or business decisions: ultimately, neoliberal globalisation has come into existence because the world's politicians have continued to support it.[6] Ironically, the founding father of neoliberalism, Friedrich von Hayek, had to confront the argument that socialism was inevitable in the 1940s because of technological advance, but he rightly argued that "it is because nearly everybody wants it that we are moving in this direction. There are no objective facts which make it inevitable."[7] The same argument could convincingly be advanced today apropos neoliberal globalisation, but only with regard to the politico-economic elite. As Jeremy Gilbert has insightfully observed, only the core neoliberal elite and key strategic sectors at its periphery (corporate management, for example) need to be recruited to any kind of active belief in neoliberal globalisation, as long as no singular alternative wins widespread support. Thus, general dissatisfaction with neoliberalism and its social consequences is rife, but there is no popular alternative able to garner sufficient potency to challenge it.[8]

The Global Group Hug: Internationalisation's Normative "Pull"

It has been mentioned that *Doctor Who*'s commitment to international law and governance peaked in the late 1960s and early 1970s. What then was the attraction of internationalisation for the *Doctor Who* authors of the time? Two factors are readily apparent. The first relates to rationality. Una McCormack has observed that the pre-1989 programme repeatedly put faith in the power of reason to overcome injustice and achieve a

[6] Nicol, *Constitutional Protection of Capitalism*, 14.

[7] Friedrich von Hayek, *The Road to Serfdom* (London: Ark Paperbacks, 1986), Chap. IV.

[8] Jeremy Gilbert, "What Kind of Thing is Neoliberalism?", in *Neoliberal Culture*, ed. Jeremy Gilbert (London: Lawrence & Wishart, 2016), 26.

more rational social order.[9] Just as the classic series promoted scientific rationalism, so too it advocated political rationalism. National divisions were perceived as irrational. *Doctor Who*'s perennial theme of toleration of diversity derived from the experience of the Nazi and fascist regimes of the inter-war years and the Second World War. The classic series, after all, began to be broadcast a mere eighteen years after the war. In the aftermath of war, and in the midst of the Cold War, rejection of the nation could be seen as anti-racist and progressive. The programme's stance was to shun national differences and to emphasise shared humanity. Britishness was therefore portrayed as encapsulating an open-minded willingness to participate in international endeavour.

The second reason why internationalisation must have seemed an attractive option relates to the widespread perception that Britain was on a downward spiral during *Doctor Who*'s early years. The perception of Britain as a superpower vanished at the end of the Second World War, a demotion confirmed by the Suez crisis in 1956. Waning international status was accompanied by the perceived stagnation of the British economy. The era of "You've Never Had It So Good" in the late 1950s gave way to apparent economic decline. The industrial unrest of the 1970s further heightened this perception. British politicians adapted by reaching out towards international solutions. In the context of foreign policy, this took the form of strongly aligning Britain to the United States of America. Britain's politicians constructed the idea of a "Special Relationship" with the United States, based on a strong presumption that they would go along with American military initiatives. In the economic sphere, politicians came to see entry to Europe's "Common Market" as the solution to Britain's economic ills. European integration would provide the prosperity that Britain could no longer achieve alone.

These two factors—one based on principle and emotion, the other based on the perception of Britain's diminution—affected the treatment of globalisation and nation state in *Doctor Who*. In the late 1960s and early 1970s, it was striking just how fervently *Doctor Who* conveyed its pro-internationalisation message. Thereafter, however, the show's propagandising evaporated. Furthermore, in *Doctor Who*'s post-2005 reboot,

[9] Una McCormack, "He's Not the Messiah: Undermining Political and Religious Authority in New *Doctor Who*", in *The Unsilent Library: Essays on the Russell T. Davies Era of the New Doctor Who*, eds. Simon Bradshaw, Anthony Keen and Graham Sleight (London: The Science Fiction Foundation, 2011), 46.

the writers have adopted a far more critical stance, swinging radically away from the born-again internationalism of the *Doctor Who* of the past. This transformation will be assessed by examining four distinct features of the programme's development. *First*, intergalactic law serves as a metaphor for the globalisation of law; its legitimacy reaches its height during the period where the show's confidence in internationalism peaked but thereafter suffers a long decline. *Secondly*, human institutions change throughout the series. The programme's high-water mark of internationalising optimism is apparent in the centrality of the United Nations Intelligence Taskforce (UNIT) during the Doctor's exile on Earth, yet this stance is subsequently supplanted by reliance on national institutions and figures, such as Torchwood, Harriet Jones, Winston Churchill, Liz 10 and the pervasive imagery of the Union Jack.[10] *Thirdly*, globalised law's silent partners, the transnational corporations, whilst significantly absent in the programme's earliest years, increasingly come to the fore in numerous stories where corporate governance morphs into totalitarian rule. *Fourthly*, *Doctor Who*'s attitude to globalisation can also be traced through the show's stance towards the globalising effect of American hegemony and the extent to which the United States of America should be permitted to intervene in British governance. These different elements will now be examined in turn.

Intergalactic as Global

The first part of my argument is that, in *Doctor Who*, intergalactic law represents a disguised form of globalised law. At first blush, this claim may seem extravagant but in fact it is not particularly fanciful; the same argument has been advanced by other scholars. In regarding the Time Lords as a disguised globalised institution, the allegorical nature of science fiction comes to the fore. James Chapman views the Time Lords in "The War Games" (1969) as "a sort of outer space United Nations who are the last court of appeal for disputes", an assessment that, incidentally, reflects the importance of judicial institutions in globalisation

[10]On the importance of visual imagery in *Doctor Who*, see Piers Britton and Simon Barker, *Reading between Designs: Visual Imagery and the Generation of Meaning in The Avengers, The Prisoner and Doctor Who* (Austin: University of Texas Press, 2003).

arrangements.[11] Using intergalactic law to represent international law fits into the show's broader allegorical tradition.

The conclusion that international and intergalactic law in *Doctor Who* are one and the same is reinforced by the role of the Doctor in his third regeneration. Exiled to Earth, he works for UNIT to thwart alien invasions, yet he *also* works occasionally for the Time Lords when they deign to allow him to travel in the TARDIS to other times and planets on missions ("Colony in Space" (1971), "The Curse of Peladon" (1972), "The Mutants" (1972)). In his first role, the Doctor is supporting an international force, in the second, an intergalactic one, yet in both he performs rather similar functions. It is difficult to dismiss the similarity as mere coincidence. For instance, in "Colony in Space", on the planet Uxarieus he has to side with one group of humans against another (corporate) group of humans, just as he does on Earth in "The Green Death" (1973); in "The Curse of Peladon", he has to persuade different species gathered on the planet Peladon to unite, just as he has to convince hostile human factions on Earth to work together in "Day of the Daleks" (1972); in "The Mutants", he has to combat colonialism on the planet Solos just as he fights neocolonialism on Earth in "Invasion of the Dinosaurs" (1974). Thus, the Doctor's efforts on behalf of the international organisation and his toils at the behest of the intergalactic elite resemble each other rather too closely for the likeness to be dismissed as coincidence.

In "The War Games" (1969), the Time Lords put the Doctor on trial, and in so doing we are especially reminded of the United Nations. Indeed, the Doctor's trial in episode 10 is particularly significant in emphasising the legitimacy of the international sphere. Contrary to later encounters, the Time Lords in this story possess a magisterial grandeur. At trial, the Time Lords are portrayed with dignity and gravitas. Tat Wood characterises them as "an austere clergy".[12] Their displays of power reinforce their stateliness: for instance, we witness the Time Lords seemingly slowing down time by use of a force-field as the Doctor and his companions try to re-enter the TARDIS in order to escape them.

[11] James Chapman, *Inside The TARDIS: The Worlds of Doctor Who*, 2nd ed. (London: I.B. Tauris, 2013), 73–74.

[12] Tat Wood, "The Empire of the Senses: Narrative Form and Point-of-View in *Doctor Who*", in *Time and Relative Dissertations in Space: Critical Perspectives on Doctor Who*, ed. David Butler (Manchester: Manchester University Press, 2007).

A booming voice in the TARDIS summons the Doctor back to his home planet. The Doctor is put on trial, but so too is the main villain of the War Games, an alien called the War Lord. The Time Lords convict the War Lord then dematerialise him and his henchmen, so they will never have existed. They then place a force-field around his entire planet, in order to protect the rest of the universe from his warlike people. Such omnipotence lends the Time Lords a solemnity which is reinforced by the seriousness with which they are portrayed on screen.

The Time Lords' charge against the Doctor is one of having unlawfully interfered in the affairs of other planets. This dovetails with classical international law, which emphasises respect for recognised frontiers. On this reading, the Doctor's speech in his own defence is a skilful one, for he selects instances where he has saved worlds from *invaders* and *conquerors*—the Dominators, Great Intelligence, Ice Warriors, Cybermen and Daleks. Furthermore, the Time Lords' verdict on the Doctor, whilst unwelcome to the viewer, and the punishment they mete out to him—exile to Earth with his appearance changed—does not seem egregiously unjust. He knowingly violated the Time Lords' most fundamental law, and the Time Lords make concessions to his arguments in deciding their sanction. In so doing, they are partly agreeing with the Doctor's point of view. Does not such a concession on the part of the Time Lords undermine their neutral stance? Do they not become half-hearted upholders of their own supposedly fundamental law of non-interference?

In any event, in subsequent encounters, the Time Lords' gravitas spectacularly implodes. Sclerotic pomposity, corruption and treachery become the rule, and grand displays of power are replaced with ineffectual effeteness going hand in hand with their moral degradation. This is evident in such stories as "The Deadly Assassin" (1976), "The Invasion of Time" (1978), "Arc of Infinity" (1983) and "The Five Doctors" (1983). In "The Trial of a Time Lord" (1986), it is not without good reason, therefore, that the Doctor denounces the Time Lords as "decadent, degenerate and rotten to the core!" Indeed, during his exile on Earth, the frequency with which the Time Lords deploy the Doctor as their intergalactic James Bond undermines their own pretensions to non-interference. Whilst Time Lord intervention may be justified in "Colony in Space" in view of the cataclysmic potential of the Doomsday Weapon, their interference in "The Curse of Peladon" and "The Mutants" seems excessive. In the grand scheme of things, nothing much hangs on the fate of Peladon and Solos, yet Time Lord interference in these planets seems to constitute precisely the offence for which they punished the Doctor. Furthermore—as I will argue—the "good" of their intervention, certainly on Peladon, is contestable, mirroring perhaps the contestability of United Nations (UN) decision-making on issues such as Korea, and the accusation that the UN has departed from its original vaunted ideological neutrality. As Kim Newman suggests, the more we hear of the Time Lords, the less interesting they become.[13] It becomes difficult to resist the view of *Doctor Who*'s original producer, Verity Lambert, that it might have been better had we never met the Time Lords.[14]

The authors of new-series *Doctor Who* purported to dispense with the Time Lords completely, by killing them off in the Time War which occurs offscreen before the new series even begins. The universe toddles along much as before without its Platonic guardians. An alternative organisation, the Shadow Proclamation, proves entirely impotent in "The Stolen Earth" (2008). When the Time Lords finally re-emerge in "The End of Time" (2009–2010), their influence is more malign than ever: they intend to destroy the very dimension of time itself. "The End of Time" was immediately preceded by a significant episode, "The Waters of Mars" (2009), in which the Doctor claims that as last surviving Time Lord, he can now control the laws of time, so that he alone can change even fixed points in time. The Time Lords' loss of legitimacy thus leads, via their destruction, to the assumption of personal rule by the Doctor himself, which is portrayed as an illegitimate concentration of power in the hands of an individual, and one which endangers the Doctor's very sanity. The Doctor's power-grab is rejected as such by the leading one-off character in the story, Captain Adelaide Brooke, who chooses to kill herself rather than allow the Doctor to pervert the laws of time in order to save her life. The "Time Lord victorious" of "The Waters of Mars" seems a far cry from the image of the wayward time traveller of *Doctor Who*'s early years, doing good sporadically and peripherally, hither and thither, on remote planets and distant times.

[13]Kim Newman, *Doctor Who* (London: BFI TV Classics, 2005), 100.

[14]"I have never been particularly keen on the Time Lords actually, on actually seeing them. I just think it would have been better not to see them. I think some things are better kept as a mystery. I believe certain areas you should explain as little as possible." Quoted in John Tulloch and Manuel Alvarado, *Doctor Who: The Unfolding Text* (New York: St. Martin's Press, 1983), 30.

The suggestion is that, paradoxically, law's globalisation has led to too great a concentration of power at the top.

A second way in which intergalactic law acts as a metaphor for supranational law is in the pair of stories "The Curse of Peladon" (1972) and "The Monster of Peladon" (1974). These serve as a very obvious allegory for British entry to the European Economic Community (EEC), now European Union. The King of the insular planet of Peladon wishes it to join the Galactic Federation, an organisation of planets which have learnt to control their past and which has its own system of laws (which is the case with the EEC, its laws taking precedence over national laws even in the national courts).[15] Its decisions have to be unanimous (as was broadly the case in the EEC until the Single European Act, a European treaty of 1986). The Federation's delegation to Peladon comprises a motley ragbag of aliens including the previously warlike Ice Warriors. The King's ultra-conservative High Priest, Hepesh, wants the King to return to the ancient ways of Peladon, and deploys sacred monster Aggador to intimidate the King and populace out of Federation membership. The Doctor reveals that Hepesh is in league with one of the delegates, who has made a private deal with Hepesh to exploit Peladon's mineral wealth. The story thereby suggests something corrupt and secretive about bilateral trade deals, whereas fixed and open multilateral trading arrangements, buttressed by the existence of supranational organisations, are somehow more virtuous. However, this alien traitor turns out not to be an Ice Warrior. Hepesh dies, admitting in his final words that perhaps he was wrong to try to preserve the old ways.

The solidly pro-EEC stance of "The Curse of Peladon" was, however, reconsidered two years later in "The Monster of Peladon". This story rather overflows with political messages. It is primarily an allegory of the miners' strike of 1974 and the struggles between the competing moderate and left wings of the National Union of Mineworkers, the Doctor siding with the moderates. It also contains a feminist message. However, these strongly expressed themes have rather obscured the story's intriguingly unfavourable account of supranationalism. Interest lies in the swiftly diminishing legitimacy of the Galactic Federation.

---

[15] See the judgement of the Court of Justice of the European Communities in Case 26/62 *NV Algemene Transporten Expeditie Onderneming van Gend en Loos v Nederlandse Administratis der Belastingen* [1963] ECR 1 and Case 6/64 *Costa v ENEL* [1964] ECR 585.

In particular, it is amongst the ordinary people that disillusionment with the Federation is most keenly felt. The miners complain that they were told that things would get better once Peladon was in the Federation, yet life has only improved for those in the Queen's court. Federation troops are brought into replace domestic troops, and there is a threat that Federation workers will mine the minerals if Peladon miners down tools. The villains of the piece are the Ice Warriors, who appear to be manipulating the Federation for their own ends. In particular, the introduction of Federation troops seems to be a cover for an invasion by an oppressive Ice Warrior-dominated force, authorised to use any terror method. The Queen complains fruitlessly of a violation of Peladon's planetary sovereignty and laments that when her father signed treaties with the Federation, he could not have known it would lead to nothing but bloodshed; as it is, she reflects, Peladon must accept the consequences.

Of course, British membership of the EEC did not lead to invasion or bloodshed. Nonetheless, by 1974 the improvement in Britain's fortunes resulting from EEC membership must have been far from clear. Viewed as a Eurosceptic text, "The Monster of Peladon" remarkably predates the growth of Euroscepticism among the country's political elite.[16] It is also an insightful story in terms of its recognition that integration will have a different economic impact on different social classes. Agustin José Menéndez has observed that British entry into the EEC did not affect all Britons equally. Indeed, whether you derived a benefit or suffered a burden from the country's EEC membership was determined not by your being British but by your socio-economic position.[17] In any event, Edward Heath, the Conservative Prime Minister in the early 1970s who secured UK accession to the EEC, was so determined to achieve British membership that he perhaps gave rather too great a build-up to the benefits of European integration. Whatever the merits and demerits of membership, it did not lead to any great leap forwards in Britain's economic performance. "The Monster of Peladon" draws attention to the gap between political leaders who remained positive about the European adventure

[16]British Euroscepticism increased considerably as a result of the Maastricht Treaty in 1992–1993, which amended the European Community treaties so as to create the single currency and European Union. See Danny Nicol, *EC Membership and the Judicialisation of British Politics* (Oxford: Oxford University Press, 2001), Chap. 7.

[17]Agustin José Menéndez, "Whose Justice? Which Europe?", in *Europe's Justice Deficit*, eds. Grainne de Búrca, Dimitry Kochenov and Andrew Williams (Oxford: Hart, 2014).

and the general public who, whilst willing to give the benefit of the doubt to the Common Market, were rather less enthusiastic.

Human Organisation: UNIT Rule Versus UK Rule

In considering *Doctor Who*'s presentation of Britishness, Barbara Selznick has suggested that throughout the classic series, "nations are shown to be naïve at best and malevolent at worse".[18] Closer examination, however, may suggest that the depiction of nation changed over time. It reveals particularly that hostility towards the nation peaked in the *Doctor Who* stories of the late 1960s and early 1970s. It was precisely because there seemed for a time to be a viable progressive alternative—the international sphere—that *Doctor Who*'s storylines could deliver a particularly stark anti-nation message. Inclined to revere international endeavour, the authors felt able to display startling contempt for British institutions. The strength of this onslaught is so striking that it seems misguided of fans not to have viewed "classic" *Doctor Who* as political.[19] In view of this, it should be noted that the programme did not entirely abandon the idea that Britain could be a great power: stories such as "The Ambassadors of Death" (1970) draw attention to Britain's potential as a leading nation in space exploration, and "The Sea Devils" (1972) highlights British naval prowess. Rather, the pervasive theme was that national might is better constrained by international institutions.

Doctor Who gravitated towards contemporary Earth in 1970. Exiled to Earth, the Doctor becomes Scientific Adviser of UNIT, in return for the supply of scientific equipment with which to repair the TARDIS. Not everyone approved of the Doctor's involvement in this organisation. *Doctor Who* creator Verity Lambert complained of the Doctor becoming too much of an establishment figure.[20] This accusation has been

---

[18] Barbara Selznick, "Rebooting and Rebranding: The Changing Brands of *Doctor Who*'s Britishness", in *Ruminations, Peregrinations, and Regenerations: A Critical Approach to Doctor Who*, ed. Chris Hansen (Newcastle-upon-Tyne: Cambridge Scholars Publishing, 2010), 74.

[19] Alan McKee, "Is *Doctor Who* Political?", *European Journal of Cultural Studies*, vii(2) (2004): 201–217.

[20] John Tulloch and Manuel Alvarado, *Doctor Who: The Unfolding Text* (New York: St. Martin's Press, 1983), 52.

Fig. 4.1 Happy family. The Doctor with his UNIT colleagues of the early 1970s. *Doctor Who* (classic series), "Invasion of the Dinosaurs", season 11, serial 71; British Broadcasting Corporation, 1974

contested.[21] Either way, Lambert's criticism raises the question of *which* establishment the Doctor joined. Significantly, it appears to be not so much the British establishment but a newly emerging internationalised one, embodied in the show by UNIT. When we first encounter UNIT in "The Invasion" (1968), Brigadier Alastair Lethbridge-Stewart, its commanding officer, describes it as an independent intelligence group, which does not actually arrest people but merely investigates. UNIT, we are told in "Spearhead from Space" (1970), deals with the odd, the unexplained, anything on Earth or even beyond. Yet it soon becomes

[21]James Chapman is surely correct to observe that the Doctor's relationship with the establishment is constantly problematised and that he is often in conflict with both military and civilian authorities. Chapman, *Inside the TARDIS*, 81.

apparent that UNIT is not merely an investigation team but a military force, indeed a small army with notoriously expendable troops.

Figure 4.1 shows the Doctor nestled within his UNIT "family": Sergeant Benton, Captain Yates, companion Sarah Jane Smith and the Brigadier. This image, from "Invasion of the Dinosaurs" (1974), presents two poles of authority: the Brigadier, pointing at his map, and the Doctor, picking up the phone. Observe that the UNIT officers are all men: UNIT in the 1970s was depicted as almost exclusively male. In response, Sarah Jane's attire is rather masculine too. The UNIT officers wear uniforms which do not seem readily distinguishable from classic British uniforms, which might lead us to suspect that inventing UNIT merely represented a softer way of introducing a military element than invoking the national army.

Yet the programme's commitment to internationalism was more far-reaching than the rather British-style uniforms of the UNIT soldiers would suggest. UNIT's very existence presupposes that Britain has voluntarily limited its sovereignty in the highly sensitive sphere of internal coercive military activity, and has provided a legal framework to legitimise the establishment of a United Nations force within the national territory. Its status within *Doctor Who*'s Britain represents a rude bifurcation between the *Who*niverse and real life. Most of Britain's politicians have been content to shed their discretion over significant aspects of economic policy but have shown rather less willingness to hive off to a supranational forum decisions regarding military involvement. This was reflected in the Common Foreign and Security Policy of the European Union, which relies wholly on international co-operation so that if an EU Member State wishes to retain its own policy on any particular aspect of foreign policy (supporting or opposing the invasion of Iraq, for instance), it cannot be overruled by the other Member States through majority voting. On the other hand, despite their distaste for internationalising the military function, British leaders have shown no hesitation in permitting the forces of another country, the United States of America, to maintain military bases on British territory. Thus, the presence of non-national forces is not without precedent. Replacing American bases with a UNIT base can be seen as *Doctor Who* softening the realities of the Cold War, substituting a more acceptable international engagement for Britain's partial abdication of foreign and defence policy to another state.

The viewer's first encounter with UNIT in "The Invasion" (1968) places UNIT in a favourable light in comparison to British establishment figures. It is not UNIT but the Brigadier's superior in the British Ministry of Defence, Major General Rutlidge, who succumbs to the hypnotic influence of Tobias Vaughan, the tycoon who is in league with the Cybermen. A squeaky-clean, fresh-faced supranational body is thus contrasted to a corrupted national one. As the UNIT serials proliferate, this theme becomes pervasive. For the most part, UNIT derring-do is counterposed to British governmental buffoonery. In "Spearhead from Space" (1970), General Scobie, a British army officer, comes to grief because of his vanity in allowing a Madame Tussaud's waxwork to be made of himself. In "The Ambassadors of Death" (1970), the villain turns out not to be the aliens but rather a British military officer, the deranged General Carrington, Head of Britain's Space Security Department. "Ambassadors" also features a British civil servant, Sir James Quinlan, who is duped by Carrington into believing he will garner the kudos of being the first person to make contact with an alien species, whereas Carrington's real intention is to kill the aliens. In "The Claws of Axos" (1971) a British civil servant, Mr. Chinn, is a pompous, dangerous yet comical figure, his own minister evidently rating him a fool. Mr. Walker in "The Sea Devils" (1972) is a belligerent Parliamentary Private Secretary preoccupied with his meals who sanctions war with the Sea Devils. The depiction of Walker is arguably more sinister than that of Chinn for being played less comically. In the same serial, George Trenchard, buffoonish governor of the prison holding the Master, the Doctor's arch-enemy, is easily fooled by the Master. It should be noted that the British figures of fun all appear to be upper class—as well as white and male—though so too is the Brigadier.

One serial in the early 1970s actually treats us to a Cabinet meeting. This is "The Green Death" (1973), in which Cabinet proceedings are (unrealistically) interrupted so that the Minister for Ecology can take a call from the Brigadier regarding UNIT's investigation of Global Chemicals. The pair quarrel about the interpretation of a measure called the Enabling Act, presumably the British statute giving UNIT its jurisdiction within national territory. In any event, the argument is resolved by the Prime Minister, whose name is Jeremy, which suggests that the then leader of the Liberal Party, Jeremy Thorpe, had somehow made it to Downing Street. The Prime Minister takes the phone and insists that the Minister's interpretation must carry the day. The premier gets his way in spite of the Brigadier's assertion that he answers to Geneva. In so doing, the Prime Minister effectively vetoes the Brigadier's investigation into a corporation whose polluting activities have generated deadly giant maggots. The tension between international rules and national implementing measures is readily apparent. Here the national authorities prevail; they decide in favour of a private company, and their decision is disastrous. Thus, the story paints national decision-making as the chief guarantor of the commercial freedom of private enterprise, regardless of the public interest.

The show's hostility towards British political figures is further emphasised by the way in which the Doctor's verbal attacks on these characters often take the form of criticising their nationalism. He chides Chinn for wanting "England for the English"; he slates Walker for his "extremely insular point of view"; he attributes Trenchard's blunder in trusting the Master to his patriotism. The suggestion that suspicion of other countries is actually insane is inherent in General Carrington's xenophobic assumption that a foreign power is participating in the alien invasion that he is seeking to thwart.

The virulence of *Doctor Who*'s anti-British government stance is confirmed by the Doctor's startling unfairness towards Mr. Brownrose, a minor character in "Terror of the Autons" (1971). Brownrose is a British civil servant who comes to UNIT to report a series of unexplained deaths. Yet, before he has even had time to impart this information to the Brigadier, he is the victim of unmerited rudeness on the part of the Doctor. Subsequently, the Doctor refers to him as "that fool Brownrose", when we have actually been given no evidence at all of his folly. Unlike other portrayals of civil servants, the script does not make Brownrose a figure of fun nor a provider of light relief. The Doctor's kneejerk hostility towards him reflects the programme's reflex action against anyone representing national government.

The unfavourable stance towards British government officials may partly be explained by the erosion of belief in a public service ethos from the 1970s onwards. The controversy over the Crossman Diaries, one government minister's record of the 1964–1970 Labour government, laid to rest the idea of a civil service endlessly deferential to ministerial wishes and showed that civil servants would battle with ministers in the perceived interests of their departments.[22] Labour's virulence

[22] Richard Crossman, *The Diaries of a Cabinet Minister*, vols 1–3 (Worcester and London: Trinity Press, 1975–1977).

against civil servants is confirmed by the memoirs of Marcia Williams, the political secretary to the then Prime Minister Harold Wilson, who maintained that "in the offices of Whitehall and in the clubs of Pall Mall lies immense power. The electorate believes that on Polling Day it is getting a chance to change history. The reality is that in many cases the power remains with the civil servants who are permanently ensconced in Whitehall, rather than with the politicians who come and go at elections."[23] At the other end of the political spectrum, as the 1970s progressed, Hayek's denial of a public service ethos and his emphasis on the self-interested motives of the civil service gathered momentum, and was eventually reflected in the BBC comedy series *Yes Minister* (1980–1984) Denigration of civil servants and the insistence that they did not have the public interest truly at heart meant that they could safely be replaced by political advisers and private companies.

Linked to these unfavourable portrayals of national officials are the frequent power struggles between national law and United Nations law which emerge in the stories. As one might expect, the exact power relationship between UNIT and national armed forces remains vague and ambiguous in the series. Since national sovereignty has been compromised in such a sensitive area, demarcation disputes between UK law and UN law are bound to be fiercely contested. Britain is a dualist state in that international law and national law are treated as forming two separate systems.[24] This means much will depend on the UK legislation authorising UNIT activity, and on the interpretation of that legislation. Unsurprisingly, therefore, *Doctor Who* in the early 1970s featured multiple conflicts over whether national or international forces have authority on British territory. We have General Scobie and the Brigadier in "Spearhead from Space" (1970) tussling over whether the factory making the Autons is off-limits to UNIT soldiers. We have Mr. Chinn in "The Claws of Axos" (1971) having UNIT's staff arrested and placed under armed guard under an Emergency Powers Act, only for Chinn to be countermanded once the Brigadier has sent an urgent communication to UNIT headquarters in Geneva. We have General Carrington in "The

[23] Marcia Williams, *Inside Number 10* (London: New English Library, 1972), 274.

[24] See the cases of *Mortensen v Peters* (1906) SLT 227, and *Cheney v Conn* [1968] 1 All ER 779.

Ambassadors of Death" (1970) arresting the Brigadier and the rest of UNIT to stop them rescuing the Doctor.

"Invasion of the Dinosaurs" (1974) portrays British establishmentarian figures—a general, a government minister and a top scientist—as traitors to Britain and to the world. They intend to shift Earth back in time to a period before humankind evolved, allowing an elite to establish a new form of human existence. Though not stated explicitly, their New Earth will be not only an ecologically pure but also a racially pure world of white, middle- and upper-class Britons, since neither ethnic nor national diversity is apparent in the choice of the surviving elite, and there do not appear to be any working-class people among the elect. The New Earth movement has corrupted a member of UNIT, Captain Mike Yates. There is a profoundly symbolic moment when Yates points his gun at the Brigadier just at the point when the Brigadier is telephoning UNIT headquarters in Geneva. The scene therefore counterposes the insanity of nationally based figures to the rationality of international institutions. Significantly, Yates is portrayed as misguided not malevolent, having *irrationally* deserted the international fold.

By contrast to the litany of British government buffoons and villains, the Brigadier emerges as an idealised globalised Briton. Whilst Kim Newman's assessment is that the warm relationship between the Brigadier and the Doctor cools considerably once the latter is exiled on Earth,[25] James Chapman is perhaps closer to the mark in describing the relationship as being edgy at first before developing into a firm friendship.[26] Paradoxically, he can be seen as embodying Britain itself, combining as he does his plummy English accent with Scottish ethnicity, the latter being revealed in "Terror of the Zygons" (1975). For the Brigadier, globalisation does not mean abandoning Britishness but redefining it, maintaining national identity without being tied to the British government. Taking his orders from Geneva does not serve to make the Brigadier less British: rather, the best Briton is an internationalising one. Indeed, his halo only slips when he acts at the national behest, notably the blowing-up of the Silurians at the instruction of the British Ministry of Defence in "Doctor Who and the Silurians" (1970).

[25] Newman, *Doctor Who*, 67.

[26] Chapman, *Inside the TARDIS*, 81.

As the 1970s wore on, however, supranational efforts were starting to lose their lustre. EEC membership was not dramatically improving the British economy and eventually spending cuts advocated by the International Monetary Fund (IMF) served to spark industrial unrest. Proselytising zeal for all things international no longer seemed so progressive. This was lightly reflected in *Doctor Who* in the mid-1970s by a loosening of ties with UNIT, the organisation only featuring in a handful of serials. Moreover, in those stories which did involve UNIT some of the key themes that had come to characterise UNIT-orientated adventures disappear. Above all, there is no denigration of the British state. UNIT stories no longer counterposed the United Nations to the British authorities. Indeed, UNIT could easily be mistaken for part of the British army. For example, in "Terror of the Zygons" (1975), it is not the United Nations Secretary-General who telephones the Brigadier but the (female) British Prime Minister, presumably Mrs. Thatcher: the Brigadier assures her that he will be "resolute". Furthermore, UNIT's and the Doctor's opponents are no longer in cahoots with the British state. For instance, in "Robot" (1974–1975) their enemies are a clique of scientists working for an independent research centre and involved in the fascistic Scientific Reform Society. In "The Seeds of Doom" (1976), the villain Harrison Chase is in league not with a government minister or civil servant but with an embittered official of the World Ecology Bureau, presumably an international organisation.[27] All in all, it seemed that the "international good, national bad" stance had fizzled out. No doubt this reflected misgivings as to whether international endeavour would prove a beacon of progress. The United Nations had shown itself impotent to prevent the bloodshed of the Vietnam War. The EEC was going through a period of internal stagnation with little to indicate that it would be a force for egalitarianism. In 1976 the IMF pressed the 1974–1979 Labour government to make substantial cuts in public spending, arguably leading to the industrial action (the so-called "Winter of Discontent") which saw Labour thrown out of office in favour of a protracted period of Conservative rule under the premiership of Margaret Thatcher. In fact, Britain's engagement with the IMF

[27] Similarly "The Android Invasion" (1975) and "Battlefield" (1989) do not really implicate the British state or its officials.

had been unnecessary: as the then Chancellor of the Exchequer Denis Healey later conceded: “in practice … we could have done without the IMF loan if we—and the world—had known the real facts at the time. But in 1976 our forecasts were far too pessimistic”.[28] Thus, Labour’s surrender of economic policy to a supranational organisation turned out to be not a necessity but a choice based on a false premise.

Let us now contrast UNIT in the classic series with UNIT in the new series. In new *Who*, the treatment of UNIT is very different, and suggests a serious deterioration in the legitimacy of international organisations. UNIT may still defend the human race, but its reputation is no longer untarnished. Negative images abound. Cumulatively, these serve to make UNIT look very different from the benign organisation viewers once knew and loved. UNIT now stands for “Unified Intelligence Taskforce”, a more opaque and unaccountable body than its predecessor. The United Nations had at the time suffered blows to its legitimacy by being split on the matter of the Iraq invasion and by its inability to resolve the Iraq issue through peaceful means. Distancing UNIT from the United Nations at this time therefore served to make UNIT look stronger. Its uniform of black with red berets seems more alien to British eyes than the familiar khaki of classic *Doctor Who*, and when the Doctor says that the UNIT of yesteryear seemed more homespun, he might mean that UNIT originally was not only less flash but also less foreign. The Americanisation of UNIT—its emphasis on “Homeworld security”, and companion Donna Noble’s observation in “The Sontaran Stratagem” (2008) that its activities smack of Guantanamo Bay—further alienates the organisation from the viewer. Subsequent adventures serve to reinforce this portrayal.

Furthermore, UNIT seems over-mighty. For example, in “The Sound of Drums”/“Last of the Time Lords” (2007) the United States President is able to invoke United Nations law to threaten to depose the British Prime Minister, a threat which would presumably be enforced by UNIT forces. Again, in “The Stolen Earth”/“Journey’s End” (2008), it transpires that UNIT is in control of the Osterhagen Key, a chain of twenty-five nuclear warheads placed beneath the Earth’s crust which UNIT will detonate if humanity’s fate is so without hope that self-destruction becomes the only option. Thus, UNIT holds the power of

[28] Denis Healey, *The Time of My Life* (London: Penguin, 1990), 433.

life and death over the entire planet. For good measure, UNIT controls the gargantuan sky-ship the *Valiant*, which again suggests that the low-key force of the Brigadier's day has been entirely transformed into an over-powerful militia. In "The Sontaran Stratagem"/"The Poison Sky" (2008), UNIT is portrayed as a coercive force whose gun-toting methods have to be defended by former companion Martha Jones against the Doctor's criticism. And strikingly, in "The Stolen Earth", UNIT's New York HQ prominently and repeatedly features the Stars and Stripes, a none-too-subtle hint at American domination of the organisation. There are unpleasant UNIT soldiers (Private Harris in "The Sontaran Strategem" (2008), Colonel Karim in "Death of the Doctor", a 2010 episode of the *Doctor Who* spin-off *The Sarah Jane Adventures*) as well as pleasant ones. Even in stories where UNIT has only a cameo role, as in "The Bells of Saint John's" (2013), its strong-arm, visceral image dominates even its fleeting appearance. This forms a stark contrast from the ordinary blokes in military uniform of classic *Who*'s UNIT stories.

When Steven Moffat became showrunner, it seemed as though there might be a restoration of UNIT's reputation. Notably, we learn in "The Power of Three" (2012) that Brigadier Lethbridge-Stewart's daughter, Kate Stewart, has taken the helm within the organisation (dropping her full surname in order to avoid being promoted on nepotistic grounds). Whilst Kate is a sympathetic character and putting her in charge of UNIT could have heralded a nostalgic return to the good old internationalist UNIT of the 1970s, in fact the organisation nonetheless never quite recovers its esteem. Its legitimacy is repeatedly compromised in ways that resonate with the UN's peacemaking failures and with Western aggression in Iraq and elsewhere. Its shortcomings under Kate's leadership include her own willingness to blow up London in order to stop an arsenal of weapons falling into the hands of the alien Zygons ("The Day of the Doctor (2013)), UNIT's subsequent undue enthusiasm to bomb rebel Zygons ("The Zygon Invasion" (2015)) and the organisation's invisibility in an episode which features the killing of the UN Secretary-General ("The Pyramid at the End of the World" (2017)).[29]

[29] During Moffat's stewardship of the programme, the Brigadier himself dies of natural causes only for his corpse to be transformed into a Cyberman in "Death in Heaven" (2014). In Cyberman form, however, he not only saves Kate's life but sacrifices himself in order to help destroy a cloud which would have turned all of humanity into Cybermen. His ending thereby rounds off the Brigadier's narrative with a course of action that benefits humanity as a whole, reinforcing his character as an internationalist Briton.

In post-2005 *Doctor Who*, faith in UNIT is replaced to a significant extent by an emphasis on British organisations and figures—Torchwood, Harriet Jones, Liz 10, Winston Churchill. Contrasting UNIT with Torchwood is particularly enlightening since Torchwood is the organisation that replaces UNIT in some of the stories, and which is also a rival to UNIT. Believing that Great Britain has enemies beyond imagination from which it must be defended, Queen Victoria creates Torchwood at the end of "Tooth and Claw" (2006). Whether the Queen would have had power to do so under the royal prerogative is controversial.[30] The organisation's first substantive appearance in contemporary times, in "Army of Ghosts"/"Doomsday" (2006), feels satirical. Torchwood's leader, Yvonne Hartman, envisages a second British Empire and a return to imperial measurements. Yet, remarkably, Hartman manages to retain her allegiance to sovereign and nation despite being converted into a Cyberman.

The organisation Torchwood shifts from villain to hero in the *Doctor Who* spin-off *Torchwood* (2006–2011). Under the leadership of Captain Jack Harkness, Torchwood seemingly loses its imperialist dimension and battles heroically to save the world from aliens who emerge from a rift in time and space located around Cardiff. The tension between Torchwood and UNIT is sketched in one such episode. In "Fragments" (2008), Toshiko Sato (Tosh) who later becomes a member of staff of Torchwood Cardiff, is abducted by UNIT. She is told: "This is a UNIT facility. Your rights as a citizen have been taken away." Later, she is informed that UNIT intends to keep her indefinitely. Indefinite detention would have had particular resonance during this period, because of the controversy over the Belmarsh detainees, suspected terrorists imprisoned indefinitely without trial in Belmarsh prison in South East London, an

[30]Substantial royal influence in politics declined after the 1840s but did not vanish until the end of the century. See Stanley Chrimes, *English Constitutional History*, 2nd ed. (Oxford: Oxford University Press, 1953), 183. Bagehot insisted that the rights of constitutional monarchs were to advise, encourage and warn (though these rights could be exercised in such a way as to make royal power considerable). See Walter Bagehot, *The English Constitution* (Oxford: Oxford University Press, 2009), Chap. 3. Dicey, writing in 1885, emphasised the way in which the royal prerogative augmented *ministerial* power vis-à-vis Parliament. See Albert Venn Dicey, *Introduction to the Study of the Law of the Constitution* (London: Macmillan, 1962), 465. Perhaps the Queen would have been more likely to have influenced the relevant minister to establish an organisation such as Torchwood, rather than having done so herself.

arrangement eventually declared contrary to human rights by the British courts.[31] "Fragments" thereby destroys at a stroke the overwhelmingly favourable image that UNIT enjoyed under the sway of Brigadier Lethbridge-Stewart.

As the new series developed, UNIT was sidelined in favour of greater reliance on national figures. These included Harriet Jones (a British Prime Minister), Liz 10 (a British sovereign) and Winston Churchill. Harriet Jones emerges as a compassionate backbench MP in "Aliens of London" (2005), and has become Prime Minister in "The Christmas Invasion" (2005). As premier, she has made a noticeable difference to her country. Harriet Jones' ideology seems to combine a redistributive economic policy—this is "Britain's golden age", where working-class people like Rose's mother Jackie feel discernibly better off—with robust nationalism. In her prime ministerial broadcast, Jones is flanked with Union Jacks and a photograph of the Queen, a more nationalistic background than that encountered in any real-life broadcast. With her fierce rejection of American interference, the unifying ideal is that of Britain as an *independent* political nation. Despite her merits, the Doctor machinates to have Jones deposed after she orders missiles to be fired on a retreating alien spaceship. The notion of destroying a retreating ship is plainly intended to recall Mrs. Thatcher's sinking of the *General Belgrano* during the Falklands War. Yet the Doctor's coup against Jones backfires spectacularly. His arch-enemy the Master comes to power and becomes the British Prime Minister in the political space created by Jones' fall. Her reputation is substantially restored by her heroic final appearance in "The Stolen Earth"/"Journey's End" (2008).

The patriotic theme continues in "The Beast Below" (2010), where British independence has been secured by the populace leaving Earth on Starship UK (minus the Scots who insisted on a spaceship of their own). It transpires that Starship UK is in fact a police state with bogus democracy; this story will be considered in depth in Chap. 7. For present purposes, we need only observe that in the end the nation state proves to be reformable, thanks to Amy's (more than the Doctor's)

[31] See Adam Tomkins, "Parliament, Human Rights and Anti-terrorism", in *The Legal Protection of Human Rights: Sceptical Essays*, eds. Tom Campbell, Keith Ewing and Adam Tomkins (Oxford: Oxford University Press, 2011).

intervention.[32] The enigmatic Liz 10 turns out to be Queen Elizabeth X, the country's mixed-heritage, über-cool sovereign. Whatever the merits or demerits of Liz 10's decision-making in the story, one should have regard for the importance of the constitutional monarch as a *symbol*: the identification of being British with being mixed-race is a powerful one. This linking of Britishness with mixed ethnicity is further emphasised by the street scenes which combine an ethnically diverse citizenry with walkways bedecked with Union Jacks. Emphasis on Britain's multi-ethnic nature serves to undermine the progressive rationale for supranational governance.

More generally throughout new *Who*, the Union Jack appears as a pervasive theme in a way which would have been taboo in the late 1960s and early 1970s, when its use would actually have had fascist overtones. Britain's flag features prominently in "The Empty Child" (2005), "The Christmas Invasion" (2005), "Fear Her" (2006), "The Beast Below" (2010), "Victory of the Daleks" (2010) and "Thin Ice" (2017) among others. So frequently does the national flag appear in *Doctor Who* that its treatment may correspond to Michael Billig's idea of banal nationalism, whereby it is the flag hanging unnoticed on the public building, the image of the nation which is not even consciously registered, that is particularly significant in building a sense of national identity. The programme's constant use of the Union Jack is on all fours with Billig's theory of flagging, in that its appearance on *Doctor Who* has become so commonplace as to provide a continuous "flagging", or reminding, of nationhood.[33]

Moreover, in stark contrast to the UNIT heyday, in new *Who*, British officialdom is not always to be depicted unfavourably: quite the opposite. Consider the sympathetic portrayal of Mr. Llewellyn, Harriet Jones' adviser, who sacrifices himself in "The Christmas Invasion" (2005), and that of Professor Edwin Bracewell, top scientist to the Churchill government in "Victory of the Daleks" (2010). Neither of these heroic Britons is English; they are Welsh and Scottish respectively, each reflecting the origins of the *Doctor Who* showrunner of the day.

[32] On Amy's role see Chap. 3. See also Piers D. Britton, *TARDISbound: Navigating the Universes of Doctor Who* (London: I.B. Tauris, 2011), 206–210.

[33] Michael Billig, *Banal Nationalism* (London: Sage Publication, 1995), 8–9.

Doctor Who's "patriotic turn" was belatedly reflected on the British political scene by a growing hostility towards supranational governance among sections of the public. Some demanded an end to Britain's EU membership by supporting the United Kingdom Independence Party (UKIP) at elections, prompting the party's victories in the Clacton and Rochester by-elections in 2014. Others were concerned at international big business taking over the National Heath Service by dint of the Transatlantic Trade and Investment Partnership (TTIP). The mood in favour of greater independence culminated in the "Leave" vote in the 2016 referendum on European Union membership. It is easy to see the 2013 *Doctor Who* Christmas Special, "The Time of the Doctor", as celebrating the possibility of Britain's splendid isolation. In this adventure, the Doctor settles down to defend a nostalgic, cut-off town on a planet sealed off from hostile forces by a none-too-effective force-field.

"Praise the Company!": Globalisation by Corporation

We now turn our attention to perhaps the most important part of my argument: the role of transnational companies in *Doctor Who*. The evolution of these companies is inextricably linked to globalisation. Indeed, private enterprise has fashioned globalisation's very design. Even in its early stages, globalisation led to a significant advance in the position of transnational companies in relation to the state. In their strengthened position, companies have been empowered to press politicians for further intensifications of globalisation—in the form of binding supranational law—to the benefit of their commercial interests. These changes can be properly considered constitutional, since they comprise durable restrictions on the legislative freedom of the nation states. Since most politicians, certainly over the last thirty years, have given pride of place to the concerns of business, companies could rest assured that the global constitution would be changed in their favour, often in accordance with companies' own proposals.[34]

[34]Wayne Sandholtz and John Zysman, "1992: Recasting the European Bargain", *World Politics*, 42 (1989): 95. Sandholtz and Zysman argue that the content of the first major revision of the European Community Treaties (the "Single European Act" of the mid-1980s) was substantially influenced by the demands of lobbyists for transnational corporations such as the Kangaroo Group.

Significantly, the earliest years of the programme were characterised by an absence of corporation-bashing. The state, not private companies, was seen as the problem. Thus, in the second *Doctor Who* adventure set on contemporary Earth, "The War Machines" (1966), the Doctor and companion Dodo encounter a renegade computer built by the state in the newly constructed Post Office Tower. "The War Machines" was preceded by "The Savages" (1966), a story which featured an exploitative state on another planet, with no hint of corporate organisation. Nowadays, such stories would almost certainly centre around private companies. They were, however, written in the wake of the 1940s nadir of private enterprise, when government and parliament agreed to the nationalisation of public services where it felt that private ownership was failing the test of service to the nation. This "national service" test—rather than assuming that what was good for companies was good for the country—focused on the economic and social interests of the broad mass of the British people. On this basis, gas, electricity, coal and rail were taken out of private hands and the National Health Service was established as a taxation-funded service free at the point of need. Only gradually did private companies recover their position and legitimacy, such as to merit being the focus of science fiction as a perceived threat. The first serial to feature corporate power was "The Invasion" in 1968, where magnate Tobias Vaughan deploys the power of his company, International Electromatics, to help the Cybermen conquer Earth. Thereafter, stories which make private companies the villain of the piece come thick and fast. They include "Colony in Space" (1971), "The Green Death" (1973), "The Sun Makers" (1977), "The Power of Kroll" (1978) and "The Caves of Androzani" (1984). Even the Daleks become entrepreneurs, buying up an intergalactic funeral home in "Revelation of the Daleks" (1985).

The rise of the transnational corporation had already started in earnest by the 1970s. Economist Stuart Holland argued that the emergence of multinational companies constituted a fundamental change in the structure of capitalism, whereby power was now concentrated in the hands of a miniscule class of enormously powerful top managers.[35] This globalisation, he contended, rendered ineffective the traditional Keynesian means of governmental control of the economy. The position of these

[35] Stuart Holland, *The Socialist Challenge* (London: Quartet, 1975).

corporations was subsequently strengthened by the creation of supranational laws that essentially bestowed upon companies fundamental human rights of free trade—the free movement of capital, the right of direct foreign investment, the free movement of services and goods. World and regional trade regimes, including the European single market and World Trade Organization (WTO), were thereby fashioned for the benefit of these corporations, which played an essential role in determining their very design.[36] Thus, globalised law promoted the further empowerment and enlargement of the transnational corporations.

Is it possible to have "benign" globalisation without corporate takeover? In the late 1960s and early 1970s, *Doctor Who*'s authors clearly thought so. They assumed that internationalisation would liberate people rather than companies. Yet there are compelling arguments to the effect that globalisation is not politically neutral but is always likely to be subject to corporate capture. This is because democracy, the organic counterbalance to capitalism, is only achievable in a much-weakened form at the international level.[37] Thus, national constitutions have always offered limited scope for changing the balance of power in favour of corporations, since considerations of democratic legitimacy would make it difficult to entrench pro-corporation policies. By contrast, supranational constraints offered greater scope, binding political communities for the future whilst masquerading as the "low politics" of technical trade deals.[38] To be sure, there are scholars who believe that globalisation can be detached from corporate capture. Some believe, for instance, that a World Social Organisation could be created which would act as counterweight to free trade groups such as the WTO.[39] But this would mean transferring the right to balance social concerns against the interests of business—traditionally, the very essence of government—to an unaccountable organisation.[40] Another group of scholars believe that state-based politics could and should be replaced by a politics of global civil

[36] See e.g. Nicol, *Constitutional Protection of Capitalism*, 97–99.

[37] On globalisation's sidelining of democracy, see Joseph Stiglitz, *Globalization and its Discontents* (London: Penguin, 2002), Chap. 3.

[38] Nicol, *Constitutional Protection of Capitalism*, 153.

[39] Noreena Hertz, *The Silent Takeover: Global Capitalism and the Death of Democracy* (London: Arrow, 2001).

[40] Carol Harlow, *Accountability in the European Union* (Oxford: Oxford University Press, 2002), 144.

society—they advocate a rejection of national politics and political parties and instead urge a focus on the transnational social movements which bubble up "from below".[41] But these nebulous ideas are also unconvincing. Insofar as an effective democracy exists at all in relation to corporations, it does so at the national and sub-national level.[42] Furthermore, it can convincingly be argued that the actions of transnational movements have a limited effect on politics, tending to leave control in the hands of the powerful. Thus, globalisation remains corporation-dominated. On this reading, the rejection of state-based politics is a cover for unwillingness to engage in political contestation per se.[43]

The inseparability of globalisation and corporate power was reflected in the post-2005 revival of *Doctor Who*, which witnessed an intensification of criticism of private enterprise. The sinister side of big business looms large in "The End of the World" (2005), "Dalek" (2005), "The Long Game" (2005), "The Lazarus Experiment" (2007), "Planet of the Ood" (2008), "The Rebel Flesh"/"The Almost People" (2011) "The Bells of Saint John" (2013), "Time Heist" (2014), "Sleep No More" (2015), "The Return of Doctor Mysterio" (2016) and "Oxygen" (2017). Kim Newman observes that new *Who*'s writers had created "a surprising number of villains whose schemes boil down to unethical profit-chasing".[44] But why should it be surprising? By 2005, Britain had experienced quarter of a century of neoliberalism, the variety of capitalism ushered in by Margaret Thatcher and Ronald Reagan. This had effected a profound change in Britain as a country. In the early 1970s, the trade unions had been considered one of the great estates of the land, governments routinely according the Trades Union Congress as much importance as the Confederation of British Industry, or at least purporting to do so.[45] But the 1980s onwards witnessed the decline and

[41] Iris Marion Young, *Global Challenges* (London: Polity, 2007), 141; Michael Hardt and Antonio Negri, *Multitude: War and Democracy in the Age of Empire* (London: Penguin, 2005), 237–38.

[42] Leo Panitch, "Rethinking the Role of the State", in *Globalisation: Critical Reflections*, ed. James Mittelman (Boulder, CO: Lynne Rienner, 1997), 109.

[43] David Chandler, "Deconstructing Sovereignty: Constructing Global Society", in *Politics without Sovereignty*, eds. Christopher Bickerton, Philip Cunliffe and Alexander Gourevitch (London: UCL Press, 2007).

[44] Newman, *Doctor Who*, 116–117.

[45] The importance of the trade unions was reflected in television coverage during the 1970s and 1980s: the televising of the week-long Trades Union Congress in its entirety (and at a time when there were only three or four television channels) was an annual ritual.

fall of British unions to the point of irrelevance in some sectors. This went hand-in-hand with the cultivation of an ethos of entrepreneurship, with more and more aspects of British life becoming dominated by private enterprise. In 1988, the Labour Party published a policy review that moved them further towards the new Thatcherite orthodoxy. Thereafter, all main parties tended to favour private-sector solutions and were content to tolerate a growing wealth gap. This propagandising effort was reinforced by television programmes such as *The Apprentice* (2005–present) and *Dragon's Den* (2005–present), which promoted a vision of the British as competitive entrepreneurs. *Doctor Who*'s sustained onslaught on the corporation therefore forms a striking contrast to the cult of the entrepreneur promoted by successive governments of both parties as well as by the mass media.

As a matter of theory, neoliberalism is commonly seen as involving "an almost doctrinal fixation on free trade, privatization and small government, and unfettered markets to foster economic growth and wealth generation, as opposed to government action and collective bargaining to promote social and economic equality".[46] But David Harvey has argued that, in fact, there are actually *two* competing interpretations of neoliberalism.[47] *The first conception of neoliberalism relates to this utopian theoretical design*, based on "a model of societal relations in which government regulation and social welfare guarantees are reduced in order to foster the play of market forces driven by private enterprises pursuing profit maximization".[48] However, the *second interpretation of neoliberalism* put forward by Harvey is very different: it perceives neoliberalism as *a political project designed to restore the power of economic elites*. In other words, neoliberalism is essentially about the promotion of *class* interests, not about adherence to free market *principles*. Harvey argues that, in practice, it is this second conception of neoliberalism that is dominant. Indeed, he contends

[46] Gregory Shaffer, *Defending Interests: Public–Private Partnerships in WTO Litigation* (Washington, DC: Brookings Institution Press, 2003), 5. The ideological founding father of this grand design of neoliberalism was Friedrich von Hayek, whose books *The Road to Serfdom* and *The Constitution of Liberty* ran against the grain of socialist and social democratic thinking in the 1940s and 1950s.

[47] David Harvey, *A Brief History of Neoliberalism* (Oxford: Oxford University Press, 2005), 19.

[48] Shaffer, *Defending Interests*, 4.

that the theoretical utopianism of neoliberal argument works primarily as a system of justification and legitimation for whatever needs to be done to achieve the goal of restoring the power of an economic elite, even if such actions conflict diametrically with neoliberal orthodoxy. On this reading, the dominant role of private enterprise is not some natural, organic order of things. Rather, it is an order which has been created and maintained as a matter of public policy and governmental power. As Antinori has observed, "laissez-faire is a myth, and the question is never between government regulation of the economy and no government regulation: the question is always what type of government regulation".[49] Accordingly, neoliberal theory is essentially window-dressing: it provides the indispensable normative basis for neoliberalism, the arguments of principle based on liberty and democracy which seek to justify the system of private enterprise. But when neoliberal principles clash with the need to sustain elite power, then such principles are either abandoned or are twisted out of all recognition.

The banking crisis of 2008 may be interpreted as confirming that neoliberalism's real focus is class interests, not free market principles. The bank bailouts were needed in order to maintain the economic elite in the wake of its calamitous "herding" in favour of investment in subprime mortgages. Free market principles would have insisted upon making firms pay the price of their business mistakes. Instead, governments opted for economic state intervention in the form of lavish state aid and temporary nationalisation, the very sort of state intervention reviled by those neoliberals who insist upon utopian principles of competition.[50]

In view of the compelling argument that neoliberalism is based not on "small government" principles but on class interests, it is significant that in new *Who* some stories presuppose inseparability or interweaving between state and private corporation. The state supports and sustains private enterprise by paying for private-sector services rather than maintaining large public-sector employment. In "The Rebel Flesh"/"The

[49] Michael Antinori, "Does *Lochner* Live in Luxembourg? An Analysis of the Property Rights Jurisprudence of the European Court of Justice", *Fordham International Law Journal*, 18 (1994–1995): 1778, 1838, 1846.

[50] Nicol, *Constitutional Protection of Capitalism*, 4, 124.

Almost People" (2011), the company Morpeth Jetsan is linked to the Ministry of Defence. It is this company that creates the "gangers", living facsimiles of human beings who ultimately rebel against the human race in response to being treated as highly disposable. In "The Bells of Saint John" (2013), a private company is linked to its seemingly sole "client", the Great Intelligence, a form of *alien* governance. It abducts humans by uploading them to the internet. These links between business and "state" reflect the post-Thatcher mode of government of public–private partnerships, outsourcing and the private finance initiative.

The virtual elimination of the trade unions from public life is a further reminder of neoliberalism's fundamentally *class* nature. On this reading, neoliberalism's only real "principle" is to widen the gap between the rich and the remainder of society. *Doctor Who*'s recognition of this reality is reflected by making the Doctor's first companion in the new show—Rose Tyler—a working-class young woman, whereas the vast majority of earlier companions were middle class. Rose's modest origins are often counterposed to the vast wealth of those she meets on her adventures with the Doctor, the issue of the class divide being emphasised in episodes such as "The Unquiet Dead" (2005), "The End of the World" (2005) and "New Earth" (2006). Rose's class status is equally highlighted by other characters perceiving her as coming from a higher social class than is the case. Thus, Rose has to give permission to Raffalo the plumber to speak in "The End of the World", and Gwyneth the maid in "The Unquiet Dead" also treats Rose as a social superior. At the other end of the spectrum, leaders and managers are often aliens (the Slitheen pose as the British government in "Aliens of London" (2005), the editor-in-chief turns out to be the monstrous Jagrafess in "The Long Game" (2005)). The ruling elite are not just a class apart but a species apart. As noted earlier, it is also significant that several subsequent companions, whilst not overtly working class, are nonetheless in less secure and lower-status employment compared to classic-series predecessors, reflecting the new hard-nosed capitalism's effects on the economic security of the middle class.

It is only to be expected, therefore, that post-2005 *Doctor Who* accords prominence to corporations. Doing so reflects the resilience of neoliberalism after Mrs. Thatcher left office. Simon Jenkins, in his book *Thatcher and Sons*, convincingly argues that the Major, Blair and Brown governments, far from relinquishing Thatcherism, actually pursued it with revolutionary zeal.[51] Indeed, the change of term from "Thatcherism" to "neoliberalism" shows how Mrs. Thatcher's system of beliefs outlived her. Part of this collective ideology has been the cult of the entrepreneur and the corresponding disparagement of the public-sector ethos, or the outright denial of its existence. New *Who*'s corporation-bashing can be seen as a response to this political tidal wave.

"He's Not My Boss": Globalisation and the United States of America

The United States of America is a globalising power par excellence. American administrations played a significant role in creating the United Nations. They helped prompt the shift in international law away from an emphasis on ideological neutrality and the equality of states and in favour of greater intervention in the name of human rights—the controversial "obligation to protect". They built the North Atlantic Treaty Organization (NATO), encouraged the establishment of the European Economic Community and transformed the General Agreement on Tariffs and Trade (GATT) into the World Trade Organization (WTO). This promotion of globalised solutions was carefully conceived to advance American domination and business interests.[52]

In an essay entitled "TARDIS at the OK Corral", Nicholas J. Cull considers the relationship between *Doctor Who* and the USA.[53] He argues that post-war Britain's relationship with the United States is a pervasive theme both in terms of the rise and fall of the classic series and as a regular passing reference within its storyline. He contends that the triumph of brains over brawn in the Doctor's adventures signifies the British belief that we can keep muddling through without John Wayne-style gunpower. At the same time, however, Cull observes that the sparring with American culture is at a low level in classic-series *Doctor Who*, the scripts taking only occasional pot-shots at the United States. This is borne out by the sporadic and muted criticism of Americans in the serials "The Tenth Planet" (1966) and "The Tomb of the Cybermen" (1967).

---

[51] Simon Jenkins, *Thatcher and Sons* (London: Penguin Books, 2006).

[52] Peter Gowan, *The Global Gamble* (London: Verso, 1999).

[53] Nicholas J. Cull, "TARDIS at the OK Corral: *Doctor Who* and the USA", in *British Science Fiction Television: A Hitchhiker's Guide*, eds. John Cook and Peter Wright (London: I.B. Tauris, 2006).

Cull mentions that, particularly in the early 1970s, the series seemed comfortable with an American presence, as exemplified by the American character, Bill Filer, in "The Claws of Axos" (1971).

Let us consider Bill Filer a little more closely. It is revealing that the classic series' most sympathetic one-off portrayal of an American coincided with the period in which the programme was most enamoured of internationalisation. In "The Claws of Axos", Bill Filer has been sent from Washington to deal with the Doctor's arch-enemy, the Master. He helps the Doctor and Jo Grant, and is cast in a heroic light. Overall, his portrayal in the story is highly sympathetic. He befriends Jo and comes up against the dead hand of British officialdom, being warned by the civil service buffoon Mr. Chinn that the visit from the Axons is an internal British matter and that he (Filer) will be arrested if he does not leave immediately. Instead of leaving he enmeshes himself in the fight against the Axons, which combined with his favourable depiction suggests that American intervention is justified. As the story unfolds, the Axons create a bogus Filer and the two Filers fight each other, a special effect which serves to accentuate the American's humanity.

This strikingly sympathetic depiction of an American character would actually fit well with the series' belief in internationalisation in the early 1970s, bearing in mind the pivotal American role in fashioning the post-war international order. In the 1970s, the Cold War made it easier to retain a favourable view of the USA's role since the alternative was the dictatorship of the Soviet Union. Furthermore, the country's reputation for capitalistic "rugged individualism" was somewhat softened by the Great Society era of President Lyndon B. Johnson, in which reforms such as Medicare and Medicaid revealed limits to even American faith in private enterprise. Moreover, the "special relationship" between Britain and the USA at that time was not characterised by any sense of British subservience. The Johnson, Nixon, Ford and Carter presidencies witnessed significant irritants and tensions in the "special relationship", intensified by personality clashes between British and American leaders. For example, Harold Wilson, whilst voicing strong support to President Johnson on Vietnam, was determined to keep British forces out of that war.[54] Indeed, it has been argued that by the close of the 1960s, much of the economic

[54] John Dumbrell, *A Special Relationship: Anglo-American Relations from the Cold War to Iraq*, 2nd ed. (Basingstoke: Palgrave Macmillan, 2006), 75, 82.

and defence framework within which Anglo-American co-operation had flourished since the Second World War had disappeared.[55]

From the 1980s onwards, however, under the presidency of Ronald Reagan and his successors, the USA embraced an increasingly hardline neoliberal policy. In particular it advanced a more extreme form of globalisation on terms favourable to its corporations, through the intensification of global free trade, the free movement of capital and foreign direct investment. Thus, American statesmen were pivotal in refashioning the low-profile GATT into the more powerful and wider-reaching WTO. The United States arguably also deployed foreign policy and military intervention to pursue those same global business aims. These changes did not alter the perspective of Britain's politicians, who were more fervent than ever in support of the "special relationship", since they now shared neoliberal ambitions with their American counterparts. But the same changes allowed a far freer rein in the new show to *Doctor Who*'s traditional deep nationalistic concerns about rampant American capitalism.[56] For good measure, the disintegration of the Soviet Union reduced the need to cling to the USA for fear of something worse. The highly controversial interventions in Afghanistan and Iraq were examples of British foreign policy being uncomfortably close to American foreign policy.

So new-series *Doctor Who* took a more stridently anti-American line than the classic series, certainly in respect of American leaders and the American domination of Britain. Two stories can be used to illustrate this stance. The first is "The Christmas Invasion" (2006), in which Britain has a seemingly ideal prime minister in the form of Harriet Jones, who had emerged as a heroine as a backbench MP in the earlier story "Aliens of London/World War Three" (2005). The mild ribbing of the USA in the classic series is replaced with a fierce hostility in new *Who*. Faced with an alien invasion, Harriet Jones instructs the president of the United States to be informed: "in these exact words, he is not my boss and he's certainly not turning it into a war". She is the architect of "Britain's golden age" of egalitarian prosperity—her economic policy also suggests a robust departure from the so-called "Washington

[55] Alan Dobson, *Anglo-American Relations in the Twentieth Century: Of Friendship, Conflict and the Rise and Decline of Superpowers* (London: Routledge, 1995), 138.

[56] Selznick, "Rebooting and Rebranding", 73.

consensus" of privatisation and entrepreneurial freedom. Rose Tyler's mother Jackie Tyler praises Jones, mentioning that her income has gone up, and it is remarkable to British ears to hear any member of the public, let alone a working-class person, saying something nice about any government. Wilf Mott, grandfather of companion Donna Noble, also seems proud to have voted for her.

In the second story to feature Americans—"The Sound of Drums/ Last of the Time Lords" (2007)—aggression towards American leaders assumes a positively murderous form. In this story, the Doctor's success in having Harriet Jones removed from office has seriously backfired, with the appalling consequence of ultimately bringing the Doctor's arch-enemy, renegade Time Lord the Master, to power. Styling himself as Harold Saxon, the Master's party wins the election and he becomes prime minister. He then orchestrates "first contact" with an alien race, the Toclafane. The Master then proceeds to behave so outrageously as to bring about a threat from American President-elect Winters to remove him from office under United Nations authority. The American President thereby seizes control of the meeting with the Toclafane. "So America is completely in charge?" quizzes the Master. "Since Britain elected an ass, yes!" retorts the President. When the meeting with the Toclafane takes place, the Master announces: "I'm taking control, Uncle Sam. Kill him!" at which point the Toclafane obliterate the President. Significantly, there is nothing to make the viewer feel sympathy for the President, not even in the face of a monster like the Master. For good measure, at the end of the adventure, the Doctor puts everything right by reversing the flow of time, but thereby obliterates everything *after* the assassination of President Winters—an astonishingly anti-American finale. The idea raised by the story that United Nations law could be deployed to effect regime change in a democratic country is an allegorical extension of its existing potential to do so in respect of less democratic regimes.

Superficially, the plot of "The Impossible Astronaut"/"Day of the Moon" (2011) places Americans in a kindlier light. Insofar as the treatment of the Americans is more favourable, it is surely because the story concerns friendly co-operation between sovereign states rather than American domination of Britain. The adventure takes place on American soil, and far from involving an American intrusion into British sovereignty it concerns the "British" (the Doctor and companions River Song, Amy Pond and Rory Williams) meddling in events on American territory. Indeed, the plot implies British intellectual domination over the Americans. James Chapman has argued that the favourable depiction of President Richard M. Nixon can be seen as making amends for the assassination of President-elect Winters in the earlier story.[57] On the other hand, though, "The Impossible Astronaut"/"Day of the Moon" may be read as a particularly extreme manifestation of the programme's perennial tendency to counterpose British brainpower with American firepower ("Do you think you can just shoot me?" asks the Doctor; "They're Americans!" quips River. At a later stage, the FBI purport to shoot the Doctor's companions and transport them in body bags). The Doctor and his companions pose as a special detachment from Scotland Yard and help the hopeless but trigger-happy Americans battle against a species known as the Silence, who rule the world through hypnotic suggestion. The Scotland Yard cover-story reinforces the Doctor's claim to Britishness, if any such boost were needed. Although President Nixon is indeed portrayed reasonably sympathetically, the only useful thing he does is to let the Doctor and his companions get on with it. The only unequivocally positive portrayal of an American is that of ex-FBI agent Canton Everett Delaware III, who can be seen as a countercultural figure owing to his desire to marry a black man. By the time of "The Return of Doctor Mysterio" (2016), after eight years of Barack Obama's moderate presidency, *Doctor Who* seemed to return to gently ribbing the difference between Americans and the British. The Doctor accidentally transforms an American boy into a classic all-American superhero possessing the usual superhuman powers and strength. Whilst the superhero and his "love-interest" journalist employer are sympathetically drawn, the episode nonetheless satirises American superheroes and the story's ending contrasts *par excellence* the Doctor's "British" brainpower with American brawn.

As if further evidence were needed, American domination also features in the *Doctor Who* spin-off *Torchwood*. As Martin Griffin and Rosanne Welch have observed, in the five-part serial "Torchwood: Children of Earth" (2009), "General Pearce—a mere three-star general, it would appear—commands the operations of the British government in a brusque manner designed to conjure up a long cultural and political history of the post-World War Two era and the irreversible decline of

[57] Chapman, *Inside the TARDIS*, 287–288.

British power and global force projection to the advantage of the United States".[58]

These stories should not imply that new-series *Doctor Who* portrays all Americans in an unfavourable light. Rather, the show tends to concentrate its fire on the country's ruling and business elite. In "Dalek" (2005), for example, an American magnate almost destroys the world by reviving the (supposedly) sole remaining Dalek. The story suggests that this tycoon has the American presidency in his gift, thereby emphasising business domination of American politics. By contrast, in "Daleks in Manhattan"/"Evolution of the Daleks" (2007), the working-class Americans of the Great Depression are portrayed sympathetically, and small-town Americans of the nineteenth century are similarly depicted in "A Town Called Mercy" (2012). But occasionally, the show cannot resist a generalised pot-shot at Americans, as is apparent in "The Angels take Manhattan" (2012) where no American character is depicted favourably.

Significantly, the new series' critical approach towards the USA is remarkably at odds with the stance of Britain's political elite, who have nurtured a "special relationship" with the USA from 1945 onwards. The "special relationship" endured the major tensions of the late 1960s and early 1970s and was fully re-established by dint of the close friendship between Margaret Thatcher and Ronald Reagan in the 1980s.[59] United with their American colleagues by the common adherence to neoliberalism, Thatcher's successors continued to pursue this close relationship, despite the controversial nature of some American-inspired military interventions and the growing sense of American corporate domination. *Doctor Who* was reborn in the wake of the contentious adventures in Iraq and Afghanistan, and the show displays the gulf between politicians and public as to the appropriate degree of closeness to the USA. The "special relationship" had been born of a British strategy to benefit from American power, yet the end of the Cold War deprived it of much of its rationale.[60] There was resentment at British subservience to the USA, and feelings of a neo-imperialist tinge to the USA's relationship

[58] Martin Griffin and Rosanne Welch, "Crisis of Authority/Authoring Crisis: Decision and Power in Torchwood—'Children of Earth'", in *Torchwood Declassified: Investigating Mainstream Cult Television*, ed. Rebecca Williams (London: I.B. Tauris, 2013), 108.

[59] Dumbrell, *A Special Relationship*, 5.

[60] Dumbrell, *A Special Relationship*, 5, 13.

to Britain.[61] This was exacerbated by Tony Blair's premiership. Peter Riddell suggests that Blair had an underlying strategy of going along with whatever President George W. Bush wanted, on the grounds that by remaining steadfast as American's closest ally, the USA in return would "listen back" on issues such as the Middle East peace process, global warming and engagement with the United Nations. Riddell concludes that this policy of "hug them close" ultimately delivered few benefits but much pain for Blair himself. The bargain was lopsided; the British Prime Minister earned the right to be consulted by the American President, but that influence was seldom crucial.[62] New-series *Doctor Who* has sought to correct this imbalance by imagining a more independent Britain and a relationship with the USA which is more one between equals.

Conclusion: Globalisation's Fall from Grace

Doctor Who of the late 1960s and early 1970s tended towards a "national bad/international good" depiction of politics. The programme's striking commitment to internationalisation during that period manifested itself in a remarkably strong kneejerk hostility towards national governance. British institutions were seen as irretrievably blighted and had to be replaced by supranational ones. The international realm would somehow rescue humanity from the corrupted nation state.

But as Tom Nairn has observed, what passed for internationalism in the 1970s was in truth an abstract and narrow creed, resting on a pious and selective acceptance of certain establishment ideas.[63] By contrast, new-series *Doctor Who* has tended to reject the assumption of inherent badness of the national scene and inherent goodness of the supranational. To be sure, contemporary *Doctor Who* does not exchange one fantasy for another: it has no illusions about British politics, and recognises its tendency to become corrupted. At the same time, perhaps it sees

[61] Dumbrell, *A Special Relationship*, 2–3.

[62] Peter Riddell, *Hug Them Close: Blair, Clinton, Bush and the "Special Relationship"* (London: Politicos, 2004), 15.

[63] Tom Nairn, "*Break-Up*: Twenty-Five Years On", in *Scotland in Theory: Reflections on Culture and Literature*, eds. Eleanor Bell and Gavin Millar (Amsterdam and New York: Rodopi, 2004), 17–34.

the less remote governance of the nation state as being more susceptible to redemption. The occasional nostalgic lapse aside, the contemporary show has displayed a striking scepticism towards globalised regimes. This scepticism serves to highlight the compromised nature of international law after the adventures in Afghanistan and Iraq, the far more contested nature of European integration than was originally anticipated and the fear of corporate and American neoliberal capture of global institutions. Above all, new-series *Doctor Who* has had to be mindful of the extent to which globalisation has turned out to be a Trojan horse for corporate power. This rejection of remote rule and unaccountability also underpins the modern show's pervasive British patriotism, which highlights that, though national governance can sometimes lead to equally egregious authoritarian outcomes, its relative nearness to the people lends it a greater chance of being corrected. These insights are valuable in bringing to the fore the remarkable isolation of our own hyper-globalising political elite vis-à-vis the country they purport to represent.

Bibliography

Antinori, Michael. "Does Lochner Live in Luxembourg? An Analysis of the Property Rights Jurisprudence of the European Court of Justice." *Fordham International Law Journal* 18 (1994–1995): 1778–1794.

Bagehot, Walter. *The English Constitution*. Oxford: Oxford University Press, 2009.

Billig, Michael. *Banal Nationalism*. London: Sage Publications, 1995.

Britton, Piers and Simon Barker. *Reading Between Designs: Visual Imagery and the Generation of Meaning in The Avengers, The Prisoner and Doctor Who*. Austin: University of Texas Press, 2003.

Britton, Piers D. *TARDISbound: Navigating the Universes of Doctor Who*. London: I.B. Tauris, 2011.

Chandler, David. "Deconstructing Sovereignty: Constructing Global Society." In *Politics without Sovereignty: A Critique of Contemporary International Relations*, edited by Christopher Bickerton, Philip Cunliffe and Alexander Gourevitch. London: UCL Press, 2007.

Chapman, James. *Inside the TARDIS: The Worlds of Doctor Who*, 2nd ed. London: I.B. Tauris, 2013.

Chrimes, Stanley. *English Constitutional History*. Oxford: Oxford University Press, 1953.

Crossman, Richard. *The Diaries of a Cabinet Minister*, vols 1–3. Worcester and London: Trinity Press, 1975–1977.

Cull, Nicholas. "TARDIS at the OK Corral: *Doctor Who* and the USA." In *British Science Fiction Television: A Hitchhiker's Guide*, edited by John Cook and Peter Wright, 52–70. London: I.B. Tauris, 2006.

Dicey, Albert Venn. *Introduction to the Study of the Law of the Constitution*. London: Macmillan, 1962.

Dobson, Alan P. *Anglo-American Relations in the Twentieth Century: Of Friendship, Conflict and the Rise and Decline of Superpowers*. London: Routledge, 1995.

Dumbrell, John. *A Special Relationship: Anglo-American Relations from the Cold War to Iraq*, 2nd ed. Basingstoke: Palgrave Macmillan, 2006.

Gilbert, Jeremy. "What Kind of Thing is Neoliberalism?" In *Neoliberal Culture*, edited by Jeremy Gilbert, 10–32. London: Lawrence & Wishart, 2016.

Gowan, Peter. *The Global Gamble*. London: Verso, 1999.

Griffin, Martin and Rosanne Welch. "Crisis of Authority/Authoring Crisis: Decision and Power in *Torchwood*—'Children of Earth'." In *Torchwood Declassified: Investigating Mainstream Cult Television*, edited by Rebecca Williams, 104–119. London: I.B. Tauris, 2013.

Hardt, Michael and Antonio Negri. *Multitude: War and Democracy in the Age of Empire*. London: Penguin, 2005.

Harlow, Carol. *Accountability in the European Union*. Oxford: Oxford University Press, 2002.

Harvey, David. *A Brief History of Neoliberalism*. Oxford: Oxford University Press, 2005.

Hayek, Friedrich von. *The Constitution of Liberty*. Chicago: University of Chicago Press, 1960.

Hayek, Friedrich von. *The Road to Serfdom*. London: Ark Paperbacks, 1986.

Healey, Denis. *The Time of My Life*. London: Penguin, 1990.

Henkin, Louis. *How Nations Behave: Law and Foreign Policy*. New York: Columbia University Press, 1979.

Hertz, Noreena. *The Silent Takeover: Global Capitalism and the Death of Democracy*. London: Arrow, 2001.

Holland, Stuart. *The Socialist Challenge*. London: Quartet, 1975.

Jackson, John. *The World Trade Organization: Constitution and Jurisprudence*. London: Pinter, 1998.

Jenkins, Simon. *Thatcher and Sons*. London: Penguin Books, 2006.

Kennedy, David. "The Move to Institutions." *Cardozo Law Review* 8 (1986–1987): 841–988.

McCormack, Una. "He's Not the Messiah: Undermining Political and Religious Authority in New *Doctor Who*." In *The Unsilent Library: Essays on the Russell T. Davies Era of the new Doctor Who*, edited by Simon Bradshaw, Anthony Keen and Graham Sleight, 45–62. London: The Science Fiction Foundation, 2011.

McKee, Alan. "Is *Doctor Who* political?" *European Journal of Cultural Studies* vii(2) (2004): 201–217.

Menéndez, Agustin José. "Whose Justice? Which Europe?" In *Europe's Justice Deficit*, edited by Grainne de Búrca, Dimitry Kochenov and Andrew Williams, 137–152. Oxford: Hart, 2014.

Nairn, Tom. "*Break-Up*: Twenty-Five Years On." In *Scotland in Theory: Reflections on Culture and Literature*, edited by Eleanor Bell and Gavin Millar, 17–33. Amsterdam and New York: Rodopi, 2004.

Newman, Kim. *Doctor Who*. London: BFI TV Classics, 2005.

Nicol, Danny. *EC Membership and the Judicialisation of British Politics*. Oxford: Oxford University Press, 2001.

Nicol, Danny. *The Constitutional Protection of Capitalism*. Oxford: Hart, 2010.

Panitch, Leo. "Rethinking the Role of the State." In *Globalisation: Critical Reflections*, edited by James Mittelman, 83–113. Boulder, CO: Lynne Rienner, 1997.

Riddell, Peter. *Hug Them Close: Blair, Clinton, Bush and the "Special Relationship"*. London: Politicos, 2004.

Sandholtz, Wayne and John Zysman. "1992: Recasting the European Bargain." *World Politics* 42 (1989): 95–128.

Selznick, Barbara. "Rebooting and Rebranding: the Changing Brands of *Doctor Who*'s Britishness." In *Ruminations, Peregrinations and Regenerations: A Critical Approach to Doctor Who*, edited by Chris Hansen, 68–84. Newcastle-upon-Tyne: Cambridge Scholars Publishing, 2010.

Shaffer, Gregory. *Defending Interests: Public–Private Partnerships in WTO Litigation*. Washington, DC: Brookings Institution Press, 2003.

Tomkins, Adam, "Parliament, Human Rights and Anti-Terrorism." In *The Legal Protection of Human Rights: Sceptical Essays*, edited by Tom Campbell, Keith Ewing and Adam Tomkins, 13–39. Oxford: Oxford University Press, 2011.

Tulloch, John and Manuel Alvarado. *Doctor Who: The Unfolding Text*. New York: St. Martin's Press, 1983.

Vibert, Frank. *The Rise of the Unelected: Democracy and the New Separation of Powers*. Cambridge: Cambridge University Press, 2007.

Williams, Marcia. *Inside Number 10*. London: New English Library, 1972.

Wood, Tat. "The Empire of the Senses: Narrative Form and Point-of-View in *Doctor Who*." In *Time and Relative Dissertations in Space: Critical Perspectives on Doctor Who*, edited by David Butler, 89–107. Manchester: Manchester University Press, 2007.

Young, Iris Marion. *Global Challenges*. London: Polity, 2007.

CHAPTER 5

Is the Doctor a War Criminal?

The Doctor is the star of *Doctor Who*. It is natural and understandable that he be considered the programme's hero.[1] At the same time, interference lies at the heart of the show. The Doctor's status as hero derives from his nature as "incorrigible meddler". His interventions give *Doctor Who* its bite. Yet the moral worth and lawfulness of the Doctor's interference is constantly in question. These doubts in turn reflect concerns about Britain's contemporary role in the world. This chapter puts forward four arguments in this regard.

First, it contends that whilst, for the most part, the Doctor may fight for good and against evil, the merits of his interventions have from the outset been highly questionable on a number of occasions. As the show's hero, it apparently remains the BBC's expectation that viewers should love him.[2] This matches the Doctor's self-image: in "The Doctor Falls" (2017) he explains to two incarnations of his arch-enemy the Master that

[1]The Doctor was played by male actors from 1963 to 2017 until the casting of Jodie Whittaker: I therefore refer to him in the masculine.

[2]"Yes we all love the Doctor" proclaims the BBC's *Official Miscellany* (Cavan Scott and Mark Wright, *Doctor Who: The Official Miscellany* (London: BBC Books, 2013), 175). John Fiske observes that "the BBC is specific and precise about the morality of the show—the Doctor must be clearly good, and his adversaries clearly bad." (John Fiske, "Dr Who: Ideology and the Reading of a Popular Narrative Text", *Australian Journal of Screen Theory*, 14 (1983): 69–100.) Companion Clara Oswald, in "The Time of the Doctor" (2013), conveys the official line when she tells the Time Lords that if they love the Doctor, *and they should*, then they must save him. They do so, by granting him a new cycle of regenerations.

D. Nicol, *Doctor Who: A British Alien?*,
https://doi.org/10.1007/978-3-319-65834-6_5

he does what he does because it is kind, and he urges them to "just be kind" too. This vision of the Doctor, coupled with the forgiving nature of the programme's fans,[3] lends the Doctor a veneer of virtue which cannot be sustained by each and every *Doctor Who* story. Viewed with a greater sense of detachment, his judgement is fallible, and sometimes goes badly awry often due to the very "dislike for the unlike" which he would criticise in others, and which the programme itself has ostensibly condemned since the phrase was uttered by companion Ian Chesterton in the 1963–1964 serial "The Daleks". This chapter rejects the familiar argument attributing the Doctor's loss of his moral compass to the absence of companions. Quite the opposite: the predominantly human or humanoid nature of his companions serves to accentuate the Doctor's unjustifiable siding against "the unlike".

Secondly, the chapter highlights a distinction between classic and new *Who*. In the classic series, the innate controversy of the Doctor's encounters is often (but not always) glossed over. In the post-2005 reboot, the rightfulness of the Doctor's actions is challenged far more frequently. This may not happen on every occasion, and criticism may be terse, but nonetheless, criticism is made. As Gabriel McKee has observed, the Doctor's actions are no longer held up as singularly heroic, but viewers are led to question his choices rather than assume that he is doing the right thing.[4] It is to the show's credit that it thereby engages viewers more actively in considering the rights and wrongs of the Doctor's deeds.

Thirdly, bearing in mind *Doctor Who*'s allegorical nature, it will be argued that, in the new series, the trend towards greater criticism of the Doctor's actions serves as a metaphor for qualms over Britain's foreign policy in the twenty-first century—in particular the country's interference in Iraq and Afghanistan. This will be offered as

---

[3] Joshua Vasquez, "The Moral Economy of *Doctor Who*: Forgiving Fans and the Objects of Their Devotion", in *Ruminations, Peregrinations and Regenerations: A Critical Approach to Doctor Who*, ed. Chris Hansen (Newcastle-upon-Tyne: Cambridge Scholars Publishing, 2010).

[4] Gabriel McKee, "Pushing the Protest Button: *Doctor Who*'s Anti-authoritarian Ethic", in *Time and Relative Dimensions in Faith: Religion and Doctor Who*, eds. Andrew Crome and James McGrath (London: Darton, Longman and Todd, 2013), 22.

an explanation for the difference between classic and new *Who*. The Iraq and Afghanistan adventures were—and remain—highly controversial. The invasion of Iraq in particular represented a very important moment in British politics. It revealed a sharp division between the general public who were hostile to meddling, and their political leaders who were more easily convinced of the merits of intervention. In so doing, it highlighted the more general phenomenon of the gulf between the British people and their ruling elite, a theme explored in Chap. 7. Furthermore, the propensity of "interference" to backfire—rather a common occurrence when Britain intervenes in the affairs of other countries—is also repeatedly evidenced in new-series *Doctor Who* stories. The theme has particular resonance now that the country's engagement in Iraq has morphed into a seemingly permanent conflict against a section of the Islamic Arab world, presently in the form of the campaign against Islamic State/ISIS/Daesh. On this reading, *Doctor Who* prompts us to question Britain's role in the world.

Fourthly, from time to time, *Doctor Who* also poses the issue of whether, if the Doctor *is* acting wrongly, his actions should be considered criminal. In this regard, the programme raises vital questions concerning the appropriate frontiers of politics and law. Should blame for conflict be contested in the realm of politics or in the courtroom? Does shifting conflict to the judicial arena actually militate in favour of a more "just" outcome? Conversely, the realisation that in debating war and peace we are dealing with controversial, contestable issues, might actually compel us to question the very notion of war crimes. In raising this issue, *Doctor Who* tackles a question which has been shunned in British political discourse, where calls for leaders such as Tony Blair to be prosecuted for war crimes have not been matched by voices actually casting doubt on the entire war crimes concept.

In writing this chapter I am not arguing for a "goody two-shoes" Doctor. If he were to intervene only when the case for doing so was wholly incontestable, this would likely make for a dull programme. Rather, I am arguing for the contestability of the Doctor's actions to be fully acknowledged in the show, something which has already happened to some extent and which has added to *Doctor Who*'s allure. I would like the programme to recognise *all* instances of the Doctor's "dislike for the unlike" and to engage the viewer in debate, however terse, on all of them.

Court Lewis' Case for Interference

For some academic commentators, however, hero worship seems the order of the day. Thus, a more favourable assessment of the Doctor is put forward in an essay by Court Lewis entitled "Interference, the Doctor and the Good Life".[5] Lewis argues that the Doctor's interference teaches viewers how to live "the good life". The good life, Lewis contends, is one in which (a) one's rights are respected and (b) one in turn respects the rights of others. This means, as companion Rose Tyler puts it in "The Parting of the Ways" (2005), "you don't just let things happen. You make a stand. You say 'no'. You have the guts to do what is right when everyone else just runs away!" Lewis insists that the Doctor is kind even to his enemies and that the punishments he metes out to them are compassionate. Lewis philosophises that we are all entitled to our "natural preferables"—the things that are part of our lives simply by virtue of having been born—such as life and health. He advocates "the flourishing life" whereby one *balances* respecting others' rights to their preferables and having one's own rights to one's preferables respected. He believes that the Doctor undertakes this balancing exercise. Killing, maintains Lewis, is not something the Doctor does lightly. He contends that, for the Doctor, killing someone cannot be an easy thing to do: the Doctor tends to take the kinder option. Crucially, this means the Doctor is compassionate even towards his adversaries. The Doctor's interference, according to Lewis, is a manifestation of his compassion, selflessness and respect for the rights of others. The Doctor promotes the flourishing of all life in the universe, even when innocents are harmed. It will be readily apparent that Lewis' analysis is remarkably uncritical of the Doctor—ironic given that his essay is published in a volume subtitled *A Critical Approach to Doctor Who.*

Lewis then cites examples to prove his point, devoting particular attention to "Human Nature"/"The Family of Blood" (2007), but deploying more briefly "The Caves of Androzani" (1984), "Planet of the Spiders" (1974) and others. No attempt will be made here to contradict Lewis' conclusions that the Doctor is basically doing good in these

[5] Courtland Lewis, "Interference, the Doctor and the Good Life", in *Ruminations, Peregrinations and Regenerations: A Critical Approach to Doctor Who*, ed. Chris Hansen (Newcastle-upon-Tyne: Cambridge Scholars Publishing, 2010).

stories.[6] Rather, it will be argued that Lewis fails to appreciate that a war criminal who does a lot of good things is still a war criminal. Reeling off a list of the Doctor's good deeds will not therefore acquit the Doctor of unjustified interferences or even war crimes or genocide. Thus, Lewis appears not to realise that the onus on him is far more daunting than he seems to assume. For his argument to succeed, he must show that the Doctor's conduct is entirely bereft of instances of unjustifiable interference, a task which would require a review of *all* his adventures from the show's outset. To put it another way, Lewis needs to show complete consistency in the Doctor's compassion. By contrast, the onus on those taking a less rose-tinted view of the Doctor is far less burdensome, requiring only compelling evidence that the Doctor's adventures *include* some in which the Doctor's actions are highly questionable.

Ironically, the notion that a war criminal who does goodly deeds nonetheless remains a war criminal is heavily emphasised in the *Doctor Who* episode "A Town Called Mercy" (2012). Alien humanoid Kahler-Jex cites his philanthropic work in an American frontier town in order to excuse his past actions on another planet in turning members of his own species into deadly cyborgs. Jex accuses the Doctor of being bewildered by the paradox that he could be both the creator of killing machines, and the physician dedicating his life to serving the town. The Doctor retorts that Jex has simply chosen his own punishment for the atrocity he has committed, and that doing so does not constitute justice.

Oblivious to his methodological error, Lewis justifies his uncritical stance by a selective viewing of the Doctor's adventures. In so doing, perhaps in his zeal to furnish evidence of the Doctor's virtue, Lewis even mistells stories. He asserts, for example, that no-one dies in the episode "World War Three" (2005), in order to emphasise the Doctor's joy at everyone surviving. One wonders if Lewis is getting his *Doctor Who*

[6]Nonetheless, the attempt could be made. For instance, as regards "Human Nature"/"The Family of Blood", K. Jason Wardley observes that the Family of Blood's onscreen reaction to the punishment meted out by the Doctor sees them screaming and bound in thick metal chains which are pulled backwards, and that this forms a marked contrast to the Doctor, who watches coldly and unemotionally before walking away. It is rather difficult to share Lewis' view that this constitutes a compassionate response. K. Jason Wardley, "Divine and Human Nature: Incarnation and Kenosis in *Doctor Who*", in *Time and Relative Dimensions in Faith: Religion and Doctor Who*, eds. Andrew Crome and James McGrath (London: Darton, Longman and Todd, 2013).

stories mixed up, for at the end of "World War Three" all but one of the Slitheen family is wiped out.[7] It is curious that Lewis overlooks this fact, since the extermination of the Slitheen is heavily emphasised in the subsequent episode, "Boom Town" (2005), where we meet the sole survivor. The Slitheen's fate reveals a mentality, no matter how unconscious, whereby lives are accorded varied value. This is significant because it tallies with real-life experience: consider, for instance, the attention routinely devoted by British news media to an American gun rampage compared to the coverage accorded to an Iraqi market bombing. This differentiation is highly significant where first-world, Western powers such as Britain are accused of unjustifiable interferences in other countries. Decisions to intervene in third-world, non-white, non-Christian countries such as Afghanistan and Iraq—decisions involving the very balancing exercises which Lewis extols—are taken on the basis of a devaluation of the lives of "the unlike". In any event, Lewis' portrayal of the Doctor as wholly good is not particularly compelling: a more convincing account would need to be less flattering and more nuanced.

Yet Lewis is not alone. A similarly rosy view of the Doctor is presented by David Layton in his book *The Humanism of Doctor Who*. Layton praises the Doctor as the antithesis of the all-American "shoot first" hero, and claims that he conscientiously avoids violence and strives for co-operation.[8] The Doctor, he insists, represents the open-minded alternative to closed-minded nationalism.[9] It will be argued that, in fact, the Doctor's dislike of the unlike sets a limit to this vaunted open-mindedness. Similarly Matt Jones lauds the universal relevance of "the Doctor's strategies of non-violent resistance".[10] Bonnie Green and Chris Wilmott praise the Doctor for displaying a hesitancy to kill, and Laura Brekke argues that he represents "the best of empathy".[11] These authors appear

[7] Perhaps Lewis has confused "World War Three" with "The Doctor Dances" (2005).

[8] David Layton, *The Humanism of Doctor Who: A Critical Study in Science Fiction and Philosophy* (Jefferson, NC: McFarland, 2012), 20–24.

[9] Layton, *Humanism of Doctor Who*, 274.

[10] Matthew Jones, "Fluid Links: That's What I Like", *Doctor Who Magazine*, 238 (1996) Marvel Comics, London, 20, cited in Matt Hills, *Triumph of a Time Lord: Regenerating Doctor Who in the Twenty-First Century* (London: IB Tauris, 2010), 7.

[11] Bonnie Green and Chris Willmott, "The Cybermen as Human.2", in *New Dimensions of Doctor Who: Adventures in Space, Time and Television*, ed. Matt Hills (London: I.B.

to have swallowed hook, line and sinker the establishment line that the Doctor is, as the Master once put it, "so despicably good, so insufferably compassionate" ("The Deadly Assassin" (1976)).

Contestability of the Doctor's Actions: His Questionable Political Morality from the Outset

One argument of this chapter is that the Doctor's questionable political morality, far from being a recent phenomenon, has been a recurring feature of the show since its inception.[12] With this in mind, the argument proceeds by considering four stories from different points in the show's history in which the Doctor puts forwards militaristic solutions to situations of conflict without exhausting the possibilities for a more compassionate alternative. The criticism would be not so much that the Doctor fails to succeed in getting more compassionate compromises accepted, but rather that he does not attempt to do so in the first place. Too often, he fails point blank to put forward a solution which would accommodate both humans/humanoids and "the unlike". In so doing, he displays an unjustified favouritism for "the like", one which runs counter to his pretension that "it's part of a Time Lord's job to insist on justice for all species" ("The Masque of Mandragora" (1976)). Thus, for example, in "The Evil of the Daleks" (1967), in answer to Jamie's charge that he is callous, the Doctor says that he cares about human beings. In "The Power of Three" (2012), the Doctor states that humans and the planet Earth are precious to him and he will defend them with his dying breath. Yet why should an alien like the Doctor be so partisan in favour of our own kind, such as to skew his judgement? Might it be a case of humans and Gallifreyans resembling each other physically, a liking for the like? Against this backdrop, let us consider some instances where the Doctor's activities are, on a critical reading, difficult to justify.

Tauris, 2013); Laura Brekke, "Humany, Wumany: Humanity versus Human in *Doctor Who*", in *Time and Relative Dimensions in Faith: Religion and Doctor Who*, eds. Andrew Crome and James McGrath (London: Darton, Longman and Todd, 2013).

[12] See generally Alec Charles' characterisation of the Doctor as killer in Alec Charles, *Out of Time: The Deaths and Resurrections of Doctor Who* (Oxford: Peter Lang, 2015), 101–109.

The Doctor's Misdeeds #1: The Daleks (1963–4)

In the earliest *Doctor Who* stories, the Doctor was deliberately portrayed not as a hero but as a morally ambiguous character. Thus, the Doctor removes his granddaughter's schoolteachers Ian Chesterton and Barbara Wright from their own world and time, knowing that it is far from certain whether he will ever be able to return them ("An Unearthly Child" (1963)); he lies to them in order to compel them to undertake a risky visit to an alien city ("The Daleks" (1963–1964)), and he even threatens to expel them from the TARDIS ("The Edge of Destruction" (1964)). It seems appropriate to take an example such as "The Daleks" from this short-lived period, since it prompts a comparison: was the ostensibly kinder Doctor of subsequent years actually any more compassionate in his treatment of "unlike" species? "The Daleks" also merits attention because it is widely acknowledged that the Daleks serve as a metaphor for the Nazis.[13] Apropos of this, the Doctor's companion Ian Chesterton attributes the Daleks' hostility towards the humanoid Thals to a "dislike for the unlike"; the Daleks fear the Thals because they are different from them. "The Daleks", however, raises the intriguing issue of whether the Doctor himself, and indeed *Doctor Who* as a programme, has a dislike of the unlike. In this regard, Fig. 5.1 highlights the difference between the two species which we meet in the serial, the Thals and the Daleks. It is an image from the final throes of the war between the two races. We see two Thals manhandling two Daleks in the run-up to the final destruction of the Dalek race. We should note the depiction of *contrasts*: the humanoids' visceral struggle is so different from the pepperpot passivity of the Daleks. The grimacing face of the Thal facing the camera contrasts with the lack of faces of the Daleks. There is no doubt that the Thals are the species with whom viewers should identify. We should also observe that the Thals have the upper hand in physical combat: the early Daleks were literally a pushover compared to their new-*Who* equivalents.

"The Thals are no concern of ours" says the Doctor in episode 4, "We cannot jeopardise our lives to get involved in an affair which is none of our business." Thus "The Daleks" raises in striking form the issue of interference and non-interference. However, in assessing "The Daleks",

[13] Richard Scully, "*Doctor Who* and the Racial State: Fighting National Socialism Across Time and Space", and Alec Charles, "The Allegory of Allegory: Race, Racism and the Summer of 2011", both in *Doctor Who and Race*, ed. Lindy Orthia (Bristol: Intellect, 2013).

Fig. 5.1 Manhandling the unlike. Two Thals get physical with two Daleks. *Doctor Who* (classic series), "The Daleks", season 1, serial 2; British Broadcasting Corporation, 1963–1964

we need to be careful to deprive ourselves of the benefit of hindsight. We must clear our minds of the Daleks' subsequent (and frequent) designs for conquest of the universe and focus exclusively on the plot of this early adventure. This is because, significantly, in "The Daleks" the Daleks have no imperialistic intentions beyond their home planet of Skaro. They want their planet, and they want it free of the Thals, but they express no desire to invade other worlds. Indeed, the only character to moot the idea that the Daleks might travel in time and space is the Doctor himself, when he tries to bargain for his and granddaughter Susan's lives after having been recaptured by the Daleks.

In "The Daleks", the TARDIS materialises on a seemingly dead planet, later identified as Skaro. The Doctor, Susan, and Ian and Barbara make a cursory exploration of their surroundings and discover a city. Selfishly, the Doctor deceives his companions by insisting that an essential part of the TARDIS, its fluid link, has run out of mercury, which will need to be replenished if the TARDIS is to function, forcing them to investigate the city in search of mercury. There they encounter the Daleks—grotesque beings inhabiting metal shells—who imprison them. They learn that the Daleks have lived in their city, unable to leave it, for some five centuries since their war with the Thals. Following that, there has been no hostility between Daleks and Thals because they have been oblivious of each other's survival for centuries.

Meanwhile, the Thals have migrated towards the Dalek city following drought and famine. After the Daleks ambush the Thals and exterminate some of them, the Doctor and his companions manage to escape with the Thals, who are beautiful blond humanoids. Significantly, the Doctor and his companions come very close to non-intervention midway through the story: they are all set to re-enter the TARDIS and leave the Daleks and Thals to their fate. Only the discovery that the Daleks have confiscated the fluid link, immobilising the TARDIS, prompts the time travellers to turn the Thals into "a ready-made army" to fight the Daleks, the Doctor arguing that this is no time for morals and that it is just common sense to use the Thals to attack the Daleks. For their part, the Daleks think it is only logical that the time travellers would side with the Thals and attack the Daleks. They assume a "liking for the like", which is borne out. Ian is at least honest in remarking that the Thals would basically be fighting and dying for a fluid link.

It is therefore to regain the fluid link that the Doctor sides with the Thals against the Daleks. To this end, his companions persuade the Thals to relinquish their pacifism in order to fight. Thus, "The Daleks" can be seen as containing an anti-pacifist message, Ian remarking that "pacifism only works when everybody feels the same". Indeed, the story equates pacifism with cowardice. Notably, one of the Thals, Antodus, seems to want to abandon the war against the Daleks out of fear. Yet this slur serves to undermine rational argument. From the point of view of their own self-interest, the Thals' decision to go to war against the Daleks is based on rather thin justification. They have been the victims of an ambush in which some Thals (including their leader) died, but not many. They fear that the Daleks will find a way of existing outside their city, yet they are in no position to know whether doing so is an imminent Dalek priority. Therefore, their war against the Daleks can be seen as a form of pre-emptive defence. For his part, the Doctor presents himself as a war leader: "With me to lead them, the Thals are bound to succeed." No war aims are specified: presumably, then, the Thals' war aim is much the same as those as the Daleks in orchestrating the ambush—extermination. In any event, no lesser war aim is articulated.

Many of the most significant aspects of the plot only come to light well into the latter half of the story. In particular, the Daleks discover that they have become conditioned to radiation, and that the level of radiation on Skaro is falling. This means that the entire Dalek race is in danger. We witness in episode 5 the deaths of Daleks from the Thals' anti-radiation drugs. These deaths are poignant and gruelling to watch, provided one feels a similar compassion for Daleks as one would for humanoids. In this regard, the story perhaps relies on the viewer's lack of empathy with the Daleks, the viewer's own dislike for the unlike. For the Daleks, the anti-radiation drug is a poison and radiation is essential for their very survival. The explosion of another neutron bomb is therefore not in fact intended to eliminate the Thals but is rather an absolute necessity if the Daleks are not to die. They need radiation as the Thals need air.

It has been argued that the Daleks should be regarded as evil because Daleks lack empathy for other Daleks. Robin Bunce has contended that "the Thals are good because they love each other. The Daleks don't, and that's why they are evil."[14] But this argument is rather unconvincing. It is impossible to know that the Daleks are not upset by the deaths of those Daleks who have taken the Thals' anti-radiation drug. After all, Bunce's argument obliges us to presuppose that Thals and Daleks are predisposed to the same degree of emotional demonstrativeness; it makes no allowances for the emotional impact on the Daleks of their bunker mentality and it assumes the existence of an appropriate distribution of concern for the individual as against the collectivity. In any event, Bunce's underlying idea is questionable. Do we human beings love each other where no family or friendship ties exist? Is love for one's own species to be counterposed with non-love for the "Other"? Does love for members of one's own species actually matter that much? Above all, even if the Daleks do not conform to the criterion of sufficiently loving individual members of their own species, is this a good enough reason to exterminate them?

[14] Robin Bunce, "The *Evil* of the Daleks", in *Doctor Who and Philosophy: Bigger on the Inside*, eds. Courtland Lewis and Paula Smithka (Chicago and La Salle, IL: Open Court, 2010).

Either way, the Thals are wholly unaware of the Daleks' plan to explode their bomb. Indeed, the Doctor and Susan only discover the plan well after the war against the Daleks has begun. Thus, the Thals' decision to go to war against the Daleks is not the result of the Daleks' decision to make Skaro's atmosphere poisonous to the Thals. The Thals are equally oblivious to the Daleks subsequently abandoning the bomb idea on the grounds that it will take too long and instead opting to bombard the atmosphere with radiation from the Daleks' nuclear reactors. When he hears of this plan, the Doctor, in a fine display of humbug, denounces "this senseless evil killing" of the Thals, when in fact he has already planned the killing of the Daleks through war.

The idea that without radiation the Dalek race will die is one that undermines the Dalek-Nazi metaphor. Objectively, the German people would have soldiered on without *Lebensraum* and the Holocaust. But there is nothing in "The Daleks" to make us doubt the validity of the Daleks' assessment that without radiation the Daleks would indeed perish. The Daleks, therefore, must disseminate radiation or else commit collective suicide. On the face of it then, for both Daleks and Thals to survive is problematic. If we return to Courtland Lewis' claim that the Doctor is compassionate even to his opponents, there would have been a range of compassionate responses that the Doctor could have put forward in "The Daleks", which could have attempted to accommodate the interests of Daleks and Thals alike. The Daleks could have made part, not all, of Skaro radioactive; or they might have settled for living in a large radioactive dome; or, at a pinch, the Doctor might simply have bundled the Thals into the TARDIS and taken them to another habitable planet, allowing the Daleks to create an atmosphere conducive to their continued existence. No doubt such compromises would have been doomed to fail on the rock of Dalek intransigence, but we do not know this at the time; we only know it with the impermissible benefit of hindsight. Crucially, we establish for sure that the Daleks' sole interest in the Thals is in their total extermination only after the Thals have started their war against the Daleks.

Yet the Doctor proposes no compromise; he does not test the limits of the Daleks' bunker mentality. He does not, as David Layton claims, test whether the tyrant will relent.[15] Instead, he tells Ian Chesterton that

[15] David Layton, *Humanism of Doctor Who*, 311.

this is no time for morals and treats us to a good dose of warmongering. Thus, the Doctor gives us no higher normative aspiration than the destruction of the enemy. In this regard, the Thal leader's words at the conclusion of the story—"if only there'd been some other way"—ring true: the Doctor had done nothing to explore any other way.

The Doctor's Misdeeds #2: The Macra (1967)

The example of "The Daleks" might conceivably be dismissed as one of the earliest *Doctor Who* stories in which the Doctor's credentials as anti-hero were being established before his character "softened". It was perhaps from the mid-1960s to the early 1970s that the show presented the Doctor most unequivocally as a force for good. With the Cold War maturing into normality, perhaps this black-and-white view reflected confidence in the moral superiority of British liberalism in the face of both Soviet dictatorship and American bellicosity. Even if Britain were fading both economically and as a world power, the British still had right on their side.

Of the four examples of the Doctor's misdeeds cited here, "The Macra Terror" (1967) is the only story focusing on a human colony on another planet. Given *Doctor Who*'s frequent use of metaphor to comment upon Britain, it would seem that human colonialism symbolises British colonialism. Scholars have been critical of the show's treatment of colonialism, not least in the edited collection *Doctor Who and Race*.[16] In fact, whatever the inadequacies and inconsistencies, the programme at least consistently raises doubts, however limited sometimes, over Britain's colonising role. But "The Macra Terror" is an exception. Certainty, not doubt, imbues the Doctor's and eventually the colonists' treatment of the Macra. The Macra are the colonised who do not know their place.

In "The Macra Terror", the TARDIS materialises on a planet on which there has been a human colony for several centuries. The Doctor and companions Ben Jackson, Jamie McCrimmon and Polly discover that the colony practises "healthy happiness" and "hard work and happiness" and has the aura of a fun-loving holiday camp with ample singing and dancing. At the same time, however, the colony also seems to

[16] Lindy Orthia, ed., *Doctor Who and Race* (Bristol: Intellect, 2013).

have characteristics of a police state. This police state is designed to conceal the fact that the colony is being run not by its apparent leaders but by the Macra, giant crab-like beings, who exploit the humans for the gas they mine, gas on which the Macra depend. The Macra have lulled the colonists into believing that they are mining the gas for the benefit of the colony's industry and activity. Ostensibly, the colony is run by its Control Centre and its Controller, aptly referred to as "Control", who insists over the colony's tannoy that "Control must be believed and obeyed!" To this end, the colony's population are brainwashed in their sleep (a fate which befalls Ben), and are indoctrinated with the belief that "Control knows best". If (like one individual, Medok) they see and report the existence of the Macra, they are considered to have suffered hallucinations and are treated as disturbed. Such dissidents are consigned to hospital. Only as a last resort does a "shoot to kill" policy apply.

The viewer is kept ignorant of the Macra's history. With no suggestion that the Macra have travelled from another planet, they are quite probably the indigenous sentient species of the planet. We are not told otherwise, and the Doctor freely admits that he cannot tell when the Macra arrived in the first place. Indeed, he suggests that the Macra are likely to come from the planet's interior and that they find the atmosphere too inhospitable for life on the surface. Despite the likelihood that the Macra are indigenous, the Doctor nonetheless describes them in the language of illness: they are germs in the human body, parasites, a disease, the evil forces at the heart of the colony. Significantly, the Doctor's utterances echo those of Adolf Hitler, who variously denounced Jews as "parasites, plague, cancer, tumour, bacillus … and racial tuberculosis".[17] Medok condemns the Macra as "horrible things … creatures … infesting this camp at night". These various characterisations of the Macra all appeal to the viewer's dislike for the unlike. For their part, the Macra can hardly defend themselves, remaining silent throughout the serial.

[17] Kristine Larsen, "'They Hate Each Other's Chromosomes': Eugenics and the Shifting Racial Identity of the Daleks", in *Doctor Who and Race*, ed. Lindy Orthia (Bristol: Intellect, 2013).

It is clear that the Macra need the gas in order to stay alive; without it, they would perish. This fact is emphasised when the Macra flood one of the mines with gas not in order to kill Jamie, who happens to be there, but to rescue one of their own. Yet the story fails to tease out the implications of the Macra's imperative need for gas, which places them in a similar situation to that of the Daleks vis-à-vis radiation. The plot presupposes that the Macra are more technologically advanced than the humans, as well as more wily. But the Doctor does not rise to the challenge of concocting a solution which could somehow accommodate both the Macra's and the humans' divergent needs and make use of their different talents. Instead he machinates to secure the elimination of "the unlike".

It is evident that more general themes of the freedom of the individual and the passive acceptance of authority are at play in "The Macra Terror". The Doctor's companions are put through a process of deep-sleep adaptation, whereby a voice tells them: "You must obey orders. The leaders of the colony know what is best. You will be glad to obey. You will question nothing in the colony." Ben is successfully brainwashed, and asserts that the Doctor, Jamie and Polly should learn to obey; the Doctor, however, gives short shrift to such unquestioning uniformity: "Don't be obedient! Always make up your own mind!" Ultimately, Ben regains his ability to decide for himself, and significantly, having reclaimed his autonomy, it is he who creates an explosion which destroys the Macra. This morality tale is suspect: Ben uses his revived freedom of choice in order to destroy a species.

Must one annihilate one's oppressors? To be sure, the Macra exploit the humans, but is genocide appropriate? We do not know how many humans die in the "danger gangs" who extract gas for the Macra, but, in fact, only one human, Medok, actually dies during the course of the serial. Within the *Doctor Who* canon itself, the Doctor's treatment of the Macra contrasts unfavourably with that meted out to the Elders in "The Savages" (1966), a story written by the same author as "The Macra Terror", Ian Stuart Black. In "The Savages", one group of humanoids (the Elders) oppresses another group of humanoids (the Savages). The Doctor merely destroys the means of that oppression, and encourages companion Steven to remain with the Elders and Savages as their new leader in order to foster reconciliation. "The Savages" indicates rather clearly that the Macra would have had a different fate had they been humanoids. So much for the claim that the Doctor gives all sentient and intelligent species the same standard of treatment based on the rights that existing gives them.[18]

Comparing "The Macra Terror" to the real world, one could argue that, in a sense, humans in the Macra colony are actually better off than black people in apartheid-era South Africa (and of course those who enforced apartheid were subjected not to extermination but to a Truth and Reconciliation Commission). Unlike those who suffered under apartheid, in "The Macra Terror", the colonists are subjectively very happy due to mind control, even if their contentment may not be objectively justified. This is reflected in a particularly heavy irony: the identical nature of the beginning and end of the story. In both, the colony's majorettes strut their stuff to a catchy jingle, and this entertainment is enjoyed by the colony's members. This serves to indicate that, in one sense, little has changed in the colony, yet the script does not emphasise this irony, and viewers may well not pick up on it.

The Doctor's Misdeeds #3: The Vervoids (1986)

The particular irony of "Terror of the Vervoids" is that it is a story related by the Doctor in his own defence when he is put on trial for the second time by the Time Lords for interference in the affairs of other peoples and planets in episodes 9–12 of "Trial of a Time Lord" (1986). Yet it constitutes one of the most clear-cut instances of the Doctor committing genocide. The Doctor and companion Mel Bush answer a mayday call sent by someone on the space liner Hyperion III. On board, they encounter among the passengers Professor Sarah Laskey and her colleagues Doland and Bruchner. It transpires that these three scientists are secretly transporting a sentient plant species, the Vervoids, to the planet Earth. We discover that, unbeknown to his colleagues, Doland is in cahoots with a consortium intending to exploit the Vervoids as slave labour once this consignment reaches Earth: the Vervoids will run Earth's factories at practically no cost since they only require sunlight and water. When challenged by the Doctor that this would constitute slave labour, Doland retorts that the most enduring and spectacular empire, Rome, was based on slave labour.

---

[18] Layton, *Humanism of Doctor Who*, 309.

For their part, the Vervoids, once awakened from their dormant state, set about killing "animalkind" on Hyperion III, since they regard all animals as their enemy. To this end, they heap all the human corpses into a pile. When Mel expresses the view that this is obscene, the Doctor responds: "Not to a Vervoid!" To the Doctor, it is a matter of perspective: in her cottage at home, Mel would have put weeds on the compost heap. By the same token, explains the Doctor, the Vervoids are merely obeying instinct, a compulsive following of the lifecycle. At the same time, the Doctor considers that since all animalkind consume plant life, co-existence between Vervoids and humans is impossible. He therefore uses a substance called vynesium, which generates intense light and carbon dioxide, in order to accelerate the Vervoids' lifecycle by aping spring, summer and autumn. In one fell swoop, by dint of this ingenious plan, the Doctor destroys every Vervoid. He justifies this destruction by contending that if even a single leaf had survived and fallen on fertile soil, a Vervoid would have grown, threatening human life on Earth. Against this backdrop, the prosecutor in the trial, the Valeyard, declares that the Doctor has proved himself guilty of genocide, a far more serious crime than mere interference, and—rather astonishingly, in mid-trial—this charge is forthwith added to the charges against him. Significantly the Doctor puts forward no evidence at all to contradict the charge.[19] Eventually, the trial is stopped out of the Time Lords' gratitude to the Doctor, not because he has been acquitted on the evidence.

The extent to which the Gallifreyan Doctor favours humans over Vervoids again suggests a dislike for the unlike, particularly since the Vervoids are not "true" invaders: they are being forcibly transported to Earth by humans for scientific and profit-making motives. The Vervoids can even lay claim to some moral superiority over humans: one of the few things we are told about them is that they do not kill their own kind, leaving them able to condemn human "animalkind" for having no respect for any form of life. Apart from that, as in the case of the

[19] The objection may be advanced that ultimately "The Trial of a Time Lord" suggests that the Valeyard has tampered with the matrix, the Time Lords' depository of knowledge from which the court obtains its information on the Doctor's adventure with the Vervoids. A benevolent interpretation might be that this casts some doubt on the Doctor's guilt. I would argue, however, that in court the Doctor does not deny the basic facts which constitute the genocide. He seems not to grasp that he has done anything wrong in killing off the Vervoids.

Macra, we learn remarkably little about the Vervoids. And whilst the Doctor may be right in asserting that Vervoids and humans cannot share a planet, he makes scant effort to find the Vervoids alternative means of survival.

The Doctor's Misdeeds #4: The Silence (2011)

New-series *Doctor Who* has highlighted the Doctor's moral ambiguity far more explicitly than classic-series *Doctor Who*. As we shall see, the years leading up to "The Impossible Astronaut"/"Day of the Moon" (2011) were replete with challenges to the rightness and justice of the Doctor's choices. In this context, Tim Jones has argued that it is when the Doctor lacks companions that his moral compass goes awry,[20] yet in this story he has no fewer than three or possibly four companions.

In this adventure, the Doctor and his companions discover a completely unknown network of tunnels running underneath the entire planet Earth, with a particularly high concentration under the United States of America. These caves are occupied by a species known as the Silence, creatures who edit themselves out of the memories of humans as soon as humans stop looking at them. The Doctor reveals that the Silence are not invaders, but that they have been influencing human behaviour on a global scale for thousands of years, as a result of which people have suffered and died. "This isn't an alien invasion", he emphasises, "They live here". To stress the point, in answer to the accusation of being invaders, a Silent answers "This world is ours. We have ruled it since the wheel and the fire". It is not specified that the Silence have an extraterrestrial origin at all, but even if they have, when does the immigrant become indigenous? When does the settler become legitimate? In light of this, it is telling that the story is set in the USA, an immigrant state where most people's forebears have not resided in the national territory for thousands of years. In such a context, one can make too much of the "we were here first" argument.[21]

---

[20] Tim Jones, "Breaking the Faiths in 'The Curse of Fenric' and 'The God Complex'", in *Time and Relative Dimensions in Faith: Religion and Doctor Who*, eds. Andrew Crome and James McGrath (London: Darton, Longman and Todd, 2013), 49.

[21] See Layton, *Humanism of Doctor Who*, 274.

It could be said in the Doctor's defence that he at least gives the Silence a warning before launching his attack on them. Melissa Beattie has argued that, Daleks aside, giving warnings and a chance to surrender has become part of the Doctor's routine wartime morality.[22] Piers Britton has noted the new series' "predictable trope" of the Doctor offering his opponents one last chance to mend their ways which they inevitably refuse and thus get destroyed. He notes how this has gone hand in hand with the Doctor becoming self-appointed arbiter of justice, pitiless in the retribution he metes out to his adversaries.[23] In any case, warnings are only useful as a means of preventing slaughter if one's enemies have an inkling of one's strength as an opponent, and that is not the case here. Moreover, the Doctor does not even establish whether the particular Silence whom he encounters are in any position to speak for their species on matters of war and peace.

Swiftly judging that the Silence are "way out of time" to surrender, the Doctor ensures that a subliminal message is repeatedly broadcast during the televised landing on the Moon. This consists of one of the Silence incanting the words "you should kill us all on sight". The Doctor thereby incites ordinary human citizens to destroy the Silence. In so doing he promotes a kind of vigilante, gun-culture genocide against this species. This is hardly morally uplifting. Furthermore, it is ironic that "The Impossible Astronaut"/"Day of the Moon" mercilessly lampoons American gun culture, yet ends up putting forward a violent solution based on the right of the citizen to bear arms.

Yet is this death sentence merited? The charge-sheet against the Silence could hardly be more sketchy. The Doctor proffers no examples of how "people have suffered and died" as a result of the Silence's influence. How much have people suffered? How many have died? There is no clear idea of the extent to which the Silence have ruled our lives, and we have to take it entirely on trust that their influence is malign, not benign. The example of the Silence's influence put forward by the story hardly convinces us of their evil. The Silence compel the human race to venture to the moon in order that they can obtain a space suit.

[22]Melissa Beattie, "Life during Wartime: An Analysis of Wartime Morality in *Doctor Who*", in *The Mythological Dimensions of Doctor Who*, eds. Anthony S. Burdge, Jessica Burke and Kristine Larsen (Crawfordville, FL: Kitsune Books, 2013).

[23]Piers D. Britton, *TARDISbound: Navigating the Universes of Doctor Who* (London: I.B. Tauris, 2011), 204.

If this is the best the Doctor can do by way of convincing us that the Silence merit extermination, it is rather pathetic. It could indeed be argued that the Silence were doing humans a favour. In any event, it is scarcely adequate justification to annihilate a species. Like the Macra, the problem with the Silence is not that they kill human beings but, in the Doctor's words, that "they have been running your lives for a very long time now". Domination, rather than extermination, is their business, so is extermination an appropriate response? Is it legitimate for the Doctor to be harder on the Silence than he is on the Silurians, some of whom harbour genocidal intent towards humanity?[24]

Following the fate of the Silence, a portrayal of the Doctor as intergalactic criminal was put forward in stark terms in a polemic in *The Guardian* by Chris Weston, who deemed him "a murdering hypocrite who should be extradited to the Hague on charges of genocide ... [he is] some kind of intergalactic Ratko Mladić ... hellbent on cleansing the Earth of all non-humanoid immigrants and will happily kill to achieve this end—although he prefers to manipulate others to do his dirty work for him".[25] Yet, as regards the Silence, Weston actually understates the case: "The Impossible Astronaut"/"Day of the Moon" heavily emphasises that the Silence are neither immigrants nor invaders. Rather, they have occupied their tunnels under the Earth's surface and been influencing human behaviour for millennia. Nonsensically, however, conceding their legitimate residence on Earth does not lead the Doctor to concede their right to continue to live. Yet, despite this genocide, in "The Time of the Doctor" (2013), the Doctor has made friends with the Silence and they are his allies against the Daleks. This all seems rather familiar in terms of American and British foreign policy, whereby the portrayal of a foreign leader can change from bogeyman to ally and vice versa. This in turn reinforces the possibility that the Silence might serve as a metaphor for Islam, since in a subsequent story, "Let's Kill Hitler" (2011), it is revealed that the Silence are in fact not a species but a religious order.

---

[24] "Doctor Who and the Silurians" (1970), "The Hungry Earth"/"Cold Blood" (2010) Perhaps the Doctor differentiates between instances when evolution takes its "natural" course (Silurians, Sea Devils, Thals) and when it does not (Silence, Daleks, Professor Lazarus), but then, who is the Doctor to judge? Indeed in "Time and the Rani" (1987) he fought a renegade Time Lord who had pretensions to determine the "true" course of evolution.

[25] *The Guardian*, August 20, 2011.

This reminds us of how the "threat" allegedly posed by specific rogue states blurred into one posed by extremist Muslims of all nationalities.

Daleks, Macra, Vervoids, Silence—Does Doctor Who *Criticise the Doctor?*

Insofar as the programme itself expresses a view on its central character's actions, it does so by putting words in the mouths of either the Doctor's friends (often the companions) or his enemies. However, in none of the examples considered above does the Doctor's eradication of his enemies provoke discussion or debate by other characters as regards the rightness or wrongness of the Doctor's actions. In fact, in the classic series, from which three of our four examples come, aside from the Doctor's two trials for interference, there is generally a striking lack of critical comment regarding the Doctor's deeds from other characters. It is difficult to prove the presence of an absence, but a startling example is the destruction of the Daleks' home planet Skaro in "Remembrance of the Daleks" (1988). In this story, the Doctor outwits the Daleks by giving them the Hand of Omega, a weapon which he has pre-primed to bring about the planet's destruction and with it the deaths of a great many Daleks. This genocide is particularly ironic in view of the laudable anti-racist theme which pervades "Remembrance of the Daleks". If, as Piers Britton convincingly argues, "Remembrance" restores the Daleks' ideological significance as Nazi figures obsessed with racial purity, then the Doctor's mass extermination of them is all the more astonishing.[26] Yet his annihilation of an entire planet inspires no criticism from the other characters. The story ends with the Doctor's companion, Ace, asking "We did good, didn't we?" to which the Doctor replies, "Perhaps. Time will tell. It always does." Ace's comment may connote uncertainty but hardly constitutes scepticism, let alone criticism. If anything, the Doctor's own lack of certainty is more intriguing: however, it is all too subtle, especially in view of the then lead actor's image as "the Dark Doctor".[27]

[26] Britton, *TARDISbound*, 66.

[27] James Chapman, *Inside the TARDIS: The Worlds of Doctor Who*, 2nd ed. (London: I.B. Tauris, 2013), 165.

Increased Questioning of the Doctor's Deeds in New-Series *Doctor Who*

By contrast, new *Who* contains considerably more independent criticism of the Doctor. Indeed, a neat contrast with the classic series is apparent in the new-series episode "Journey's End" (2008) in which Davros—the creator of the Daleks who had featured in "Remembrance of the Daleks" twenty years earlier—characterises the Doctor as "destroyer of worlds", thereby advancing criticism of the Doctor's destruction of Skaro two decades after "Remembrance" was broadcast. Davros' condemnation of the Doctor as "the Time Lord who butchered millions" is surely not without foundation: what is interesting is the contrast between the classic series' reluctance to articulate criticism of the Doctor and the new series' readiness to do so.

New *Who*'s willingness to cast doubt on the Doctor's political morality is readily apparent. This may take the form of general comments on the Doctor's nature. In "The Name of the Doctor" (2013), the Great Intelligence describes the Doctor as "the cruel tyrant ... the slaughterer of the ten billion". When the Doctor's friend Madame Vastra defends him by denying the charge that the Doctor is "blood-soaked", the Great Intelligence retorts "Tell that to the leader of the Sycorax, or Solomon the Trader, or the Cybermen, or the Daleks!" In "Journey's End" (2008), Davros points out the Doctor's hypocrisy as the man who ostensibly abhors violence yet fashions ordinary people such as his companions into weapons, into murderers. Davros' view that the Doctor is "the destroyer of worlds" forms a stark contrast to Vastra's belief that he saves worlds.[28] In the *Doctor Who* spin-off *Class*, alien king Corakinus refers to the Doctor as "the great destructor of the universe".[29]

Sometimes, the Doctor's opponents make comments aimed *inter alia* at persuading the Doctor to spare them. One of the most sustained attacks on the Doctor's politics is made by the Slitheen Margaret Blaine/Blon in "Boom Town" (2005). In a previous adventure ("Aliens of London"/"World War Three" (2005)), the Doctor had defeated the attempt of the alien Slitheen family to reduce the world to molten slag in

[28] "The Doctor is not kind. He doesn't interfere in the world. He was different once: kind, a hero even, saving worlds", "The Snowmen" (2012). Thus, Vastra associates interference with kindness.

[29] "For Tonight We Might Die" (2016).

order to create fuel to sell for profit. The family are killed, save for a sole survivor who somehow becomes Mayor of Cardiff. In "Boom Town", the Doctor thwarts Margaret Blaine/Blon's plan to create a nuclear explosion in the city which would have powered her attempt to escape from Earth. The Doctor's instinct is to return her to her own planet, but it transpires that the Slitheen family were sentenced to death in their absence on their home planet, so returning her there means sending her to her death. She asks the Doctor not to do so, on the grounds that she has changed and become a better person. She cites the fact that she has recently spared a young pregnant woman: the Doctor scoffs, arguing that letting the occasional victim go salves the conscience of those who slaughter millions.

> MARGARET: Only a killer would know that. Is that right? From what I've seen, your funny happy-go-lucky little life leaves devastation in its wake. Always moving on because you dare not look back. Playing with so many people's lives, you might as well be a god. And you're right, Doctor. You're absolutely right. Sometimes you let one go. Let me go.

Thereby, Margaret convincingly likens the Doctor to the enemies he is forever fighting. After this, criticisms of the Doctor's political morality come thick and fast from opponents and companions alike. In "The Vampires of Venice" (2010), Rosanna, mother-leader of an alien species which the Doctor is poised to destroy, asks the Doctor whether his conscience can carry the weight of another dead race. In "The Lazarus Experiment" (2007), Professor Lazarus questions the Doctor's legitimacy to judge him. Having turned himself into the Lazarus monster, who is the Doctor to decide that Lazarus is an evolutionary option which evolution rejected? Lazarus sees his mutation as "progress". In "Asylum of the Daleks" (2012), the Doctor is appalled that the Daleks find hatred beautiful, only for the Dalek Prime Minister to retort, "Perhaps that is why we have never been able to kill you!".

Sometimes, both adversaries and companions have criticised the Doctor's political morality in one and the same episode. For instance, in "Dalek" (2005) the universe's sole surviving Dalek says that the Doctor would have made a good Dalek, and companion Rose Tyler asks the Doctor what the hell he is changing into as he points a weapon at the Dalek. Similarly, in "A Town Called Mercy" (2012) the confirmed war criminal Jex tells the Doctor that "looking at you is like looking in the mirror", yet when the Doctor tries to dispose of Jex, companion Amy Pond attacks the Doctor for considering killing to be an option: "we can't be like him; we have to be better than him!".

Critical comment on the Doctor reaches its logical conclusion in "A Good Man Goes to War" (2011). Here, the Doctor dragoons his friends and allies to form an army to rescue Amy, only to discover that his very name has been reinterpreted to mean "mighty warrior", and that this is how he is seen by the opposing army. Companion River Song draws attention to how the meaning of his name has changed from "healer" and "wise man", and how he can turn armies around at its very mention. *Doctor Who*'s 2014 run made its pervasive theme the question of whether the Doctor was "a good man", a question to which, as we shall examine shortly, the Doctor ultimately gives an inadequate answer. All in all, therefore, when, in "The Name of the Doctor" (2013), the Great Intelligence says that "the Doctor lives his life in darker hues, day upon day", this rather sums up how the new show has portrayed the Doctor.

The new series' questioning approach towards the Doctor's conduct is commendable. But sometimes, an important instance of the Doctor's "dislike for the unlike" slips under the radar. The genocide against the Silence is one example. Another prize example relates to "Asylum of the Daleks" (2012). In this adventure, the Doctor and his companions are rescued from a planet on which the Daleks have dumped the mentally deranged members of their species, thanks to the advice and help of a marooned young woman, Oswin Oswald, who thinks she is locked inside her own spaceship. It transpires, however, that Oswin has in fact been turned into a Dalek, though her character, personality and intelligence clearly remain her own. Yet because her outward form is that of a Dalek, the Doctor writes her off.[30] It never for a moment occurs to him that Oswin might actually have all the makings of a companion, despite her

[30] In this regard, the Doctor's physical appearancism matches his approach in "The Evil of the Daleks" (1967), where he treats numerous Daleks with the "human factor", giving them the power to think independently and criticise the Dalek leadership, but then seems happy that all the Daleks have apparently killed each other in a civil war. Why did the Doctor not come to the aid of the "human" Daleks? In the event, none of the Doctor's human companions questions their destruction despite the "human" Daleks' earlier displays of affection for the Doctor. By contrast, the Doctor is more sympathetic to those with *human* form but some aspects of Dalek mentality in "Evolution of the Daleks" (2007).

Dalek form.[31] What better repudiation of racism could there have been than to have a Dalek companion for the Doctor?

The Parallel with British Foreign Policy

The Doctor's contestable choices in differentiating those who are good from those who are evil mirrors the same sustained practice on the part of British governments. We can see *Doctor Who* once again serving as a metaphor for Britain. Specifically in this instance, the Doctor's conduct reflects the country's foreign policy.

There has been a long tradition among *Doctor Who*'s writers of using the show to pass comment on how Britain conducts itself vis-à-vis the rest of the world. Thus, the classic series' pervasive theme was Britain's discarding of Empire.[32] The show's approach varied from story to story but with a loose common theme was that it was wrong to treat the colonised in an unkind fashion. Even this message is pursued with varied degrees of enthusiasm, as shown in the account of *Doctor Who* plots involving colonisation given in Chap. 2. It will be readily apparent that *Doctor Who*'s colonialism stories do not advance a consistent normative position. From one perspective, the underlying political messages are sometimes disappointing; decent treatment of alien species sometimes considered to be of a "lower order" is not the same as equality and mutual respect for each other's way of life.[33] On the other hand, from the perspective of a country only just discarding its empire, a more sympathetic assessment is possible, insofar as the pervasive message is,

[31] This is despite the fact that past companions have included the robot dog K9, whom John Fiske has aptly described as "a domesticated Dalek" (Fiske, "Dr. Who: Ideology", 76). A further example is suggested by the political activist and blogger "Fire Fly". The Doctor commits genocide against the Racnoss in "The Runaway Bride" and this forms a contrast with his own inconsolable grief when the Master dies, suggesting that characters who do not resemble white men are not worth grieving over (Fire Fly, "The White Doctor", in *Doctor Who and Race*, ed. Lindy Orthia (Bristol: Intellect, 2013), 15–20).

[32] See Maura Grady and Cassie Hemstrom, "Nostalgia for Empire 1963–74", in *Doctor Who in Time and Space: Essays on Themes, Characters, History and Fandom, 1963–2012*, ed. Gillian I. Leitch (Jefferson, NC and London: McFarland, 2013), 125.

[33] John Vohlidka arges that "often these stories fell into the racist trap: arguing against imperialism but from a pro-Western view". See John Vohidka, "*Doctor Who* and the Critique of Western Imperialism", in *Doctor Who and Race*, ed. Lindy Orthia (Bristol: Intellect, 2013), 125–139.

generally speaking, at least one of sympathy for the colonised, whatever the shortcomings of the show's stances.

In any event, *Doctor Who*'s pervasive theme of colonisation reflects Empire's deep ramifications in British politics. Whilst the end of Empire was certainly not the sole focus of British foreign policy in the aftermath of the Second World War, it nonetheless had a profound bearing on it. Whilst the Suez crisis of 1956 is commonly seen as marking the end of Britain's time as a great power, some scholars argue that the country's decline was actually longer and subtler than that.[34] Against the backdrop of this protracted decline, many aspects of long-term British policy can be seen as flowing from Britain's loss of imperial greatness and the longstanding preoccupation of the British political elite with the country remaining a "great power". These aspects include the "special relationship" with the United States, the determination to possess and retain nuclear weapons, and the desire to be in the European Community/Union.[35] Empire's *covert* centrality would thus make sense of the preponderance of stories involving empire in *Doctor Who*.

In *Doctor Who*'s post-2005 reboot, concerns regarding the British Empire have been superseded by criticism of a neo-imperial foreign policy. Even long after the abandonment of the British Empire, the country's politicians retain a taste for Britain to "punch above its weight" and to remain one of the relatively few countries which can make its influence felt around the world.[36] This particularly manifested itself in British interventions during Tony Blair's premiership. These conflicts, especially the Iraq invasion, dominated the British political scene and were quite naturally reflected in *Doctor Who*. Thus, the questions constantly articulated in new *Who* as to the rightness and justice of the Doctor's actions mirror the unease expressed by many critics, including on occasion the majority of the British people, regarding British meddling in foreign countries, notably Iraq and Afghanistan. The Doctor's controversial

[34] David Dilks, "Introduction", in *Retreat from Power: Studies in Britain's Foreign Policy of the Twentieth Century. Volume Two, After 1939*, ed. David Dilks (London and Basingstoke: Macmillan, 1981), 33.

[35] Margaret Gowing, "Britain, America and the Bomb", in *Retreat from Power: Studies in Britain's Foreign Policy of the Twentieth Century. Volume Two, After 1939*, ed. David Dilks (London and Basingstoke: Macmillan, 1981), 130–131.

[36] Laurence Martin and John Garnett, *British Foreign Policy: Challenges and Choices for the 21st Century* (London: Pinter, 1997), 139.

belligerence and questionable political morality reflect the aggressive approach pursued by British leaders. Some authors dwell on the continuity between the Blairite policy and the earlier British imperial mindset. Coates and Krieger, for example, perceive Blair's actions as "pure Ernest Bevin—instincts of Atlanticism and the imperial use of UK military power". They argue that having left its colonialist past behind, it is unfortunate that the British political class finds it so difficult to shed the residues of the attitude which once sustained the Empire. These include the staggering arrogance whereby British governments expect gratitude and support from the "liberated" when they rearrange the political architecture of a country, something which if done to Britain would legitimately be repelled as a simple matter of aggression.[37] The Doctor displays similar arrogance in rearranging the political architecture of planets. Indeed, Alec Charles is right to point out that the Doctor, by consistently violating the (vaunted) Time Lord policy of non-interference, repeatedly reinstates the very imperialist agendas and alibis which the character's liberal humanism purports to oppose.[38] It could, however, be argued that what is true of the Doctor is equally true of Britain. The country's leaders conceal their neo-imperialism beneath a veneer of concern for the indigenous population, a narrative that often does not bear scrutiny.

The connection between the Doctor's political morality and Britain's military exploits was strengthened by *Doctor Who*'s 2014 story arc (series 8). The series was broadcast against the backdrop of Britain's withdrawal from Afghanistan. This end of British engagement inevitably prompted reflection on whether Britain's participation had been worthwhile. There had been considerable loss of life, including on the British side; furthermore, there was every likelihood that the Taliban (whom America and Britain had removed from power) would simply carry on where they left off once the foreigners had departed. It was questionable, therefore, whether the British had done any good. By the same token, *Doctor Who* focused with renewed vigour on the rights and wrongs of the Doctor's intervention, with the pervasive question, "Am I a good man?"

[37] David Coates and Joel Krieger, *Blair's War* (Cambridge: Polity, 2004), 124.

[38] Alec Charles, "The Ideology of Anachronism", in *Time and Relative Dissertations in Space: Critical Perspectives on Doctor Who*, ed. David Butler (Manchester and New York: Manchester University Press, 2007), 117.

The connection between the Doctor's actions and British soldiering is particularly strong due to the role of Danny Pink, boyfriend to the Doctor's companion Clara Oswald: a schoolteacher haunted by his military past in Afghanistan. The series persistently draws parallels between Danny and the Doctor.[39] Danny repeatedly suggests that if he is a soldier then the Doctor is an officer, indeed a "blood-soaked old general" ("The Caretaker" (2014), "Death in Heaven" (2014)). The series finale sees Missy, the recently introduced (and female) incarnation of the Doctor's arch-enemy, the Master, offering the Doctor a ready-made army of Cybermen. She argues that armies are for people who think they're right, and no-one thinks they are more right than the Doctor. An army will help him stop the bad guys winning all the wars, enabling him to "go and get the good guys back!". The Doctor retorts that he is neither a good man nor a bad man but an idiot with a box and a screwdriver, "passing through, helping out, learning". He does not require an army because he has "them, always them", pointing to Clara and Danny.

The Doctor's defence of himself is actually rather weak. He talks in terms of "helping out" to justify his interventions. Yet, in countries such as Iraq, "helping out" one group required crushing another, so little is added to the argument by deploying the gentle-sounding spin of "helping out". As for the Doctor not needing an army since he can rely on the humans whom he encounters, one is reminded of Davros' incisive observation in "Journey's End" (2008) that the Doctor fashions his companions into weapons. The Doctor uses different language to make the same point as Davros: his companions constitute a metaphorical army.

Furthermore, just as it is controversial whether Britain's activist foreign policy in Afghanistan, Iraq and elsewhere has ultimately achieved "good" results, so too new *Who* has repeatedly questioned whether the Doctor's deeds actually have the benign consequences he intends. Thus, the Doctor's deposing of British Prime Minister Harriet Jones, architect of Britain's golden age, in "The Christmas Invasion" (2005) creates the political space for the Master, in the guise of Harold Saxon, to ascend to Downing Street in "The Sound of Drums" (2007). Similarly, the Doctor's efforts in the distant future to liberate Satellite 5 from an alien

[39] To emphasise the theme, the Doctor encounters other soldiers in some stories, e.g. "Into the Dalek" (2014), "Mummy on the Orient Express" (2014).

despot in "The Long Game" (2005) result in the space station being taken over by the Daleks in "Bad Wolf" (2005). Vanquish the mighty Jagrafess and end up with the Daleks; vanquish the mighty Saddam and end up with Islamic State. When Andrew O'Day observes that the new state of equilibrium sought by the Doctor fails to emerge,[40] the same could be said of how high-minded talk of an "ethical foreign policy" in New Labour's early years failed to achieve the lofty "equilibrium" of "human rights, civil liberties and democracy" that the then Foreign Secretary Robin Cook had in mind.[41] In fact, New Labour's invasions had the effect of relegitimising Al-Qaeda and its offshoots and equivalents throughout the Arab world, and it is questionable whether they have made Britain safer.[42]

From Misdeeds to Crimes? the Doctor as War Criminal

In new *Who*, therefore, the Doctor's political morality is heavily contested. Can we go further and allege that he is presented as acting unlawfully? What would be added by making an accusation of illegality? After all, the Doctor's very first comment on law is rather insightful: "one man's law is another man's crime", he observes to Ian Chesterton in "The Edge of Destruction" (1964). It could, however, be argued that *Doctor Who*'s role as an allegory for Britain and Britishness makes the question of war crimes in the show altogether more intriguing. If the Doctor qualifies as a war criminal, what is that suggesting about our own British government? War crimes emerged as a form of law in the wake of the Second World War, and Britain's leaders were deeply involved in their evolution. In a sense, indeed, British politicians have had a more consistent record than their American counterparts in supporting the development and enforcement of war crimes legislation, since Britain, unlike the USA, has accepted the jurisdiction of the International Criminal Court in respect of its own nationals. At the same time, however, the question of whether

[40] Andrew O'Day, "Towards a Definition of Satire in *Doctor Who*", in *Ruminations, Peregrinations and Regenerations: A Critical Approach to Doctor Who*, ed. Chris Hansen (Newcastle-upon-Tyne: Cambridge Scholars Publishing, 2010).

[41] Mark Wickham-Jones, "Labour's Trajectory in Foreign Affairs: The Moral Crusade of a Pivotal Power?", in *New Labour's Foreign Policy: A New Moral Crusade?* eds. Richard Little and Mark Wickham-Jones (Manchester: Manchester University Press, 2000), 3–4.

[42] Coates and Krieger, *Blair's War*, 120–121.

the actions of British leaders—notably Tony Blair in the context of the invasion of Iraq—would themselves constitute war crimes, remains deeply contentious. Yet if British leaders enjoy a *de facto* immunity from war crimes prosecutions, this serves to undermine the very concept of war crimes by compromising the law's objectivity. If *Doctor Who*'s satire reflects these controversies, the show could be seen as offering an even more critical reading of Britain and of the world system it has helped to fashion.

Let us assume, therefore, that questions of war crimes may be of allegorical interest: what would count as illegality in *Doctor Who*? In the programme's early years, the show's writers took time to get to grips with the idea of intergalactic law. At first, the programme's stance was that interfering in the course of established history was scientifically impossible ("The Aztecs" (1964), "The Reign of Terror" (1964)). Yet this position lacked coherence; if the Doctor could not change the course of history on Earth how could he change the history of Skaro by helping the Thals against the Daleks? Moreover, given the programme's lack of deference towards the concept of "the present", any substantial interference at any specific point in time is likely to change the course of history: so, for instance, the Doctor transforms Earth's "future history" by thwarting the Dalek conquest of the planet ("The Dalek Invasion of Earth" (1964)). Swiftly, therefore, the scientific impossibility became a golden rule of *law*, one which *ought* to be obeyed. Hence, the Doctor defeats the time-meddling Monk in his bid to change the result of the Battle of Hastings ("The Time Meddler" (1965)), and refuses companion Steven a wholesale rescue of new-found friends who are fated to meet their deaths on the occasion of an anti-Protestant massacre in France ("The Massacre of Saint Bartholomew's Eve" (1966)). The logic of "non-interference as law" was that this law might sometimes need to be enforced. In "The Time of the Doctor" (2013), the Doctor confesses to having constantly flouted the principal law of his own people, and on two occasions his own people have considered the lawfulness of his activities—episode 10 of "The War Games" (1969) and "The Trial of a Time Lord" (1986).

Would the Doctor's Activities Violate Earth's International Criminal Law?

Under the law of his own people, therefore, bare interference with other peoples and planets is subject to criminal sanction. The question of whether the Doctor would be a war criminal under *human* international criminal law might be considered of limited interest: the Doctor is not human, his adversaries are usually not human, and a good many of his adventures take place on other planets. Nonetheless, the categories of crime created by international criminal law correspond to those courses of action that the international community has viewed as particularly worthy of censure. After all, there needs to be a particularly strong and broad consensus in order for conduct to be criminalised internationally. It would, therefore, cast the Doctor in a particularly bad light if he were guilty of conduct that would amount to war crimes here on Earth. So it may be enlightening to know whether *Doctor Who*'s hero has committed any of these offences, because a reading of *Doctor Who* which pays regard to the Doctor's possible war crimes may prompt us to take a more critical approach to the character of the Doctor. Conversely, bringing together popular culture and legal debate may well cause us to view war crimes in different, perhaps more critical, ways.

If one cuts the show some metaphorical slack, there are four offences that the Doctor is likely to have committed: war crimes involving prohibited *methods* of warfare, war crimes involving prohibited *means* of warfare, crimes against humanity, and genocide.

War Crimes Involving Prohibited Methods of Warfare

Article 8(b)(i) and (ii) of the Rome Statute of the International Criminal Court 1998 confirms that it is unlawful to intentionally launch an indiscriminate attack affecting a civilian population or civilian objects in the knowledge that such attack will cause excessive loss of life, injury to civilians or damage to civilian objects.[43] It could be argued that the Doctor's actions in "Remembrance of the Daleks" (1988) would violate this prohibition. In this serial, the Doctor joins forces with a detachment from the British army against two antagonistic Dalek factions. The Doctor could therefore loosely be said to be involved in "armed conflict" against the Daleks, a necessary ingredient for this offence. Both factions come to Earth not to conquer the planet but to find and take a weapon that the Doctor left when he was on Earth in 1963. This weapon, styled "the Hand of Omega", was created by a Time Lord stellar engineer called Omega who used it to create the supernova that powered the Time Lords' time-travelling experiments. It is a remote stellar

[43] Antonio Cassese et al., *Cassese's International Criminal Law*, 3rd ed. (Oxford: Oxford University Press, 2013), 73.

control-manipulator, a device that can customise stars. The two Dalek factions battle it out for this prize, until one group, the Imperial Daleks, are victorious and take it away to their spaceship. Unbeknownst to them, however, the Doctor has perpetrated a massive deception. He has pre-programmed the Omega device to fly to the Daleks' solar system, transform Daleks' home planet Skaro's sun into a supernova and vaporise Skaro. This is indeed what transpires, and the Doctor seems content to have turned Skaro into "a burnt cinder circling a dead sun". The question could usefully be posed whether all the Daleks killed on Skaro were soldiers. Whilst a crude description of the Daleks might see them purely as a military race, it is clear from "The Daleks" (1963) that they have a multiplicity of needs. They grow food; they require power supplies; it would seem inevitable that some are involved in non-combat activities. In any event, the Doctor makes no effort to see whether he is killing non-combatant Daleks. Nor does he bother to establish whether any other sentient species on the planet (such as the Thals) will be annihilated by Skaro's destruction. The jurisprudence suggests that such gross or culpable negligence may suffice to provide the requisite mental element for this offence; in other words, there is no need to prove an intention to kill civilians.[44]

War Crimes Involving Prohibited Means of Warfare

Article 8(b)(xvii)–(xx) of the Rome Statute gives the Court jurisdiction to hear prosecutions for war crimes involving prohibited means of warfare. This includes using weapons of a nature likely to cause superfluous injury or unnecessary suffering, using chemical, biological or blinding laser weapons. It is therefore unlawful to employ poison or poisonous gases, and bullets which expand within the body.

It requires a special feat of imagination to divine what weapons might be classed as unlawful in the intergalactic field. After all, Earth prohibitions are not always logical: the international taboo on chemical weapons animated President Obama and others to threaten a broader intervention in the Syrian civil war, yet far more civilians had been killed in that conflict through conventional than through chemical means. A fair guess

[44] Cassese et al., *Cassese's International Criminal Law*, 75–76.

at a prohibited weapon might be the Time Destructor, which features in "The Daleks' Master Plan" (1965–1966), and which—as its name suggests—destroys time itself. Indeed, the Doctor spends most of the twelve-part serial being chased around the galaxy trying to make sure that the Daleks do not get hold of a terranium core needed to power the Time Destructor. Yet in the final episode, it is the Doctor, not the Daleks, who activates the Time Destructor on the planet Kembel, annihilating the Daleks along with all other life there (and, depending on the weapon's range, perhaps on worlds beyond Kembel as well).[45]

Crimes Against Humanity

Article 7 of the Rome Statute defines crimes against humanity as acts, including murder and extermination, that are committed as part of a widespread or sustained attack directed against any civilian population with knowledge of that attack. In intergalactic terms, we would need to translate "humanity" into "sentient beings". This would not be a particularly fanciful translation: the Doctor himself in "Genesis of the Daleks" (1975) argues that if he wipes out an *intelligent* form of life like the Daleks, he will be no better than the Daleks. On this assumption, the Doctor's transgression in "Remembrance of the Daleks" might be seen as a violation, and it would be easier to secure a conviction for the destruction of Skaro under this head than under that of a war crime. This is because, as Theodor Meron has pointed out, in the case of crimes against humanity, no nexus to armed conflict needs to be shown; they are as applicable in peacetime as in wartime. One does not even require proof of discrimination against the targeted (Dalek) population.[46] Indeed, Meron observes that crimes against humanity overlap with some violations of fundamental human

[45] It would, however, be borderline whether the requisite state of armed conflict exists in this instance: according to the International Criminal Tribunal on the former Yugoslavia, "an armed conflict exists whenever there is a resort to armed force between states or protracted armed violence between governmental authorities and organised armed groups or between such groups within a state". *Boškoski and Tarčulovski* judgement 2010 of the ICTY Appeal Chamber.

[46] Theodor Meron, *War Crimes Law Comes of Age* (Oxford: Oxford University Press, 1998), 305.

rights, which thus become criminalised under a multilateral treaty. Antonio Cassese and others emphasise that crimes against humanity must be of a large scale or massive nature, which would be the case here.[47] Alternatively, the Doctor's earlier acts against the Daleks on Skaro and Kembel could be cited as evidence of the "systematic" nature of the attack; in other words, that it is part of a sustained pattern of conduct on the part of the Doctor against them.

Genocide

The international crime that the Doctor most frequently perpetrates is undoubtedly genocide. Whilst the intention to destroy entire groups of people recurs throughout the history of humankind, the word "genocide" was only coined in 1944 and acquired a legal meaning in the Genocide Convention 1948. According to Article II of the Convention, the perpetrator must intend to destroy a national, ethnical, racial or religious group in whole or in part. The crime is then committed when he *inter alia* kills members of the group.[48] Furthermore, punishable acts include not only genocide itself but also conspiracy and complicity to cause genocide (relevant in the case of the Daleks and the Vervoids),[49] and direct and public incitement to commit genocide (relevant in the case of the Silence).[50] Genocide is also committed where measures are imposed intended to prevent births within a group.[51] In "The Twin Dilemma" (1984), the Doctor sabotages an incubator full of the eggs of giant Gastropods, telling the race's leader, "I'm not having your sluggy eggs spread all over the Universe causing havoc, nor will I allow you to destroy what was once a very beautiful planet". His unwillingness to entertain a Gastropod empire stands in marked contrast to the apparent praise which he lavishes for the "great and bountiful human empire"

[47] Cassese et al., *Cassese's International Criminal Law*, 92.

[48] Article II (a).

[49] Article III (a) and (e).

[50] Article III (c).

[51] Article II (d).

in "The Long Game" (2005). It should be noted that genocide is not a war crime in the strict sense, so there need not be a state of armed conflict in order for genocide to be committed. To secure a conviction for genocide, it must be shown that the perpetrator has genocidal intent—he must harbour the specific intent to destroy the group while carrying out any of the genocidal acts. In real life, this intent does not require the defendant to be somehow like Hitler. In *Eichmann in Jerusalem*, Hannah Arendt comments that it would have been comforting to believe that Adolf Eichmann, who was convicted of participation in the Holocaust, was a monster: in fact, "the trouble with Eichmann was precisely that so many were like him, and that the many were neither perverted nor sadistic, that they were, and still are, terribly and terrifyingly normal".[52] All in all, therefore, we may conclude that there is indeed evidence to suggest that the Doctor could be convicted for several types of international crime if Earth law applied intergalactically.

Trials of a Time Lord—Casting Doubt on War Crimes?

The Doctor has twice been put on trial by the Time Lords for intergalactic crimes—namely for interfering in the affairs of other peoples and planets: in episode 10 of "The War Games" (1969) and in the fourteen-part story "The Trial of a Time Lord" (1986). The show itself has thereby explicitly flagged up the possibility of the Doctor as intergalactic criminal. Should these trials be considered akin to war crimes trials? On one level, the Time Lords are merely applying their domestic law to one of their own. Yet on another level, the focus on the Doctor's interventions on other planets lends the trials an element of extraterritoriality; he is abducted from outside Time Lord territory in order to face trial,[53]

[52] Hannah Arendt, *Eichmann in Jerusalem: A Report on the Banality of Evil* (New York: Penguin, 1994), 276.

[53] In the case of Adolf Eichmann, Hannah Arendt considers that his abduction from Argentina constituted the feature of the trial least entitled to become a valid precedent. Arendt, *Eichmann*, 263–265.

and the trials have the grandiose feel of war crimes trials.[54] Moreover, the modern trend is to encourage national authorities to prosecute war crimes as first port of call. As Charles Anthony Smith has observed, the jurisprudence on war crimes has emerged from both transnational/international and domestic legal environments.[55] In episode 10 of "The War Games", the seamlessness of transition from the trial of the War Lord—unequivocally for war crimes—to the Doctor's trial for interference, would also seem to approximate the Doctor's offences to war crimes. In "The Trial of a Time Lord" (1986), the parallel with a war crimes trial is made manifest not least by the decision to belatedly add genocide to the list of charges against the Doctor.

If the Doctor's trials are akin to war crimes trials, can they also be said to be show trials? In *Law, War and Crime*, Gerry Simpson argues that war crime trials are haunted by the spectre of show trials, and that these two types of trial share structural similarities such as a lack of procedural justice, a grand theatricality, and a belief by the participants that they are immersed in matters of great political moment whilst simultaneously being somehow "above politics".[56] The Doctor certainly sees his second trial as a show trial, denouncing the proceedings as "a farce … a farrago of trumped-up charges!"

Undoubtedly, both trials highlight the proximity of law and politics rather strikingly. In episode 10 of "The War Games", the Time Lords at first blush appear to operate a highly formal, black-letter system of law. Thus, any interference in the affairs of other peoples and planets merits a severe penalty, seemingly without much room for argument. This portrayal of law as an inflexible system would have chimed with the perception of law in the 1960s and earlier, as a more black-letter system than it is today. Furthermore, whilst a court, during that era, could hear copious argument as to how a law should be interpreted, it could not entertain any argument at all as to whether that law should actually be on the

---

[54] In this respect, the style of the two trials can be contrasted with the Doctor's trial in "The Deadly Assassin" (1976) for the assassination of the Lord President of the High Council of Time Lords which is a low-profile, almost intimate, hearing under purely domestic criminal law.

[55] Charles Anthony Smith, *The Rise and Fall of War Crimes: From Charles I to Bush II* (Cambridge: Cambridge University Press, 2012), 9–10.

[56] Gerry Simpson, *Law, War and Crime: War Crimes Trials and the Reinvention of International Law* (London: Polity, 2007), 106–115.

statute book.[57] The Doctor, by contrast, argues that Time Lord policy is entirely misconceived and that the Time Lords are guilty of doing nothing in the face of the evils of the universe. The Time Lords' legalistic stance thereby contrasts with that of the Doctor, who can be seen to be treating the question of interference as a question of politics—one that is open to being argued about—rather than a question of law—one where the substantive policy argument has been settled and the emphasis instead is on interpretation, application and enforcement. Gerry Simpson has in fact convincingly argued that war crimes prosecutions are a form of displaced politics. They involve, he believes, a general juridification of politics, whereby criminal law can be applied to people with whom we have sharp political disagreements. Such a juridified diplomacy, he argues, constitutes a depoliticised politics. Against this backdrop, he contends, the criminalisation of aggression is a sort of anti-politics which tends to criminalise our enemies because they *are* our enemies. Once a state has been condemned as an aggressor, all sorts of judgements can be suspended.[58]

In fact, the Time Lords do not actually keep to their legalistic stance. Whilst they initially appear to dismiss the Doctor's arguments as irrelevant, when they actually arrive at their verdict, they accept the Doctor's plea that there is evil in the universe that must be fought and that the Doctor has a part to play in that battle. This in turn justifies the leniency of their punishment. But more profoundly, the Time Lords' concession to the Doctor's argument casts doubt on their professed commitment to their supposedly principal law. Certainly, they fail to give a reasoned judgement which explains how the Time Lords balance non-interference against a measure of agreement with the Doctor. Indeed, it could be argued that their acceptance of the Doctor's position that it is right to fight evil in the universe essentially destroys the non-interference policy. This is confirmed by the Time Lords' subsequent conduct. As mentioned in the previous chapter, the number of occasions on which the Time Lords deploy the Doctor as their intergalactic secret agent during his exile on Earth serves to emphasise that their commitment to

[57] See the judgement of Lord Morris of Borth-y-Gest in *British Railways Board v Pickin* [1974] AC 765. Currently, by contrast, due to section 4 of the Human Rights Act 1998, the higher courts can flag up to parliament that legislation is incompatible with human rights and that lawmakers should therefore consider changing the offending provision.

[58] Simpson, *Law, War and Crime*, 158.

non-intervention was only skin deep. Similarly, in "The Trial of a Time Lord", it transpires that the Time Lords have moved planet Earth light-years from its established position in the universe in order to protect certain scientific secrets. Thus, when it comes to meddling, the Time Lords want the Doctor to do as they say, not as they do.

Furthermore, the aftermaths of both trials also serve to highlight the close connection between law and politics. In "The Three Doctors" (1972), the Doctor saves the Time Lords from their arch-enemy Omega and as a result they lift his punishment; so the Doctor's "political" rescue of the Time Lords obliterates the judicially imposed sentence proclaimed at the end of "The War Games". In "The Trial of a Time Lord", the Time Lords once again accuse the Doctor of interference, and at a later stage they add genocide to their list of charges. Yet, at the end of the trial, the Doctor absconds from the courtroom in order to rescue the Time Lords from his arch-enemy the Master. Ultimately, the Doctor saves the Time Lords and as a result the trial is abandoned without a verdict having been reached. Thus, the legal process is truncated out of extra-legal gratitude, enforcing the law having become politically inexpedient. In real-world war crimes tribunals, too, the pursuit of justice is often sidelined for reasons of expediency.[59]

Doctor Who, therefore, gives rather an unfavourable portrayal of war crimes trials, emphasising how, for all their image of judicial purity, they are in fact saturated with political motives. It seems unlikely that "The War Games" and "The Trial of a Time Lord" were intended specifically to satirise Nuremberg's shortcomings, since rose-tinted images of the Nuremberg trials prevailed throughout the twentieth century. An entire generation blissfully assumed that justice had been done to World War II's evil perpetrators, whereas the true state of affairs was rather different. Whilst the Doctor's trials cannot therefore be taken to be a satire of Nuremberg, *Doctor Who* usefully highlights the *inevitability* of politics seeping into war crimes trials as part of the reality of superpower domination.

This is a valuable insight, and one that reflects historical experience. The classic objection to war trials, that they constitute "victors' justice", is no less valid merely because the complaint is perennially made.

[59]At the Tokyo war crimes trials, for example, the Japanese chemical and biological weapons unit were not prosecuted because the USA wanted their expertise and was willing to trade this expertise for immunity, a move which substantially undermined the trial's legitimacy. The Emperor of Japan and Japanese industrialists also escaped prosecution.

For example, the legitimacy of the Nuremberg trials is rarely challenged, yet many aspects were highly questionable. Even supporters of war crimes trials acknowledge that the victors' justice tag remains potentially applicable more than half a century after Nuremberg.[60] James Owen has argued that the myth surrounding Nuremberg—that the trials constituted a model act of justice where the defendants were sentenced to well-deserved fates—masks a more complex reality.[61] In particular, the charges levelled against the defendants had not existed as crimes at the time they were committed. This was the most powerful legal objection to the entire prosecution, since creating retrospective criminal offences constitutes a flagrant breach of the rule of law. For instance, the crime of "launching an aggressive war" was unknown in international law at the time. In addition, the American legal concept of conspiracy was controversially deployed as a catch-all, with the consequence that someone who had not participated in a crime could nonetheless be found guilty of it. In effect, its use meant that *all* the defendants could be blamed for *every* invasion and atrocity. Furthermore, there were no guides in international law as to who should determine the verdict and pronounce sentence on those found guilty of the violations of these "laws".[62]

Most astonishing was the choice of defendants, a choice that kept changing even once the trial had begun, as the victorious nations haggled over who to indict. Specifically, the Allies came to the conclusion that they should indict at least one defendant representative of each odious aspect of the Nazi regime. There would, therefore, be one defendant to represent Nazi propaganda, one to symbolise anti-Semitism, another to represent finance and so forth.[63] This bizarre arrangement resulted in highly dubious decisions: with Goebbels dead, the Allies picked an obscure broadcaster to stand for propaganda; to represent anti-Semitism, they plumped for a Nazi who had been under house arrest since 1941; and the defendant selected to represent finance had been sent

---

[60] Howard Ball, *Prosecuting War Crimes and Genocide: The Twentieth-Century Experience* (Lawrence, KS: University Press of Kansas, 1999), 49.

[61] James Owen, *Nuremberg: Evil on Trial* (London: Headline, 2006), 1.

[62] Ball, *Prosecuting War Crimes*, 49.

[63] Richard Overy, "The Nuremberg Trials", in *From Nuremberg to The Hague: The Future of International Criminal Justice*, ed. Philippe Sands (Cambridge: Cambridge University Press, 2003), 12.

to a concentration camp by the Nazis on suspicion of plotting against them. Thus, the final list of defendants had the feel of a lucky dip.[64] Even Nuremberg's most doughty supporters acknowledge its due process defects, and the lack of equality between prosecution and defendants.[65]

Breaches of procedural fairness likewise permeate the Doctor's trials. In "The War Games", he is given no time to prepare his defence. In "The Trial of a Time Lord", the High Council of Time Lords excises certain areas of testimony, believing that it is not in the public interest to reveal all the evidence. The Inquisitor, presiding over the trial, says she cannot conduct a proper trial under these circumstances. Unwisely, however, the Doctor elects to make no formal objection, so the trial proceeds. It is hardly in the interests of justice to allow a defendant to opt for an unfair trial. For good measure, as previously mentioned, genocide, a charge which carries a death penalty, is added to the charges against the Doctor in mid-trial.

Quite apart from procedural deficiencies, the maintenance of double standards appears to be inherent in the practice of war crimes trials. For instance, at Nuremberg, the Western powers accepted that Allied actions that might now be regarded as crimes should be immune from review in the trials. The decision to include German bombing as part of the indictment was quietly dropped so as to avoid any focus on Allied bombings.[66] The Soviets were establishing concentration camps just as the trial was hearing about the Nazi camps.[67] The Americans insisted that the new-fangled offence of crimes against humanity could only be perpetrated in a state of armed conflict, otherwise the USA could have been liable for the treatment of black people within its national territory.[68] *Doctor Who* raises acutely this question of legitimacy, along with the problem of the prohibition of the *tu quoque* defence—the argument that the victorious or dominant power was doing much the same thing as the accused. The Doctor's speech towards the end of "The Trial of a Time Lord" (1986)

---

[64] Owen, *Nuremberg*, 3–13.

[65] Meron, *War Crimes Law*, 199.

[66] Overy, "The Nuremberg Trials", 25.

[67] Overy, "The Nuremberg Trials", 26.

[68] Andrew Clapham, "Issues of Complexity, Complicity and Complementarity: From the Nuremberg Trials to the Dawn of the New International Criminal Court", in *From Nuremberg to The Hague: The Future of International Criminal Justice*, ed. Philippe Sands (Cambridge: Cambridge University Press, 2003), 43.

directly challenges the Time Lords' right to try him on the grounds that they practise the very incorrigible meddling of which they accuse him:

> In all my travellings throughout the universe, I have battled against evil, against power-mad conspirators. I should have stayed HERE! The oldest civilization: decadent, degenerate and rotten to the core! ... Daleks, Sontarans, Cybermen—they're still in the nursery compared to us! Ten million years of absolute power—that's what it takes to be really corrupt!

The Time Lords' transportation of Earth across the universe in "The Trial of a Time Lord" in order to protect their scientific secrets, the very sort of interference of which they accuse the Doctor, can be seen as satirising the *tu quoque* dilemma. So too can the incident in "The Trial of a Time Lord", when the Time Lords place one of the characters—King Yrcanos—temporarily in a time bubble, so that they can use him to assassinate all those involved in an experiment whereby the mind of one being is transferred into the brain and body of another (the Doctor's companion Peri Brown).[69] The Doctor's assessment that the Time Lords "took it upon themselves to act like second-rate gods" seems reasonable. The allegation that the Time Lords are as prone as he is to interference, corresponding as it does to *tu quoque* claims, has a delegitimising effect on the trial. The Nuremberg and Tokyo trials were deliberately structured to avoid *tu quoque* defences. Even then, the legitimacy of the trials was compromised. For instance, at the Tokyo trial the dissenting Judge Pal condemned the Allies for hypocrisy in having prosecuted the defendants when their own record of colonialism and the Hiroshima and Nagasaki bombings were far more iniquitous.[70]

Closely related to *tu quoque* as a delegitimising device is the problem of selective prosecution. Why should those Time Lords who covered up Earth's removal not be put on trial? Selectivity has dogged international criminal tribunals from their inception to the present day; why, for example, were those who bombed German population centres during the Second World War not brought to book?[71] This question is raised in

[69] It subsequently emerges that the Time Lords' record of events has been distorted to the extent that somehow King Yrcanos has married, not killed, Peri.

[70] Robert Cryer, *Prosecuting International Crimes: Selectivity and the International Criminal Law Regime* (Cambridge: Cambridge University Press, 2011), 207.

[71] Cryer, *Prosecuting International Crimes*, 208.

the *Doctor Who* serial "The Curse of Fenric" (1989). More recently, in 2000 the prosecutor for the International Criminal Tribunal on the former Yugoslavia (ICTY), Carla del Ponte, announced her decision not to investigate NATO's conduct during the conflict, a decision that caused much controversy.[72] Del Ponte deployed the dubious argument that it was unlikely that sufficient evidence could be acquired. This was despite the fact that the ICTY had broad powers for securing evidence. Her decision effectively shunted the judges to the sidelines, since they could not adjudicate if she did not prosecute; the decision provoked persistent criticism even at the heart of the Tribunal.[73]

Some legal scholars have argued that "[selective] justice is better than no justice at all. Half a loaf is better than pie in the sky".[74] It cannot be denied that selectivity is inevitable in any justice system and does not of itself compromise that system's legitimacy. Selectivity would be tolerable were it random. However, the remarkable feature of war crimes trials is that selectivity is systematic. In particular, it is difficult to imagine leaders of Britain and of the United States of America ever being punished for war crimes, no matter how bad the atrocities they commit. It may well be that the creation of the International Criminal Court (ICC) will further institutionalise American and British impunity if the ICC's performance so far is anything to go by, since "on the Court's record, crimes against humanity and war crimes are acts committed by non-Westerners".[75] Thus, although the ICC was intended to remove the "victors' justice" accusation by introducing universality, its creation provided no triumph for the international penal process, since the international justice system does not operate in a vacuum but is subject to the realities of superpower domination.[76] The resulting systematic selectivity profoundly undermines the legitimacy of war crimes.

[72]Cryer, *Prosecuting International Crimes*, 215.

[73]Pierre Hazan, *Justice in a Time of War: The True Story Behind the International Criminal Tribunal for the Former Yugoslavia* (Texas: Texas A&M University Press, 2004), 133.

[74]Cassese et al., *Cassese's International Criminal Law*, 260.

[75]Tor Krever, "Dispensing Global Justice", *New Left Review*, 85 (2014): 67–97, 94.

[76]Jackson Nyamuya Maogoto, *War Crimes and Realpolitik* (Boulder, CO: Lynne Rienner, 2004), 203–223.

"The Trial of a Time Lord" also usefully highlights the role of a war crimes trial in writing history.[77] The Time Lords wish to tell a story which pitches themselves as an austere clergy, eternally above the whirligig of interfering. The trial reveals that the opposite is the case: the Time Lords have essentially rewritten the history of the planet Ravolox (previously Earth) as part of a cover-up. The story highlights how, in war crimes trials, questions of individual guilt and innocence are inevitably bound up with larger contestations regarding historical narratives.[78] All in all, therefore, the story appears to confirm that the purpose of such trials is to accomplish not justice but political consolidation.[79] At the same time, it shows how dissenting texts which challenge the authorised view of history can be transmitted during and beyond the trial as correctives to historical orthodoxy.[80] For instance, Madoka Futamura reveals how the Tokyo trials, unlike Nuremberg, did not contribute to settling the history of a traumatic and controversial period for Japan.[81] As Gary Jonathan Bass observes, war crimes tribunals have no monopoly on truth-telling.[82]

Doctor Who's insight regarding the inevitability of unjust trials in a world of superpower domination is particularly valuable because if the prosecution of war crimes were suspect in the wake of the Second World War, it is even more so today. In particular, it is difficult to take the idea of war crimes seriously when the invasions of Afghanistan and Iraq go unpunished. The British and American espousal of "preventative war" in those cases undermined the core international law prohibition on aggressive warmaking.[83] It sat uncomfortably with the United Nations

---

[77] William A. Schabas, "Building the Narrative", in *The Scene of the Mass Crime: History, Film and International Tribunals*, eds. Christian Delage and Peter Goodrich (Abingdon: Routledge, 2013), 28.

[78] Schabas, "Building the Narrative", 31.

[79] Charles Anthony Smith, *The Rise and Fall of War Crimes Trials* (Cambridge: Cambridge University Press, 2012), 266, 289–290.

[80] Simpson, *Law, War and Crime*, 94.

[81] Madoka Futamura, *War Crimes Tribunals and Transitional Justice: The Tokyo Trial and the Nuremberg Legacy* (London and New York: Routledge, 2008), 147.

[82] Gary Jonathan Bass, *Stay the Hand of Vengeance: The Politics of War Crimes* (Princeton, NJ and Oxford: Princeton University Press 2000), 302–303.

[83] Richard Falk, Irene Gendzier and Robert Jay Lifton, eds., *Crimes of War: Iraq* (New York: Nation Books, 2006), xvii.

commitment of all states to respect the territorial integrity and political independence of other states.[84] Although the United States of America was the chief architect of the Nuremberg and Tokyo war crimes trials, the same country used its power to exempt its leaders from accountability for aggressive warmaking by refusing to make its own nationals subject to the ICC.[85] Yet the USA had no hesitation about imposing such legal accountability upon its enemies such as Slobodan Milošević and Saddam Hussein.[86]

The disappearance of the Time Lords in new *Who* corresponds to the diminution of the United Nations' legitimacy following its failure to prevent the invasion of Iraq, a watershed in British politics. The "warlike humanitarianism" of NATO's Kosovo intervention had already eroded the primacy of the territorial integrity of states, discarding an organising principle of the international system in a way reminiscent of the Time Lords' jettisoning of their own cherished dogma of non-interference.[87] Afghanistan and Iraq saw the principle of territorial integrity being revised still further in favour of a "new traditionalism" of pre-emptive defence, entitling states to invade rogue states threatening their security, a right of pre-emptive action wherever a state judged a threat to be justified or accurate.[88] Just as Iraq damaged the legitimacy of the United Nations as a peacekeeping organisation, so too in "The End of Time", the Time Lords divest themselves of such legitimacy as they might still possess by planning to destroy time itself. In their place, we find rather weak, *ad hoc* surrogate institutions such as the Judoon, the Shadow Proclamation and Teselecta (a mobile court shadowing the mobile nature of *ad hoc* criminal courts in the recent past)—which correspond to the seemingly fragmented international system post-Iraq.

The idea explored in "The Waters of Mars" (2008)—that, with the Doctor now the sole surviving Time Lord, the laws of time are under his

[84]Article 2(4) United Nations Charter: "All Members shall refrain in their international relations from the threat or use of force against the territorial integrity or political independence of any state, or in any other manner inconsistent with the purposes of the United Nations".

[85]Falk, Gendzier and Lifton, *Crimes of War: Iraq*, 4.

[86]Falk, Gendzier and Lifton, *Crimes of War: Iraq*, 4.

[87]Coates and Krieger, *Blair's War*, 21.

[88]China Miéville, "Anxiety and the Sidekick State: British International Law After Iraq", *Harvard International Law Journal*, 46 (2005): 441–458.

control—reflects the perception in the immediate aftermath of the Cold War that there was one sole superpower, the United States of America. In "The Waters of Mars", the Doctor wishes to change the course of established history by saving some of the people known to have died in a disaster at a human colony on Mars in 2059. In so doing, he reminds us that he is the last of the Time Lords, and asserts that the Time Lords having died, so too have their rules. From now on, the laws of time are the Doctor's, and those rules will obey the Doctor. He is unmoved by the argument that his new omnipotence is wrong. Yet if the Doctor is to determine the laws of time, his track record is hardly encouraging. Like the superpower he now is, the Doctor has long differentiated good guys from bad guys, and picked fights with the latter; and his judgements, as we have seen, are contestable.[89]

Conclusion

This chapter has argued that an uncritical approach towards the Doctor is not really justified. Since the programme's inception, the Doctor has not incontestably been on the side of good and has often been driven by a dislike for the unlike. What has varied over the years is the show's own accompanying narrative: the extent to which *the programme* portrays the Doctor as an unsullied agent of good or otherwise through the words of his friends and enemies. It is not difficult to perceive a reading of Britain in the Doctor's actions. Like the Doctor, Britain's leaders tend to differentiate groups into "good" and "evil", without much room for grey areas. More often than not, groups most unlike ourselves are the most likely to be classed as the enemy.

If we look at the definitions of war crimes and adapt them by feat of imagination to the intergalactic scale, then it is rather difficult to acquit the Doctor. But are legal formulae the right yardstick by which to judge him? The Doctor's trials reflect the danger of law being deployed as a surrogate for political debate on whether conflict is right or wrong. The questionable legitimacy of the Doctor's trials reflects the inevitability of illegitimate justice when superpowers prosecute war crimes, and it

[89] In the event, rather like the USA, the Doctor's superpower status is to some extent illusory; one of the would-be beneficiaries of his control of the laws of time, Captain Adelaide Brooks, elects to commit suicide rather than to allow the Doctor to change a fixed point in time.

is good that *Doctor Who* provides such insights. It shows that a superpower-controlled war crimes tribunal is inevitably something of a show trial. Where the leaders of a weaker power are arraigned at the behest of stronger powers, then there will always be some justification for Judge Pal's dissenting dictum at the Tokyo trials that "only a lost war is a crime".[90]

Against that backdrop, we should therefore beware of allowing smug legalism to obscure political criticism.[91] We should also be wary of hiving off the resolution of such controversies to a judicial elite. Yet the suspect nature of the trials should not push us towards an indiscriminate heaping of praise upon the Doctor. It is to new-series *Doctor Who*'s credit that it so often places question marks over the merits of the Doctor's interference. We can see this as a metaphor for the British public's own scepticism about recent British adventures, notably the Iraq invasion. It is to be hoped that the programme will continue to raise doubts about the Doctor, and to do so even more vigorously, since the new series' more explicit permanent debate over the rights and wrongs of his actions adds greatly to the richness of *Doctor Who*.

Bibliography

Arendt, Hannah. *Eichmann in Jerusalem: A Report on the Banality of Evil.* New York: Penguin, 1994.

Ball, Howard. *Prosecuting War Crimes and Genocide: The Twentieth-Century Experience.* Lawrence, KS: University Press of Kansas, 1999.

Bass, Gary Jonathan. *Stay the Hand of Vengeance: The Politics of War Crimes.* Princeton, NJ and Oxford: Princeton University Press 2000.

Beattie, Melissa. "Life During Wartime: An Analysis of Wartime Morality in *Doctor Who*." In *The Mythological Dimensions of Doctor Who*, edited by Anthony S. Burdge, Jessica Burke and Kristine Larsen, 85–104. Crawfordville, FL: Kitsune Books, 2013.

Boister, Neil and Robert Cryer. *The Tokyo International Military Tribunal: A Reappraisal.* Oxford: Oxford University Press, 2008.

[90] Neil Boister and Robert Cryer, *The Tokyo International Military Tribunal: A Reappraisal* (Oxford: Oxford University Press, 2008), 121.

[91] Miéville, "Anxiety and the Sidekick State", 453.

Brekke, Laura. "Humany, Wumany: Humanity versus Human in *Doctor Who*." In *Time and Relative Dimensions in Faith: Religion and Doctor Who*, edited by Andrew Crome and James McGrath, 94–105. London: Darton, Longman and Todd, 2013.

Britton, Piers D. *TARDISbound: Navigating the Universes of Doctor Who*. London: I.B. Tauris, 2011.

Bunce, Robin. "The *Evil* of the Daleks." In *Doctor Who and Philosophy: Bigger on the Inside*, edited by Courtland Lewis and Paula Smithka, 339–350. Chicago and La Salle, IL: Open Court, 2010.

Cassese, Antonio, Paola Gaeta, Laurel Baig, Mary Fan, Christopher Gosnell and Alex Whiting. *Cassese's International Criminal Law*, 3rd ed. Oxford: Oxford University Press, 2013.

Chapman, James. *Inside the TARDIS: The Worlds of Doctor Who*, 2nd ed. London: I.B. Tauris, 2013.

Charles, Alec. "The Ideology of Anachronism." In *Time and Relative Dissertations in Space: Critical Perspectives on Doctor Who*, edited by David Butler, 108–122. Manchester and New York: Manchester University Press, 2007.

Charles, Alec. "The Allegory of Allegory: Race, Racism and the Summer of 2011." In *Doctor Who and Race*, edited by Lindy Orthia. Bristol: Intellect, 2013.

Charles, Alec. *Out of Time: The Deaths and Resurrections of Doctor Who*. Oxford: Peter Lang, 2015.

Clapham, Andrew. "Issues of Complexity, Complicity and Complementarity: From the Nuremberg Trials to the Dawn of the New International Criminal Court." In *From Nuremberg to the Hague: The Future of International Criminal Justice*, edited by Philippe Sands, 30–67. Cambridge: Cambridge University Press, 2003.

Coates, David and Joel Krieger. *Blair's War*. Cambridge: Polity, 2004.

Cryer, Robert. *Prosecuting International Crimes: Selectivity and the International Criminal Law Regime*. Cambridge: Cambridge University Press, 2011.

Dilks, David. "Introduction." In *Retreat from Power: Studies in Britain's Foreign Policy of the Twentieth Century. Volume Two, After 1939*, edited by David Dilks, 1–34. London and Basingstoke: Macmillan, 1981.

Falk, Richard, Irene Gendzier and Robert Jay Lifton, eds. *Crimes of War: Iraq*. New York: Nation Books, 2006.

Fire Fly. "The White Doctor." In *Doctor Who and Race*, edited by Lindy Orthia, 15–20. Bristol: Intellect, 2013.

Fiske, John. "Dr. Who: Ideology and the Reading of a Popular Narrative Text." *Australian Journal of Screen Theory* 14 (1983): 69–100.

Futamura, Madoka. *War Crimes Tribunals and Transitional Justice: The Tokyo Trial and the Nuremberg Legacy*. London and New York: Routledge, 2008.

Gowing, Margaret. "Britain, America and the Bomb." In *Retreat from Power: Studies in Britain's Foreign Policy of the Twentieth Century. Volume Two, After*

1939, edited by David Dilks, 119–137. London and Basingstoke: Macmillan, 1981.

Grady, Maura and Cassie Hemstrom, "Nostalgia for Empire, 1963–74." In *Doctor Who in Time and Space: Essays on Themes, Characters, History and Fandom, 1963–2012*, edited by Gillian I. Leitch, 125–143. Jefferson, NC and London: McFarland, 2013.

Green, Bonnie and Chris Willmott. "The Cybermen as Human.2." In *New Dimensions of Doctor Who: Adventures in Space, Time and Television*, edited by Matt Hills, 54–70. London: I.B. Tauris, 2013.

Hazan, Pierre. *Justice in a Time of War: The True Story Behind the International Criminal Tribunal for the Former Yugoslavia*. Texas: Texas A&M University Press, 2004.

Hills, Matt. *Triumph of a Time Lord: Regenerating Doctor Who in the Twenty-First Century*. London: I.B. Tauris, 2010.

Jones, Matthew. "Fluid Links: That's What I Like." *Doctor Who Magazine* 238 (1996) Marvel Comics, London: 20.

Jones, Tim. "Breaking the Faiths in 'The Curse of Fenric' and 'The God Complex'." In *Time and Relative Dimensions in Faith: Religion and Doctor Who*, edited by Andrew Crome and James McGrath, 45–59. London: Darton, Longman and Todd, 2013.

Krever, Tor. "Dispensing Global Justice." *New Left Review* 85 (2014): 67–97.

Larsen, Kristine. "'They Hate Each Other's Chromosomes': Eugenics and the Shifting Racial Identity of the Daleks." In *Doctor Who and Race*, edited by Lindy Orthia, 233–250. Bristol: Intellect, 2013.

Layton, David. *The Humanism of Doctor Who: A Critical Study in Science Fiction and Philosophy*. Jefferson, NC: McFarland, 2012.

Lewis, Courtland. "Interference, the Doctor and the Good Life." In *Ruminations, Peregrinations and Regenerations: A Critical Approach to Doctor Who*, edited by Chris Hansen, 299–311. Newcastle-upon-Tyne: Cambridge Scholars Publishing, 2010.

McKee, Gabriel. "Pushing the Protest Button: *Doctor Who*'s Anti-Authoritarian Ethic." In *Time and Relative Dimensions in Faith: Religion and Doctor Who*, edited by Andrew Crome and James McGrath, 16–31. London: Darton, Longman and Todd, 2013.

Maogoto, Jackson Nyamuya. *War Crimes and Realpolitik*. Boulder, CO: Lynne Rienner, 2004.

Martin, Laurence and John Garnett. *British Foreign Policy: Challenges and Choices for the 21st Century*. London: Pinter, 1997.

Meron, Theodor. *War Crimes Law Comes of Age*. Oxford: Oxford University Press, 1998.

Miéville, China. "Anxiety and the Sidekick State: British International Law After Iraq." *Harvard International Law Journal* 46 (2005): 441–458.

O'Day, Andrew. "Towards a Definition of Satire in *Doctor Who*." In *Ruminations, Peregrinations and Regenerations: A Critical Approach to Doctor Who*, edited by Chris Hansen, 264–282. Newcastle-upon-Tyne: Cambridge Scholars Publishing, 2010.

Orthia, Lindy. ed. *Doctor Who and Race*. Bristol: Intellect, 2013.

Overy, Richard. "The Nuremberg Trials." In *From Nuremberg to The Hague: The Future of International Criminal Justice*, edited by Philippe Sands, 1–29. Cambridge: Cambridge University Press, 2003.

Owen, James. *Nuremberg: Evil on Trial*. London: Headline, 2006.

Schabas, William A. "Building the Narrative." In *The Scene of the Mass Crime: History, Film and International Tribunals*, edited by Christian Delage and Peter Goodrich, 28. Abingdon: Routledge, 2013.

Scott, Cavan and Mark Wright. *Doctor Who: The Official Miscellany*. London: BBC Books, 2013.

Scully, Richard. "*Doctor Who* and the Racial State: Fighting National Socialism Across Time and Space." In *Doctor Who and Race*, edited by Lindy Orthia, 179–196. Bristol: Intellect, 2013.

Simpson, Gerry. *Law, War and Crime: War Crimes Trials and the Reinvention of International Law*. London: Polity, 2007.

Smith, Charles Anthony. *The Rise and Fall of War Crimes: From Charles I to Bush II*. Cambridge: Cambridge University Press, 2012.

Vasquez, Joshua. "The Moral Economy of *Doctor Who*: Forgiving Fans and the Objects of Their Devotion." In *Ruminations, Peregrinations and Regenerations: A Critical Approach to Doctor Who*, edited by Chris Hansen 233–248. Newcastle-upon-Tyne: Cambridge Scholars Publishing, 2010.

Vohlidka, John. "*Doctor Who* and the Critique of Western Imperialism." In *Doctor Who and Race*, edited by Lindy Orthia, 125–139. Bristol: Intellect, 2013.

Wardley, Jason K. "Divine and Human Nature: Incarnation and Kenosis in *Doctor Who*." In *Time and Relative Dimensions in Faith: Religion and Doctor Who*, edited by Andrew Crome and James McGrath. London: Darton, Longman and Todd, 2013.

Wickham-Jones, Mark. "Labour's Trajectory in Foreign Affairs: The Moral Crusade of a Pivotal Power?" In *New Labour's Foreign Policy: A New Moral Crusade?* edited by Richard Little and Mark Wickham-Jones, 3–33. Manchester: Manchester University Press, 2000.

CHAPTER 6

From Davos to Davros: Corporate Power in Britain and in *Doctor Who*

Nothing epitomises the power of private corporations better than the World Economic Forum held each winter at Davos in Switzerland. Business and political leaders congregate at this annual gathering in order to shape global and national policies—a form of governance that British politicians have embraced. *Doctor Who* merits study in this regard because it has spanned Britain's transformation from a social democratic country into a neoliberal one. During the programme's lifetime, belief among Britain's politicians in the centrality of the welfare state, a significant public sector, full employment and a measure of social equality has been replaced with zeal for private enterprise, a cult of the entrepreneur and a cheery toleration of the widening gap between rich and poor. Yet the emergence of this strong neoliberal consensus among the country's political elite actually followed an economic change: the rise of transnational corporations. Concerns over the size and power of large-scale capitalist enterprises made them an important focus for science fiction, including in *Doctor Who*. As shown in Chap. 1, the earliest days of the series did not actually feature corporate villains at all. This changed with "The Invasion" in 1968, after which the number of *Doctor Who* stories featuring corporate enemies multiplied, and corporate domination became a theme to which the programme returned time and again.

This chapter argues that, despite *Doctor Who* being a multi-authored television programme, there are some remarkable recurring themes in the Doctor's numerous engagements with companies and magnates. Intriguingly, one of the earliest and best-known pieces of *Doctor Who*

D. Nicol, *Doctor Who: A British Alien?*,
https://doi.org/10.1007/978-3-319-65834-6_6

scholarship tackled the very question of *Doctor Who*'s relationship with capitalism. In a celebrated 1983 article entitled "Dr. Who: Ideology and the Reading of a Popular Narrative Text", John Fiske argues that *Doctor Who* advances a pro-capitalist ideology.[1] He does so by singling out for analysis the four-part serial "The Creature from the Pit" (1979). This chapter puts the case against both Fiske's methodology and his conclusion. It will be argued, *contra* Fiske, that *Doctor Who* has persistently adopted a *critical* approach towards corporations, albeit one which falls short of being socialist. The chapter aims to show that *Doctor Who* stories tend to attribute a number of unfavourable common features to the corporate system. In so doing, the programme satirises both Britain's imperial past and its neoliberal present.

Doctor Who's Turning-Point: "The Invasion"

As shown in Chap. 4, "The Invasion" was the first *Doctor Who* serial in which a corporation and its owner played a prominent villainous role. Yet "The Invasion" was broadcast in 1968, which meant that *Doctor Who* had been on the air for five years before corporate domination started to become a pervasive theme. What might have inspired *Doctor Who*'s authors to turn their fire on the private sector? The most obvious explanation is that, until the latter half of the 1960s, companies were not really perceived as overmighty and threatening, and were not therefore the stuff of science fiction. Rather, at the height of the Cold War, the overwhelming threat to the citizen was perceived as coming from the state. Concern about the abuse of governmental power was reflected in "The War Machines" (1966), a story in which the British state, albeit inadvertently, creates a computer which sets about eliminating humans from the planet. This perception—that the threat to liberty came from governments rather than from companies—changed as a result of a merger boom in the latter half of the 1960s. Startlingly, by the early 1970s, the top hundred manufacturing firms in Britain now controlled some half of net manufacturing output, whereas in 1950 they had controlled only a fifth, and in 1910 only 15%.[2] There had, therefore, been

[1] *Australian Journal of Screen Theory*, 14 (1983): 69–100.

[2] Stuart Holland, *The Socialist Challenge* (London: Quartet, 1975), 49.

a dramatic concentration of economic power in the hands of a relatively small number of top firms.

Companies were changing in another sense too: they were becoming more multinational.[3] A system in which international trade was conducted between different firms in different countries was being replaced by one in which such trade was actually conducted within the *same* firm, by its subsidiaries from different countries trading with each other. Furthermore, their multinational nature gave firms the ability to relocate investment and jobs outside Britain. Companies thereby gained the power to bargain terms for their operations within Britain which suited them more than they suited the British government. Indeed, by the 1970s, the multinational nature of companies was serving to substantially undermine the effectiveness of the monetary and fiscal policies of governments everywhere.[4] Thus, as early as 1973, the Steuer Report concluded that it would be difficult for governments to pursue *any* policy which could effectively constrain the activities of foreign companies within national territories.[5] In sum, the increasingly global operation of companies, coupled with the concentration of corporate resources into fewer giant firms, was turning corporate power into the kind of threat to human freedom with which science fiction needed to engage.

It was with this backdrop that *Doctor Who* commenced its onslaught against corporate domination in "The Invasion". In this adventure,

---

[3] Holland, *The Socialist Challenge*, 76. Holland observes that the number of firms controlling at least six foreign subsidiaries rose from thirty to fifty of the top hundred British manufacturers during the 1960s.

[4] Holland, *The Socialist Challenge*, 74–77, 79–86. The multinationality of companies undermines national *monetary* policy because they can draw funds regardless of national interest rates from the internally generated funds of their subsidiaries operating abroad, as well as from international capital markets which large multinational companies are better placed to use than national companies. Multinational companies are likewise well placed to bypass national *fiscal* policy for a variety of reasons. First, they can impede the use of fiscal measures to restrain growth since their market is not limited to the domestic market, a feature which can give them a competitive advantage over nationally based companies. Secondly, they can often secure tax concessions over national companies as a condition of their locating in the national economy concerned. Thirdly, multinational companies practise "transfer pricing", whereby their foreign subsidiaries charge them prices for products and services which are higher than the real value of those products and services. As a result, they can declare low profits and pay low taxes.

[5] Max Steuer et al., *The Impact of Foreign Direct Investment on the United Kingdom* (London: HMSO, 1973).

the Doctor is pitted against Tobias Vaughn, a magnate who owns the global corporation International Electromatics and is in league with the Cybermen. International Electromatics is a firm in the computers sector. This choice of sector was essential to the plot: the company and its Cybermen allies deploy processors concealed within transistor radios as a means of mind control in an attempt to subdue the human population into becoming Cybermen. However, the choice also reflected the real-world concentration of commercial power: in the field of computers, IBM's world domination had already become notorious.[6] Ultimately, the corporation-backed Cybermen are defeated by state power: the armed forces of different countries work together to destroy the Cyberfleet with missiles, aided by the mathematical calculations of the Doctor's companion Zoe Heriot. The "good" state is thereby counterposed to the "bad" corporation.

In the years that followed, *Doctor Who* plots increasingly portrayed corporations and their leaders as villains. The number of such stories is striking: they include "Spearhead from Space" (1970), "Terror of the Autons" (1971), "Colony in Space" (1971), "The Green Death" (1973), "The Seeds of Doom" (1976), "The Sun Makers" (1977), "The Power of Kroll" (1978–1979), "Terminus" (1983), "The Caves of Androzani" (1984), "Vengeance on Varos" (1985), "Revelation of the Daleks" (1985), "The Trial of a Time Lord" ("Mindwarp") (1986), "The End of the World" (2005), "Dalek" (2005), "The Long Game" (2005), "Bad Wolf"/"The Parting of the Ways" (2005), "Rise of the Cybermen"/"The Age of Steel" (2006), "Voyage of the Damned" (2007), "Partners in Crime" (2008), "Planet of the Ood" (2008), "The Sontaran Stratagem" (2008) "The End of Time" (2009–2010), "A Christmas Carol" (2010), "The Rebel Flesh"/"The Almost People" (2011), "The Bells of Saint John" (2013), "Time Heist" (2014) and "Dark Water"/"Death in Heaven" (2014), "Sleep No More" (2015), "The Return of Doctor Mysterio" (2016) and "Oxygen" (2017).

[6] Holland, *The Socialist Challenge*, 77.

Doctor Who and Capitalism: John Fiske's Analysis

In the context of this depiction of corporate villainy, it seems strange that the first academic analysis on the relationship between *Doctor Who* and capitalism reached the conclusion that *Doctor Who* promotes a capitalist ideology. This is the 1983 article "Dr. Who: Ideology and the Reading of a Popular Narrative Text" by John Fiske. One must certainly applaud Fiske for being the first to engage with *Doctor Who*'s treatment of this most fundamental of issues. Analysing the *Doctor Who* story "The Creature from the Pit" (1979), his argument revolves around *discourses.* He contends that the story contains political discourses which assume a high degree of consensus even in controversial areas. Whilst Fiske warns that the operation of such discourses is highly complex, this does not stop him concluding that the story advances a free trade agenda and thereby promotes the capitalist system. Furthermore, Fiske's article implies that what's true of "The Creature from the Pit" is true of *Doctor Who* as a whole.[7]

Let us pause here to dwell on Fiske's methodology: he examines *one single Doctor Who serial.* The classic series consisted of no fewer than 156 serials, and by the time of Fiske's article, the BBC had broadcast 123 of them. Yet Fiske does not seek to justify his reliance on one story alone. At best, one can discern an implicit rationale, in that he analyses the script line by line, which would not be practical on a grand scale. By the same token, such methodology would hardly have ruled out the analysis of several *Doctor Who* serials rather than just one. Had he done so, he could have chosen to study some which pit the Doctor against corporate opponents and which therefore seem highly critical of capitalism. Moreover, Fiske's reliance on one story alone seems particularly inappropriate given the multi-authored nature of *Doctor Who.* Whilst it is of course perfectly possible for a consensus to form among the show's writers, Fiske surely should at least be able to point to a reasonable number of authors to prove that this is the case.

In fact, a consensus does indeed exist among *Doctor Who*'s authors—but it takes the form of a highly critical stance towards corporations.

[7] The article's title, Fiske's comments on the discourses relating to the Doctor's character, and his lack of mention of *Doctor Who* stories which might pull in the opposite ideological direction, all suggest that his complaint of pro-capitalist bias relates to *Doctor Who* generally, rather than merely the single story which he analyses.

Furthermore, there are several *Doctor Who* adventures that were broadcast *before* "The Creature from the Pit" which show this consensus emerging, and which Fiske does not consider. Let me summarise some of them. In "The Invasion", a transnational corporation acts as a bridgehead for a Cyberman invasion force. In "Colony in Space" (1971), the Interplanetary Mining Corporation uses murder to scare off environmentally motivated colonists from a planet on which it wishes to pursue its commercial gain. "The Green Death" (1973) features a company, Global Chemicals, covertly run by a megalomaniac computer which is creating deadly giant maggots through its chemical processes. "The Sun Makers" (1977) imagines that the planet Pluto is ruled by a company that enslaves its workers through excessive taxation, oppressive criminal laws and drugged air. In "The Power of Kroll" (1979), a methane-refining company seeks to eliminate marsh-dwelling natives who are regarded as subhuman by the company's staff. Fiske does not engage with the consistently anti-corporate discourses of any of these stories. So even if we were to accept hook, line and sinker Fiske's interpretation of "The Creature from the Pit", that would not of itself provide convincing evidence that *Doctor Who* generally advances pro-capitalist propaganda.

Fiske couples his argument that "The Creature from the Pit" contains a free trade discourse with a contention that the story also promotes individualism. He marries together free trade and individualism as two values which uphold capitalism.[8] Eccentricity and individualism, he insists, should be seen as values of capitalism, whereas conformity is associated with communism.[9] Let us leave to one side the contested nature of individualism: it is a matter to which we will return later in this chapter. However we interpret individualism, in making his argument, Fiske's analysis once again suffers from the narrowness of his study. There are *Doctor Who* serials preceding "The Creature from the Pit" that portray corporate domination as hostile to individuality. Thus, in "The Green Death", capitalist uniformity is ensured by the computer which runs Global Chemicals, subjecting the company's staff to mind control, and in "The Sun Makers", workers are drugged into conformity with the company by the use of airborne chemicals.

[8] Fiske, "Dr. Who: Ideology", 73.

[9] Fiske, "Dr. Who: Ideology", 85.

My primary objection to Fiske's thesis, therefore, is that he bases himself on only one of the Doctor's adventures and, in so doing, ignores a large number of anti-corporate *Doctor Who* stories. The narrowness of his evidence base skews his depiction of the show. But there are other objections to his argument too. This book contends that *Doctor Who* often bases itself on metaphor. Scholars and fans continually put forward arguments that a *Doctor Who* story serves as a metaphor for this, that or the other social, political or legal phenomenon. As I argue at the beginning of this book, the crucial question is whether the evidence for such arguments is sufficiently *convincing*. I would contend that the metaphorical link between the plot of "The Creature from the Pit" and the economic debates in Britain in the late 1970s is not particularly compelling, and that this further weakens the argument that "The Creature from the Pit" is capitalist propaganda.

Judging whether Fiske's metaphorical link is convincing requires us to consider his argument in more depth. Fiske starts his article by relating the plot of "The Creature from the Pit". To give a condensed version: the Doctor and companion Romana land on Chloris, a planet overrun with vegetation but short of minerals. They fall into the hands of Lady Adrasta, the planet's dictator, who owns a monopoly of metal. Fearing the Doctor, Adrasta has him thrown down a pit where he encounters the Creature, a gigantic blob-shaped entity used by Adrasta to crush to death those who incur her displeasure. The Doctor discovers that the Creature is in fact Erato, an Ambassador from the planet Tythonis sent on a trade mission: the Tythonians desperately need vegetation but have a surfeit of metal. For years Adrasta has imprisoned Erato to preserve the monopoly from which her power derives. Ultimately, Erato kills Adrasta, and the two planets end up making a trading agreement.

Fiske argues that this plot contains "discourses of politics, morality, economics and individualism" which assume the existence of a high degree of consensus over controversial areas such as free trade and individualism. He concedes that the operation of discourse is potentially variable, yet he proposes that the values of the heroes in "The Creature from the Pit" are those of capitalist democracies, whereas those of the villains are those of communism. Unfortunately, Fiske does not spell out how the capitalism-versus-communism choice impacted on politics in Britain at the time the story was broadcast.[10]

Let us consider Fiske's suggestion that the story contains a free trade discourse. Insofar as Britain's political right favoured free trade more than the political left, the issue of trade has a certain resonance. But how strong is the free trade metaphor in "The Creature from the Pit"? When he mentions trade in his article, Fiske generally refers to it as "free trade". Yet, having done so, he does not go on to consider what "free trade" actually means. "Trade" simply morphs into "free trade" through Fiske's linguistic sleight of hand. In fact, a free trade area is usually taken to mean a territory within which barriers to trade are generally dismantled, as in the single market of the European Union.[11] Free trade "allows unregulated international movement of goods and services and of capital".[12] Thus, *any* quantity of *any* product can move freely across national frontiers. In the case of the European Union, free trade has come to entail a significant loss of national sovereignty, since it affects not only what happens at frontiers but also a country's internal measures.[13] The opposite of free trade is not necessarily "non-trade", autarky

[10]The choice which confronted *Britain* in the late 1970s and early 1980s was not between capitalism and communism but between (a) the new brand of radical capitalism (subsequently dubbed neoliberalism) advanced by Margaret Thatcher's Conservatives, (b) the compromised social democracy implemented by the 1974–1979 Labour government, and (c) the more radical democratic socialism propounded by the left of the Labour Party under the informal leadership of Tony Benn. The choice in favour of neoliberalism was one which would determine the political direction of the country for decades to come.

[11]At the time, this free trade area was known as the "common market" of the European Economic Community, but its fundamentals of the free movement of goods, persons, services and capital had already been established to a significant extent.

[12]Arthur McEwan, *Neo-liberalism or Democracy?* (London: Zed Books, 1999), 31, 33.

[13]Free trade involves a general eradication of both fiscal and non-fiscal barriers to trade on all products. Charges cannot be made at frontiers, internal taxation must in no way discriminate against imports, and quantitative restrictions on imports and equivalent measures must be abolished. A welter of case law from the European Union's Court of Justice confirms that the prohibition on "measures equivalent to quantitative restrictions" is interpreted very broadly indeed: for instance, it renders even regulations which apply to *all* goods—domestic and imported alike—liable to judicial review for their proportionately, and even prohibits the British government from organising "Buy British" campaigns. See *Rewe-Zentral AG v Bundesmonopolverwaltung für Branntwein* (Cassis de Dijon), Case 120/78, [1979] ECR 649; *Commission v Ireland* (Buy Irish), Case 249/81, [1982] ECR 4005.

(economic self-sufficiency) and a closed economy: indeed, in the political context of Britain in 1979, free trade was counterposed to planned trade.[14] "Planned trade" meant that there would indeed be trade with other countries but that the nature and volume of this trade would be determined by the state. The trade imagined at the conclusion of "The Creature in the Pit" is merely that one state (planet) permits the importation of *a certain specific product* from another state (planet) in return for being allowed to export *another specific product* to that other state (planet). This limited trade is in fact planned trade—the policy associated at the time with the British left—rather than free trade—the policy associated with the British right. Thus, the something-for-something exchange advocated by the story is not actually free trade.

Fiske's suggestion that *Doctor Who* advances a pro-free trade ideology has also been seriously undermined by a story broadcast six years after "The Creature from the Pit" and two years after the publication of Fiske's article. This is "Vengeance on Varos" (1985). In this adventure, the TARDIS materialises on the planet Varos to find an impoverished and authoritarian society which trades in its only natural resource, zeiton-7 ore. If "The Creature from the Pit" suggests that trade between planets/states is co-operative, egalitarian and benign, then "Vengeance on Varos" depicts trade as exploitative and oppressive. Whereas "The Creature from the Pit" posits two planets as equal trading partners, "Vengeance on Varos" imagines disequilibrium between an economically weak Varos and a powerful corporation, the Galatron Mining Corporation.

---

[14]This kind of planned trade was the official policy of the Labour government which lost power in 1979: in its election manifesto, it trod a middle way, supporting increased trade whilst rejecting a free-for-all: "We also need a programme to protect employment while the necessary changes and modernization of our industry takes place. We will not allow our industries to be wiped out by excessive imports before they have had a chance to recover their strength. The Labour Government will ensure that imports enter our market only within acceptable limits." Yet the Conservative opposition also envisaged limits on free trade. Whilst the Party's 1979 manifesto opposed in general terms the "Socialist panacea" of import controls, it nonetheless sought a revision of the General Agreement on Tariffs and Trade (GATT) in order to "give us a better defence against sudden and massive surges of imports that destroy jobs". (By contrast, within the European single market, there is no protection against import surges from other parts of the EU.) Ostensibly, therefore, the difference between Britain's two major parties on trade was merely one of degree: in the year in which "The Creature in the Pit" was broadcast, neither party expressed support for free trade as an unqualified public "good": trade policy was almost a consensus issue.

The scenario in Varos is more realistic than that in Chloris in two senses: firstly, the economic inequality between planets reflects the real-world distinction between rich and poor countries, and secondly, the fact that one of the parties is a corporation mirrors the real-world domination of economic life by the private sector—strangely, in "The Creature from the Pit", Fiske's vaunted capitalism develops in the absence of private enterprise. By contrast, in "Vengeance on Varos", we are informed that for centuries the Corporation has declared rich dividends by exploiting the planet's labour and resources. For good measure, it becomes evident that the corporation intervenes deeply into Varos' internal affairs: Sil, the company's agent, says of the Doctor and his allies: "They must be apprehended, sentenced, executed! My company is only interested in stable situations!" Sil's stance neatly encapsulates the situation under globalisation whereby transnational companies could increasingly threaten to transfer their operations from state to state in order to exact the best possible conditions from governments, including a political settlement that conforms to corporate wishes.

Of course, Fiske was in no position to know about "Vengeance on Varos". However, the liberalisation of trade also ends in tears in "Carnival of Monsters" (1973), which predates "The Creature from the Pit". Relaxing its approach to trade, a planet allows the importation of an item banned under intergalactic law—a machine containing miniaturised aliens. A huge carnivorous creature, a Drashig, escapes from the machine, and causes mayhem. Read together, the two "Peladon" stories also offer a cautionary tale against trade-based integration. In "The Curse of Peladon" (1972), *Doctor Who*'s grand allegory for British accession to the European Economic Community, the Doctor sides with those who favour the planet Peladon's accession to the Galactic Federation against a primitive and self-serving opposition. It is clear that the Federation's foundation is multilateral trade: the Doctor's enemies appear to have concocted a bilateral trade deal in opposition to Federation arrangements. However, in "The Monster of Peladon" (1974), a story broadcast only two years later, the Federation has become a source of oppression, overworking the planet's miners. Ultimately, Federation troops are brought into quell the miners' protests, in what seems a cover for an invasion by an oppressive Ice Warrior force, authorised to use any terror method. Thus, the free trade organisation turns itself against the underprivileged.

In view of all of this, it is possible to envisage a more compelling reading of "The Creature from the Pit". This interpretation would view the story as a condemnation of totalitarianism, linked to xenophobia, racism and a lack of internationalism. The refusal to trade is merely a manifestation of these reactionary stances, on a par with the act of imprisoning a foreign ambassador in a pit. This interpretation of the story chimes better with certain aspects of "The Creature from the Pit", notably the feudal rather than communistic nature of Chloris' society, the costumes and the scenery. These exude the medieval era, not Soviet greyness. In fact, they serve to make the story's theme of monopoly more reminiscent of Tudor and Stuart grievances than of communism. In the sixteenth and seventeenth centuries, the Crown granted monopolies to private corporations to engage in specific commercial activities (the most famous beneficiary being the East India Company). Monopoly was thus associated with early *capitalist* development.

Furthermore, Fiske's thesis sits unhappily with the villain, Lady Adrasta, being a woman. A study by Richard Wallace has shown that the *Doctor Who* season in which "The Creature from the Pit" was broadcast marked a turning-point in the show's history. The gender balance of the Doctor's opponents changed dramatically. The number of woman villains leapt from two in the previous season to six. Thereafter, throughout the 1980s, the Doctor was twice as likely to encounter a female villain as had been the case prior to 1979.[15] The most convincing explanation for this change is the emergence of Margaret Thatcher as a political figure. Yet if Adrasta is a Thatcher figure, as seems likely, she can hardly be a communist at the same time.

Corporations in *Doctor Who*: Common Themes

We should, therefore, be wary of Fiske's suggestion that *Doctor Who* is actively pro-capitalist. But if it is not, what are *Doctor Who*'s criticisms of corporate domination? The remainder of the chapter explores this question. Unlike Fiske, it does so by surveying the entire *Doctor Who* television canon. In so doing, we can easily discern a trope: that big business is

[15] Richard Wallace, "'The Sound of Empires Toppling': Politics, Public Service Broadcasting and *Doctor Who*", *Doctor Who: Walking in Eternity*, University of Hertfordshire, September 3–5, 2013.

portrayed as hostile to human wellbeing. Within this trope one can identify a surprising number of "sub-tropes", criticising corporate behaviour in various different respects.

Before examining these sub-tropes, it is easy to overlook the presence of an absence: the lack of *favourable* imaginings of companies in *Doctor Who*.[16] There is a striking non-existence of public-spirited private corporations and kindly private-sector employers in the Doctor's adventures.[17] In a sense, this is unsurprising. Private companies may expend some modest efforts on extolling their own philanthropic activities.[18] However, for the most part, they argue that their benefit to the country lies in producing goods and services efficiently in a climate of competition. It is precisely their profit-making which is trumpeted as being in the national interest. These pro-corporation arguments do not seem to work themselves into *Doctor Who*.

Neither does *Doctor Who* appear to promote the ideas of public interest advanced in favour of corporations by neoliberal normative theory. This theory, expounded by Friedrich von Hayek, stipulates that an economy of privately owned companies will guarantee the liberty of the individual because of competition between firms, whereas one based on public ownership and governmental economic planning involves a paternalistic desire to foist upon people a creed considered good for them.[19] Hayek was adamantly opposed to monopoly institutions, even Britain's National Health Service in the field of healthcare, seeing them as coercive. He wanted to replace them with *markets* of competing institutions.[20] But competition between corporations is rarely apparent in *Doctor Who* stories. Rather, a single corporation rules the roost and itself

---

[16]In two adventures set in hospitals the Doctor remarks he likes a little shop, but even this statement leaves open the question of whether the hospital shop is public-sector or private-sector ("New Earth" (2006), "Smith and Jones" (2007)).

[17]For such a depiction, consider e.g. the Cheeryble brothers in Charles Dickens' *Nicholas Nickleby* (Oxford: Oxford University Press, 2008).

[18]Some commentators criticise British corporations for being far less engaged in philanthropic activities than their Victorian predecessors: see e.g. *Ian Hislop's Age of the Do-Gooders*, BBC2, 29 November–13 December 2010.

[19]See e.g. Friedrich von Hayek, *The Road to Serfdom* (London: Routledge and Kegan Paul, 1986), *The Constitution of Liberty* (Chicago: University of Chicago Press, 1960), *Law, Legislation and Liberty* (London: Routledge and Kegan Paul, 1982).

[20]Hayek, *The Constitution of Liberty*, 304.

acts as a source of coercion. To be sure, *Doctor Who*'s satire exaggerates: sectors of British industry are rarely dominated by a single company. It is, however, common for a handful of companies to enjoy collective dominance in a sector. The economic phenomenon whereby only a few companies control a sector, with substantial obstacles to new firms entering the market, is known as oligopoly. The significance of oligopoly is that prices tend to rise to a supracompetitive level without the need for companies to connive. To give an example, the post-privatisation British energy industry is an oligopoly and British consumers have suffered the consequences in their gas and electricity bills.[21] Other oligopolies in the British economy include banking, supermarkets, land-line telephones, vehicle fuel retailers and bus transport. Frequently, therefore, competition does little to offset the concentration of economic power in the hands of large privately owned operators, or, for that matter, their political power. In this regard, by emphasising corporate domination over the merits of competition, *Doctor Who* provides a valuable insight.

In sum, *Doctor Who* has never projected a benign image of capitalist enterprise, nor does it promote Utopian designs of competition. Rather, *Doctor Who* has tended to attribute certain negative features to large-scale capitalist enterprise. These comprise: political rule and empire (including the very fusion of corporation and state), authoritarianism and oppression, clandestine ownership by an alien, the servicing of the super-rich and the reinforcing of the class system, the pursuit of uniformity, and finally, the cultivation of an inability to question capitalism. Let us now consider these various sub-tropes in more depth.

Sub-Trope 1: Political Rule and Empire

Corporations in *Doctor Who* frequently do not restrict themselves to business activities and exercise political power as well. Furthermore, their activities are often linked to the acquisition and expansion of empires. Evaluating *Doctor Who*'s stance on the political role of business obliges

[21] See generally Ian Bartle, *Globalisation and EU Policy-Making: The Neoliberal Transformation of Telecommunications and Electricity* (Manchester: Manchester University Press, 2005). British newspapers from both sides of the political spectrum express outrage at the conduct of the companies: "Gas bill rip-off as we freeze", *Daily Express*, January 30, 2015, "Energy fat-cats' profits up 1000 per cent", *Daily Mirror*, January 30, 2015. Yet such behaviour is inevitable in an oligopoly.

us to dwell on the role of capitalist enterprise in Britain's imperial past. It also requires us to consider *Doctor Who*'s satire of present-day political rule by corporations. Finally, it is worthwhile assessing whether *Doctor Who* storylines conform to the relationship between business and political state advocated by neoliberal normative theory.

Before tackling these questions, we should note that it is an inevitable aspect of capitalism that companies assume a political role. Their profitability substantially depends upon governmental regulation, so it is only logical for them to press for laws which favour their economic interests. The fact that businesses cannot be kept to a discrete world of business may be considered one of the internal contradictions of liberal democracy: we can vote all we like, but companies retain a disproportionate say in government policy by virtue of their economic might. Business leaders tend not to trumpet this political sway. Rather, they often like to portray themselves as remote from party politics and disdainful of politicians: they frequently seek to "depoliticise" controversial matters and have them judged according to business criteria. Doing so, however, represents not the avoidance of ideology but rather its surreptitious importation.[22] Yet, at key moments, the leaders of corporations cheerfully discard agnosticism in party politics, as shown by the support of numerous company executives for the Conservative Party during Britain's 2015 general election.[23] *Doctor Who* satirises the political influence of companies by imagining them with even more power. Thus, in some *Doctor Who* stories, companies wield enormous political power whilst not forming the government. In others, they actually rule planets.

Doctor Who's cautionary tales resonate with the historical experience of British capitalism and Empire. In particular, they serve as a reminder of the remarkable evolution of the East India Company (1600–1874), which ruled over what was essentially the British Empire in Asia for more than a century.[24] The idea that the Empire was run by a private company before it was governed by the British state is astonishing, and has largely been written out of British history. Given the peculiar amnesia hanging

---

[22] Ralph Miliband, *The State in Capitalist Society* (London: Weidenfeld and Nicolson, 1969), 56.

[23] *Daily Telegraph*, April 1, 2015.

[24] It passed over its territories to the Crown in 1858 following rebellion in India and financial collapse.

over the East India Company's story, it is unlikely that *Doctor Who*'s writers mugged up on it before concocting their anti-corporate tales. Nonetheless, the Company—which has been described as the "mother of the modern corporation"—rather strongly resembles the sort of corporations that we meet in *Doctor Who.*[25] Not least, it acted as a political ruler. From its coastal ports of Bombay, Calcutta and Madras, the Company established a huge land empire which later spread to South East Asia and parts of China and Japan, as well as the ports of Penang and Singapore. Some of these territories were acquired by military conquest, since the Company had its own armed forces; others were gained by commercial contract, a point neatly reflected in "The Sun Makers" (1977), where the alien, capitalistic Usurians have secured ownership of the human race through a "normal business transaction". Whilst the East India Company's activities have been significantly erased from the mainstream British historical narrative, in India they serve as a cautionary tale against the dangers of domination by foreign companies. This is because the Company was an enterprise which "came to trade but stayed to rule". Specifically, it was accorded a number of semi-sovereign privileges: the right to mint coins, to exercise justice and to wage war; and it could thereby practise "commerce with a sword in its hand".[26] Crucially, in 1763 the Company was granted *diwani* rights for Bengal, Bihar and Orissa. This meant that, in return for a lump sum payment, the Company secured the power to levy taxation. This proved immensely profitable. It also effectively reconstituted these territories as corporate states: very much the stuff of *Doctor Who* adventures.

In "The Sun Makers", for instance, the (nameless) Company has assumed the task of tax collection and taxes its employees (its "work units") excessively for the privilege of having their parents put to death once their usefulness as workers expires. Since the Company *is* the state, the apparatus of the state has been arranged to maximise the profitability of the Company. Whilst stories like "The Sun Makers" exaggerate for the sake of satire, the experience of the East India Company shows that *Doctor Who*'s imaginings of corporate political rule are far from fanciful. "The Sun Makers" is just one of a number of *Doctor Who* stories

[25] Nick Robins, *The Corporation That Changed the World: How the East India Company Shaped the Modern Multinational* (London: Pluto Press, 2006), xii, 5.

[26] Robins, *The Corporation That Changed the World*, 28–29.

in which a corporation actually acts as political ruler of territory, in this case the planet Pluto populated by the human race. Similarly, in "The Long Game" (2005) the space station Satellite 5 is governed by a corporation that has control of the news media throughout the human empire. Furthermore, in both stories, the growth of the company has supposedly been propelled by imperial expansion. In "The Long Game", the company has ostensibly flourished as part of the "Fourth Great and Bountiful Human Empire" which has spread across a million planets and a million species. In "The Sun Makers", we are told that humans have gone beyond "Old Earth" and that this development is best explained by a "natural progression theory". Yet in both stories, the nature of the empire proves deceptive. In "The Long Game", we discover that the real owner and ruler of Satellite 5 is the mighty Jagrafess, a huge, snarling alien. In "The Sun Makers", it transpires that the Usurians, having obtained control of humanity through a business transaction, moved dying humanity to Mars, then taxed them, then moved them to Pluto and then taxed them more. In both stories, the narrative of political empire is mere spin, concealing the reality of corporate empire.

Doctor Who has also repeatedly tackled the ownership claims of corporations over the third world. In a series of *Doctor Who* stories—"Colony in Space" (1971), "The Power of Kroll" (1978–1979), "The Caves of Androzani" (1984) and "Vengeance on Varos" (1985)—corporations own, or lay claim to, "underdeveloped" planets in order to extract their resources: they intend to establish political rule over those worlds, not merely a commercial presence. Similarly, in "Planet of the Ood" (2008), the home planet of a slave race called the Ood, known as the Ood-Sphere, seems to be owned and ruled by a human company, Ood Operations.

Furthermore, corporate claims of territorial control can trump the claims of the state. For example, "The Invasion" (1968) is an earthbound story which involves a company effectively ruling over land which, at a formal level, is part of the United Kingdom: the story opens with an agent of the United Nations Intelligence Taskforce (UNIT) trying to escape from a large site in southern England run by the company. The premises appear in practice to be subject only to the company's own political rule and law. Even though the UNIT operative escapes the company's domain, he is nonetheless hunted down and killed by company henchmen. Later in the story, a senior government military officer, Major General Rutlidge, accuses UNIT of having "trespassed" over the company's "top security site" by undertaking surveillance by helicopter. Rutlidge thereby displays a chilling deference towards the territorial and security claims of a private firm.

Let us now consider the way in which *Doctor Who* reflects our *present-day* experience of corporate domination. A major difference between today's Britain and the era of the East India Company lies in the emergence of democracy as supreme indicator of governmental legitimacy. Whereas the Company came to prominence in a pre-democratic era, nowadays the belief that only an elected regime has the right to rule is deeply ingrained. Corporations have to pay lip service to elected governments and parliaments. This does not mean that they have ceased to be political rulers but merely that corporate political rule must be pursued more surreptitiously. This does not prevent *Doctor Who* from brushing aside the window-dressing and observing that corporations, not governments, pull the strings.

The political role of companies has intensified in the last few decades, and *Doctor Who* has come to reflect this. From the 1960s onwards, the trend towards economic concentration meant that individual businesses became a force to be reckoned with. Globalisation has further intensified since the 1980s, and this has served to exacerbate these concerns. By the 1990s, it was becoming increasingly evident that markets were undermining the traditional role of governments.[27] The so-called "Washington consensus" came to dominate the politics of the main British parties. This was a political settlement based on policies which benefit corporations—namely "an almost doctrinal fixation on free trade, privatization, and small government, and unfettered markets to foster economic growth and wealth generation, as opposed to government action and collective bargaining to promote social and economic equality".[28] Whilst the Conservative governments of 1979–1997 pioneered this consensus in Britain, Labour and the Liberal Democrats fell into line. The resulting lack of distinctiveness between the parties has, for many, undermined the legitimacy of the political process. In this regard, Peter Oborne observes that in practice it makes better sense to talk of New Labour, the

[27] Walter B. Wriston, *The Twilight of Sovereignty: How the Information Revolution is Transforming Our World* (New York: Charles Scribner's Sons, 1992), 7–17.

[28] Gregory Shaffer, *Defending Interests: Public-Private Partnerships in WTO Litigation* (Washington, DC: Brookings Institution Press, 2003), 4.

Conservatives and the Liberal Democrats as a homogeneous social and economic unit. He argues that the real division is between this hegemonic political class and a disenfranchised population.[29] Britain's contemporary neoliberalism is reflected in *Doctor Who*'s treatment of privatisation and sub-contracting in such episodes as "The Rebel Flesh"/"The Almost People" (2011), where a private contracting firm, engaged by Britain's Ministry of Defence, manufactures "Gangers", quasi-humans that it uses as highly expendable slaves, despite the fact that they share the emotions and memories of the humans of whom they are facsimiles. This may be read as a reference to the driving-down of labour costs that has tended to accompany privatisation. In a looser sense, privatisation can be discerned in "The Bells of Saint John" (2013) where an alien entity, the Great Intelligence, has seemingly contracted-out to a company the task of uploading the human race to the internet. The company's ruthlessness and its flash headquarters in London's temple of capitalism the Shard, are deeply redolent of Britain's neoliberal era.

This close proximity between corporations and the political world has resulted in the growing perception that politicians are now more accountable to corporations than they are to party members or to the electorate. Against the backdrop of the increased corporate funding of political parties, it seems that the parties' true allegiance no longer lies with their members but with their financial dependency.[30] In the same vein, a "revolving doors" phenomenon has emerged, whereby retired politicians secure lucrative employment within the corporate sector. The expectation of such gain has become woven into the fabric of the political elite's career structure. The financial links between corporations and the political class is reflected in "Rise of the Cybermen"/"The Age of Steel" (2006), where, in a parallel Republic of Great Britain, the

---

[29] Peter Oborne, *The Triumph of the Political Class* (London: Simon and Schuster, 2007), 93–94.

[30] As Britain's neoliberal era developed from the 1980s onwards, the country's three main nationwide parties increasingly adopted expensive ways of fighting elections. As a result, their dependency on corporate donations also increased. Peter Oborne explains the dependency of the British political parties on business donations by observing that the parties are now husks. Their memberships are a mere 10% of what they were during the 1950s—an astonishing collapse. Unable to rely on funding by members, parties need to sell political opportunities to corporations, creating a marketplace in influence and access and enabling the capture of parties by business interests. Peter Oborne, *The Triumph of the Political Class*, Chap. 4, 92–93.

president comments that most of the public thinks that John Lumic, CEO of Cybus Industries, owns his government.

More profoundly still, this homogeneous political class has made use of its long period in office to fashion a *constitutional* restructuring designed to entrench the power of corporations, prevent political change and restrict the expression of popular discontent. This has been achieved through the growing web of supranational agreements and institutions which our political elite has established. Such regimes as the World Trade Organization and the European Union have served to entrench key aspects of neoliberalism, such as free trade, strong property rights and privatisation.[31] More recently the EU–US Transatlantic Trade and Investment Partnership (TTIP) and the EU–Canada Comprehensive Economic and Trade Agreement (CETA) have both aroused controversy for their neoliberalism. Supranationalism of this kind reduces governmental exposure to political pressure from the electorate,[32] and constrains the state to use its power to serve business interests.[33] Furthermore, the freedom of corporate action which this supranational constitution guarantees has facilitated an even greater concentration and global reach of corporate power.[34] *Doctor Who* has reflected this economic change: "Rise of the Cybermen"/"The Age of Steel" (2006) emphasises the transnational and gigantic nature of Cybus Industries, for example, the fact that it has factories in almost every country in the world turning humans into Cybermen. By contrast, in "The Invasion" (1968), whilst International Electromatics is ostensibly a global company, we never actually hear of its overseas activities, and action alternates between its London headquarters and its Hertfordshire complex.

Let us finally consider the contrast between neoliberal normative theory and *Doctor Who*'s depiction of intimacy between private sector and state. Neoliberalism's founding father, Friedrich von Hayek, sought separation of state from business. Hayek saw private enterprise as "a self-generating or spontaneous order". He believed that government should

[31] See generally Danny Nicol, *The Constitutional Protection of Capitalism* (Oxford and Portland, OR: Hart, 2010), 46.

[32] Consider, for instance, the enmeshment of Greece within the Eurozone.

[33] Colin Leys, *Market-Driven Politics: Neoliberal Democracy and the Public Interest* (London: Verso, 2001), 3.

[34] This has occurred in such sectors as finance, energy, the media, pharmaceuticals, transportation and retailing. David Harvey, *A Brief History of Neoliberalism* (London: Oxford University Press, 2005), 38.

restrict itself to enforcing and improving the rules conducive to the formation of this spontaneous order.[35] He therefore deplored the socialist era's destruction of the traditional limits on the powers of the state.[36] Hayek explicitly sought a limited democracy in which parliamentary majorities would recognise restrictions on their power.[37] In particular, he was strongly opposed to governmental efforts to "correct" the spontaneous order according to principles of justice.[38] Yet the banking crisis of 2008 provided a quite different picture of the neoliberal state. In the years running up to the crisis, the financial sector made the calamitous blunder of investing heavily in the "sub-prime" mortgage market, making home loans to people who could not actually afford them. When the bubble burst, states poured their national coffers into the sector to make up the losses. This governmental largesse led to years of austerity as British taxpayers picked up the tab. Hayekian notions of competition, whereby governments play a limited role and companies pay the price for errors by going out of business, went by the board. Moreover, government subsidy of the private sector is no one-off: taxpayers annually pay the private sector around £93 billion in subsidies, a transfer of more than £3500 per household.[39] Far from the restricted state craved by Hayek, private enterprise relies on constant state support for its very survival.[40]

Implicitly, *Doctor Who* gives short shrift to Hayekian imaginings of the limited state, since it frequently emphasises the strongest links between state and corporation, either by imagining the state as servicing corporate interests or by turning the corporation into a state. Some *Doctor Who* stories combine both these possibilities. An illustration is

---

[35] Hayek, *Law, Legislation and Liberty*, Chap. 2.

[36] Hayek, *The Constitution of Liberty*, 256.

[37] Hayek, *The Constitution of Liberty*, 117.

[38] Hayek, *Law, Legislation and Liberty*, 142.

[39] *The Guardian*, July 8, 2015.

[40] Likewise, to pursue our historical example, the East India Company, far from being part of a spontaneous order, was born of the state—it was created by Royal Charter in 1600. Its very design was determined by the state. Throughout its life, the Company had an intimate relationship with the state, whether in the form of charter renewal or periodic bail-out by the state. The corporation was born with the state. The state allowed it gradually to transform itself into a profit-making organisation of shareholders, and thereby permitted the corporation to develop as "an ingenious device for acquiring rights and shedding responsibilities". George Monbiot, *Captive State: The Corporate Takeover of Britain* (London: Macmillan, 2000), 11.

"A Christmas Carol" (2010), where the request of the planet's president to allow a spaceship to land safely, thereby saving four thousand lives, is haughtily dismissed by the super-rich Kazran Sardick, who owns the planet's sky. Another example is "The Caves of Androzani" (1984), where the planet's military forces take orders from Morgus, a civilian magnate, since "he has the Praesidium in his pocket", and it is therefore considered better to obey Morgus' commands than to appeal his decisions. Morgus has a meeting with the president, at the end of which Morgus pushes him down a lift shaft. Having murdered the president, Morgus, as chairman of the conglomerate, takes control of the peace negotiations with the story's other main protagonist, Jek. So here we witness a corporate takeover of politics. Similarly, "Rise of the Cybermen"/"The Age of Steel" (2006) sees the president of Great Britain coming to a sorry end because he resists the tycoon John Lumic. Indeed, the mass conversion of humans into Cybermen in Lumic's factories should be seen as imposing *de facto* political rule by a corporation.

Hayek's perception of business as a "spontaneous order" conveys the idea "that markets enjoyed some mystic, organic connection to the people, while governments were fundamentally illegitimate".[41] This organic connection to the people is far from apparent in *Doctor Who* stories: indeed, the people are more usually ignorant of what is going on. For instance, in "The Sun Makers" (1977) the Company's workers know that the Company exists to make a profit, but have no idea for whom, nor even who owns the Company. In "The Sontaran Stratagem" (2008), customers are unaware that the satnav system ATMOS is intended to gas them in their cars as a prelude to alien invasion. Talk of a spontaneous order also lends the impression of an ever-changing commercial landscape, yet this dynamism can be overstated. It is often the *durability* of companies that is most apparent. Many corporate giants have ruled the roost throughout our entire lifespans. They have dominated the economy since before we were born and may be expected to continue to do so long after we die. In Britain, examples include Barclays, Lloyds, RBS, BP, Tesco, Sainsburys—others have been merged, renamed and repackaged. *Doctor Who* tends to emphasise corporate longevity. In "The Long Game" (2005), for example, the Editor explains that the alien ruler of the corporation "has always been your boss, since the day

[41] Thomas Frank, *One Market Under God: Extreme Capitalism, Market Populism, and the End of Economic Democracy* (New York: Anchor, 2000), xii.

you were born". In "The Sun Makers" (1977), the company has ruled for generations, moving its human workforce over the centuries from planet to planet. This very resilience should itself prompt us to question the making of a sharp demarcation line between corporation and state. If corporations are *permanent* fixtures wielding *political* power, should we not conceive them as actually forming part of the constitution? To this end, Gavin Anderson has argued for a reimagining of the constitution in which "the principal corollary of a reconfigured state is the elevation of multinational corporations as major political actors on the global stage".[42]

Doctor Who's treatment of corporations is therefore far removed from Hayek's craving for a limited neoliberal state. The show's corporation-based stories tally more with Ralph Miliband's view of the state's role under capitalism. For Miliband, the state in a class society is primarily and inevitably the guardian of that society's dominant economic interests. Accordingly, the state's foremost purpose is to ensure the continued predominance of those interests.[43] *Doctor Who* frequently envisages such an intimate relationship between big business and the state, either by imagining the corporation as pulling government's strings or by conceiving the corporation as actually constituting the government.

Sub-Trope 2: Corporate Authoritarianism and Oppression

Doctor Who has, therefore, frequently emphasised that large corporations wield enormous political power: the next question is how they exercise this power. *Doctor Who*'s resounding charge is one of despotism. Once again, this stance forms rather a sharp contrast to the way in which neoliberalism is meant to operate according to theory. Hayek, writing in *The Road to Serfdom* in 1944, recommended an economy based on competition, private enterprise and limited governmental interference because he perceived such an economy as sole guarantor of individual liberty, whereas centralised planning and state monopolies would lead to dictatorship. By contrast, in the very first *Doctor Who* story to feature a large corporation, "The Invasion" (1968), it is the company itself which is the source of tyranny, through its chief director, Tobias Vaughn. In this

[42] Gavin Anderson, *Constitutional Rights After Globalization* (Oxford: Hart, 2005), 22.

[43] Ralph Miliband, *The State in Capitalist Society* (London: Quartet, 1973), 238.

adventure, Vaughn seeks to use his Cyberman allies so that he becomes ruler of the world: he tells the Doctor that he does not seek power for its own sake but because the world is weak and vulnerable, a mess of uncoordinated and impossible ideals: it needs, he insists, a strong man, a *leader*. This imagining of captain of industry as despot is a recurring theme of *Doctor Who*.

In this regard, four particular aspects of *Doctor Who*'s charge of corporate despotism merit attention. First, corporations or their leaders frequently kill people: sometimes outsiders who threaten their interests, sometimes their own staff. Secondly, they oppress people through economic means, such as the exploitation of economic dependence, excessive taxation and slavery. Thirdly, they manipulate information and curtail civil liberties. Fourthly, they often act unlawfully.

Let us start by considering corporate disregard for human life in *Doctor Who*. Frequently, corporate leaders or their henchmen murder (or attempt to murder) staff and outsiders alike. Those who are not company staff tend to be targeted because they endanger company objectives. For instance, in "The Invasion" (1968) International Electromatics' security guards hunt down and shoot dead a UNIT agent in order to safeguard the company's secrets. In "Colony in Space" (1971), an officer of the Interplanetary Mining Corporation (IMC) instructs a robot to kill the Doctor after he has interfered with IMC's plans. The would-be murderer consoles his intended victim with the comment that the killing is merely good business, nothing personal. Later on, IMC staff plot the death of a whole community of human colonists by forcing them to embark in an unsafe rocket. The Doctor and companion Leela's efforts to overthrow a tyrannical company in "The Sun Makers" (1977) lead to Leela being sentenced to public execution for crimes against the company, although in the event she is rescued by her fellow revolutionaries. "The Caves of Androzani" (1984) sees the chairman of a giant conglomerate murdering the planet's president. In "Partners in Crime" (2008) the alien Miss Foster, who runs Adipose Industries, uses her corporate henchmen to try to dispose of the Doctor and companion Donna Noble. Some *Doctor Who* stories even imagine a corporation's security guards morphing into a private army, as in "The Invasion" (1968), "Planet of the Ood" (2008) and "The End of Time" (2009–2010).

As for company staff, they are murdered for a variety of reasons: sometimes because they have shown a lack of effectiveness, as in "The

Invasion" (1968) and "Time Heist" (2014); sometimes because they have rebelled against tyrannical corporate aims, as in "Revelation of the Daleks" (1985), "Rise of the Cybermen"/"The Age of Steel" (2006) and "Planet of the Ood" (2008); and occasionally because they have simply outlived their usefulness to the company since the corporate objectives have largely been achieved, as in "Dark Water"/"Death in Heaven" (2014) and "The Bells of Saint John" (2013). In "Oxygen" (2017), unprofitable spacemen are killed by their own spacesuits, and in "The Long Game" (2005), being murdered is actually built into the career structure: members of staff vie with each other to be promoted, whereupon they will reside—so they believe—in the space station's luxurious "Floor 500". In fact, they are killed there, and their corpses deployed as zombie automatons to run the space station's media empire. Enforced death is also part of the corporate plan in "The Sun Makers" (1977), with each staff member being assigned a "death day".

This disregard for human life once again reflects Britain's corporate past as well as its present. As regards the past, the East India Company frequently placed its desire for profits above human life. For example, during the Bengal Famine of 1769–1770, the Company relentlessly bought up rice, to take advantage of likely soaring prices. As a result, thousands of Indians died of starvation.[44] The Company declined to temper its profit motive with any sense of responsibility towards Bengal's population.[45] Such callous exploitation of scarcity has featured in *Doctor Who*: for instance, in "The Caves of Androzani" (1984), the magnate Morgus arranges an explosion at his conglomerate's copper mine in order to inflate the price of copper; and in "The Creature from the Pit" (1979), Lady Adrasta, the dictator who enjoys a monopoly on metal, machinates ruthlessly to ensure that it remains scarce. The East India Crash in 1769, along with the Bengal Famine, resulted in millions of Bengalis losing their lives.[46]

Predictably, a corporate mentality which values profit over human beings—particularly the third-world poor—remains the way of the

---

[44] Robins, *The Corporation That Changed the World*, 91–92.

[45] Robins, *The Corporation That Changed the World*, 93. The corporation can thus be seen as an ingenious device to acquire rights and shed responsibilities; see Monbiot, *Captive State*, 11.

[46] Robins, *The Corporation That Changed the World*, 96–98.

world. One instance is the notorious Bhopal case, in which a toxic gas escaped from an underground storage tank belonging to the transnational corporation Union Carbide in India in 1984. The immediate death toll was 1800 people, but by the early 1990s this figure had risen to 4200 as a result of after-effects.[47] Over 200,000 people were injured. Other examples abound.[48] Naomi Klein has chronicled how established human rights groups, such as Amnesty International and Human Rights Watch, have increasingly reported foreign corporations soliciting, even directly contracting, local police and military forces to kill peaceful protesters, in order to safeguard the smooth flow of trade.[49]

Let us now consider the various ways in which corporations in *Doctor Who* oppress individuals through economic dependency. In real life, this dependency has increased during the period in which *Doctor Who* has been broadcast, with the decline of trade unions, growth of insecurity and encouragement of debt. In this regard, one can discern a "re-proletarianisation" of a large portion of middle-class employees. "The Sun Makers" (1977) imagines a company-run planet, Pluto, where the workforce's dependency on the company is increased by the levying of punitive taxation. The story is sometimes characterised as an attack on taxation, but this reading is rather unsophisticated; a more accurate interpretation would be that it satirises *regressive* taxation, since the company's bottom-rung employees—the "work units"—are most adversely affected. "The Sun Makers" coincided with disillusionment with the

[47] See e.g. Sudhir Chopra, "Multinational Corporations in the Aftermath of Bhopal: The Need for a New Comprehensive Global Regime for Transnational Corporate Activity", *Valparaiso University Law Review*, 29 (1994): 235–284; P.T. Muchlinski, "The Bhopal Case: Controlling Ultrahazardous Industrial Activities Undertaken by Foreign Investors", *Modern Law Review*, 50 (1987): 545–587.

[48] See e.g. Alison M. Dussias, "Indians and *Indios*: Echoes of the Bhopal Disaster in the Achuar People of Peru's Struggle Against the Toxic Legacy of Occidental Petroleum", *New England Law Review*, 42 (2008): 809–846; J. Oloka-Onyango, "Reinforcing Marginalized Rights in an Age of Globalization: International Mechanisms, Non-State Actors and the Struggle for People's Rights in Africa", *American University International Law Review*, 18 (2002): 851–914.

[49] In one report of 1997, for example, Amnesty International documented Indian villagers and tribal people being violently arrested, and some killed, for resisting the development of private power plants and luxury hotels on their land—a melding, once again, of private enterprise and state power. Naomi Klein, *No Logo* (London: Flamingo, 2001), 338–339.

1974–1979 Labour government, which had promised to "squeeze the rich till the pips squeak" but ended up making public spending cuts.[50] The taxation in "The Sun Makers" may seem peculiar: ordinarily, governments impose taxation, not companies. Yet, as James Meek insightfully observes in his study of British privatisation *Private Island*, if a payment to an authority, public or private, is compulsory, it is a tax. So electricity and water bills are taxes, as are rail fares for those who cannot get by without the railways, and university fees for those who regard a university education as essential. Viewed in this less formalistic fashion, it becomes easier to see private concerns as imposers of taxation.[51]

Doctor Who contains an array of instances of corporations exploiting the economic dependency of employees. In "Colony in Space" (1971), a member of staff of the Interplanetary Mining Corporation is pressurised by his superiors into committing murder because he is in debt. In both "Terminus" (1983) and "The Caves of Androzani" (1984), workers' economic dependency is guaranteed by their reliance on life-extending drugs supplied by the corporation. The satire in "The Long Game" (2005)—an episode broadcast when Britain had experienced two decades of neoliberalism—is rather subtler: the time travellers materialise on the space station Satellite 5 in the distant future, and the Doctor tells companions Rose Tyler and Adam Mitchell that they have arrived at a "fantastic" period in Earth's history: an era of exceptional art, culture and politics, fine food and good manners. The scene then erupts as workers almost riot in order to obtain a rushed, junk-food lunch. Their economic dependency pressurises them into an unappealing rat-race, far removed from the urbane lifestyle which the Doctor anticipated.

If "The Long Game" satirises the neoliberal way of life within Britain, then "Planet of the Ood" (2008) tackles the relationship of British corporations with the third world. The plot concerns a human-run company, Ood Operations, which trades in a slave species, the Ood, and has

---

[50] The leading ideologue of British social democracy, Anthony Crosland, writing in *The Times*, September 8, 1977, even thought that discontent with Labour might lead to revolutionary change: "We believe that the developing crisis in the capitalist system, by which we mean both economic stagnation and the social and political conflicts to which it gives rise, makes it possible to think in terms of developing a sizeable and serious revolutionary socialist party in a way that was not possible twenty or even ten years ago.".

[51] James Meek, *Private Island: Why Britain Now Belongs to Someone Else* (London: Verso, 2015), 22.

established a headquarters on the Ood's home planet, the Ood-Sphere. Companion Donna Noble is appalled by this slave-empire; but lest she draw too sharp a contrast with the Earth of her own era, the Doctor quips "who do you think made your clothes?" The story thereby emphasises the lack of a "bright line" distinguishing wage-slavery from slavery. The same theme emerges in "The Long Game" (2005), where the Editor, Satellite 5's ostensible manager, seeks to engage the Doctor in a philosophical debate on whether a slave is a slave when he does not know he is enslaved.

The unconscious slavery of which the Editor speaks brings us to our next pervasive theme: *Doctor Who* often associates corporations with the manipulative control of information. In "The Long Game", Satellite 5 is owned by a company that monopolises news broadcasting to the human race. When the Doctor notices that there are no aliens on board the space station, even though it is supposedly at the heart of the Fourth Great and Bountiful Human Empire, he asks a journalist, Cathica, why this is the case. Cathica gives a vague and muddled response. In a similar vein, in "Rise of the Cybermen"/"The Age of Steel" (2006), citizens of a parallel Earth lap up the news provided by a giant corporation called Cybus Industries. *Doctor Who*'s linkage of corporate power and news manipulation is not without foundation. Aside from the British Broadcasting Corporation itself, the mass media in Britain is dominated by large-scale private enterprise. Furthermore, the concentration of business ownership which took hold generally in the 1960s has long been evident in the media sector.[52] With a few corporations controlling some 90% of the British press and a handful owning the commercial broadcasting organisations, proprietors exercise control by their appointment of key personnel, ensuring that journalistic output conforms to the proprietor's political wishes.[53] This is reflected in "The Long Game" by the way in which the Editor can be relied upon to do the bidding of the alien Editor-in-Chief.[54]

---

[52] Miliband, *The State in Capitalist Society*, 227.

[53] Brian McNair, *News and Journalism in the UK*, 5th ed. (Abingdon: Routledge, 2009), 49–51.

[54] Matt Hills characterises "The Long Game" as "science fiction as politicised commentary" in that it attacks commercial news-gathering and defends a public-service ethos of accurate and truthful reporting. Matt Hills, *Triumph of a Time Lord: Regenerating Doctor Who in the Twenty-First Century* (London: I.B. Tauris, 2010), 168.

To be sure, the dissemination of political news has come under the control of a very small number of extremely wealthy people. Whatever their rivalries, these super-rich individuals tend to share political perspectives and deploy their resources to fight for their political aims. Party leaders are aware of this power, and feel constrained by it when formulating their programmes.[55] Increasingly therefore, party leaders have acted as clients of the media barons.[56] "The Long Game" exaggerates this situation by imagining that the media empire itself constitutes the government. In Britain, under sections 319–320 of the Communications Act 2003, the independent regulator for the communications industry (OFCOM) is obliged to set standards for television and radio programmes which ensure that news is presented with "due impartiality". This explains why Britain is not subject to news content in the style of the American channel Fox News. Nonetheless, this protection is rather thin: it will always be open to debate what degree of impartiality is "due" in any context. Furthermore, the impartiality requirement certainly does not apply to British newspapers, where a conservative preponderance is overwhelming. But in any event, the formal impartiality of television and radio news may serve to obscure an underlying reality: that the mass media's role in advanced capitalist societies is above all to promote a general acceptance of the capitalist system as natural and desirable.[57] Perhaps "The Long Game" is taking aim at this more profound bias in news reporting. This promotion of capitalism has become more brazen as a result of the neoliberalisation of the BBC, which we consider in the concluding Chap. 7. But "The Long Game" is no less critical of the passivity of the general public in lapping up this news content, the Doctor regarding them as "stupid little slaves, believing every lie".

Corporate efforts to manipulate information are not restricted to general political news. Companies may also lie about their own commercial affairs. Recent scandals have included the corporate fiddling of money markets, including the London inter-bank lending rate and the foreign exchange markets. Such manipulation creates profound difficulty for neoliberal normative theory. Fundamental to Hayek's grand design is the

---

[55] Colin Crouch, *Post-Democracy* (Cambridge: Polity, 2004), 50.

[56] Colin Seymour-Ure, *Prime Ministers and the Media: Issues of Power and Control* (Oxford: Blackwell Publishing, 2003), 106.

[57] Miliband, *The State in Capitalist Society*, Chap. 8.

role of markets in setting price: this was what made neoliberalism better than socialism, with its paternalistic assessment of needs. However, as Raymond Plant has observed, where information is concealed or distorted, there is no market price. He gives the example of the "toxic assets" held by financial institutions during the 2008 banking crisis. Many of these consisted of bundles of mortgage debts, a high proportion of which would never be paid back since they were "sub-prime". The value of these bundles was completely opaque. Banks therefore had enormous sums of money bound up in assets for which there was no market price: capitalism had created its own "calculation problem".[58] As a result, banks would not lend to each other, necessitating massive and exorbitant government intervention. It is common in *Doctor Who* for companies to lie about their activities: for instance, in "Revelation of the Daleks" (1985) the Daleks, led by their creator Davros, appear to have taken over an intergalactic funeral home, but in reality, they are recycling corpses in order to create more Daleks as well as to process as a foodstuff (a detail they will not disclose lest there be "consumer resistance"); in "Partners in Crime" (2008), a company selling slimming products is secretly using its customers' bodies to incubate baby aliens; and in "Dark Water"/"Death in Heaven" (2014), a firm purporting to give "more life" to people after death, is actually turning them into Cybermen.

Corporations in *Doctor Who* also deny civil liberties in order to conceal the truth. Thus, in "Bad Wolf"/"The Parting of the Ways" (2005), the Bad Wolf Corporation threatens to send dissidents such as the Doctor and companion Captain Jack Harkness to the Lunar Penal Colony without trial. In "Partners in Crime" (2008), the managing director of Adipose Industries, Miss Foster, imprisons journalist Penny Cooper. Significantly, in both instances, corporate denial of civil liberties is linked to the manipulation of information: the Bad Wolf Corporation dare not risk the Doctor uncovering the real nature of its activities in harvesting human bodies, and Miss Foster does not want Penny to reveal the truth about her slimming products. *Doctor Who*'s corporate deceit arguably reflects the real-world untruths that neoliberal capitalism has to conceal: the fallibility of markets, the phoniness of meritocracy and trickle-down economics, and the bogus claim of "small government" in the wake of the bank bailout.

[58] Raymond Plant, *The Neo-liberal State* (Oxford: Oxford University Press, 2010), 263.

A final aspect of corporate oppression that repeatedly features in *Doctor Who* is contempt for the rule of law. Obviously, corporate unlawfulness in *Doctor Who* is very common: whenever a magnate kills someone, he or she breaks the law. However, there are several instances in which the programme lays particularly heavy emphasis on the *illegal nature* of corporate actions. For instance, "Rise of the Cybermen"/"The Age of Steel" (2006) opens with the tycoon John Lumic killing a scientist who wants Cybus Industries to comply with the law by applying for permission from the competent authority to licence the production of Cybermen. In "The Caves of Androzani" (1984), when the magnate Morgus' crimes are finally exposed, the Praesidium charge him with some seventeen counts, including murder, treason, grand fraud and embezzlement. They freeze all his assets, including secret funds stashed away on other planets. "Partners in Crime" (2008) sees Miss Foster, an alien super-nanny, using the bodies of live humans to breed an alien species, the Adipose. The Doctor warns her that since Earth is a level 5 planet, this constitutes a violation of galactic law: her clients, the Adipose first family, ultimately do away with her in order to hide the evidence of this crime. Although the episode's title superficially seems to refer to the Doctor and companion Donna Noble, since Miss Foster refers to them as "partners in crime", the real criminal conspiracy is between Miss Foster and the Adipose.

Doctor Who's emphasis on magnates acting illegally is significant because reliance on the rule of law is so pivotal to neoliberal normative theories. Neoliberalism's founding fathers Friedrich von Hayek and Ludwig von Mises made the rule of law absolutely central to their theoretical blueprints.[59] If the rule of law lies at the heart of neoliberal ideology, one would assume that corporations themselves tend to act lawfully. Yet, in *Doctor Who*, corporate illegality is rife. This reflects a real-world trend: Harry Shutt has identified "the widespread incidence of fraud, corruption, organised crime and abuse of power" as part of the changing pattern of the world economy since the 1970s. He attributes this spread of lawlessness to the growth in the unaccountable power of

[59] Friedrich A. von Hayek, *The Road to Serfdom*, 79; Ludwig von Mises, *Bureaucracy* (New Haven, CT: Yale University Press, 1944), 76.

large corporations. Governments, he argues, have progressively removed restraints to such criminal activity and have increased incentives to engage in it.[60]

In sum, *Doctor Who* pulls no punches. It frequently presents corporations as murderous organisations which deploy a full array of economic weapons against the individual, manipulate information in their own interests, ride roughshod over civil liberties and act with contempt towards the law. This is a portrayal of capitalist enterprise that *Doctor Who* has delivered with remarkable consistency since the late 1960s.

Sub-Trope 3: Clandestine Alien Leadership

There are multiple instances in *Doctor Who* in which a corporation's workforce is human but its leader is an exploitative alien whose existence or whose alien nature is kept secret. Examples include "The Sun Makers"(1977), "The Long Game" (2005), "Bad Wolf"/"The Parting of the Ways" (2005), "Partners in Crime" (2008), "The Bells of Saint John" (2013), "Dark Water"/"Death in Heaven" (2014), "The Return of Doctor Mysterio" (2016) and arguably "The Green Death" (1973).[61] Sometimes a corporation has a semi-human, cyborg leadership, as in "The Invasion" (1968) and "Rise of the Cybermen"/"The Age of Steel" (2006). There are far fewer stories in which corporations have an openly alien leadership and humanoid underlings, as in "Vengeance on Varos" (1985) and "The Trial of a Time Lord" ("Mindwarp") (1986).

---

[60] Harry Shutt, *The Trouble with Capitalism* (London and New York: Zed Books, 1998), 167–169. In the same vein, Dave Whyte analyses the role of corporations in post-invasion Iraq and identifies "state corporate criminality" stemming from "an irresolvable contradiction in neo-liberal capitalism: the need to enforce a rule of law that preserves the viability and legitimacy of the economic system whilst reproducing an economic order that preserves the primacy and autonomy of market actors". Whyte shows how the privatisation programme of the occupying coalition forces constituted an international crime by violating the sovereign right of a people to determine their own economic and social future enshrined in Article 64 Geneva Convention 1949, Articles 55 and 43 Hague Regulations 1907. Dave Whyte, "The Crimes of Neo-liberal Rule in Occupied Iraq", *British Journal of Criminology*, 47 (2007): 177–195.

[61] There is also "Spearhead in Space" (1970) and "Terror of the Autons" (1971) where legitimate human companies are taken over by an alien entity and used to manufacture plastic killing machines.

Frequently in these adventures, the nature of the corporation's leadership is initially shrouded in secrecy and it is only through the Doctor's conflict with the corporation that its alien identity comes to light. So, for instance, in "The Sun Makers" there is widespread ignorance as to who runs the company, and it transpires that the ostensibly human managing director is in fact a Usurian, a creature whose natural form is like "a sea kale with eyes". A similar air of mystery surrounds the management of Satellite 5, the giant media company in "The Long Game". Questions of ownership and leadership are displaced by fables of Floor 500, where senior staff are thought to live in splendour. In fact, the company's Editor-in-Chief turns out to be an enormous creature, the Jagrafess, which inhabits the space station's roof. It transpires that the Jagrafess has been installed in power by a consortium of banks. In "Bad Wolf"/"The Parting of the Ways", the Bad Wolf Corporation is secretly run by Daleks. "Partners in Crime" involves a corporation run by an alien super-nanny. "The Bells of Saint John" concerns a company which uploads human souls to a data cloud. It transpires that the company, although ostensibly managed by a human, Miss Kizlet, has in fact a single client: the disembodied alien Great Intelligence, which somehow feasts on these souls. The story can be read as a satire on outsourcing arrangements where the sole client calls the shots. "Dark Water"/"Death in Heaven" is about a company called 3 W, which is converting human corpses into Cybermen.[62] 3 W's boss turns out to be a long-term Time Lord opponent of the Doctor. "The Return of Doctor Mysterio" features a multinational corporation which extracts and replaces the brains of key authority figures around the world, thereby preparing Earth for full colonisation by aliens. "The Green Death" might be considered a borderline case since the head of the company, Global Chemicals, is not actually extraterrestrial but is nonetheless non-human: a deranged computer called BOSS. Driven by its prime directive of "efficiency, productivity and profit for Global Chemicals", BOSS intends linking with other computers worldwide in order to turn humans into slave units.[63]

[62]The depiction of 3 W may be read as satirising British care homes for the elderly, which are now overwhelmingly private sector. A staff member, Dr. Chang, bemoans the frequency of government inspections. This is reminiscent of the supervision of the Care Quality Commission in UK care homes.

[63]Vanessa de Kauwe and Lindy Orthia argue that BOSS's madness and brainwashing distances it from a more banal corporate capitalism. However, such dysfunctional, oppressive conduct is, I would contend, simply too common among *Doctor Who*'s corporations to

Why then has *Doctor Who* so persistently portrayed the bosses of corporations as hostile aliens? Two explanations come to mind: one relates to class and the rise of the super-rich, the other to the weakening of national ties among business leaders. These explanations may be seen as complementary rather than competing.

First, corporate bosses lend themselves to being portrayed as "a species apart" because of the phenomenon of the super-rich and the increase in inequality in Britain. On one level, the "Otherness" of the business class in terms of social class is nothing new. As E.E. Schattschneider observed in the 1930s, "Business men collectively constitute the most class-conscious group in…society. As a class, they are more highly organised, more easily mobilised, have more facilities for communication, are more like-minded and are more accustomed to stand together in defence of their privileges than any other group".[64] What has, however, changed is the wealth gap which separates this class from the rest. Under conditions of globalisation, new processes of class formation emerged as entrepreneurial opportunities opened up and new structures of trading relations came into existence. The resulting concentration of wealth meant that by 1996 the net worth of the 358 richest people was equal to the combined income of the poorest 45% of the world's population, some 2.3 billion people.[65] At the start of the twenty-first century, a shift took place *within* the ranks of the wealthy, with the top 1% pulling away from the rest. Even among this tier of the super-super rich, the greatest gains have been at the tip of the pyramid.[66] In particular, the ultra-rich 0.1% pulled away from the remaining 0.9%.[67] Ironically, research indicates that the "one-percenters" who find themselves moored at the "bottom of the top" tend to be particularly covetous and to express low levels of

regard BOSS as distanced from the show's own extended metaphor of capitalist banality. Vanessa de Kauwe and Lindy Orthia, "Knowledge, Power and the Ethics Illusion in Classic Era *Doctor Who*", *Journal of Popular Television*, 6(2) (2018).

[64] E.E. Schattschneider, *Politics, Pressures and the Tariff* (New York: Prentice-Hall, 1935), 287.

[65] Moreover, the world's richest two hundred people had doubled their net worth in the four years to 1998. Harvey, *A Brief History of Neoliberalism*, 34–35.

[66] Chrystia Freeland, *Plutocrats: The Rise of the New Global Super-Rich* (London: Penguin, 2012), 34.

[67] Freeland, *Plutocrats*, 80.

wellbeing.[68] Be that as it may, this growing and alienating gulf between the super-rich and the rest of society was becoming a reality during the latter years of the "classic series" and was well established by the time *Doctor Who* returned to our screens in 2005.

It is well recognised that the super-rich lead lives very different from those of the rest of the population, lives in which the acquisition of investments and luxury goods loom large. Against this backdrop, it is easier for the business elite to conceive themselves as being almost a different species—superhuman compared to the sub-human of the non-rich—and this makes it easier to rationalise meting out a harsh and precarious existence to the have-nots. This contrast is well drawn in "The End of the World" (2005) where, in the distant future, a bizarre array of ultra-rich corporate aliens convenes to witness the spectacle of the Earth being destroyed by the Sun. Their vast wealth is counterposed to the lowly status of the event staff: diminutive blue beings who may not even speak without permission.

Secondly, the alien nature of corporate leaders may be viewed as stemming from globalisation. We inhabit a world in which the economic elite has lost its national ties. The firms and executives of the City of London are global citizens, not national citizens. As such, they are happy to set up shop wherever the tax breaks are the most favourable and the pickings richest.[69] William Robinson contends that the formation of a transnational capitalist class has been central to globalisation.[70] He argues that this class may be seen as an agent of change, setting out to transform countries in the 1980s and 1990s by dismantling nation-based Keynesian welfare policies and enmeshing states within supranational liberalisation structures. David Harvey contends that even under early capitalism international links were important to the economic elite, but that there has

---

[68] Freeland, *Plutocrats*, 82.

[69] Robert Peston, *Who Runs Britain?* (London: Hodder and Stoughton, 2008), 192.

[70] Willam Robinson, *A Theory of Global Capitalism: Production, Class, and State in a Transnational World* (Baltimore, MD: Johns Hopkins University Press, 2004). As early as 1974, Richard Barnet and Ronald Mueller had argued that the proliferation of multinational corporations had created a new international corporate elite. See Richard Barnet and Ronald Mueller, *Global Reach: The Power of the Multinational Corporation* (New York: Simon and Schuster, 1974). This formed a contrast to the nineteenth-century perception, when Karl Marx conceived of the capitalist class as originally national, insofar as it developed within a specific nation state.

certainly been a deepening and widening of these transnational connections in the present era.

It does not follow that the super-rich will not deploy their nationality for the advantages and protections that it affords them. However, these attachments will be no more stable than the capitalist activity they pursue, as witnessed by Rupert Murdoch's various nationalities.[71] As Aditya Mittal, Chief Financial Officer of ArcelorMittal has remarked, "the difference in [national] identity is not as significant as it used to be. For a global businessman, you can achieve the same set of objectives whether you're in London, New York, or a place like Singapore."[72] Rather than being tied to any specific nationality, the super-elite see themselves as global citizens, and this is a relatively new phenomenon.[73] Such lack of national allegiance makes it easy for them to move their operations from state to state, regardless of the interests of workers who are their fellow nationals. In Britain, such mobility on the part of the very wealthy can also be used to avoid taxation on the basis of non-domicile status.

In this respect, it is enlightening once again to contrast John Lumic, the magnate who leads Cybus Industries in "Rise of the Cybermen"/"The Age of Steel" (2006), with Tobias Vaughn, the tycoon in charge of International Electromatics in the earlier Cyberman adventure "The Invasion" (1968). Both firms are global, yet Lumic's transnational credentials are far more explicitly pronounced. He crosses an international frontier in his airship, having ordered that it set sail for Great Britain, whereas Vaughn remains in Southern England throughout. Unlike Vaughn, we are explicitly told that Lumic has factories producing Cybermen on every continent. Lumic claims a sense of attachment to his own home country yet has no hesitation in getting his Cybermen to kill Britain's head of state and turn his compatriots into Cybermen.

In sum, therefore, the non-human nature of business leaders in *Doctor Who* symbolises an economic elite shorn of national common ground with its workers and so far removed from them in terms of wealth as to seem to be almost another species.

---

[71] Harvey, *A Brief History of Neoliberalism*, 35.

[72] Freeland, *Plutocrats*, 59.

[73] Freeland, *Plutocrats*, 60.

Sub-Trope 4: Servicing the Super-Rich, Reinforcing the Class System

Doctor Who's engagements with corporations have often served to highlight the connection between the corporate system and the gap between rich and poor. The era of corporate domination which has developed during the lifetime of *Doctor Who* has indeed seen greater polarisation of wealth. As might be expected, some *Doctor Who* storylines can easily be read as critical of the way in which a society based on large corporations has generated rampant inequality.

Doctor Who started life during a period of social democratic consensus in which British politicians favoured social mobility, a significant public sector and mildly egalitarian measures. With the transition to neoliberalism at the end of the 1970s, however, the wealth of Britain's richest has greatly increased vis-à-vis the rest of the country. From the mid-1990s onwards, executive pay soared, such that the leaders of large corporations came to earn 780 times the salary of their average employees. Yet at the same time, the sense of responsibility of the company towards its workforce was starting to disintegrate; the rich were coming to see other people's precariousness in the workplace as the means to their own prosperity.[74] Astonishingly, the financial crisis of 2008 became a further exercise in the redistribution of wealth, with the super-rich according to some estimates doubling their wealth since the crisis.[75] By contrast, those at the other end of the social spectrum suffered years of austerity. Rhetoric of "we're all in this together" ultimately had to be discarded as a more socially divided society took shape. Oxfam calculated that by 2016 the richest 1% of humanity would own as much as the bottom 99%, whilst Britain, as a tax haven for the rich, now had 104 billionaires.[76]

[74] Examples would include the abandonment of final salary pension schemes for employees and the trend towards zero-hours contracts.

[75] *The Sunday Times*, April 26, 2015. Some 95% of the gains from the state bailouts went to the super-rich, while quantitative easing by central banks inflated their assets. In 2015, the wealthiest one thousand people based in Britain owned £547 billion—up from £258 billion in 2009.

[76] Emma Seery and Ana Caistor Arendar, *Even It Up: Time to End Extreme Inequality* (Oxford: Oxfam International, 2014).

Yet this degree of inequality is not quite what was promised. Some forty years ago, Margaret Thatcher as prime minister argued that whilst the promotion of entrepreneurism would cause greater inequality, there would be a "trickle-down effect", whereby economic growth and the spending of the rich would make the whole of society more prosperous. This did not materialise. Furthermore, talk of "meritocracy"—of Britain as an "aspiration nation"—turned out to be entirely window-dressing: an alibi for government by a wealthy elite.[77] In reality, the wealth of the many has been eroded while that of the super-rich has soared.[78] The enrichment of a small minority has gone hand-in-hand with a de-bourgeoisification of much of the middle class as well as the growth of an underclass.[79] The gulf between the top 1% and the rest of Britain indicates that wealth has actually trickled *up*, from the less-well-off to the richest. It is this chasm which *Doctor Who* storylines often capture.

Some *Doctor Who* stories emphasise the sheer excessive wealth of the super-rich. For example, in "The End of Time" (2009–2010), the magnate Joshua Naismith deploys his wealth and power to secure immortality for his daughter Abigail.[80] The same theme is taken up in "Dark Water"/"Death in Heaven" (2014), where the Doctor's adversary Missy runs a company somehow offering "more life" to the wealthy deceased. These stories reflect an existing inequality in lifespans: the well-to-do already outlive the poor. In 2015, male life expectancy for the British rich was assessed at 88 years, compared to 70 years for working class Britons. Excessive wealth is also emphasised in "Time Heist" (2014), where we visit the Bank of Karabraxos, the most secure bank in the galaxy. Described as "a fortress for the super-rich", we are told that if you can afford your own star system, this is where you keep it. Its visibly

---

[77] Jo Littler, "Meritocracy as Plutocracy: The Marketisation of Equality under Neoliberalism", in *Neoliberal Culture*, ed. Jeremy Gilbert (London: Lawrence & Wishart 2016).

[78] Peston, *Who Runs Britain?* 255.

[79] John Gray, *False Dawn: The Delusions of Global Capitalism* (London: Granta Books, 2002), 72, 30.

[80] The story creates an elegant parallel between the greed of the Naismiths in their efforts to cheat death and that of the Time Lords who are attempting much the same thing. They do so by seeking to end time altogether, and to become "creatures of conscience alone"—thereby exchanging their longevity for immortality. Like Abigail Naismith, the Lord President of the Time Lords is determined never to die.

Oriental, African and Arab clients reflect the globalised economic elite of the real world.

Other *Doctor Who* plots more explicitly counterpose the corporate super-rich with the poor whom they exploit. "The Sun Makers" (1977) draws a contrast between the penniless but likeable Cordo (who tries to commit suicide because of his indebtedness) and the company's owner, the Collector, who rails against "the vicious doctrine of egalitarianism" and taxes his "work units" to excess. "Vengeance on Varos" (1985) contrasts the planet Varos' ruling elite and corporate imperialist Sil with a couple of undernourished television viewers.[81] "Rise of the Cybermen"/"The Age of Steel" (2006) counterposes tycoon John Lumic with the starving poor who are hoodwinked into Cyber-conversion by promises of food.

In his book *A Brief History of Neoliberalism*, David Harvey identifies two competing interpretations of the doctrine.[82] He suggests that neoliberalism could be interpreted either as a utopian project to redesign capitalism, or alternatively it could be read as a political project to re-establish the power of economic elites. The first interpretation would correspond to the vision advanced by Hayek: that a system of competition is in the public interest as a guarantor of freedom. *Doctor Who*, however, tends to line up with the second reading, seeing the corporate system as being for the benefit of an economic elite rather than for society as a whole. When, in "The Green Death" (1974), the supposed company manager Stevens tells the Doctor "what's good for Global Chemicals is best for the world, is best for you!" this public interest argument is intended to be taken with a huge pinch of salt.[83] In *Doctor Who*, the essence of the corporate system seems to be to detach the super-rich from the rest of humanity.

[81] For good measure, Jodar, a revolutionary, claims to have discovered that Varos' officer elite enjoy luxury whilst the citizens live in poverty.

[82] Harvey, *A Brief History of Neoliberalism*, 19.

[83] Stevens' comment is based on a famous misquotation from Charles E. Wilson, who at his 1953 confirmation hearing as US Defense Secretary expressed unwillingness to dispose of his shares in General Motors since he believed that the country's and company's interests were the same.

Fig. 6.1 Corporate army. The henchmen of International Electromatics arraign companion Zoe Heriot and friend before Tobias Vaughn. *Doctor Who* (classic series), "The Invasion", season 6, serial 46; British Broadcasting Corporation, 1968

Sub-Trope 5: Uniformity

It has been said that one of the chief political messages of *Doctor Who* is to encourage non-conformity and difference.[84] To this end, the eccentric Doctor is frequently contrasted to the homogeneous Daleks and Cybermen. The idea of Britain as a country which reveres its eccentrics is an attractive one. It is, however, possible to associate such individuality with capitalism. John Fiske makes this link in his essay on *Doctor Who* and capitalist ideology, alleging that the Doctor's oddness reflects capitalist values.[85] Certainly, it is easy to contrast the drab, grey uniformity of Soviet-type totalitarianism to the capitalist freedom where one can buy what one wants, no matter how wayward, if one has the money.

Hayek indeed bases his entire ideology on the freedom of the *individual.* In *The Road to Serfdom*, he associates individualism with commerce. For him, business involves an unchaining of individual energies.[86]

---

[84] James Chapman, *Inside the TARDIS* (London: I.B. Tauris, 2013), 7.

[85] Fiske, "Dr. Who: Ideology", 72.

[86] Hayek, *The Road to Serfdom*, 10–12.

The state represents coercion, the private sector somehow does not. Pursuing Hayek's ideas within 1980s Britain, Margaret Thatcher has been said to have promoted a politics whereby "all forms of social solidarity were to be dissolved in favour of individualism".[87] Similarly, Alexander Somek argues that the European Union's governing ideology is individualism, and that this is particularly apparent from the EU's claim for regulatory authority and from the design of the European single market.[88]

Tolerance of eccentricity and diversity, however, is not actually the same thing as tolerance of corporations. Promoting an individualism inextricably linked to capitalism hardly fits with *Doctor Who*'s general onslaught on the corporate sector. Moreover, there are multiple instances in *Doctor Who* where capitalist enterprise stifles individuality *in pursuit of uniformity*—the opposite of Fiske's claim. An example is "The Invasion" (1968), where the Doctor is surprised to see that the office of Tobias Vaughn in his factory in the countryside is identical to his London office. Vaughn explains that the secret of his success is uniformity and duplication, and that his whole business empire is built on those principles. This compulsion towards uniformity is on all fours with his desire to subject the human race to cyber-conversion, the ultimate imposition of sameness. Figure 6.1 adroitly shows the contrast between corporate uniformity and non-corporate freedom of expression. Companion Zoe Heriot and her friend Isobel are arraigned in front of magnate Vaughn. They sport the fashions of the swinging sixties. Standing behind the two young women are three corporate henchmen from Vaughn's private army. Their dark uniforms lend them an air of grim anonymity which contrasts starkly with Zoe's and Isobel's cheerful attire. The men's helmets serve to remind us of the Cybermen with whom Vaughn is in league, an alien race renowned for its uniformity.

The same theme is apparent in "Rise of the Cybermen"/"The Age of Steel" (2006), where tycoon John Lumic pledges to bring about unity and uniformity. He already fosters conformity among humans by getting them to wear his earpods which feed them news and entertainment. Subsequently, the earpods are used to compel humans to march to his

[87] Harvey, *A Brief History of Neoliberalism*, 23.

[88] Alexander Somek, *Individualism: An Essay on the Authority of the European Union* (Oxford: Oxford University Press, 2008), 111–137.

factories and be converted into Cybermen. The story thereby links the indoctrination by Lumic's media empire with the drastic uniformity that he imposes through cyber-conversion. In the same vein, in "The Long Game" (2005) the Editor pours scorn on human pretensions to individuality. He berates his species for thinking they are so individual when in fact they are "just cattle". Director Karabraxos in "Time Heist" (2014) staffs her bank with clones of herself, killing those who fail to give her satisfactory service. The uniformity of a corporation's workforce is often emphasised, be it the homogeneous-seeming robots of "The Robots of Death" (1977), the "work units" of Pluto with their designated death days ("The Sun Makers" (1977), or the Gangers (doppelgangers) of the company Morpeth Jetsan, who are identical to its human employees ("The Rebel Flesh"/"The Almost People" (2011)). In "Oxygen" (2017), staff are killed off at the corporation's behest by their own spacesuits, leaving the animated spacesuits (each one gruesomely occupied by a corpse) to run the space station. The refrain of the few survivors is "Stay away from the suits!" But "suits" is also slang for business executives, so the uniformity of the spacesuits may be a derisive metaphor for the real-world uniformity (of thought as well as of attire) of those enmeshed into the higher echelons of the corporate system.

Doctor Who therefore depicts corporations as the enemies of the individual. This is not a difficult thing to do, because the neoliberal version of individualism is not actually particularly enticing. Alexander Somek detects a discomforting emptiness in neoliberal individualism, and observes that in a market society the individual, far from being able to "live their own life", is constantly required to adapt to shifting market conditions. Furthermore, Somek argues that, ironically, individualism presupposes not diversity but social homogeneity, since one has to create a social world in one's own image in order to arrive at a system of laws which will facilitate one's own autonomy. Indeed, a society based on individualism, he argues, is susceptible to authoritarianism. This is because, since homogeneity is unlikely to arise organically, absolute freedom is likely to obtain only when individuals wholly identify with the wishes of an all-powerful leader.[89] It might be argued that in *Doctor Who* this absolute rule is frequently provided by the corporate dictator.

[89] Somek, *Individualism*, 265–280.

Sub-Trope 6: Conditioning—The Inability to Question Capitalism

It will be readily apparent that *Doctor Who* places much blame on corporations for society's ills. However, on a number of occasions, the programme has been no less critical of the general public for their unquestioning acceptance of the dominant position of corporations in society. This criticism might apply with particular force in neoliberal Britain, where the gains made by the less-well-off under social democracy were given up rather easily. With the collapse of the miners' strike in 1984–1985, it seemed that trade unions generally also rather collapsed. Unions appeared powerless to resist the replacement of careers structures by casualisation, the phasing-out of final salary pension schemes and the burgeoning wealth gap between those at the top of companies and those below. On the political front, unions affiliated to the Labour Party contributed to their own marginalisation by supporting New Labour's party reforms. Once in office, New Labour—far from discarding Thatcherism—actually supercharged it.[90] As Simon Jenkins has painstakingly documented, the Blair and Brown governments drove privatisation into every corner of the public services, enthusiastically promoted welfare reform and lauded the profit motive. Partnership with corporations was pursued at every turn. As prime minister, Tony Blair had little time for unions, believing the role of government was to support business. Since Labour's affiliated unions and party members had agreed to snap the chains that bound the leader to the party, he was free to do so.[91] Wealth and power therefore shifted to the super-rich with scant resistance.

Significantly, *Doctor Who* stories differ in their portrayals of workers' responses to corporate domination according to whether they pre-date or post-date Britain's neoliberal shift. "The Sun Makers" (1977) was broadcast before the country's neoliberal transformation. In this serial, company staff are processed at a Correction Centre to make them compliant. Curiosity is a crime, punishable by "reconditioning". Above all, the "work units" are kept passive by a chemical called PCM which is pumped into the air. The Doctor says that PCM is an anxiety-inducing agent which eliminates freedom. Only senior staff are given tablets

[90] Simon Jenkins, *Thatcher and Sons* (London: Penguin Books, 2006), 206.

[91] Jenkins, *Thatcher and Sons*, Chap. 15.

which act as an antidote. At the end of the story, the rebels bring about a revolution by eliminating PCM from the atmosphere. The plot presupposes that the natural state of humankind is questioning and rebellious, and that artificial substances are required to subdue this revolutionary potential.

By contrast, "The Long Game" (2005) was broadcast in an era when neoliberalism was well established and was encountering few obstacles to its hegemony. The episode involves the space station Satellite 5, which monopolises broadcast news to the human empire. In so doing it has created a climate of fear through news manipulation, and has fashioned a society of restriction, hassle, junk food and endless jockeying for promotion. It would have been all too easy for the story to attribute humanity's passivity to brain surgery, which the workforce routinely undergoes in order to link it to the space station's giant computer. Tellingly, however, this passivity is depicted as an act of free will: rather than question the system, humans put their energies into achieving promotion so that they reach the prestigious Floor 500. The Doctor complains of a human race that does not bother to ask questions and would trot into a slaughterhouse if they believed that would advance their careers. Unlike "The Sun Makers", "The Long Game"—informed by the actual experience of a protracted period of neoliberalism—recognises that society is saturated with a deeply conservative culture. This pessimism is reinforced by the episode's sequel. When the Doctor quits the scene in "The Long Game", he says that people will start believing a lot of things about Satellite 5's misdeeds, and that human progress will accelerate. Yet when he returns to the space station some ninety years later, he finds it under the control of another oppressive corporation. Thus, in "Bad Wolf"/"The Parting of the Ways" (2005), the Doctor comments that people have turned into brainless sheep watching ten thousand television channels. By contrast to "The Sun Makers", these stories seem to recognise that there is no need for drugged air or correction centres, since people will settle for a rather harsh form of capitalism if given a life of burgers, chips and television.[92]

[92] This reading is reinforced (in the same story but back on contemporary Earth) by companion Rose Tyler's argument with her mother Jackie and her on-off boyfriend Mickey, in which she insists that the Doctor showed her a way to live which was better than the treadmill of work, home and eating chips. See Ken Chen, "The Lovely Smallness of *Doctor Who*", *Film International*, 6 (2008): 52–59.

Passivity towards corporations also emerges in several more new-series episodes. Only a tiny band of rebels resist John Lumic's activities in "Rise of the Cybermen"/"The Age of Steel" (2006): most people accept his domination and wear his earpods. The Doctor reflects that humans tend to submit to anyone who takes control: they prefer an easy life. In "Planet of the Ood" (2008), the Doctor asks one of the staff of Ood Operations whether people back on Earth know how the company treats the Ood. She says they know what is going on. When the Doctor queries this, she snaps that people do not ask, and that this amounts to the same thing. A similarly uncritical acceptance is apparent in "The Rebel Flesh"/"The Almost People" (2011), where companion Rory Williams' horror at the way in which the company Morpeth Jetsan treats its Gangers is evidently not shared by the rest of humanity. *Doctor Who*'s depiction of people's acceptance of neoliberal capitalism resonates with the work of Mark Fisher and Jeremy Gilbert. Fisher reflects that there is currently no *imaginable* alternative to neoliberal capitalism. For most young people, he considers, capitalism seamlessly occupies the horizons of the thinkable, such that the lack of alternatives to capitalism is no longer even an issue. The fact that capitalism has colonised even the unconscious—the dreaming life of the population—is taken for granted and no longer merits comment.[93] For his part, Gilbert emphasises that it is perfectly possible to recognise neoliberal capitalism's iniquitous nature without being moved to oppose it, since no popular alternative has cohered enough to gain the critical mass to challenge neoliberalism.[94]

Why *Doctor Who* Is not Socialist

There is ample evidence, therefore, to disagree with John Fiske's argument that *Doctor Who* is capitalist propaganda. Does it follow that the show is socialist propaganda? If we define socialism as the replacement of private ownership of the commanding heights of the economy with common ownership, then the answer would have to be "no". This is because the Doctor is strong on diagnosis but weak on prescription.

---

[93] Mark Fisher, *Capitalist Realism: Is There No Alternative?* (Winchester: Zero Books, 2009), 8.

[94] Jeremy Gilbert, "What Kind of Thing is Neoliberalism?", in *Neoliberal Cultures*, ed. Jeremy Gilbert (London: Lawrence & Wishart, 2006), 26.

Whilst relentlessly castigating corporations, *Doctor Who* tends not to propose an alternative to them. Vanessa de Kauwe and Lindy Orthia have observed this tendency at a higher level of generality: *Doctor Who* is generally readier to identify a tyrannical regime than to propose any political alternatives to it.[95] Thus, in the context of corporations, in the vast majority of *Doctor Who* stories, the Doctor, having vanquished the corporate leader, normally simply quits the scene and we are not told what happens next. "The Sun Makers" is a rare exception. Here, the "work units" stage a revolution, and presumably reorganise Pluto's governance in their own interests, although we do not know how successful they are. Another rare exception is "Oxygen" (2017), which envisages a rebellion leading to the abolition of capitalism throughout space. In some other adventures, the solution to corporate domination is a nostalgic return to an agrarian, egalitarian past-that-never-was. This can be seen in "Colony in Space" (1971) and "Revelation of the Daleks" (1985). In a highly industrialised country like Britain, this is a pipedream. Similarly, the replacement of one villainous corporation in "The Long Game" (2005) by another villainous corporation in "Bad Wolf"/"The Parting of the Ways" (2005) perhaps implies that resistance to corporations is futile.

Doctor Who's non-socialism is particularly well exemplified by the conclusion of "The Rebel Flesh"/"The Almost People" (2011). Having resolved a murderous conflict between the human staff of the company Morpeth Jetsan and their sentient facsimiles the Gangers, the Doctor wants humans and Gangers to knuckle down and work together. To this end, he transports two Gangers to the company's press conference in the touching belief that they will somehow convince Morpeth Jetsan to eschew profit in favour of a policy of compassion and equality towards Gangers. The Doctor's habit of rarely tying up loose ends proves convenient here. Always moving on, he does not trouble himself with ascertaining whether Morpeth Jetsan actually accepts the Gangers' pleadings before he dematerialises in the TARDIS. *Doctor Who*'s highly critical approach to corporations is remarkable: but it might still be considered compatible with a system of corporate domination so long as no viable alternative is presented as being possible. On this reading, *Doctor Who* merely provides a safety valve for neoliberalism's discontents.

[95] Vanessa de Kauwe and Lindy Orthia, "Knowledge, Power and the Ethics Illusion", *Journal of Popular Television*, 6(2) (2018).

This chimes with Jeremy Gilbert's observation that the most common response to neoliberalism is explicit rejection of its norms coupled with a resigned compliance with its demands.[96]

Conclusion

Considered as a whole, *Doctor Who* is far more critical of the corporate system than John Fiske's famous study of "The Creature from the Pit" would have us believe. It frequently presents corporations as controlling or even constituting government; it portrays them as lawless entities, contemptuous of the value of human life, ready to deploy their economic weapons to coerce, and as corrosive of truth and civil liberties. *Doctor Who* often paints the leaders of corporations as a hostile, alien species. It depicts private-sector domination as a source of rampant inequality, crushing individuality rather than fostering it. All in all, *Doctor Who*'s view of corporations is far less starry-eyed than that of the British political class. To be sure, *Doctor Who* rarely posits an actual alternative to capitalism and cannot therefore be regarded as socialist. But conversely, it in no way shares the political elite's love affair with big business. Rather, *Doctor Who*'s authors persistently adopt a far more cynical view of large-scale private enterprise, a stance which may be considered an essential component of *Doctor Who*'s Britishness.

Bibliography

Anderson, Gavin. *Constitutional Rights After Globalization.* Oxford: Hart, 2005.

Barnet, Richard and Ronald Mueller. *Global Reach: The Power of the Multinational Corporation.* New York: Simon and Schuster, 1974.

Bartle, Ian. *Globalisation and EU Policy-Making: The Neoliberal Transformation of Telecommunications and Electricity.* Manchester: Manchester University Press, 2005.

Chapman, James. *Inside the TARDIS: The Worlds of Doctor Who*, 2nd ed. London: I.B. Tauris, 2013.

Chen, Ken. "The Lovely Smallness of *Doctor Who*." *Film International* 6 (2008): 52–59.

[96] Gilbert, "What Kind of Thing is Neoliberalism?", 18.

Chopra, Sudhir. "Multinational Corporations in the Aftermath of Bhopal: The Need for a New Comprehensive Global Regime for Transnational Corporate Activity." *Valparaiso University Law Review* 29 (1994): 235–284.

Crouch, Colin. *Post-Democracy*. Cambridge: Polity, 2004.

de Kauwe, Vanessa and Lindy Orthia. "Knowledge, Power and the Ethics Illusion in Classic Era *Doctor Who*." *Journal of Popular Television* 6(2) 2018.

Dickens, Charles. *Nicholas Nickleby*. Oxford: Oxford University Press, 2008.

Dussias, Alison M. "Indians and *Indios*: Echoes of the Bhopal Disaster in the Achuar People of Peru's Struggle Against the Toxic Legacy of Occidental Petroleum." *New England Law Review* 42 (2008): 809–846.

Fisher, Mark. *Capitalist Realism: Is There No Alternative?* Winchester: Zero Books, 2009.

Fiske, John. "Dr. Who: Ideology and the Reading of a Popular Narrative Text." *Australian Journal of Screen Theory* 14 (1983): 69–100.

Frank, Thomas. *One Market Under God: Extreme Capitalism, Market Populism, and the End of Economic Democracy*. New York: Anchor, 2000.

Freeland, Chrystia. *Plutocrats: The Rise of the New Global Super-Rich*. London: Penguin, 2012.

Gilbert, Jeremy. "What Kind of Thing is Neoliberalism?" In *Neoliberal Cultures*, edited by Jeremy Gilbert, 10–32. London: Lawrence & Wishart, 2006.

Gray, John. *False Dawn: The Delusions of Global Capitalism*. London: Granta Books, 2002.

Harvey, David. *A Brief History of Neoliberalism*. Oxford: Oxford University Press, 2005.

Hayek, Friedrich von. *Law, Legislation and Liberty*. London: Routledge and Kegan Paul, 1982.

Hayek, Friedrich von. *The Constitution of Liberty*. Chicago, IL: University of Chicago Press, 1960.

Hayek, Friedrich von. *The Road to Serfdom*. London: Ark Paperbacks, 1986.

Hills, Matt. *Triumph of a Time Lord: Regenerating Doctor Who in the Twenty-First Century*. London: I.B. Tauris, 2010.

Holland, Stuart. *The Socialist Challenge*. London: Quartet, 1975.

Jenkins, Simon. *Thatcher and Sons*. London: Penguin Books, 2006.

Klein, Naomi. *No Logo*. London: Flamingo, 2001.

Leys, Colin. *Market-Driven Politics: Neoliberal Democracy and the Public Interest*. London: Verso, 2001.

Littler, Jo. "Meritocracy as Plutocracy: The Marketisation of Equality under Neoliberalism." In *Neoliberal Culture*, edited by Jeremy Gilbert, 73–100. London: Lawrence & Wishart, 2016.

McEwan, Arthur. *Neo-liberalism or Democracy?* London: Zed Books, 1999.

McNair, Brian. *News and Journalism in the UK*, 5th ed. Abingdon Oxon: Routledge, 2009.

Meek, James. *Private Island: Why Britain Now Belongs to Someone Else*. London: Verso, 2015.
Miliband, Ralph. *The State in Capitalist Society*. London: Weidenfeld and Nicolson, 1969.
Mises, Ludwig von. *Bureaucracy*. New Haven, CT: Yale University Press, 1944.
Monbiot, George. *Captive State: The Corporate Takeover of Britain*. London: Macmillan, 2000.
Muchlinski, Peter T. "The Bhopal Case: Controlling Ultrahazardous Industrial Activities Undertaken by Foreign Investors." *Modern Law Review* 50 (1987): 545–587.
Nicol, Danny. *The Constitutional Protection of Capitalism*. Oxford: Hart, 2010.
Oborne, Peter. *The Triumph of the Political Class*. London: Simon and Schuster, 2007.
Oloka-Onyango, J. "Reinforcing Marginalized Rights in an Age of Globalization: International Mechanisms, Non-State Actors and the Struggle for People's Rights in Africa." *American University International Law Review* 18 (2002): 851–914.
Peston, Robert. *Who Runs Britain?* London: Hodder and Stoughton, 2008.
Plant, Raymond. *The Neo-liberal State*. Oxford: Oxford University Press, 2010.
Robins, Nick. *The Corporation that Changed the World: How the East India Company Shaped the Modern Multinational*. London: Pluto Press, 2006.
Robinson, William. *A Theory of Global Capitalism: Production, Class, and State in a Transnational World*. Baltimore, MD: Johns Hopkins University Press, 2004.
Schattschneider, E.E. *Politics, Pressures and the Tariff*. New York: Prentice-Hall, 1935.
Seery, Emma and Ana Caistor Arendar. *Even It Up: Time to End Extreme Inequality*. Oxford: Oxfam International, 2014.
Seymour-Ure, Colin. *Prime Ministers and the Media: Issues of Power and Control*. Oxford: Blackwell Publishing, 2003.
Shaffer, Gregory. *Defending Interests: Public–Private Partnerships in WTO Negotations*. Washington, DC: Brookings Institution Press, 2003.
Shutt, Harry. *The Trouble with Capitalism*. London and New York: Zed Books, 1998.
Somek, Alexander. *Individualism: An Essay on the Authority of the European Union*. Oxford: Oxford University Press, 2008.
Steuer, Max, Peter Abell, John Gennard, Morris Perlman, Raymond Rees, Barry Scott and Ken Wallis. *The Impact of Foreign Direct Investment on the United Kingdom*. London: HMSO, 1973.

Wallace, Richard. "'The Sound of Empires Toppling': Politics, Public Service Broadcasting and *Doctor Who.*" Paper, *Doctor Who: Walking in Eternity*, University of Hertfordshire, September 3–5, 2013.

Whyte, Dave. "The Crimes of Neo-liberal Rule in Occupied Iraq." *British Journal of Criminology* 47 (2007): 177–195.

Wriston, Walter B. *The Twilight of Sovereignty: How the Information Revolution is Transforming Our World.* New York: Charles Scribner's Sons, 1992.

CHAPTER 7

Conclusion: *Doctor Who*'s Post-Democratic Britain

Doctor Who's cheery evocation of all things British—Queens, tea, chips and cosmopolitanism—is, we have seen, regularly punctuated with a darker, more political, projection of British identity. In this regard, it is readily apparent that *Doctor Who*'s vision of Britain and Britishness departs significantly from the sense of national identity promoted in recent times by the country's leaders. In particular, *Doctor Who* depicts a country more doubtful of Britain's foreign adventures, more cynical of Britain's level of democracy, and more critical of the role of corporate giants in British life.

This concluding chapter reviews what we have established about *Doctor Who* and Britishness. Against that backdrop, it then explores the concept of a "hidden transcript", an idea developed by James C. Scott to identify how the marginalised give vent to their grievances. It argues that *Doctor Who* may be viewed as a hidden transcript. It then goes on to consider how best to characterise the distress to which *Doctor Who*'s hidden transcript gives vent, finding a compelling answer in Colin Crouch's concept of post-democracy.

Let us begin by recapitulating what we have learned about *Doctor Who*'s Britishness. *Doctor Who*, we should recall, frequently expresses Britishness by projecting both the British *as they are*, and the British *as they ought to be*, and by differentiating between the empirical and the normative. The programme has made rather extensive use of this device, notably to reject the ideal of the British as buccaneering entrepreneurs. Profit-taking is portrayed as ignoble: public service—including

D. Nicol, *Doctor Who: A British Alien?*,
https://doi.org/10.1007/978-3-319-65834-6_7

that performed by the Doctor and by his companions through their adventures—is depicted as virtuous. Furthermore, unlike some heritage dramas on British television, the show for the most part tends to frown upon oppressive class structures. In this regard, it criticises not only the harsh class divides of Britain's past but also the contemporary gap between the super-rich and the have-nots, a gap that has widened under globalisation. Far from placing the super-rich on a pedestal, the show favours (predominantly) the British middle class and (to a lesser extent) the working class. Indeed, in recent years, the precarious position of the middle class has become a recurring theme. In addition, *Doctor Who* and its spin-offs have introduced quite a number of important characters who are bisexual, lesbian and gay, turning non-straight sexuality almost into a signifier of Britishness. The contemporary show also celebrates the multiracial nature of Britain at every turn, though unfortunately this celebration has not been coupled with any consistency in casting the top roles in a racially diverse way, with sluggishness in repeating the experiment of a non-white companion and the role of Doctor remaining a white preserve. As for gender, whilst the dolly-bird companions of some of the classic series gave way to the feistier women of new *Who*, masculine dominance on the part of the Doctor has remained the normal state of affairs. Yet continued male domination in *Doctor Who* sat awkwardly in a country which has had two women prime ministers and an array of women party leaders. The male monopoly on playing the Doctor until the casting of Jodie Whittaker for the role in 2017, has meant that, as regards gender, *Doctor Who* has projected a rather archaic vision of Britishness. It sells Britain short, not even representing the country as it is, let alone the country as it ought to be.

In other areas, *Doctor Who*'s portrayal of Britishness is more progressive. As tensions have risen between the four nations of the United Kingdom under neoliberalism, new *Who* responded by atoning for some of the sins of classic *Who*. It has given greater prominence to Scottish and Welsh characters, accorded them more agency and credited them with greater competence. It has thereby portrayed Scottishness and Welshness in ways more conducive to the continued unity of Britain. New *Who*'s subtle favouring of the maintenance of the union between the British nations coincides with the official stance the British state. Yet, in other respects, *Doctor Who* flies in the face of the official consensus. In particular, by the mid-1970s the programme seemed to lose faith in the international, globalised sphere. Strikingly, this happened just at the time when the British political class was forming an ever-tighter consensus in favour of extensive engagement in globalisation and supranational organisations. Part of *Doctor Who*'s resistance to globalisation lies in its satire of the British relationship with the United States of America. The show's endless ribbing of Americans—sometimes affectionate, frequently less so—again sits unhappily with the stance of Britain's elite. Since 1945, the country's politicians have, with greater or lesser degrees of enthusiasm, pursued a pro-American foreign policy, regardless of whether Labour or the Conservatives formed the governing party. British leaders clung to American coat-tails particularly tightly in the run-up to the launch of new *Who*, with the interventions in Afghanistan and Iraq. The excessive closeness of British and American elites during these wars seemingly inspired *Doctor Who*'s authors to delineate Britishness by emphasising difference between British characters and the American Other. Quite apart from the American element, however, *Doctor Who* also raises questions as to the sheer aggression of British foreign policy, especially in new *Who*, which was, after all, broadcast during British participation in a litany of interventions in Arab and Middle East countries. By constantly engaging in debate over whether the Doctor is a "good man", new *Who* places metaphorical question marks over whether *Britain's* meddling is justified. The programme was thereby able to reflect public misgivings about recent interventions, most notoriously the invasion of Iraq.

Doctor Who also defies British political orthodoxy through its relentless hostility towards corporations. The consensus among British leaders has long been that, under globalisation, transnational companies are there to be enticed. British governments must vie with foreign governments to attract corporations to our shores. Firms are to be wooed by lowering worker expectations and curbing egalitarian policies. *Doctor Who* takes an entirely different position. Instead of projecting corporations as Britain's economic saviours, *Doctor Who* sees them as murderous entities, dissembling, crushing liberty and individuality, and fostering severe inequality. *Doctor Who*'s stance marks a sharp and striking contrast to the British political elite's decades-long love affair with the private sector. The argument of this chapter is that, on matters such as big business, foreign policy and globalisation, *Doctor Who* through its metaphors forms a hidden transcript which answers back to the political hegemony of the age.

Doctor Who as Hidden Transcript

The concept of the hidden transcript was introduced by James C. Scott in 1992. Scott has argued that, under condition of domination, people tend to fashion "hidden transcripts" which conflict with the "public transcript". The public transcript consists of the flattering *self*-portrait of dominant elites, depicting them as they would have themselves seen. Designed to impress, the public transcript aims to affirm and legitimise elite rule. In particular, the elite use the public transcript to advance the ideological case that they rule, to a degree, *on behalf of* their subjects.[1] By contrast, the hidden transcript—a reaction to the domination legitimised by the public transcript—displays a sharply dissonant political culture. Scott contends that, where a whole stratum of society systematically suffers a series of affronts, this may generate a collective cultural product.[2] This hidden transcript represents a critique of power; it carves out a public space for the cultural expression of dissent. It is spoken to power.[3] The possibility that *Doctor Who* quite literally "talks to power" has been underlined by an exchange between British Prime Minister Theresa May and the actor who played the twelfth Doctor, Peter Capaldi, in December 2016. May revealed that she was looking forward to watching the *Doctor Who* Christmas special, prompting Capaldi to respond that he hoped that she would take to heart *Doctor Who*'s message of kindness, compassion and tolerance.[4]

Scott's account of a hidden transcript contains a number of features which enable us to envisage *Doctor Who* as falling within its parameters. According to Scott, creating a hidden transcript necessitates setting a course at the very perimeter of what authorities are obliged to permit or are unable to prevent.[5] In the case of *Doctor Who*, "the authorities" include the British Broadcasting Corporation, Britain's public-sector television and radio provider. The BBC is legally obliged to be politically impartial, although, as we shall see, the idea that it is actually

[1] James C. Scott, *Domination and the Arts of Resistance* (New Haven, CT and London: Yale University Press, 1992), 18.

[2] Scott, *Domination*, 9.

[3] Scott, *Domination*, 166.

[4] *Daily Telegraph*, December 16, 2016.

[5] Scott, *Domination*, 138–139.

impartial is fiercely contested. Furthermore, hidden transcripts by definition need to be hidden. Such is the *quid pro quo* for the daring messages they transmit. Fashioning hidden transcripts therefore requires a grasp of the arts of political disguise. Cultural expression, Scott observes, lends itself to disguise by virtue of metaphor. As we have seen, *Doctor Who* is notable for its extensive use of metaphor. Another feature which often characterises hidden transcripts is that the underdog outwits his normally dominant antagonist.[6] Similarly, in *Doctor Who*, the Doctor's battles are not trials of strength: indeed, the Doctor regularly triumphs over superior firepower. He frequently confronts entire armies of Daleks, Cybermen and others (examples include "The Dalek Invasion of Earth" (1964), "The Invasion" (1968), "The Stolen Earth"/"Journey's End" (2008) and "Nightmare in Silver" (2013)) and prevails because of his intelligence.

Doctor Who does not, however, conform to Scott's hidden transcript in one respect: Scott assumes that the hidden transcript is always fashioned by the poor and oppressed themselves, whereas *Doctor Who* is the product of writers and production teams, some of whom are well-to-do. Nonetheless, the idea of the hidden transcript can surely be extended to embrace instances where authors represent the underprivileged despite not being particularly disadvantaged themselves, at least not in a material sense. A criticism of hidden transcripts is that they merely serve as a safety valve, and thereby operate as an evasion from effecting radical change. For his part, however, Scott argues that in fact hidden transcripts actually sustain resistance: they are a condition of practical resistance rather than a substitute for it.[7]

Doctor Who and Post-Democracy

The merit of reading *Doctor Who* as a hidden transcript becomes apparent when one considers the striking degree of "fit" between the show's themes and the theory of post-democracy expounded by Colin Crouch.[8] Crouch's alarming thesis is that whilst the forms of democracy remain fully in place—and indeed have in some respects been

[6] Scott, *Domination*, 166.

[7] Scott, *Domination*, 191.

[8] Colin Crouch, *Post-Democracy* (Cambridge: Polity, 2004).

strengthened—politics and government are actually increasingly slipping back into the control of privileged elites in a manner characteristic of pre-democratic times. Crouch attributes this to the homogeneity of political parties, which is in turn closely connected to the rise of corporate elites. Indeed, Crouch emphasises that the growing sway of the firm has been *the* fundamental change driving the advance of post-democracy.[9] *Doctor Who* may be seen as a cry against post-democracy, insofar as the programme engages with multiple features of the post-democratic phenomenon.

Crouch's theory clearly raises profound questions regarding the political life of the British nation. Whilst the term "post-democracy" may not have entered everyday language, the substance of Crouch's critique nonetheless resounds powerfully in everyday life in Britain. It is reflected in the popular sentiments that politicians are all motivated by private gain, are all untruthful and are all the same.[10] Anger against the political elite reflected in the "Leave" vote in Britain's EU referendum of 2016 further indicates the growing discontent with the mass–elite gap that post-democracy has fostered. So too does the trend towards populism. We would of course expect science fiction to engage with such a fundamental change in Britain's politics as the passing of the democratic era. After all, quite apart from reflecting the political misgivings of *Doctor Who*'s authors, the programme needs to confront the burning issues of the day if it is to resonate with viewers. Engaging with the main features of post-democracy is therefore "a logical accommodation to the need for ratings success".[11]

In post-democracy, argues Crouch, the form of democracy is maintained as its substance is undermined: for example, global firms may, through threats not to invest, prompt all major parties to support the same policy reform, effectively depriving the public of democratic choice. In such instances, the effective instigator of change has been neither the electorate nor parliament but the global firms. Indeed, large companies enjoy a host of political advantages; they have privileged access to politicians and civil servants. This combines with the increasing concentration

---

[9] Crouch, *Post-Democracy*, 13.

[10] Peter Oborne, *The Rise of Political Lying* (London: Free Press, 2005); Peter Oborne, *The Triumph of the Political Class* (London: Simon and Schuster, 2007).

[11] Graham Murdock, "Authorship and Organisation", *Screen Education*, 35 (Summer 1980): 28.

of control of news and information media in the hands of a very small number of extremely wealthy individuals. As well as dominating the economy, therefore, the corporate class has increasingly become the class that dominates the running of government.[12] As a result, argues Crouch, we are steadily moving towards the establishment of a new, dominant, combined economic and political class.[13]

Post-democracy has assumed a particularly severe form in Britain, not least because of the thoroughgoing homogeneity of the parties over three decades.[14] In the mid-1980s competition between the main British parties became limited as all of them came to adopt a firmly pro-business orientation. This consensus grew so strong that, on one reading, we may conceive it as a form of one-party rule. In any event, it placed the business elite in a powerful position in Britain to pursue their core political objective of combating egalitarianism. A widening wealth gap between haves and have-nots is therefore not merely a symptom of post-democracy but its very *raison d'être.*

Doctor Who's Britain and Britishness has engaged with a range of post-democracy's key features. Classic *Who* came to an end just as the British political parties were converging on a pro-corporate ticket, but new *Who*, by contrast, came into existence when Britain had had a fulsome dose of post-democracy. Accordingly, multiple elements of post-democracy loom large in the contemporary programme and can be taken to be part of the show's hidden transcript. To give a few examples: the show has engaged with post-democracy's ***hollowing-out of democracy***, and particularly on the growing ***divergence between democratic form and democratic substance***. This is prominent in "The Beast Below" (2010)—an episode that we have already considered from the point of view of its projection of Britishness, Scottishness and the role of the female companion. The story also engages head-on with key features of post-democracy. Set in the distant future, the Doctor and companion Amy Pond land on Starship UK, a vessel in which the British people have abandoned Earth and are searching the galaxy for a new home. The Starship's secret is that it has no engine but relies instead on a vast alien creature—a Star Whale—which the government tortures in order to propel the Starship

[12] Crouch, *Post-Democracy*, 44.

[13] Crouch, *Post-Democracy*, 52.

[14] Crouch, *Post-Democracy*, 64–73.

Fig. 7.1 A mad man with a mask. The Master as British Prime Minister Harold Saxon. *Doctor Who* (new series), "The Sound of Drums"/"Last of the Time Lords", series 3, episodes 12 and 13; British Broadcasting Corporation, 2007

through space. The government has created a repressive police state in order to preserve this secret. Yet at the same time, Starship UK presents a veneer of democracy. It allows citizens to vote every five years on whether to endorse or reject the British practice of torturing the Star Whale. When Amy finds herself in a voting cubicle, she is informed by computer of "the truth about Starship UK and what has been done to safeguard the British people". She is then given the choice of whether to "*Protest*" about the treatment of the Star Whale or to "*Forget*", in which case all memories of the information that the computer has imparted are instantly wiped from the voter's mind. Amy chooses to forget, as almost everyone apparently does. Yet with the Star Whale's existence shrouded in secrecy, there can be no debate on Starship UK over the rights or wrongs of how the Star Whale is treated. The façade of voting thereby masks a denial of genuine democracy. This paradox resonates with Britain's post-democratic era, whereby governments have provided additional opportunities to vote (referendums, devolved assemblies, elected mayors), yet this has gone hand-in-hand with a corporate domination which makes democracy phoney. The key feature is the gulf between democratic *form* and democratic *substance.*

Post-democracy has also been characterised by *the degeneration of parliamentary government*, and this is readily apparent in the satire of "The Sound of Drums"/"The Last of the Time Lords" (2007). Here *the cult of the individual* is a prominent theme. The Doctor's long-term adversary the Master has become the British Prime Minister, using the name Harold Saxon. He has come to power by subjecting the electorate to some form of hypnosis; this suggests an inability of the political elite to connect with the people in the absence of bewitching powers. Saxon's cabinet consists of MPs who have betrayed their own parties in order to support him. At his first cabinet meeting, Saxon kills off these ministers using poisonous gas. Figure 7.1 shows Saxon, having released the gas, sticking his thumbs up in agreement as one of his dying ministers blurts out the words "You're mad!" The image adeptly conveys the notion of political leadership as performance (comic performance in the Master's case) and emphasises the role of the neoliberal politician as celebrity and showman. It also raises in satirical fashion the crucial issue of whether a concentration of power at the top of government does indeed foster a drift on the part of a leader from political acumen to hubris to mental illness, a pattern into which some British Prime Ministers have been accused of falling.

The narrative of Saxon's rise to power reflects elements of post-democracy which came to the fore during Tony Blair's period as prime minister: *the personalisation of politics and the growing pre-eminence of the prime ministerial role*. Paul Webb and Thomas Poguntke have argued that there has been a presidentialisation of politics, involving a shift from collective to individual power. They see this as including a rejection of collegiality and as a harking-back to elitist models of politics.[15] To be sure, post-democracy tends to rely upon the claimed charismatic qualities of the party leaders whilst fostering a weakening of formal party structures: it favours a monopoly of power at the top of parties.[16] The defection of Saxon's parliamentary supporters from their former parties reflects *the waning of party ties*, another element of post-democracy. The Saxon Cabinet thereby reflects the post-democratic perception of

[15] See Paul Webb and Thomas Poguntke, "The Presidentialization of Contemporary Democratic Politics: Evidence, Causes, and Consequences", in *The Presidentialization of Politics*, eds. Thomas Poguntke and Paul Webb (Oxford: Oxford University Press, 2005).

[16] Peter Mair, "Partyless Democracy", *New Left Review*, 2 (Mar–Apr 2000): 21–35.

politicians as "in it for themselves" and "all the same". Subsequently, Saxon becomes a tyrant, hyperbole perhaps for the "control freakery" which typified the early years of Tony Blair's premiership before it ultimately backfired, contributing both to Blair's downfall and to the fraying of party loyalty among backbenchers.[17] Certainly, Saxon's fondness for dancing around to Brit pop seems on all fours with the Blairite use of popular culture to cultivate a "cool Britannia" persona. With its focus on a leadership cult, the Saxon narrative also reflects *the rise of populism* as a reaction to post-democracy, as exemplified in the election of Donald Trump as American President and the improved showing of far-right parties in some European countries.

Finally, the theme of *the corrosive effects of corporate power on democracy* is satirised in numerous episodes, not least "Rise of the Cybermen"/"The Age of Steel" (2006), which has a particular focus on the relationship between a giant company and the British state. Set in a parallel Republic of Great Britain, the tale emphasises the political might of a global corporation, Cybus Industries. The country's president has to die because he resists the corporate demand to permit the development of the Cybermen. With the president's death, the company effectively *becomes* the state, as the British people line up for cyber-conversion. It may not be entirely fanciful to regard the immense physical strength of the (corporate-)Cybermen in this and other new-*Who* episodes as being a metaphor for the increased might of the transnational corporation under globalisation. In this respect, a comparison between classic *Who* and new *Who* is instructive: enemies which could be easily pushed around ("The Daleks" (1963–1964)) or overpowered ("The Tomb of the Cybermen" (1967)) in early serials were raised to the level of near-invincibility in the contemporary show ("Dalek" (2005), "Nightmare in Silver" (2013)). The underlying assumption is that the hostile forces ranged against ordinary people are far more powerful than in the past. This would tally with Mark Fisher's acute observation that "for most people under twenty in Europe and North America, the lack of alternatives to capitalism is no longer even an issue. Capitalism seamlessly occupies the horizons of the thinkable .... The fact that capitalism has colonized the dreaming life

[17] The trend towards MPs cross-voting is well covered by Philip Cowley, *The Rebels: How Blair Mislaid his Majority* (London: Politicos, 2005).

of the population is so taken for granted to that is no longer worthy of comment".[18]

It is significant that in all three of these adventures that engage so intimately with features of post-democracy—"The Beast Below", "The Sound of Drums"/"The Last of the Time Lords" and "Rise of the Cybermen"/"The Age of Steel"—*Doctor Who* for the most part pits British middle-class (and occasionally working-class) companions and allies against elite figures. Furthermore, in typical new *Who* fashion, these companions and allies are diverse in terms of race as well as in terms of English-Scottish-Welsh identity. They include: Rose and Pete Tyler (London English), Mrs Moore (Welsh), Amy Pond (Scottish), Martha Jones and her family (London black British), Liz 10 (mixed-race British sovereign) Jake (north-east English) and Mickey/Ricky (London black British).[19] The diversity of these characters echoes this book's argument regarding *Doctor Who*'s projection of Britishness. As well as racial diversity, it is notable that these characters are drawn from all three nations of Great Britain. Regardless of the playfulness with which tensions between the English, Scots and Welsh are handled, the three nationalities are persistently portrayed as being on the same side, reflecting the more egalitarian unionism which new *Who* projects. The programme pits "the people" against "the elite", without wishing to divide the former too much on the basis of to which of Britain's nations they belong. In doing so, *Doctor Who* underlines its disdain for the elite and its preoccupation with middle-class concerns. Here again, *Doctor Who*'s Britain differs notably from the public transcript, which depicts the middle class as having identical interests to the elite, a position constantly reflected in the BBC's business and economic news output. Indeed, Crouch explains that post-democracy denies the privilege of the elite class and the subordination of the classes below. In particular, post-democracy tends to define the interests of the middle class as *entirely at one* with the interests of business. Post-democratic politicians do not articulate wider concerns of the middle classes which might be uncomfortable for the corporate

[18] Mark Fisher, *Capitalist Realism: Is There No Alternative?* (Winchester: Zero Books 2009), 8–9.

[19] In making these designations, I am treating Englishness as an ethnicity: some black people choose to treat Englishness as a nationality and describe themselves as English rather than British.

elites: it is therefore in relation to middle Britain that manipulative politics is most extensively used.[20]

It is also intriguing—and again in line with the findings of this book—that new *Who* does not present supranational organisations as offering much relief from post-democracy's discontents. In "Rise of the Cybermen"/"The Age of Steel", there is no international body to rescue the country from Cybus Industries and its Cybermen (a Geneva protocol on bioethics is effortlessly brushed aside in the story's opening seconds), whereas the corporation's transnational nature poses an additional challenge for the Doctor's allies; and in "The Sound of Drums"/"Last of the Time Lords" UNIT is itself post-democratic: over-mighty, imperious and American-dominated. Its supranationalism is replaced by Saxon's worldwide dictatorship, another form of globalisation. As for "The Beast Below", we can conceive Starship UK itself as representing the rejection of the supranational. The episode shows that isolationism is no panacea, yet neither does it mourn supranationalism. Rather, the target of the episode's condemnation is the failure to embrace the Star Whale into the Britishness fold as part of the diversity and tolerance to which the country should aspire. New *Who*'s sceptical stance towards supranationalism matches Crouch's argument that the present supranational organisations, far from bringing about a compromise between democracy and capitalism, are mainly in the business of breaking down barriers to corporate freedom by creating global oligopolies.[21] On his reading, the supranational organisations have contributed to post-democracy rather than having softened it.

Doctor Who and the BBC: Two Stories of Britishness?

Doctor Who therefore holds an unflattering mirror to Britain's post-democracy and the programme may be viewed as a hidden transcript which lays bare post-democracy's extremes. Yet *Doctor Who* is a BBC programme and, intriguingly, the BBC as an organisation sings from an altogether more orthodox hymn-sheet. Indeed, there is rather compelling evidence that it has tended to play a major role in sustaining post-democracy. For instance, its news and documentary output treats

[20] Crouch, *Post-Democracy*, 59–60.

[21] Crouch, *Post-Democracy*, 106.

the dominant role of the transnational corporation as incontestable. At the same time, it has rarely sought to unmask the homogeneity of the British political parties and the implications for democracy of that commonality.

Yet the BBC's connivance with post-democracy goes hand-in-hand with a formal obligation to impartiality, to which much importance is attached. According to Brian McNair, part of the BBC's "civilising message" to the world as a whole is the cultural value of impartiality and balance in its news reporting.[22] However, even before British capitalism adopted its neoliberal sheen, Ralph Miliband, writing in 1969, argued that BBC impartiality was quite artificial. Miliband noted the claims of democratic diversity made on behalf of the "open societies" of advanced capitalism but contended that, in reality, the free expression of ideas and opinions mainly meant the free expression of ideas and opinions which were helpful to the prevailing system of power and privilege. The mass media in general, he maintained, had assumed the role of rendering mass publics conformative to the social and economic status quo, thereby reinforcing the system of dominance. Focusing on television and radio in particular, Miliband conceded an *appearance* of a rich diversity of views and opinions alongside passionate debate, and that on a formal level a high degree of political objectivity and impartiality was required. Yet, he insisted, in most ways impartiality and objectivity operated only with regard to political formations which, while divided on many issues, were nonetheless part of a basic, underlying consensus. The BBC sought to maintain the appearance of impartiality between the main British political parties provided they supported this consensus. This did not, however, preclude a steady stream of propaganda aimed at countering any views which fell outside it. British television, he contended, was therefore steeped in an official environment and permeated by an official climate, which ensured that in political and ideological terms it fulfilled a conformist rather than a critical role. In short, impartiality stopped where political consensus ended.[23]

---

[22] Brian McNair, *News and Journalism in the UK*, 4th ed. (London: Routledge, 2004), 150.

[23] Ralph Miliband, *The State in Capitalist Society* (London: Weidenfeld and Nicolson, 1969), 223–224.

As British social democracy gave way to neoliberalism in the late 1970s, the BBC refashioned its "common sense" political consensus to embrace a stronger pro-business stance. As a result, even the pretence of even-handedness between companies and the much-diminished trade unions evaporated. In *The BBC: Myth of a Public Service* (2016), Tom Mills traces the intensification of the BBC's role as an integral part of Britain's post-democratic establishment. He suggests that, since Miliband's day, the BBC has been transformed from a pillar of social democracy into a neoliberal, pro-business organisation. Contending that the BBC has never been independent of the state in any meaningful sense, Mills argues that its relative autonomy from private companies and the market has been steadily eroded since the 1980s.[24] In any event, he argues, the concept of independence is a poor starting-point from which to analyse the BBC's place in British society. Focusing attention on the rare instances of BBC disobedience to government obscures collusion and cohesion with the elite. It serves to hide the extent to which the BBC is the product of the same ideological forces that have shaped post-democracy. A more fruitful approach, Mills contends, is to ask what social forces have shaped the BBC's structure and culture and how these have impacted on its journalism.[25] He states that the BBC overwhelmingly reflects the ideas and interests of elite groups, and that it marginalises alternative and oppositional perspectives. The BBC is thus an integral part of the establishment, and impartiality is routinely construed in a manner skewed towards the interests of powerful groups.[26]

There are, however, shades of grey. The BBC has not always functioned like a straightforward instrument of Britain's governing class. Rather, it has always occupied a grey area—sometimes darker, sometimes lighter—between government and civil society. For example, the liberal and radical upheavals of the 1960s saw some pockets of critical reporting, socially conscious drama and biting satire.[27] By contrast, Mills relates how, in the late 1980s, the BBC was reorganised through a cull of senior news staff and the introduction of an internal market ("Producer Choice")—a

[24] Tom Mills, *The BBC: Myth of a Public Service* (London: Verso, 2016), 9.

[25] Mills, *The BBC*, 28.

[26] Mills, *The BBC*, 2.

[27] Mills, *The BBC*, 4.

process of neoliberalisation.[28] This went hand-in-hand with a fundamental reshaping of the BBC's economics reporting, whereby the economy was reported entirely from the perspective of the business elite, a small yet increasingly powerful section of society. This shift was connected to the much broader neoliberal consolidation of British public life following Labour's neoliberal turn in the mid-1980s, which created a consensus that favoured privatisation.[29] Mills' argument is reinforced by Georgina Born, who identifies the 1990s as a time when the BBC was manoeuvred to become a quiescent organisation in the face of neoliberal hegemony, bringing BBC journalism under greater control to minimise political flak and changing its internal governance in such a way as to display zeal for marketisation.[30] Its adhesion to establishment ideas was further reinforced by the way in which it came under almost daily attack for its reporting of the Iraq invasion.[31] All in all, the BBC's constant playing-down of the homogeneity of the main parties, public distrust of politicians and public disengagement from politics has made it "part of the neoliberal business-dominated establishment, a central institution of Britain's post-democratic settlement", by which "the BBC is unable to resist or to articulate a notion of the public interest which is out of step with the imperatives of the corporate-state elite".[32] On this reading, the BBC may be seen as a major actor in establishing and nurturing post-democracy, fulfilling what Chrys Ingraham sees as a central objective of the mass media: to reproduce the ruling order.[33] In a similar vein, Jim McGuigan suggests that British network television generally should be seen as "ideological state apparatus".[34]

Doctor Who clearly does not fit this template. As Matt Hills observes, the show frequently assumes a progressive narrative role, revolving around making a positive difference in the world, highlighting

---

[28] Mills, *The BBC*, 140–166.

[29] Mills, *The BBC*, 167–205.

[30] Georgina Born, *Uncertain Vision: Birt, Dyke and the Reinvention of the BBC* (London: Secker & Warburg, 2004), 57–60.

[31] Philip Knightley, *The First Casualty: The War Correspondent as Hero and Myth-Maker from the Crimea to Iraq* (Baltimore: Johns Hopkins University Press, 2003), xii.

[32] Mills, *The BBC*, 214.

[33] Chrys Ingraham, *White Weddings: Romancing Heterosexuality in Popular Culture* (New York: Routledge, 2008), 174.

[34] Jim McGuigan, *Cool Capitalism* (London: Pluto Press, 2009), 149.

Fig. 7.2 His master-race's voice. British Commander Millington is too close to Nazism for comfort. *Doctor Who* (classic series), "The Curse of Fenric", season 26, serial 155; British Broadcasting Corporation, 1989

power imbalances and challenging forms of oppression and prejudice.[35] Whatever doubts one may entertain about the Doctor's own consistency in this regard, *Doctor Who* as a programme frequently brings us to worlds in which post-democracy is seen for what it is, and is challenged. On this reading, whilst BBC business and economics reporting forms something of a public transcript, this contrasts with the hidden transcript of *Doctor Who*.

But what makes *Doctor Who* a *hidden* transcript? What modes of disguise are used to tone down the show's criticisms of contemporary Britain? Two methods of softening *Doctor Who*'s political message are apparent from classic *Who* and new *Who* alike. The first is the

[35] Matt Hills, *Triumph of a Time Lord: Regenerating Doctor Who in the Twenty-first Century* (London: I.B. Tauris, 2010), 18, n. 14.

programme's extensive use of metaphor, which brings with it an inherent ambiguity. The second is that the Doctor, having defeated a tyrannical regime, typically flies off in the TARDIS, and we are left somewhat in the dark about the nature of the new government brought to power by his intervention. Let us consider these aspects in turn.

The Camouflage of Science Fiction Metaphor

Whilst *Doctor Who*'s metaphor tends to be overt, metaphor nonetheless contains by definition an inherent ambiguity. It is easy to find examples of this ambiguity of metaphor within *Doctor Who.* In "The Curse of Fenric" (1989), set in the Second World War, one of the villains is Commander Millington, a high-ranking British officer. Millington discovers a particularly deadly poison. Believing that the Russians, not the Germans, are the country's true enemy, he plots to allow Russian soldiers to steal a code-breaking machine containing the poison which will, at a suitable time, be released into the atmosphere back in Moscow. There are several ways of reading Millington. One interpretation is to confine his character very much to the serial and to see no metaphor at all: he is merely a villain in a work of fiction. A second interpretation would perceive Millington's narrative as a way a retelling the Second World War. His character is a corrective to the orthodox narrative that views the Germans as the war's aggressors from beginning to end. This interpretation is reinforced by the character of the vicar in "The Curse of Fenric", the Reverend Wainwright, who harbours grave doubts over the rightfulness of British bombs destroying the populations of German cities. This reading draws academic support from James Chapman, who suggests that the serial is revisionist in questioning the received popular narrative of the War.[36] Figure 7.2 highlights the way in which visual similarities between Millington and Adolf Hitler are skilfully provided. The setting is a room at a British army centre deliberately made up to look like an office of German High Command. But the image goes further. We note that Millington himself wears a moustache which, though not the same as Hitler's, is not too dissimilar either. His hairstyle is also somewhat reminiscent of Hitler's. On the front of his desk is the name

[36] James Chapman, *Inside the TARDIS: The Worlds of Doctor Who*, 2nd ed. (London: I.B. Tauris, 2013), 167.

plaque "Commander A.H. Millington", initials reminiscent of Adolf Hitler. Visual imagery is therefore deftly utilised to align Millington with Britain's wartime enemy.

A final interpretation involves removing Millington from the serial's epoch, and arguing that he represents the British elite at the time the serial was broadcast rather than at the time the story is set. Despite *glasnost*, the 1980s were still a high point of the Cold War, in which tensions were exacerbated by the Soviet invasion of Afghanistan and by President Ronald Reagan's "star wars" initiative. By choosing the Russians over the Germans as Britain's true enemy and by sending them a weapon of mass destruction (one which, we ultimately establish, would spread death beyond Russia's frontiers and kill Britain's own nationals), one can piece together enough metaphorical material to align Millington to the leaders of late 1980s Britain. Yet, by the same token, any accusation that *Doctor Who* is spreading propaganda against the Cold War can be met with the argument that such a reading is fanciful. To be sure, claims of metaphor can sometimes mislead: "The Happiness Patrol" (1988) imagines a planet ruled by a dictator, Helen A, who has made sadness illegal. The part of Helen A was played by Sheila Hancock in a way which served to remind the viewer of Margaret Thatcher, leading to the serial being seen as a satire on the Thatcher governments. Yet Helen A's policies—death squads, executions and the extensive state establishment of sugar factories—bear no relation to Thatcher's, making claims of a Thatcher metaphor less convincing.

More generally, we must be ever mindful of John Street's caution against interpreting popular culture too readily as political resistance[37]; but on the other hand, Jane Espenson, a writer for *Battlestar Galactica*, has commented that the thicker the metaphor and the more distractions there are for the viewer, the more the writer of a science fiction programme can "get away with" by way of political messages.[38]

[37] John Street, *Politics and Popular Culture* (London: Polity, 1997), 16.

[38] P.A. Chow-White, D. Deveau and P. Adams, "Media Encoding in Science Fiction Television: Battlestar Galactica as a Site of Critical Cultural Production", *Media Culture and Society*, 37(8) (2015): 1210–1225.

The Replacement Regime Ambiguity

Another way in which *Doctor Who* hides its political transcript is identified by Vanessa de Kauwe and Lindy Orthia in an article entitled "Knowledge, Power and the Ethics Illusion in Classic Era *Doctor Who*". The authors argue that *Doctor Who* plots often emphasise the need to eliminate a tyrant, yet downplay the nature of the new regime which the Doctor's intervention helps bring to power. This practice, they contend, militates against an ethical evaluation of the new regime. Accordingly, there is an ethics illusion, because the impression is created that the new regime is morally good merely because it has replaced a tyrannical one, the narrative being structured to take attention away from the new regime's nature. De Kauwe and Orthia analyse "The Krotons" (1968–1969), "The Green Death" (1973) and "Terminus" (1983) to prove their point, but there are many other instances.[39] Another prize example would be "The Monster of Peladon" (1974). This serial involves a struggle between oppressed miners of the planet Peladon and the Galactic Federation, an organisation that has become despotic under the sway of the Ice Warriors. The Doctor defeats the Ice Warriors, and then he and companion Sarah Jane Smith persuade the Queen of Peladon to appoint one of the miners, Gebek, as her chancellor. This goes against the traditions of Peladon's class system and seems a progressive, egalitarian move. Yet the kind of government which Gebek will usher in is left teasingly obscure. Gebek could represent the interests of the miners and foster greater equality on Peladon. But equally, Gebek is a noted "moderate", the story counterposing him to more radical elements among the miners—so he could just as well emerge as a pillar of the ruling establishment. Notably, there is no apparent plan to turn Peladon into a democracy, Gebek serving at the Queen's pleasure. All in all, therefore, we are rather left in the dark over what sort of new government the people of Peladon will enjoy or endure.

Sometimes, *Doctor Who* seems to have come close to itself satirising the Doctor's tendency to flit off in the TARDIS with scant attention being given to what-happens-next. Notably, in "The Long Game" (2005), set in a giant space station, the Doctor eliminates a huge, tyrannical monster which, unbeknownst to its human inhabitants, is

[39] Vanessa de Kauwe and Lindy Orthia, "Knowledge, Power and the Ethics Illusion in Classic Era *Doctor Who*", *Journal of Popular Television*, 6(2) (2018).

controlling the space station along with its broadcasting of news to the entire human empire. Subsequently, in "Bad Wolf"/"The Parting of the Ways" (2005), he returns to the same craft at a point in time some ninety years later. He finds that the political void left by the monster's destruction has been filled with oppressive and clandestine rule by the Daleks. The Doctor feels guilty, but the replacement of one tyranny by another *in this particular instance* should give us pause for thought. What sorts of regimes come to power as a consequence of the Doctor's interventions *far more generally*? If *Doctor Who* were too specific about the sorts of government that replace the regimes defeated by the Doctor, there would be a danger that the show's political message would be not a hidden transcript but a manifest one, and *Doctor Who* would risk condemnation for political bias. The ambiguity over what kind of government replaces the tyrannical one is therefore another device to soften *Doctor Who*'s politics.

Yet, for all the softening of the show's political message, it is nonetheless possible to identify at least some elements of a positive manifesto from the new *Who* episodes which have engaged most intimately with the post-democratic condition. For example, "Rise of the Cybermen"/"The Age of Steel" promotes the need for surveillance of and resistance to the corporate over-reach that plays a seminal role in the creation of post-democracy. Citizens need to overcome the power of companies if they are to escape the post-democratic trap. "The Sound of Drums"/"Last of the Time Lords" serves to flag up the ease with which post-democracy collapses into totalitarianism. The story warns us to pre-empt and resist populism and dictatorship, because post-democracy may place us on the road to despotism as the public reacts illogically to its discontents. "The Beast Below" may be read as a clarion call against state secrecy. The people need to know how society works, otherwise democratic opportunities are meaningless. In this regard, David Yuratich argues that the episode sends a sceptical message that distrusts the ability of any authority figure to satisfactorily resolve issues. On this reading, "The Beast Below" pleads for a citizen-focused democracy, in which an active citizenry involves itself in the negotiation of its constitutional arrangements.[40] Yet the ideal of an active citizenry that participates

[40]David Yuratich, "'The Beast Below': *Doctor Who* and the Popular Negotiation of Constitutional Values", *Journal of Popular Television*, 6(2) (2018).

in informed debate is the polar opposite of post-democracy, in which citizens' discontents are more manipulated than addressed. A unifying theme is reflected in the Doctor's retort to the Master in "Last of the Time Lords" that he cannot stop people *thinking*. Post-democratic homogeneity is thereby counterposed to the non-conformism, nay rebelliousness, of thought that *Doctor Who* tends to advocate.[41]

Conclusion

In sum, *Doctor Who* holds a science fiction prism to Britain's post-democratic quandary. If we return to Liesbet van Zoonan's wider definition of the political, whereby works of popular culture actually *are* politics, we can see that *Doctor Who* not only reflects British identity but also contributes to it, helping to constitute it. In so doing, the programme forcefully echoes the people's discontent with the political establishment and their growing alienation from the processes of representation. To be sure, *Doctor Who*'s dissent is contained behind the fuzzy wall of metaphor and the programme is reluctant to offer much by way of a blueprint to remedy the country's predicament by way of a "replacement regime". Nonetheless, viewed as a hidden transcript, its very act of persistently putting forward worlds of post-democracy and portraying the British as trying to cope with it and resisting its excesses lends powerful resonance to *Doctor Who*'s imaginings of Britishness.

Bibliography

Born, Georgina. *Uncertain Vision: Birt, Dyke and the Reinvention of the BBC.* London: Secker & Warburg, 2004.

Chapman, James. *Inside the TARDIS: The Worlds of Doctor Who*, 2nd ed. London: I.B. Tauris, 2013.

Chow-White, P.A., D. Deveau and P. Adams. "Media Encoding in Science Fiction Television: Battlestar Galactica as a Site of Critical Cultural Production." *Media Culture and Society* 37(8) (2015): 1210–1225.

[41] Consider, in a similar vein, the independence of thought of human-Dalek hybrids in "Evolution of the Daleks" (2007) and "The Evil of the Daleks" (1967); contrast this to the Doctor's criticism of human passivity in "The Long Game" (2005), perhaps connoting that corporate capitalism brainwashes more durably than the state fascism associated with the Daleks.

Cowley, Philip. *The Rebels: How Blair Mislaid His Majority*. London: Politicos, 2005.
Crouch, Colin. *Post-Democracy*. Cambridge: Polity, 2004.
de Kauwe, Vanessa and Lindy Orthia. "Knowledge, Power and the Ethics Illusion in Classic Era *Doctor Who*". *Journal of Popular Television* 6(2), 2018.
Fisher, Mark. *Capitalist Realism: Is There No Alternative?* Winchester: Zero Books, 2009.
Hills, Matt, ed. *New Dimensions of Doctor Who: Adventures in Space, Time and Television*. London: I.B. Tauris, 2013.
Hills, Matt. *Triumph of a Time Lord: Regenerating Doctor Who in the Twenty-first Century*. London: I.B. Tauris, 2010.
Ingraham, Chrys. *White Weddings: Romancing Heterosexuality in Popular Culture*. New York: Routledge, 2008.
Jowett, Lorna. "The Girls Who Waited: Female Companions and Gender in *Doctor Who*." *Critical Studies in Television* 9 (2014): 77–94.
Knightley, Philip. *The First Casualty: The War Correspondent as Hero and Myth-Maker from the Crimea to Iraq*. Baltimore: Johns Hopkins University Press, 2003.
Mair, Peter. "Partyless Democracy." *New Left Review* 2 (2000): 21–35.
McGuigan, Jim. *Cool Capitalism*. London: Pluto Press, 2009.
Miliband, Ralph. *The State in Capitalist Society*. London: Weidenfeld and Nicolson, 1969.
Mills, Tom. *The BBC: Myth of a Public Service*. London: Verso, 2016.
Murdock, Graham. "Authorship and Organisation." *Screen Education* 35 (1980): 123–143.
Oborne, Peter. *The Rise of Political Lying*. London: Free Press, 2005.
Oborne, Peter. *The Triumph of the Political Class*. London: Simon and Schuster, 2007.
Scott, James C. *Domination and the Arts of Resistance*. New Haven, CT and London: Yale University Press, 1992.
Street, John. *Politics and Popular Culture*. London: Polity, 1997.
Tomkins, Adam. *Our Republican Constitution*. Oxford: Hart, 2005.
Webb, Paul and Thomas Poguntke. "The Presidentialization of Contemporary Democratic Consequences: Evidence, Causes and Consequences." In *The Presidentialization of Politics*, edited by Thomas Pogunke and Paul Webb, 336–356. Oxford: Oxford University Press, 2005.
Yuratich, David. "'The Beast Below': *Doctor Who* and the Popular Negotiation of Constitutional Values." *Journal of Popular Television* 6(2), 2018.

Index

A
"Abominable Snowmen, The", 65
Ace (companion), 47, 67, 179
Adelaide Brookes, Captain, 125
Adric (companion), 19
Afghanistan and Iraq invasions, 63, 160, 184, 186, 201, 202, 261, 276
Afghanistan, withdrawal from, 185
"Aliens of London"/"World War Three", 11, 63, 118, 139, 150, 180
Allegory, 2, 7, 8, 10, 11, 117, 126, 166, 187, 218
Alvarado, Manuel, 7, 8, 12, 13, 17, 18, 23, 30, 125, 128
"Ambassadors of Death, The", 9, 128, 131, 133 134
Amy-Chinn, Dee, 68, 71
"Amy's Choice", 105
Andrzejewski, Matteusz (character), 51
"Angels Take Manhattan, The", 153
The Apprentice, 145
"Arc of Infinity", 45, 124
Arendt, Hannah, 193
"Ark, The", 59
"Army of Ghosts"/"Doomsday", 96, 138
Ashildr (character), 71, 74
"Asylum of the Daleks", 181, 182
Authorship, 22, 264
"Aztecs, The", 188

B
"Bad Wolf"/"The Parting of the Ways", 47, 162, 187, 212, 237, 239, 240, 251, 253, 278
Banking crisis 2008, 118, 146, 228, 237
Barron, Lee, 67, 68
Bass, Gary Jonathan, 201
"Battlefield", 31, 53, 135
"Beast Below, The", 15, 35, 45, 53, 68, 99, 101, 139, 140, 265, 269, 270, 278
Beattie, Melissa, 21, 30, 59, 108, 177
Bell, Eleanor, 89, 99, 101, 154
"Bells of Saint John, The", 53, 137, 144, 147, 212, 226, 232, 239, 240
Benton, Sergeant (character), 93, 130
Bhopal (Union Carbide) disaster, 233
Billig, Michael, 2, 4, 140
Billy Elliot, 33

D. Nicol, *Doctor Who: A British Alien?*,
https://doi.org/10.1007/978-3-319-65834-6

Black British, 6, 7, 54, 269
Blair, Tony, 12, 32, 33, 63, 87, 98, 154, 161, 184, 188, 250, 267, 268
Blue, Journey (character), 57
Bond, James, 6, 124
"Boom Town", 98, 164, 180, 181
Bracewell, Professor Edwin (character), 102, 140
Bradney, Anthony, 5
Brassed Off, 33
Brekke, Laura, 164, 165
Brexit (British exit from the European Union), 51
British Broadcasting Corporation (BBC), 1, 7, 14, 17, 20, 36, 47, 51, 74, 77, 97, 101, 111, 133, 129, 159, 167, 213, 235, 236, 247, 262, 266, 269–274
  and neoliberalism, 33, 272
Britishness, 1, 2, 4, 6–8, 12, 13, 15–21, 24, 29–37, 42, 43, 46, 48, 49, 51, 53, 55, 57, 58, 63, 64, 67, 71–73, 75–77, 83, 84, 86–88, 94, 99, 101, 102, 105, 108, 109, 112, 113, 121, 128, 134, 140, 152, 187, 254, 259–261, 265, 269, 270, 279
  as brand image, 30, 32, 33
  as hybrid, 21, 48, 54, 69, 112, 113
  as normative, 1, 29, 30, 35, 57, 60, 64, 75, 76, 93, 259
  as political, 128, 276
British self-government, 117
Britton, Piers, 13, 21, 37, 43, 47, 108, 109, 122, 140, 177, 179
Brown, J.P.C., 12, 17, 76
Brown, Peri (companion), 19, 199
Bush, Mel (companion), 174
Byrne, Aidan, 10

C
Cameron, David, 31, 34
"Caretaker, The", 53, 57, 186
"Carnival of Monsters", 218
Cassese, Antonio, 189, 190, 192, 200
"Caves of Androzani, The", 142, 162, 212, 224, 229, 231, 232, 234, 238
Chapman, James, 7, 13, 16, 66, 72, 109, 122, 123, 129, 134, 152, 179, 247, 275
Charles, Alec, 63, 165, 166, 185
Chesterton, Ian (companion), 41, 160, 166, 170, 187
Chips, 19, 75, 251, 259
"Christmas Carol, A", 212, 229
"Christmas Invasion, The", 15, 19, 46, 139, 140, 150, 186
Churchill, Winston (character), 101, 102, 122, 138, 139
"City of Death", 18, 19, 50
Civil servants, British, 131, 132, 135
Class, 1, 11, 12, 19, 21, 29, 30, 33, 38, 39, 42–48, 51, 53, 74, 76, 90, 93, 95, 105–108, 110, 118, 131, 134, 139, 142, 145–147, 151, 153, 180, 185, 221, 226, 227, 230, 233, 241, 242, 244, 245, 254, 260, 261, 264, 265, 269, 272, 277
"Claws of Axos, The", 131, 133, 149
Coal Hill School, 53, 110
Cold War, 11, 121, 130, 149, 153, 171, 203, 210, 276
Colin Crouch, 236, 259, 263
Colley, Linda, 20, 83, 86
"Colony in Space", 60, 123, 124, 142, 212, 214, 224, 231, 234, 253
Commonwealth, 20, 49, 86
Companions, female, 64, 69, 70, 71, 76, 265
Connell, Liam, 89
Cook, Jon, 64, 87
Cook, Robin, 187
Cooper, Gwen (character), 96, 97
Corbyn, Jeremy, 32
Corporate capture of globalisation, 143

Corporate control of the media, 224
Corporate despotism, 231
Corporate empires, 224
Corporations, 33, 37, 118, 122, 141, 143, 144, 147, 150, 209, 210, 212, 213, 219–227, 230, 231, 233–235, 237–242, 244, 248–250, 252–254, 261
"Creature from the Pit, The", 210, 213–219, 232, 254
Crimes against humanity, 189, 191–192, 198, 200
"Crimson Horror, The", 74, 106, 107, 110
Crossman Diaries, 132
Cull, Nicholas J., 16, 41, 148
"Curse of Fenric, The", 9, 53, 176, 200, 274, 275
"Curse of Peladon, The", 10, 47, 50, 123, 124, 126, 218
Cybermen/Cyberman, 35, 36, 43, 45, 52, 65, 70, 103, 124, 131, 137, 138, 142, 164, 180, 186, 199, 212, 214, 227, 229, 231, 237, 238, 240, 243, 247–249, 263, 268, 270

D
"Daemons, The", 96, 105
"Dalek", 20, 37, 41, 47, 54, 55, 65, 102, 109, 112, 124, 142, 144, 153, 166–170, 172, 173, 177–183, 187–192, 199, 212, 232, 237, 240, 247, 263, 268, 278
"Dalek Invasion of Earth, The", 188, 263
Dalek-Nazi metaphor, 170
Daleks as British, 20, 47
"Daleks in Manhattan"/"Evolution of the Daleks", 55, 112, 153, 182, 279
"Daleks, The", 83, 160, 166–171, 190, 191, 268
"Dark Water"/"Death in Heaven", 212, 232, 237, 239, 240, 245
Davies, Russell T., 15, 22, 44, 69, 72, 94, 121
"Day of the Daleks", 123
"Day of the Doctor, The", 46, 111, 137
"Deadly Assassin, The", 45, 124, 165, 194
"Death of the Doctor", 112, 137
"Deep Breath", 74, 104
de Kauwe, Vanessa, 240, 241, 253, 277
Del Ponte, Carla, 200
"Delta and the Bannermen", 88, 94, 98
de Sousa, Lady Christina (character), 47
Dictatorships, 10, 149, 171, 230, 270, 278
Doctor–Donna, The (character), 69
Doctor, the ninth, 108–110
Doctor, the seventh, 103
Doctor, the twelfth, 103, 104, 262
Doctor Who and Race, 12, 18, 48, 52, 53, 55, 58, 59, 166, 171, 172, 183
Doctor Who studies, 16, 21–23, 64, 84, 128
Doctor Who The Movie, 8, 15
Dodson, Linnea, 55
Downton Abbey, 33, 42, 43
Dragon's Den, 145
Duncan, Andy, 69
Duncan, Sydney, 69

E
East India Company, 219, 222, 223, 225, 228, 232
"Eaters of Light, The", 75, 104
Eccleston, Christopher, 108, 109
Edensor, Tim, 2, 4, 9
"Edge of Destruction, The", 166, 187
Eichmann, Adolf, 193

Elizabeth I, Queen, 46
Elizabeth II, Queen, 46, 73
Empire, 7, 17, 18, 31, 33, 41, 48, 49, 51–53, 58–63, 76, 86, 87, 123, 138, 174, 183–185, 192, 219, 221–224, 232, 235, 236, 248, 249, 251, 278
"Empress of Mars", 15, 54
"Empty Child, The"/"The Doctor Dances", 14, 45, 72, 84, 86
"End of the World, The", 42, 144, 147, 212, 242
"End of Time, The", 44, 45, 125, 202, 212, 231, 245
Englishness, 29, 84, 105, 269
Entrepreneurism, 34, 41, 245
EU–Canada Comprehensive Economic and Trade Agreement (CETA), 227
European Convention on Human Rights, 119
European single market, 50, 143, 217, 248
European Union, 10, 13, 49–51, 84, 87, 117, 119, 126, 127, 130, 141, 143, 216, 227, 248
European Union referendum 2016, 13, 50, 51, 117, 118, 141, 264
"Evil of the Daleks, The", 52, 65, 103, 112, 165, 169, 182, 279
"Exit Wounds", 96
"Extremis", 75

F
The Fall, 111
Farron, Tim, 32
"Father's Day", 68
"Fear Her", 53, 140
Fisher, Mark, 252, 268, 269
Fiske, John, 22, 35, 38, 159, 183, 210, 213, 247, 252, 254
"Flatline", 68, 70, 110
Flint, Jenny (character), 73
Flynn, Kate, 35, 100, 101
Foreman, Susan (Doctor's granddaughter), 75
Franke, Alyssa, 71
Free trade, 118, 119, 143, 145, 150, 213–218, 225, 227
Full Monty, The, 33
"Fury from the Deep", 65, 92
Futamura, Madoka, 201

G
Gender, 1, 13, 22, 30, 53, 64, 67, 68, 70–72, 76, 77, 96, 101, 104, 219, 260
"Genesis of the Daleks", 191
Genocide, 163, 173–175, 177–179, 182, 183, 189, 192–193, 194, 196–198
Gerhardt, Sue, 39
"Ghostlight", 53
Gilbert, Jeremy, 120, 245, 252, 254
Gilroy, Christine, 59
"Girl Who Died, The", 74
Globalisation, 1, 4, 5, 13, 87, 99, 117–122, 126, 134, 141–144, 148, 150, 154, 155, 218, 221, 225, 241, 242, 260, 261, 268, 270
  of corporations, 1, 118, 122, 142, 143, 144, 150, 218, 225, 261, 268
Globalised law, 118, 119, 122, 143
"Good Man Goes to War, A", 74, 104, 182
Grady, Maura, 7, 16, 61, 183
Grant, Jo (companion), 10, 65, 66, 112
"Greatest Show in the Galaxy, The", 53, 63
Green, Bonnie, 164
"Green Death, The", 44, 88, 91–94, 98, 112, 123, 131, 142, 212, 214, 239, 240, 246, 277

Greenfield, Steve, 5
Green, John Paul, 108
Gwyneth (character), 95, 147

H
"Happiness Patrol, The", 10, 44, 52, 276
Harkness, Captain Jack (companion), 19, 72, 96, 97, 138, 237
Harvey, David, 145, 227, 241–243, 246, 248
Hayek, Friedrich A. von, 120, 145, 220, 227, 238
Healey, Denis, 136
"Hell Bent", 45, 53, 54, 71, 74, 112
Hemstrom, Cassie, 7, 16, 61, 73, 183
Heriot, Zoe (companion), 19, 65, 103, 212, 247, 248
Hernandez, Mike, 58
Hidden transcript, 259, 261–263, 265, 270, 274, 278, 279
Hiebert, Janet, 23, 24
"Highlanders, The", 65, 88, 90–95, 99, 102, 103, 105
Hills, Matt, 7–9, 13, 17, 21, 109, 164, 235, 273, 274
"Horror of Fang Rock", 44, 66
"Human Nature"/"The Family of Blood", 45, 162, 163
Hybridity, 54, 55, 69, 90, 111, 112

I
"Idiots' Lantern, The", 15
Imperialism, 17, 44, 48–50, 58, 62, 63, 89, 138, 167, 183–185, 190, 210, 222, 224, 246, 270
"Impossible Astronaut, The"/"Day of the Moon", 19, 151, 152, 176–178
Individualism, 18, 35, 36, 38, 39, 149, 214, 215, 247–249
Individuality, 35, 214, 247–249, 254, 261
Industrial revolution, 6, 35, 91, 106, 107
"Inferno", 10, 46
Ingraham, Chrys, 273
"Inside the Dalek", 57, 111, 186
Interference/interventions by the Doctor, 1, 9, 46, 63, 124, 125, 139, 140, 159–163, 166, 174, 175, 179, 180, 185, 186, 188, 193–196, 199, 204, 230, 261, 275, 277, 278
International Criminal Court, 187, 189–191, 198, 200, 202
International Criminal Tribunal on the former Yugoslavia, 191, 200
Internationalisation, 117, 118, 120, 121, 143, 149, 154
International Monetary Fund (IMF) loan, 135, 136
Interpretation of *Doctor Who*, 2, 22–24
"Invasion of the Dinosaurs", 123, 129, 130, 134
"Invasion of Time, The", 45, 66, 124
"Invasion, The", 65, 103, 129, 130, 142, 209–211, 214, 224, 227, 230, 231, 239, 243, 247, 248, 263
"Invisible Enemy, The", 50

J
Jackson, Ben (companion), 44, 47, 65, 90–93, 171–173
Jackson, Ellen-Raïssa, 89
James, Oliver, 39
Jenkins, Simon, 147, 148, 250
Jones, Harriet (character), 46, 122, 138–140, 150, 151, 186
Jones, Ianto (character), 73, 96, 97
Jones, Mark, 10, 15

Jones, Martha (companion), 19, 41, 42, 45, 53, 55–57, 69, 70, 137, 269
Jones, Matt, 12, 164
Jones, Matthew, 12, 16, 21, 62, 164
Jovanka, Tegan (companion), 19
Jowett, Lorna, 13, 16, 64, 68–70, 72, 77, 96
Judoon, 202

K
"Kill the Moon", 70, 110
"Kinda", 17, 18, 62, 63
Klein, Naomi, 233
"Knock Knock", 40, 75
Knox, Simone, 16, 17, 43
"Krotons, The", 47, 103, 277

L
Labour Party and neoliberalism, 145
Lambert, Verity, 125, 128
Law, 2, 5, 11–13, 23, 24, 46, 61, 85, 88, 117–120, 122–126, 133, 136, 138, 141, 143, 146, 148, 151, 155, 161, 187–203, 216, 218, 220, 222, 224, 228, 233, 238, 239, 249
Layton, David, 109, 164, 170, 174, 176
"Lazarus Experiment, The", 42, 144, 181
Leela (companion), 66, 67, 231
Leith, Murray, 94, 95, 104
Leonard, Mark, 30, 32, 34, 48, 57, 77
Lethbridge-Stewart, Brigadier Alistair (companion), 93, 129, 137, 139
"Let's Kill Hitler", 112, 178
Lewis, Courtland, 23, 162–164, 169, 170
Lisa Kerrigan, 29
Liz 10 (Queen Elizabeth X) (character), 47, 100, 140
"Long Game, The", 37, 144, 147, 187, 193, 212, 224, 229, 232, 234–236, 239, 240, 249, 251, 253, 277, 279
Lynda (character), 47

M
"Macra Terror, The", 171, 173, 174
MacRury, Iain, 23, 100
Maley, Willy, 99, 104
"Mark of the Rani, The", 43, 91, 106, 107, 110
Marquand, David, 31, 49, 87
Mason, Paul, 105
"Masque of Mandragora, The", 165
"Massacre of Saint Bartholomew's Eve, The", 188
Master/Missy as British, 20, 46, 55, 66, 103, 104, 106, 131, 132, 139, 149, 151, 159, 165, 183, 186, 191, 196, 266, 267, 274, 279
McArthur, Colin, 91
McCormack, Una, 21, 30, 44, 59, 108, 120, 121
McCrimmon, Jamie (companion), 103, 171
McCrone, David, 9, 99
McGuigan, Jim, 2, 3, 32, 33, 273
McKee, Alan, 2, 18, 22, 128
McKee, Gabriel, 37, 160
McLaughlin, Noah, 70
McNair, Brian, 20, 235, 271
"Media "due impartiality", 236
Meron, Theodor, 191
Metaphor, 2, 8, 10, 11, 17, 45, 50, 58–60, 63, 67, 70, 91, 103, 109, 110, 122, 126, 160, 166, 170, 171, 178, 183, 186, 189, 204, 215, 216, 241, 249, 261, 263, 268, 275, 276, 279

Miliband, Ralph, 222, 230, 271
Millington, Commander (character), 9, 274–276
"Mindwarp", 212, 239
Miners' strike 1984–5, 250
Mises, Ludwig von, 238
Missy (character), 20, 104, 186, 245
Mitchell, Adam (companion), 37, 234
Mittal, Aditya, 243
Moffat, Steven, 94, 99, 104, 112, 137
"Monster of Peladon, The", 10, 47, 50, 66, 126, 127, 218, 277
Monsters, 6, 8, 9, 21, 24, 61
"Moonbase, The", 65
"Mummy on the Orient Express", 45, 47, 186
Murdoch, Rupert, 243
"Mutants, The", 60, 61, 123, 124

N
Nairn, Tom, 154
Naismith, Joshua (character), 44, 245
"Name of the Doctor, The", 71, 74, 110, 180, 182
Nathanael, Tanja, 84
National Health Service, 6, 56, 64, 86, 142, 220
National identity, 1–7, 9, 12, 13, 19, 29–35, 49, 58, 62, 64, 86, 93–95, 104, 106, 134, 140, 243, 259
Nationalisation, 142, 146
NATO, 148, 200, 202
Neely, Sarah, 99
Neo-imperialism, 17, 185
Neoliberalism, 17, 33, 34, 37, 39, 47, 63, 68, 84, 87, 120, 144–148, 153, 216, 226, 227, 230, 234, 237, 238, 241, 243–246, 248, 251–254, 260, 272
"New Earth", 42, 134, 147, 220
New Labour, 11, 32–34, 98, 187, 225, 250
Newman, Kim, 125, 134, 144
"Nightmare of Eden", 50
"Night Terrors", 37, 39
Noble, Donna (companion), 41, 44, 47, 53, 54, 56, 69, 136, 151, 235, 238
Non-conformity, 16, 37, 52, 72, 73, 247
Non-Western cultures, 18, 49, 59, 62
Northern Englishness, 15, 83, 106, 108–110, 113
Northern Irishness, 29
Nuclear war, 136
Nuremberg trials, 196–198
Nyssa (companion), 19, 41, 47

O
Oborne, Peter, 11, 12, 225, 226, 264
O'Day, Andrew, 8–10, 17, 43, 71, 187
Oligopoly, 221
Olympics Opening Ceremony 2012, 6, 7, 35, 49, 77
Orthia, Lindy, 12, 18, 48, 49, 52, 53, 55, 58, 59, 62, 166, 171, 172, 183, 240, 241, 253, 277
Orwell, George, 106
Osborn, Guy, 5
Oswald, Clara (companion), 19, 41, 47, 53, 54, 58, 64, 68, 70, 74, 109, 110, 112, 159, 182, 186
"Other", 9, 58, 63, 169
Outsourcing, 147, 240
Owen, James, 197, 198
"Oxygen", 19, 144, 212, 232, 249, 253

P
Parallel universes, 10
"Partners in Crime", 212, 231, 237–240

Perkins (character), 47
"Pilot, The", 74, 75
Pink, Danny (character), 19, 186
"Pirate Planet, The", 67
Plaid Cymru The Party of Wales, 86, 87
"Planet of the Dead", 47
"Planet of the Ood", 10, 18, 44, 62, 63, 69, 144, 212, 224, 231, 232, 234, 252
Planets as states, 10
Political parties, homogeneity in UK, 264, 271
Political role of corporations, inevitability, 221, 222
Politics, 1–5, 7, 10, 12, 13, 16, 22, 24, 30, 35, 49, 50, 67, 68, 71, 72, 77, 87, 118, 127, 138, 141, 143, 144, 153, 154, 161, 180, 184, 194–196, 201, 202, 215, 216, 219, 222, 225, 227, 229, 234, 241, 248, 264, 267, 270, 273, 276, 278, 279
Polly (companion), 35, 36, 65, 171, 173
Pond, Amy (companion), 15, 19, 41, 47, 56, 58, 68, 69, 99, 101, 109, 112, 151, 182, 265, 269
Popular culture, 1–7, 14, 24, 71, 189, 268, 273, 276, 279
Postcolonialism, 89
Post-democracy, 236, 259, 263–265, 267–274, 278, 279
Post-feminism, 71
Postman, Neil, 21
Potts, Bill (companion), 19, 20, 40, 47, 54, 56, 57, 74, 75, 104
"Power of Kroll, The", 61, 67, 142, 212, 214, 224
"Power of Three, The", 137, 165
Presidentialisation of politics, 267
Pride, 13, 19, 20, 33, 141
Pritchard (character), 37, 40, 41
Public service ethos, 30, 35, 42, 76, 132, 133, 235
Purcell (character), 37, 39–41
"Pyramid at the End of the World, The", 75, 137

R

Race, 1, 6, 11, 12, 18, 19, 30, 35, 44, 48, 52–55, 57–60, 73, 75–77, 95, 99, 103, 112, 136, 140, 147, 151, 166, 169–172, 177, 181, 183, 190, 192, 223, 224, 226, 234, 235, 248, 251, 269, 274
"Random Shoes", 96
Rattigan, Luke (character), 41
"Rebel Flesh, The"/"The Almost People", 144, 146, 212, 226, 249, 252, 253
Rebels, 9, 10, 251, 252, 268
"Reign of Terror, The", 188
"Remembrance of the Daleks", 52–54, 179, 180, 189, 191
"Return of Doctor Mysterio, The", 144, 152, 212, 239, 240
Revelation of the Daleks, 142, 212, 232, 237, 253
"Ribos Operation, The", 67
Richards, Jeffrey, 36
Riddell, Peter, 154
"Rise of the Cybermen"/"The Age of Steel", 10, 45, 68, 212, 226, 227, 229, 232, 235, 238, 239, 243, 246, 248, 252, 268–270, 278
Rita (character), 56, 57
Robinson, Timothy Mark, 55, 56
"Robot", 42, 135
"Robots of Death, The", 249
Romana (companion), 19, 47, 67, 215

Rome Statute of the International Criminal Court 1998, 189
"Rose", 68
Rustin, Michael, 23, 100

S

Sarah Jane Adventures, The, 21, 30, 42, 59, 108, 112, 137
Satire, 2, 7–10, 12, 35, 42, 45–47, 91, 98, 118, 187, 188, 196, 221–223, 234, 240, 261, 267, 272, 276
"Savages, The", 44, 142, 173
Saxon, Harold (character), 151, 186, 266–268, 270
Scottish independence, 84, 88, 103, 105
Scottish independence referendum 2014, 84, 105
Scottish National Party, 87, 104
Scottishness, 29, 87, 88, 99, 102, 104, 260, 265
Scott, James C., 259, 262, 263
"Sea Devils, The", 11, 128, 131
Seaton, Jean, 20, 77
"Seeds of Doom, The", 135, 212
Selznick, Barbara, 12, 16, 33, 34, 42, 43, 76, 109, 128, 150
Semiotic thickness, 23
Sexuality, 1, 13, 30, 53, 71, 72, 75, 98, 260
Shadow Proclamation, 125, 202
"Shakespeare Code, The", 46, 53
Silence, The, 152, 176–178, 182, 192
"Silver Nemesis", 6, 46, 50
Simpson, Gerry, 194, 195, 201
Slade, Rickston (character), 37, 38
"Sleep No More", 144, 212
Sleight, Graham, 9, 21, 44, 61, 69, 72, 121
"Smile", 6, 104
"Smith and Jones", 6, 42, 220
Smith, Charles Anthony, 194, 201
Smith, Mickey (companion), 53, 57, 68
Smith, Sarah Jane (companion), 41, 42, 66, 130, 277
Social democracy, 32, 34, 216, 234, 250, 272
Somek, Alexander, 248, 249
Song, Professor River (character), 70, 75, 112, 151, 152, 182
"Sontaran Strategem, The"/"The Poison Sky", 41, 137
Soule, Daniel, 94, 95, 104
"Sound of Drums, The"/"Last of the Time Lords", 55, 136, 151, 266, 267, 269, 270, 278
South Africa, 174
"Space Museum, The", 44, 65
"Spearhead from Space", 37, 90, 129, 131, 133, 212
Special relationship between UK and USA, 121, 148, 149
"State of Decay", 18, 44, 61
"Stolen Earth, The"/"Journey's End", 54, 97, 136, 139, 263
Street, John, 1, 3, 24, 276
Suez crisis 1956, 121, 184
Sullivan, Harry (companion), 41
"Sun Makers, The", 66, 142, 212, 214, 223, 224, 229–234, 239, 240, 246, 249–251, 253
Super-rich, 40, 221, 229, 236, 241–246, 250, 260
"Survival", 53

T

"Talons of Weng-Chiang, The", 52
TARDIS, 6–8, 13, 15, 16, 19, 24, 35, 37–39, 41, 48, 56, 57, 60, 65, 66, 69–72, 76, 99, 103, 106, 109, 112, 123, 124, 128, 129, 134, 148, 152, 166–168, 170, 171, 179, 217, 247, 253, 275, 277

Taylor, Steven (companion), 19
Tea, 15, 17, 19, 20, 56, 259
"Tenth Planet, The", 36, 149
"Terminus", 212, 234, 277
"Terror of the Autons", 20, 52, 66, 111, 132, 212, 239
"Terror of the Vervoids", 174
"Terror of the Zygons", 88, 91–93, 95, 99, 102, 134, 135
Teselecta, 202
Thals, 166–170, 178, 188, 190
Thatcherism, 34, 84, 148, 250
Thatcher, Margaret, 107, 135, 144, 153, 216, 219, 245, 248, 276
"Thin Ice", 54, 57, 140
"Three Doctors, The", 196
"Time Heist", 144, 212, 232, 245, 249
Time Lords, 45, 46, 54, 55, 58, 61, 109, 112, 122–125, 159, 174, 175, 189, 193–196, 198, 199, 201–203, 245, 279
"Time Meddler, The", 188
"Time of the Doctor, The", 141, 178, 188
"Time Warrior, The", 66
Tokyo trials, 199, 201, 204
"Tomb of the Cybermen, The", 52, 149, 268
"Tooth and Claw", 46, 95, 96, 98, 138
Torchwood, 21, 30, 46, 56, 59, 69, 72, 73, 96–98, 108, 122, 138, 152, 153
  "Torchwood: Children of Earth", 152
  "Torchwood: Miracle Day", 97
"Town Called Mercy, A", 102, 103, 153, 163, 181
Transatlantic Trade and Investment Partnership (TTIP), 141, 227
"Trial of a Time Lord, The", 124, 174, 188, 193, 196, 198, 199, 212, 239
Trump, Donald, 268
Tulloch, John, 7, 8, 12, 13, 18, 23, 30, 125, 128
Turlough (companion), 19
"Twin Dilemma, The", 192
Tyler, Jackie (character), 68
Tyler, Rose (companion), 15, 19, 37, 42, 47, 53, 55, 57, 68, 108, 147, 181

U

"Under the Lake", 37, 40
"Unearthly Child, An", 166
Unified Intelligence Taskforce (UNIT), 56, 69
Union Jack, 6, 14, 15, 19, 20, 38, 64, 84, 101–103, 122, 140
Unionism, 85, 88, 90, 93, 94, 103, 113, 269
Union of England and Scotland 1707, 85
United Kingdom Independence Party (UKIP), 141
United Nations, 75, 122, 123, 125, 130, 133, 135, 136, 148, 151, 154, 201, 202
United Nations Intelligence Taskforce (UNIT), 37, 55, 69, 91, 92, 111, 122, 123, 128–140, 196, 224, 231, 270
United States of America, 121, 122, 130, 148, 176, 200, 202, 203, 261
"Unquiet Dead, The", 95, 147
Upstairs, Downstairs, 33, 42

V

"Vampires of Venice, The", 181
Van Statten, Henry (character), 41
Van Zoonen, Liesbet, 1, 3

Vastra, Madame (character), 73, 104, 106, 180
Vaughn, Tobias (character), 212, 230, 243, 247, 248
"Vengeance on Varos", 10, 212, 217, 218, 224, 239, 246
Vicki (companion), 19, 65
Victoria, Queen, 46, 96, 98, 138
"Victors' justice" argument, 196, 200
"Victory of the Daleks", 15, 20, 68, 86, 101, 102, 140
"Vincent and the Doctor", 104
Vohlidka, John, 48, 183
"Voyage of the Damned", 6, 37, 38, 46, 212

W

Wallace, Richard, 65, 219
War crimes, 161, 163, 187–191, 193–198, 200–204
"War Games, The", 45, 58, 122, 123, 188, 193, 194, 196, 198
"War Machines, The", 76, 142, 210
"Warriors' Gate", 67
Washington consensus, 151, 225
Waterfield, Victoria (companion), 65
"Waters of Mars, The", 46, 125, 202
Wealth gap, 241, 250
Weapons of mass destruction, 12, 63
Welsh independence, 13
Welshness, 29, 87, 88, 97, 260
Whovian Feminism, 71
Williams, Chris, 89, 111, 112
Williams, Marcia, 133
Williams, Rhys (character), 97
Williams, Rory (companion), 56, 69, 103, 112, 152
Wilmott, Chris, 164
Wilson, Harold, 133, 149
Winter of Discontent 1978–1979, 135
"Woman Who Lived, The", 53
World Trade Organization, 119, 143, 148, 150, 227
World War I, 86
World War II, 15, 20, 45, 73, 86, 87, 119, 121, 150, 152, 184, 187, 199, 201, 275
Wright, Barbara (companion), 41, 166

Y

Yates, Captain Mike (character), 134
Yes Minister, 133
Yuratich, David, 278

Z

"Zygon Invasion, The"/"The Zygon Inversion", 55, 63

Zeitfracht Medien GmbH
Ferdinand-Jühlke-Straße 7
99095 Erfurt, Deutschland
produktsicherheit@kolibri360.de